GEORGE PARKES

"How vast is Thy sea, O Lord; and how small is my boat . . ."

—A Fishermen's Prayer

WHERE THE WIND BLOWS

BREAKWATER

Canada

Production of this guide was partially funded by the National Search and Rescue Secretariat.

Design and Production: GDA Inc., Halifax, Nova Scotia
    Additional artwork produced by
    Immedia visual communications and
    GulfStream Graphics

Cover photography: Phyllis Blades, Atlantic Stock Images

Canadian Cataloguing in Publication Data

Bowyer, Peter J.

    Where the wind blows
    ISBN 1-55081-119-3
1. Marine meteorology—Atlantic Coast (Canada)
I. Title.

QC994.2.B68 1995   551.69163' 44   C95-950092-8

Published by authority of the Minister of the
Environment
© Minister of Public Works and Government Services
Canada, 1995
ISBN 1-55081-119-3
Catalogue No. En 56-112/1995E

Published in co-operation with Environment Canada by:
Breakwater Books Ltd.
100 Water Street, P.O. Box 2188
St. John's, Newfoundland
Canada
A1C 6E6
Tel: (709) 722-6680
Fax: (709) 753-0708
1-800-563-3333

ALL RIGHTS RESERVED. No part of this work covered by the copyright hereon may be reproduced or used in any form or by any means–graphic, electronic or mechanical–without the prior written permission of the publisher. Any request for photocopying, recording, taping or information storage and retrieval systems of any part of this book shall be directed in writing to the Canadian Reprography Collective, 6 Adelaide Street West, Suite 900, Toronto, Ontario M5C 1H6. This applies to classroom usage as well.

ACKNOWLEDGEMENTS

EDITOR:
PETER J. BOWYER

In addition to the new and original materials, this guide incorporates the contents of the first four associated publications, namely: the *East Coast Marine Weather Manual* (1989), the *Gulf of St. Lawrence Marine Weather Guide* (1991), the *Scotia / Fundy Marine Weather Guide* (1992), and the *Newfoundland & Labrador Marine Weather Guide* (1993). The original authors, considered as major contributors to this guide, are: Peter J. Bowyer, John M. Gray, Dermott Kearney, Andrew Lancaster, Ted McIldoon, Steve Miller, George Parkes, and Doug Steeves. In all, nearly three dozen meteorologists and weather service specialists from the Atlantic region's Atmospheric Environment Branch have helped to produce these books.

I would like to thank the more than 150 respondents who wrote us over the last five years with suggestions for improving the first four books. As well, I would like to thank again the many people who contributed to the success of those publications: in particular, the more than 200 mariners who were interviewed (from the Canadian Coast Guard, Federal and Provincial Fisheries, Canadian Marine Rescue Auxiliary, Canadian Power and Sail Squadrons, Department of National Defence, and local fishermen); and the Canadian Hydrographic Services for their expertise and the use of their charts, books, and photographs.

It is vital in such a publication to have the manuscript critically reviewed by people with specialized knowledge and varying levels of expertise. In this regard, I would like to thank: Ted McIldoon, Steve Miller, and George Parkes for critically reviewing the entire manuscript and offering hundreds of suggestions to tighten up both the general content and the meteorology; Ross Brown of the Canadian Climate Centre for reviewing the section on *Vessel Icing*; Phil Cote and Brian Veale of Environment Canada's Ice Centre, for reviewing the section on *Ice*; and Captain Greg MacNeill of the Nova Scotia School of Fisheries for reviewing the *Introduction* and section on *Marine Meteorology* from the perspective of an experienced instructor.

MARINE METEOROLOGY EDUCATION KITS

Environment Canada has developed a comprehensive package of visual teaching aids used by marine meteorology teachers in Power Squadron courses and Coast Guard College courses. The package includes: nine instructional videos (six of which are available separately from the educational kits); 157 graphic images on both overhead transparency and 35mm slide format (many images from this guide); 168 35mm photo-slides of weather phenomena, satellite imagery, weather instruments, and more. Included with the package is a detailed instructor's manual and a copy of this guide.

For more information on either the educational teaching package or the videos, or to submit any additions or corrections for future editions of this guide, please contact:

Director,
Atmospheric Environment Branch,
Environment Canada, Atlantic Region,
1496 Bedford Highway,
Bedford, Nova Scotia   B4A 1E5
Tel. (902) 426-9120
Fax (902) 426-9158

TABLE OF CONTENTS

ACKNOWLEDGEMENTS v

TABLE OF CONTENTS vi

HOW TO USE THIS MANUAL viii
   How To Read A Weather Map viii

INTRODUCTION x
   Physical Geography x

   Scales And Detail—
   The Mariner And The Meteorologist x

   The Role Of Mariners In Weather Forecasts xi
      Weather Observations
      Forecast Tailoring

   Marine Weather Services xii
      Observations and Data
      Routine Bulletins
      Warnings
      Special Forecasts
      Dissemination

   Be Prepared—The Checklist! xiii

MARINE METEOROLOGY 1

The Basics 1
   Where It All Starts—The Sun
   Air Masses
   Lows and Troughs
   Highs and Ridges
   Fronts
   Frontal Lows
   Trowals and Upper Fronts
   The Conveyor-Belt Model

Wind 9
   Offshore Winds
      The Effect Of Pressure (Geostrophic Wind)
      The Effect Of Friction
      The Effect Of Stability
      The Real Marine Wind
      Squalls
   Near-Shore Winds
      Winds Blowing From The Land
      Coastal Convergence / Divergence
      Cornering Effects
      Sea and Land Breezes
      Funnelling, Channelling, and Gap Winds
      Katabatic and Anabatic Winds
      Small-scale Troughs and Lows
      Cliff Effects
      Mountain Waves
   Summary on Wind Forecasting

Sea State 22
   Deep Water
      Wind-Waves and Swell
      Significant Wave Height
      Beaufort Scale
      Crossing Seas
      Seiches
   Shallow Water
      Shoaling-Breakers and Surf
      Refraction of Waves
      Tsunamis
      Tides
      Tidal Rips
      Longshore Currents and Rip Currents
      Wind-Wave-Tide-Current Interaction
      Sheltering

Clouds 31
   How Clouds Form
   Types of Clouds
   Signposts in the Sky

Vessel Icing 33
   Freezing Sea Spray
      Environmental Conditions
      Vessel Characteristics
      Vessel Activities
   Freezing Rain
   Ice Fog

Fog 35
   Radiation Fog
   Sea Fog
   Precipitation Fog or Frontal Fog
   Ice Fog

Storm Surge 37

Ice 39
   Sea Ice or Pack Ice
      Formation of Sea Ice
      Movement of Sea Ice
   Icebergs
      Movement of Icebergs
      Extent of Iceberg Drift

Storms 43
   Frontal Storms
      Typical Winds With a Mature Frontal Storm
      Typical Winds With an Occluding Frontal Storm
      Typical Winds With a Cold Low System
      Typical Sea States With a Mature Frontal Storm
   Thunderstorms
      Air Mass Thunderstorms
      Line or Frontal Thunderstorms
      Waterspouts
   Cold-Air Storms
      Cold-outbreaks
      Polar Lows
   Hurricanes and Tropical Storms
      Stages of Development
      How Hurricanes Develop
   Be Prepared—Checklist

TABLE OF CONTENTS

MARINE WEATHER CLIMATOLOGY 53

Wind
Wave Heights
Vessel Icing
Fog
Precipitation
Air Temperatures
Sea Surface Temperatures
Sea Ice
Icebergs
Frontal Lows
Tropical Cyclones
Ocean Currents
Tides

LOCAL WEATHER 63

Fundy 64
    Fundy Northwest
    Saint John River
    Upper Fundy
    Fundy Southeast

Atlantic Nova Scotia 80
    Southwest Nova Scotia
    Southeast Nova Scotia
    Eastern Shore

Cape Breton 90
    Cape Breton East
    The Bras D'Or Lakes
    Cape Breton West

Northumberland Strait 98
    Northumberland East
    Northumberland West

N. B. and P.E.I.—North 104
    New Brunswick North and Gaspé
    Prince Edward Island North

Southeast Gulf 109
    St. Paul Island
    Magdalen Islands

Newfoundland West 112
    Belle Isle
    Northeast Gulf
    Gulf-Port au Port

Newfoundland South 120
    Southwest Newfoundland
    Fortune
    Placentia Bay
    Avalon South

Newfoundland East 135
    Avalon East
    Trinity-Bonavista
    Notre Dame
    Newfoundland North

Labrador 154
    Labrador South
    Hamilton Inlet
    Labrador North

APPENDICES 167

A. Conversion Tables
B. Wind-Chill Factor
C. Ice Terminology
D. Cold Water Survival
E. Naming of Hurricanes

GLOSSARY 174

BIBLIOGRAPHY 178

HOW TO USE THIS MANUAL

Prior knowledge of marine weather or local weather effects in Atlantic Canada is not required to use this guide, but readers should familiarize themselves with the *Introduction* to use the book most efficiently. I have tried to organize the material so that readers can pick-and-choose their topics of interest.

The *Introduction* serves as a "primer" for the main text. It explains the basics of reading a weather map as well as what an "accurate forecast" really means. The role of mariners in the forecast process is discussed as well as the ever-changing marine weather services in the region. An overview of the physical geography of eastern Canada and its tie-in to local weather conditions prepares the reader for the section on local weather.

The section on *Marine Meteorology* can be understood by the layman, but also provides detailed explanations for those with a more technical interest. Special "technical boxes" are occasionally included for those interested, but skipping them won't deprive you of basic information. A detailed list of the specific topics can be found in the *Table of Contents*, and there is a *Glossary* of meteorological and oceanographic terms near the back of the book.

The section on *Marine Weather Climatology* discusses the variability of marine weather and oceanographic conditions in the region with respect to a variety of elements such as wind, sea state and temperature.

The section on *Local Weather* has been divided into 10 coastal regions, each with its own chapter describing the known weather conditions along that stretch of coastline. To find the stretch of coastline that interests you, refer to the Table of Contents or the colour-coded map on the inside back cover. If you want to learn more about the hows and whys of marine weather, you can read the whole guide. If your interest lies only with a certain bay or inlet, you need only refer to that section. The maps in this section use symbols to represent various weather effects. The legend for these symbols is found on the inside foldout of the front cover.

The *Local Weather* section is not intended to be exhaustive in describing the local weather effects within each region; nor can the many multiple-effects be depicted by one symbol. As well there are countless local-effects that we don't even know about. Hopefully, the more important details of local weather within Atlantic Canada have been highlighted.

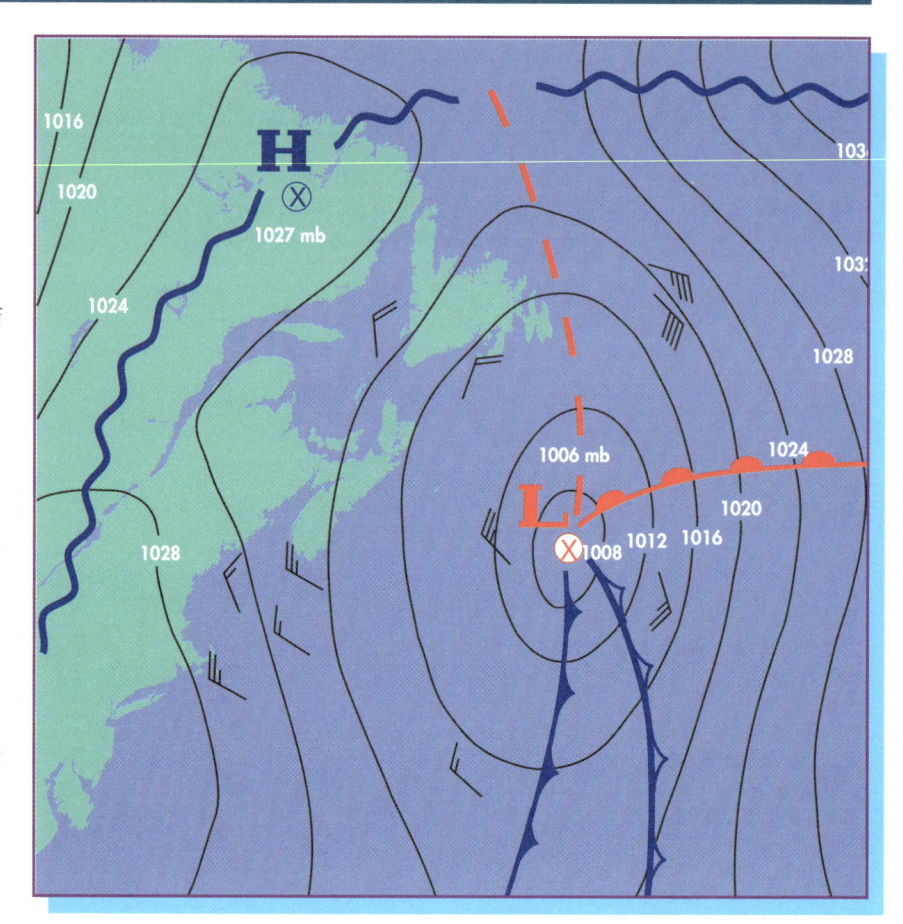

NUMBERS CONVENTION

This type of book creates a dilemma: what number units and convention should be used? The formal convention for units in Canadian publications is metric (imperial). The traditional convention for mariners is a mix of nautical and imperial units. To include all three units each time a number is presented would make the material tedious. With this difficulty in mind the following convention has been chosen:

Units
(see Table of Conversions in Appendix A)
• Distances, for the most part, are given in nautical miles (but expressed simply as, miles).
• Speeds of wind, currents, and vessels are expressed in knots (nautical miles per hour).
• Heights of waves are expressed in metres, except for heights less than 1 metre (which are expressed in feet).
• Heights of mountains and clouds are expressed in kilometres.

Abbreviations
• Feet or foot = ft.
• Metre(s) = m
• Kilometre(s) = km
• Mile(s) will be written in full.

HOW TO READ A WEATHER MAP

The weather map is as important to a meteorologist as a compass is to a mariner: both are vital tools of the trade. Mariners can also benefit from understanding the basic elements of a weather map. The numbers and symbols on a weather map show the location and strength of current weather systems.

To help you read the weather maps in this guide, as well as the actual maps received over facsimile machines, the symbols used on a weather map are shown on the next page. A complete list of symbols is provided, many of which are rarely seen on a map.

HOW TO USE THIS MANUAL

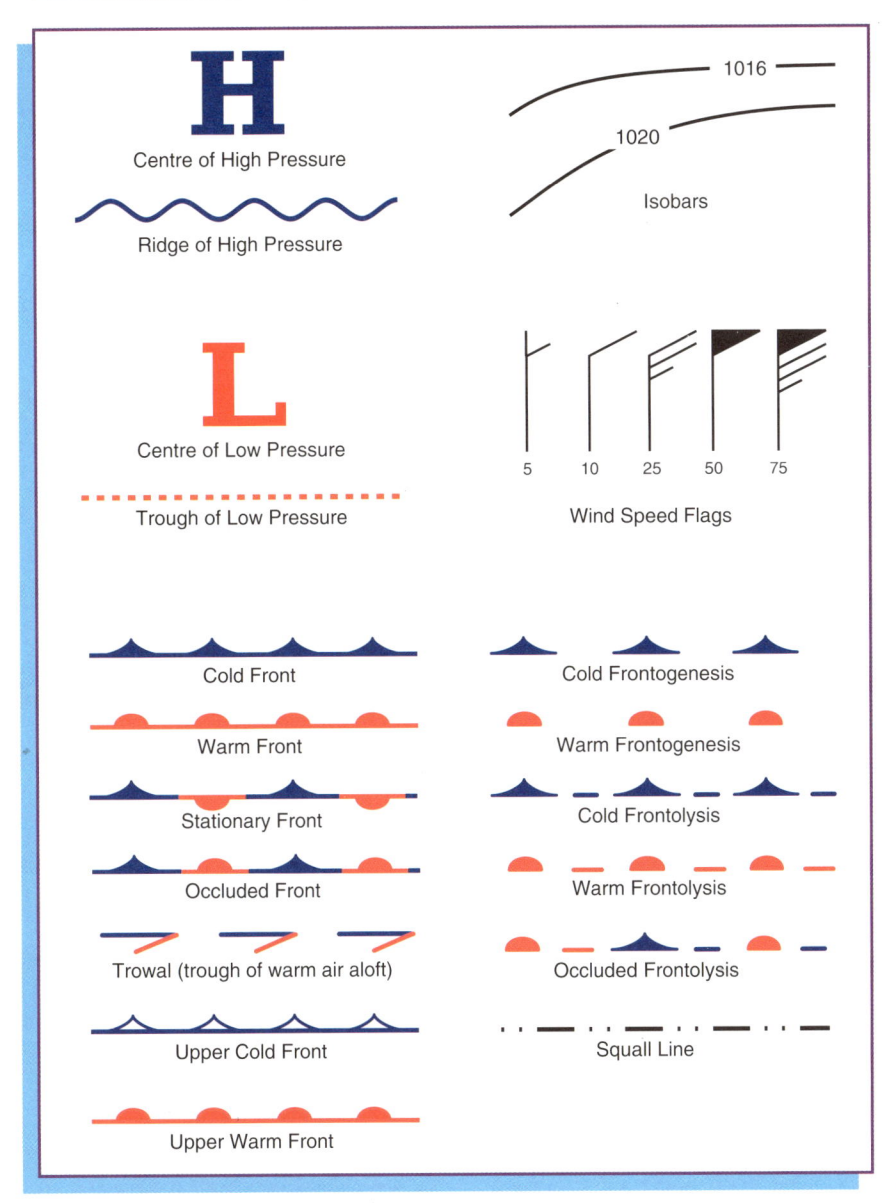

ally moves southeastward. "Icicles" on the map point away from the cold air.

Warm Front The leading edge of an advancing warm air mass (or trailing edge of a retreating cold air mass), which usually moves northeastward. "Raindrops" on the map face away from the warm air.

Wind Speed Flags The shaft of the arrow represents the direction from which the wind blows. The wind speed, in knots, is given by the number of barbs and/or flags on the shaft.

Stationary Front A front that has no discernible motion. Alternate cold and warm front symbols on opposite sides of the front designate the lack of motion.

Occluded Front A front (warm or cold) that has occluded (pulled-away from) its associated low-pressure centre. Alternate cold and warm front symbols on the same side of the front are used to designate the occlusion.

Trowal (TRough Of Warm air ALoft) A specific type of occlusion in which the warm sector has been completely displaced above the earth's surface. The "hooks" on the TROWAL point towards the warm air.

Upper Cold Front A cold front in the upper atmosphere, not reaching the surface. Quite often, this carries the weather of a surface cold front, but not the wind shifts or pressure changes. It usually precedes a surface cold front.

Upper Warm Front A warm front in the upper atmosphere, not reaching the surface. Quite often, this carries the weather of a surface warm front, but not the wind shifts or pressure changes.

Frontogenesis The formation—or "genesis" stage—of a front, is designated with the normal frontal symbology, but with no connecting line between the "icicles" or "raindrops."

Frontolysis The dying stage of a front is designated with the normal frontal symbology, with breaks along the line to show the dissipation of the front.

Squall Line A continuous line of significant convective weather (usually thunderstorms) apart from a cold front.

Centre of High Pressure An area where pressure decreases in all directions out from the centre. Central pressure values are given in millibars. Simplistically, high-pressure centres are often associated with fair weather.

Ridge An elongated region of higher pressure in which the pressure decreases in directions perpendicular to the ridge. Like highs, ridge are often associated with fair weather.

Centre of Low Pressure An area where pressure increases in all directions out from the centre. Central pressure values are given in millibars. Simplistically, low-pressure centres are often associated with poor weather.

Trough An elongated region of lower pressure in which the pressure increases in directions perpendicular to the trough. Like lows, troughs are often associated with poor weather.

Isobars Lines joining places of equal pressure, usually drawn at intervals of 4 millibars. Isobars are similar to contour lines on a relief map in that "highs" can be thought of as "hills," "lows" can be thought of as "bunkers," "troughs" can be thought of as "valleys," and "ridges" can be thought of as terrain "ridges." The closer the isobars, the stronger the wind.

Cold Front The leading edge of an advancing cold air mass, which usu-

INTRODUCTION

PHYSICAL GEOGRAPHY

Topography (physical shape of the land) and bathymetry (physical shape of the sea bed) have a profound influence on both the general climate and the local weather along Atlantic Canada's coastlines. The combination of rugged landscape and generally cold seas can produce some of the harshest marine weather conditions imaginable—sometimes with tragic consequences.

Mountainous terrain in Labrador, northwestern Newfoundland, and the Cape Breton Highlands produces katabatic winds and lee-wave effects that can cause winds from gale to hurricane force. Fjordic inlets and narrow bays can funnel and channel the winds. Bold capes and prominent headlands are subject to cornering effects and wave refraction. The shape and depth of the sea bed, together with adjacent coastlines, can give rise to unusual tides, strong currents, shoaling, and treacherous tidal rips: all of which are made worse by opposing winds and seas. The many freshwater rivers flowing into the ocean can create unpredictable wave and current effects. Freshwater discharges, along with varying depth of ocean water throughout the region, affect water temperatures and sea ice cover.

SCALES AND DETAIL—THE MARINER AND THE METEOROLOGIST

Forecasts are prepared by meteorologists who have had extensive training in synoptic-scale meteorology. This scale deals with weather systems such as high- and low-pressure areas, air masses and fronts, that extend from hundreds to thousands of miles, and last from hours to days. The Environment Canada meteorologists issue their forecasts based on the future behaviour of these synoptic-scale systems. They then describe the effects that these systems will have on the weather.

Mariners, however, operate in an environment that may have significant weather differences over a distance of a few miles or less. Meteorologists refer to these differences as effects on the mesoscale. Thunderstorms, sea breezes and valley-winds are examples of mesoscale phenomena. This is the scale of the local weather effects described in this guide. An even smaller scale of weather events—ones that happen on the microscale—are unforecastable, yet can bring weather of significant consequences. Dust devils and wind fluctuations across the bow of a boat are examples of microscale events.

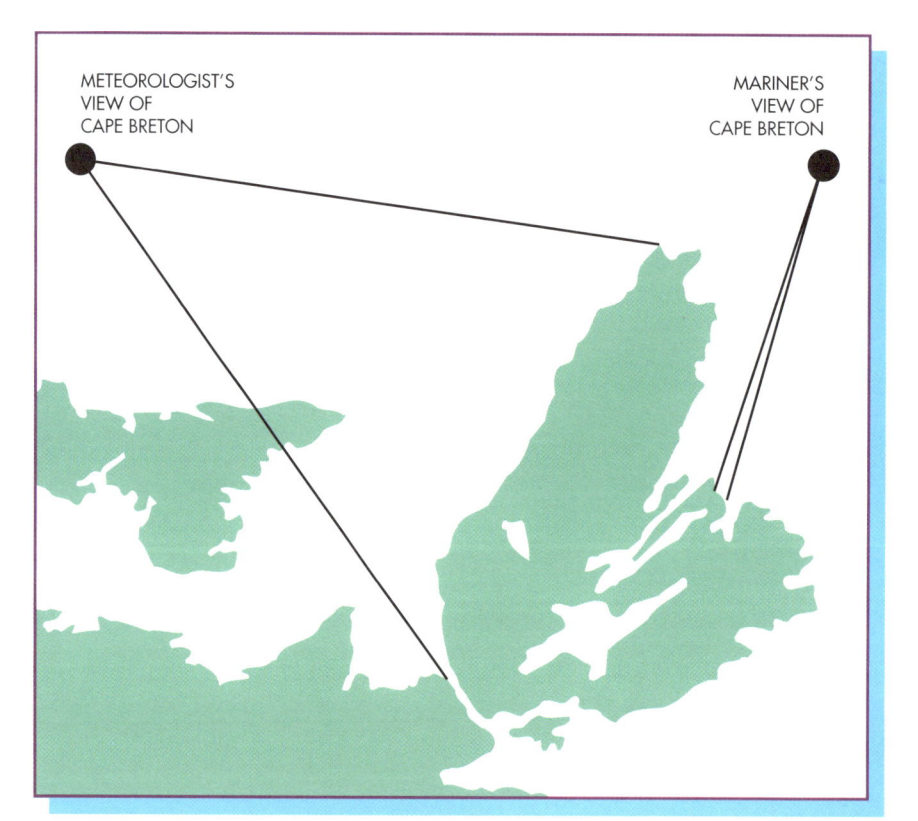

METEOROLOGIST'S VIEW OF CAPE BRETON

MARINER'S VIEW OF CAPE BRETON

INTRODUCTION

An attempt is often made to include the larger mesoscale effects in marine forecasts. However, you, the end-user of the forecast should always incorporate your own knowledge of the area. It is important for you to decide what level of detail you require on a particular day, and to tailor the forecast as necessary. For example, if a large cargo ship can operate under all but lengthy storm-force conditions, the synoptic-scale forecasts from the weather office will be all it needs. However, the board-sailor in a small bay will not only want to hear the latest marine forecast, but will also want to fine tune it for mesoscale effects such as sea breezes or local areas of stronger wind. A forecast without these details will satisfy the cargo vessel captain but not the board-sailor. Clearly, the notion of an "accurate forecast" is intimately related to the user's need.

A word of caution to mariners about consulting this guide for weather conditions on lakes and rivers in Atlantic Canada. The subjects covered in **Marine Meteorology** apply to the ocean or near-shore waters. In many cases, the basic principles may be applied to lakes and rivers, however, there are significant differences. The weather that occurs on the smaller scale of lakes and rivers is beyond the scope of this guide, even with regard to climatology.

THE ROLE OF MARINERS IN WEATHER FORECASTS

Weather Observations

Despite great leaps in forecasting technology in recent years, weather observations from transient vessels at sea still play a large role in the forecasting process. Indeed, the marine community is an essential part of the forecasting team. Mariners use the forecasts, and also supplement the data on which those forecasts are based. Without weather observations from individuals at sea, forecast quality suffers. For example, there may be hundreds of vessels in Atlantic Canadian waters at any one time, but meteorologists analyzing a weather map at 4:00 a.m. will find only a handful of weather observations. The early morning forecast is regarded by many as the most important one, yet that is when fewest reports are received from vessels at sea. The ability to predict the weather hinges in part on knowing what is happening now. Such knowledge depends on receiving observations from vessels at sea.

Weather observations are the result of international cooperation. Most countries that receive weather reports share them freely with the rest of the world. The Canadian Coast Guard marine radio relays observations to meteorologists and other users of weather information—reports that fill in missing pieces of the forecasting puzzle.

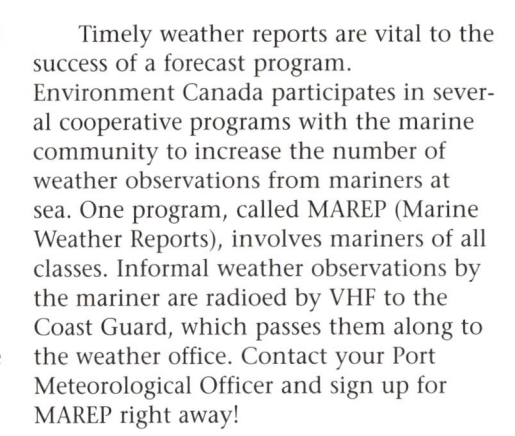

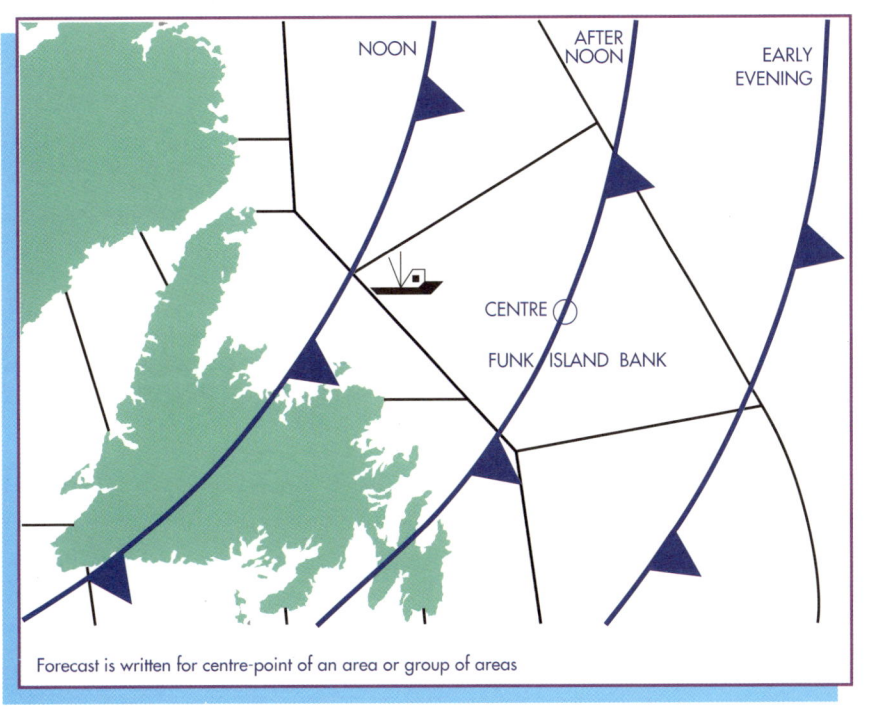

Timely weather reports are vital to the success of a forecast program. Environment Canada participates in several cooperative programs with the marine community to increase the number of weather observations from mariners at sea. One program, called MAREP (Marine Weather Reports), involves mariners of all classes. Informal weather observations by the mariner are radioed by VHF to the Coast Guard, which passes them along to the weather office. Contact your Port Meteorological Officer and sign up for MAREP right away!

Forecast Tailoring

It is often thought that the meteorologist and the mariner compete to see who can "read" the weather better. On the contrary, their cooperation produces the best forecast. The meteorologist tracks and forecasts synoptic-scale weather systems for many days through marine forecast areas as large as a million square kilometres. Experienced mariners, however, often know the signs accompanying these large-scale systems, which create the local weather experienced on a scale of a few miles or less; and they know where high winds or choppy seas develop under certain weather conditions. If the mariner doesn't participate in the forecasting process, the value of the forecast is diminished. Therefore, the mariner is expected to adjust the synoptic-scale forecast, and reduce it to the mesoscale—or his own more practical, local scale. This guide should help both the less experienced and the "old salt" who knows what to expect but can't explain why.

To be truly useful, a forecast must be tailored to fit designated marine areas. However, the weather seldom respects the boundaries between these areas. Meteorologists sometimes split the areas in half, but even this leaves hundreds of square miles described as having uniform weather.

For example, imagine a cold front moving through the Newfoundland marine area called Funk Island Bank. The front is moving at such a speed that it enters the western tip of the area at noon and does not reach the easternmost edge until early evening. It is well known that significant wind changes take place along a cold front, so the timing of its passage is important. However, the meteorologist will usually treat the area as if it were a single point, for the sake of timing and format constraints. Therefore, the forecast might refer to wind changes taking place in the after-

Forecast is written for centre-point of an area or group of areas

INTRODUCTION

noon—an average time for the entire area. Knowing this, mariners can adjust the forecast, depending on their location in the area.

If a mariner is operating in the extreme western part of Funk Island Bank, he would expect the wind change to occur a bit sooner than forecast. He would also be listening to the forecast for the adjacent marine areas since the weather may carry over from one area to another. It is minor but significant adjustments such as these that the meteorologist hopes the mariner will make.

Besides these "timing problems," the mariner must also understand that the meteorologist has to keep the forecasts brief. Because most forecasts are received by radio, those that include all weather changes are often too long and make listening tedious. To provide the most useful service to mariners, marine meteorologists have to be both concise and accurate.

When writing forecasts, the meteorologist considers what are called "significant thresholds." One example is wind shifts through only eight points of the compass: a forecast may mention a northerly or a northeasterly wind, but never a north northeasterly wind. Another example is wind events lasting three hours or more: if a non-threatening wind-event is expected to last less than three hours it is unlikely to show up in a forecast. A case in point would be a low-pressure centre passing close to, but just north of, a location. The winds might shift from easterly gales to southeasterly gales to light southerlies (when the low is very close) to strong southwesterlies—all within a three-hour period. The forecast will simply talk about easterly gales veering to strong southwesterlies. In general, a forecast that tries to incorporate every wind change would be too lengthy. The mariner needs to be aware of such constraints in order to extract the most information from the forecasts.

MARINE WEATHER SERVICES

Marine Weather Services are provided throughout Atlantic Canada by Forecast Centres in Bedford, Gander, and Fredericton. With both public demand and government spending in a state of flux, information about regional weather services quickly becomes out-of-date. Therefore, only an outline of these services is provided here. For a comprehensive list of available services, call the Port Meteorological Officers in Halifax or St. John's.

Observations and Data

Since the publication of the *East Coast Marine Weather Manual* in 1989, most lighthouses in Atlantic Canada have been automated, and weather information from them is no longer available. Many coastal staffed weather observing stations have been replaced by automatic stations. As well, there are many new automatic stations which are invaluable to meteorologists. Weather buoys deployed in offshore waters continue providing a vital service to the forecast centres. Remote sensing equipment like satellites and radar also provide continuous weather data for forecasters, and technological advances make this source of information foundational to forecasting programs.

Routine Bulletins

The following forecasts and bulletins are routinely available:

Marine Forecast Forecasts for the 38 marine areas (see map, inside back cover) are issued four times daily from both Bedford and Gander. The bulletins are valid for two days with a third-day outlook of general wind conditions. Included in the forecasts are:

Wind–Wind directions are given at eight points of the compass. Wind speeds are in knots.

Weather–Weather is given if it is expected to reduce visibility.

Visibility–Visibility is given using descriptive terms: **Good** means greater than 6 miles; **Fair** means 1 to 6 miles; and **Poor** means less than 1 mile.

Freezing Spray–This is included in the forecast when moderate or heavy ship icing is expected.

Temperature–Actual values (in °C) are given when the temperature is near or below zero; otherwise, only a temperature trend is given.

Marine Synopsis When a forecast is issued, a synopsis is included, and is usually broadcast first. The synopsis gives the broad weather picture and tells how and where weather systems are located and moving. It also lists the warnings that are in effect and discusses any tropical storms or hurricanes north of 30°N. An experienced mariner can fine tune the forecasts for an area once the general weather picture is known.

Technical Synopsis This bulletin is issued four times daily by the Maritimes Weather Centre. It gives the latitude, longitude, and movements of all weather systems within the area: 30°N to 60°N and 50°W to 90°W.

Sea State Forecast Deep water (defined as 50 m deep or greater) significant wave-height forecasts, valid for 24–30 hours, are prepared twice daily for all marine areas (except Northumberland Strait, Chaleur-Miscou, and Lake Melville, which have considerable shallow water.) Wave heights are given in metres.

Ice Forecasts Bulletins for Nova Scotia, P.E.I., and Newfoundland fishermen are available during the ice season. As well, a bulletin is issued for the Gulf of St. Lawrence throughout the ice season. All bulletins are prepared by the Ice Centre of Environment Canada in Ottawa.

Warnings

The following special bulletins are issued by the Weather Centres when forecast conditions warrant. All warnings are broadcast immediately by all participating radio stations and are mentioned in the appropriate marine synopsis and marine forecast.

Marine Weather Tip
*Wind directions given in the marine forecast are "true" as opposed to "magnetic." For example, a forecast westerly would be true westerly, or magnetic southwesterly. An easy way to remember that wind directions are "true" is to remember this simple fact: **everything from the weather office is always true!***

INTRODUCTION

Gale Warning
Issued for winds in the range of 34–47 knots during the forecast period.

Storm Warning
Issued for winds in the range of 48–63 knots during the forecast period.

Hurricane Force Wind Warning
Issued for winds exceeding 63 knots during the forecast period.

Hurricane or Tropical Storm
A statement is issued when a hurricane or tropical storm is forecast to give gale-force winds or higher to any of the 38 marine areas within 72 hours. The warning is issued by the Canadian Hurricane Centre in Bedford, N.S. and contains general information about the location and movement of the storm, as well as the wind speeds reported and forecast. When a storm is forecast within 48 hours, more frequent statements are issued.

The following warnings are **not** issued as separate bulletins:

Freezing Spray Issued when moderate or heavy vessel icing is expected due to freezing sea spray. The degree of icing depends on the size and type of vessel, as well as its motion. The freezing spray warning is therefore a general statement of the potential for vessel icing—specifically, for a vessel not following avoidance procedures. This is mentioned in both the synopsis and forecast.

Small Craft Issued by the Maritimes Weather Centre for Maritime coastal waters when winds are forecast to be 20–33 knots. This warning is mentioned only in the synopsis.

Storm Surge Mariners are advised of the potential for storm surge in the marine synopsis when unusually high water levels, at least 2 ft. above normal, are forecast along the coast.

Ice Issued by the Ice Centre in Ottawa when ice pressure poses a threat to marine operations. Details are carried in the synopsis.

Special Forecasts
The changing character of the marine community has created a growing need for specialized or detailed forecast services. Both of the marine forecast centres can provide these services upon requests to the Officer-in-Charge. For specialized services in Maritime waters call the Maritimes Weather Centre at (902)-426-9200. For specialized services in Newfoundland or Labrador waters call the Newfoundland Weather Centre at (709)-256-6610.

Dissemination
Perhaps the greatest changes in marine weather services in recent years have been in the area of information dissemination. These changes will continue as traditional methods of receiving weather information are further supplemented by a growing number of media. Environment Canada's Weatheradio, Canadian Coast Guard Marine Radio, AM/FM radio broadcasts, radio facsimile, and alpha-numeric broadcasts are no longer the only way forecasts reach the public. Weather centres now employ A.T.A.D.s (Automatic Telephone Answering Devices) for both regular and cellular telephone customers; Coast Guard's NAVTEX weather forecasts give mariners a more concise but detailed forecast in hard-copy form; television weather presentations are growing in popularity; and the explosion of information through INTERNET is making worldwide weather information available to any PC-user.

BE PREPARED - THE CHECKLIST!
Here is a checklist that can help make forecasts more useful, anywhere marine forecasts are available:

What is the present weather?
Listen to reports from along the route you are planning. Keep a "weather-eye" open.

What is the forecast trend—worse, the same, or better?
Consider how long you will be at sea.

What marine warnings are in effect or forecast?
Interpret the warnings as they apply to you:
- are forecast conditions beyond my limits?
- will local effects create conditions beyond my limits, even if no warning is in effect?

What is the weather summary?
Consider the location and forecast movement of fronts and pressure systems described in the synopsis.

What forecast areas are important to you?
Where are you?
- Make sure you listen to the right forecast.
- Also listen to the forecast for adjacent areas.
- If you are near one end of the area, you may need to adjust the time when the weather is going to affect you, depending on where it's coming from.

Where are you going?
- The reports and forecasts for all areas through which you are going to travel should be monitored.

Where is the weather coming from?
- Listen to reports from areas where the significant weather is now.

Are you offshore or near shore?
- If offshore, you can probably use the forecast with only a few minor adjustments.
- If near shore, you may need to make your own adjustments to the forecast.

MARINE METEOROLOGY *The Basics*

Don't let a word scare you. Meteorology is the term for the science of weather and weather forecasting, but everyone has some knowledge—or at least an opinion—about the weather.

Marine meteorology is the study of weather that affects larger lakes and the oceans. A basic understanding of marine weather helps mariners to know when and where hazardous weather may occur—a key to boating safety.

In the past, meteorologists have too often used technical terms and concepts unfamiliar to the public. This section is written for those who want to learn the basics of marine weather—but without the mystery.

WHERE IT ALL STARTS—THE SUN

When talking about the weather, we are most interested in what occurs in the atmosphere, at or near the earth's surface. The weather that we experience draws its energy from one basic source: the sun. The sun heats the earth, which, in turn, heats the atmosphere from below. The real catalyst for the "weather machine" is not so much the heating of the earth's surface, but, rather, its "uneven" heating. Since the sun is the "heat engine" that drives this machine, it's worth learning a bit about how it gets everything started.

Varied surfaces of land and ocean differently absorb and reflect the sun's rays. Snow and ice reflect most of the sun's rays back to space, while deserts and forests absorb much of the sunshine. The angle at which direct sunshine strikes the earth's surface also depends upon the "lay of the land." Southern slopes receive more direct rays, whereas northern slopes may be entirely in shade. The possible hours of sunshine in a deep valley may be greatly reduced by surrounding hills. These factors alone can explain many "hot" and "cold" spots around the world.

Another important factor is how direct sunshine on the earth's surface varies with time and location. In particular, this depends on the distance between the earth and the sun, the angle of the sun's noon rays on the earth, the transparency of the atmosphere, and the daily duration of sunlight. Here is a simple explanation of each of how each of these considerations affects the Northern Hemisphere.

Ironically, the sun is closest to the earth in winter; this makes for greater heating potential, but other factors counteract it.

The effect of the varying angles at which the sun's rays strike the earth can be seen in the course of the day. At "high noon," the intensity of direct sunshine is greatest; in the morning and evening, when the sun is low on the horizon, less heat is generated. The same principle has a broader application with respect to latitudes and seasons. In winter and at high latitudes, even the noon sun's angle is low; in summer and at low latitudes, it is almost directly overhead. The rays of the low-angle sun are spread over a greater surface than are vertical rays and, consequently, heat the surface less. As well, the earth's tilted axis means that we lean towards the summer sun and away from the winter sun.

MARINE METEOROLOGY *The Basics*

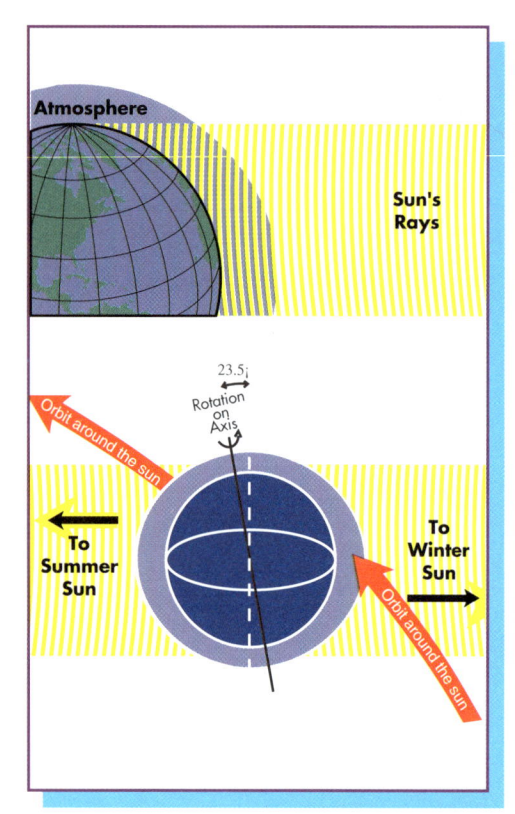

The clearer the atmosphere, the more direct sunshine reaches the earth's surface. Dust, clouds, moisture, and certain gases all reflect, scatter and absorb the sun's rays. Therefore, the farther the sun's rays pass through the atmosphere, the greater the "filtering" effect, which decreases the heating of the surface. This is seen in middle and high latitudes, where the sun's rays pass through the atmosphere at a lower angle than in tropical latitudes—the result being warmer tropics and a colder polar region. This effect varies with the seasons, being greatest in winter when the sun's rays are lowest on the horizon and at a shallow angle to the higher latitudes.

Duration of sunlight also varies with latitudes and the seasons; the longer the period of sunlight, the greater the heating. At the equator, day and night are always equal. In the polar region the daylight period lasts up to 24 hours in summer and plunges to zero hours in winter. At the summer solstice, when the sun is at its farthest point north, the north polar region receives more direct sunshine each day than other latitudes, although the net amount used for heating is reduced by the reflective qualities of ice and snow surfaces.

This uneven heating creates hot and cold spots across the globe—an interesting phenomenon for meteorologists because of a vital characteristic of the air: it has weight! Although the air consists of invisible gases, it has a definite weight, which puts pressure on the earth's surface. The heavier the air: the greater the pressure.

Most people sense that colder air is denser, or heavier, than warmer air. In meteorological jargon, warmer air is said to be more buoyant than colder air. Air pressure is simply a measure of the weight of a column of air over a given area, and as we have just seen, it is directly related to air temperature. Therefore, the "hot" and "cold" spots around the world generally correspond to low- and high-pressure spots.

But one thing that basic physics teaches us is that nature abhors differences in conditions such as temperature and pressure; the atmosphere quickly acts to try to smooth them out. This "action" is the weather that we experience. Whether it takes the form of vicious hurricanes, gentle sea breezes, blinding snowstorms, or pea-soup fogs, all our weather can ultimately be linked to differences in air pressure. For example, low-pressure centres travel thousands of miles in an attempt to even out the pole-equator temperature difference, shunting warm air northward while allowing cold air to flood south.

AIR MASSES

Besides weight, another important quality of the air is its tendency to take on the characteristics of the underlying surface. No matter where air originates, its temperature and moisture quickly conform to that of the surfaces over which it travels. When the earth's surface is heated by the sun, the air in immediate contact with the surface is also heated. If the earth's surface loses heat, the air also cools.

An air mass is a large body of air that is uniform in properties such as temperature and moisture. Air masses move about the face of the earth trying to even out global differences in temperature and moisture. Colder air masses are heavier and exert more pressure on the surface than warmer ones. Therefore, air tends to move from areas of higher pressure to areas of lower pressure. It is this motion of the air—called *wind*—that most concerns mariners.

Meteorologists once gave air masses a whole series names—*maritime polar, continental arctic, tropical*, etc. Today they seldom refer to air masses by name, except for occasional use of generic terms such as arctic (for sub-zero weather) or tropical (for very warm moist weather). This is not to say that air-mass classification is unimportant; accurate identification of an air mass' characteristics is too important to handle sloppily. That's why meteorologists analyze and diagnose each air mass daily, rather than relying on an oversimplified classification system. Accordingly, air masses will not be named in this book.

LOWS AND TROUGHS

When the earth's surface is heated by the sun, low-level air is also heated. This warmer air, more buoyant than the surrounding air, begins to rise, reducing the weight, or force, being exerted on the surface. The result: *low pressure*. The rising air causes a deficit of air near the surface, and surrounding air rushes in—converging on the lower pressure to fill the void. If the air rises quickly, then the surrounding air will also rush in quickly—creating strong winds.

Lows are of greatly varying intensities and are usually associated with bad weather—much cloud and precipitation, often with strong or gale-force winds. As a low develops, the central pressure drops, or "deepens." As well, the pressure pattern strengthens and the system is said to be intensifying. If the system becomes intense enough it can become a "storm." A weakening low centre that is rising in pressure is said to be "filling." The pressure increases in all directions away from the low. A low on a weather map is similar to a "dugout" or "bunker" on a contoured relief map.

A trough is an elongated region of lower pressure. Like the low, it is generally associated with unsettled weather. Winds can be strong on either side of a trough, and sharp wind shifts are common. Troughs on a weather map are similar to "valleys" on a contoured relief map.

MARINE METEOROLOGY *The Basics*

HIGHS AND RIDGES

Alternatively, if air is *cooled* by the surface, it becomes heavier than the surrounding air: the cooler air sinks, building up at the surface. This build-up of air adds to the weight, creating *high pressure*. It also causes air to spread out and move away from the area—the atmosphere's attempt to decrease the build-up (nature not only abhors vacuums; it also abhors excesses.) The typical high-pressure centre shown on weather maps began as an air mass that remained over a region for a time (Meteorologists say it was "stagnant,") developing generally uniform qualities. Highs are usually benign and are seldom cause for concern.

Pressure patterns with highs are weak, and winds are always light near the centre. Weather is usually quiet, dry, and settled. The cloudless skies associated with highs make ground fog and frost likely—in season (see **FOG**). High-pressure systems are usually slow-moving, compared with other systems, and can remain stationary for long periods. A high is said to "build" as the pressure within the system rises; when pressure falls, it is said to be "weakening." The pressure decreases in all directions away from a high. A high on a weather map is similar to a "hill" on a contoured relief map.

A ridge is an elongated region of higher pressure. Like a high, it is generally associated with fair weather and usually has light winds along its axis. Pressure ridges on a weather map are similar to "ridges" on a contoured relief map.

FRONTS

As discussed, highs and lows form because of "hot" and "cold" spots around the world. Air masses move about the surface in an effort to even out temperature differences. Sometimes, when air masses crowd each other, the boundary between them becomes constricted. What started out as a graduating temperature difference over a thousand miles is now compacted into only hundreds, or even tens, of miles. This narrow band is called a *front*.

A front is an elastic, ever-changing barrier between heavy, colder air on one side and lighter, warmer air on the other. A cold front occurs when the air on the cold side is advancing. Conversely, it's called a warm front if the air on the warm side is advancing while the cold air is retreating. Along either type of front there is a constant clash between cold and warm air, which creates a unique brand of weather. The "jet stream" often mentioned by TV weathercasters is simply the front at very high altitudes. It derives its strength from the front's temperature contrast.

COLD FRONTS

A cold front is like an advancing wedge of cold air, with the thin edge of the wedge arriving first. A cold front's slope is usually steep, causing sudden and sometimes severe weather. Since a cold front slopes away from the direction it is travelling, little notice can be expected before it arrives.

WARM FRONTS

Warm fronts slope in the direction they are moving: the highest part of the front arrives first and the lowest part—that nearest the ground—last. As warm air overtakes colder air, it starts a long, steady climb over the cold. The first sign of a warm front is the wispy cirrus "mares' tails" at the top of the slope. Spotting them warns you well in advance that, the base of the front is on its way, but still a good way off. The slope of a warm front is usually much shallower than that of a cold front. Its slope may extend several hundred miles and bring drizzle or continuous rain or snow for 12–24 hours.

The forward and backward slopes of warm and cold fronts show how greatly the advance notice of their approach varies. So does this verse:

The warm front sends criers far ahead
To make itself early known.
The cold front will lean over backwards instead
To hide its presence until it has blown.

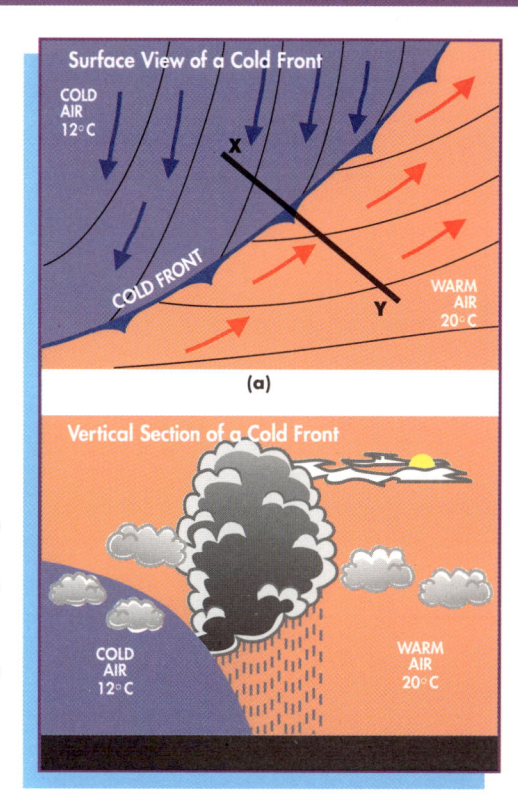

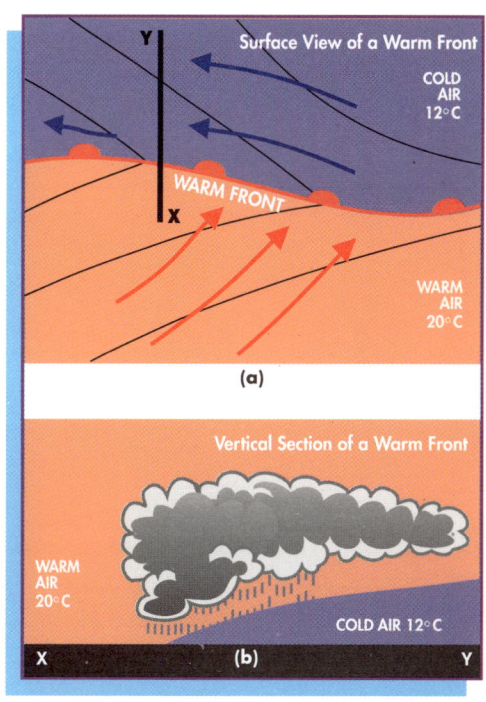

3

MARINE METEOROLOGY *The Basics*

It is important for a mariner to know what to expect when a front approaches or passes. The following tables describe the typical weather sequences that accompany warm and cold fronts. Note that detailed descriptions of the cloud formations are provided in the **CLOUDS** section.

TYPICAL SEQUENCE OF WEATHER WITH A COLD FRONT

	Front Approaching	*As it Passes*	*Behind Cold Air*
Wind	backs and increases close to front	sudden veer and often includes gusts or squalls	can back slightly, then steady its direction
Cloud	stratus and stratocumulus thickening to nimbostratus	towering cumulus and/or cumulonimbus	often total clearance; cumulus develops
Rain	heavy rain near front	heavy rain, perhaps hail and thunder	usually fine for an hour or two, then showers
Visibility	moderate or poor, perhaps fog	poor in rain	very good
Pressure	falls near front	rises suddenly	rise gradually levels off
Dewpoint	little change	falls suddenly	little change

TYPICAL SEQUENCE OF WEATHER WITH A WARM FRONT

	Front Approaching	*As it Passes*	*Behind Warm Air*
Wind	increases and often backs	veers	direction steady
Cloud	sequence of: cirrus, cirrostratus, altostratus, nimbostratus, stratus	nimbostratus	stratus, stratocumulus
Rain	becomes heavier and more continuous	stops or turns to drizzle	occasional drizzle or light rain
Visibility	deteriorates slowly as rain gets heavier	deteriorates	moderate or poor, fog likely
Pressure	falls at increasing rate	stops falling	falls if low centre deepening, otherwise steady
Dewpoint	little change	rises	little change

MARINE METEOROLOGY *The Basics*

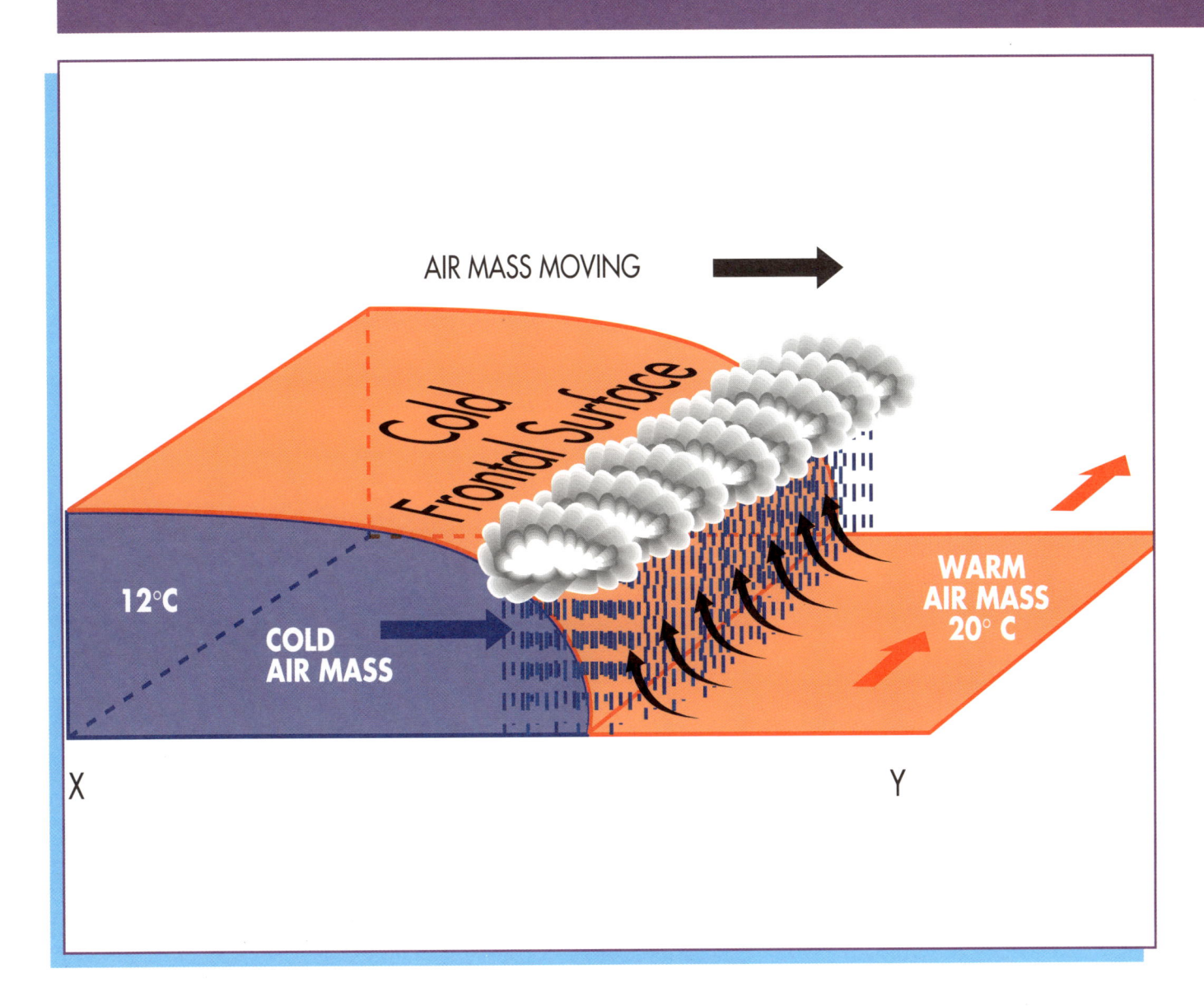

FRONTAL LOWS

The life cycle of a frontal low begins with a stationary frontal zone being disturbed by some atmospheric phenomenon. This causes a tiny bump, or wave, to form, and then move, along the front. The combination of warm and cold air around the wave results in rising warm air (and sinking cold air), which, as we have seen, creates low pressure at the surface. As the low moves and deepens in pressure, strong winds develop. The more interesting low-pressure centres—those usually referred to in marine synopses—are those that exist on fronts. The main area of activity on fronts is near these low centres that are born, grow to maturity, and then die when they become separated from the front.

It has been suggested that introducing concepts which challenge traditional understanding will confuse the longtime student. While this may be partly true, there can be no apology for updating our knowledge, even if it means revising ideas that have been held for half a century. Indeed, we would only need apologize if nothing new had been learned in five or six decades. While much of this section on frontal lows covers traditional territory, the discussion of trowals and upper fronts will likely be new to many readers. In particular, it is anticipated that the section on the *conveyor-belt model* will be completely new even to longtime students of marine meteorology.

3-D CROSS VIEW OF A COLD FRONT

Mariners accustomed to seeing fronts on weather maps are reminded that these features are not simple lines of weather but three-dimensional structures that have height, width, and depth. The change in weather from one side of the front to the other may be gradual or abrupt, depending on the contrast in temperature and moisture.

MARINE METEOROLOGY *The Basics*

EVOLUTION OF A FRONTAL LOW

1. Stationary front—Cold air lies north and warm air lies south.

2. Wave develops and fronts move—A disturbance in the atmosphere creates a wave on the front. This causes the cold air to advance south and the warm air to move along the front, which itself begins to move. The advancing cold air is called a cold front and the advancing warm air—a warm front.

3. Low pressure forms—The cold air pushes against the warm air, undercutting it and pushing it aloft. The rising warm air leaves a deficit at the surface: a low is born. Air rushes in to fill the void—and wind results.

4. Wave/Low moves along the front—The wave/low advances along the front—being directed by the winds at high altitudes.

5. Mature low—The frontal-low system is now fully cranked up and going. Air rushes in at an increasing rate and may reach gale, storm, or even hurricane force.

6. Warm air occludes—At some point in the system's evolution, the warm air will begin to "pull away," or occlude, from the low; the fronts become detached. If the occlusion is pushed aloft, it is called a trowal. An occlusion marks the "beginning of the end" for the low. During the occlusion process, most of the significant weather often pulls away from the low, accompanying the wedge of occluding warm air.

7. Low fills and warm air retracts—With no battle of air masses taking place, the low centre becomes flooded with cold air. Since cold air is heavier than warm, the pressure rises (or the low fills). As well, friction winds down the converging winds, allowing the low to fill.

8. Cold low remains—The low will often sit, stationary, for days.

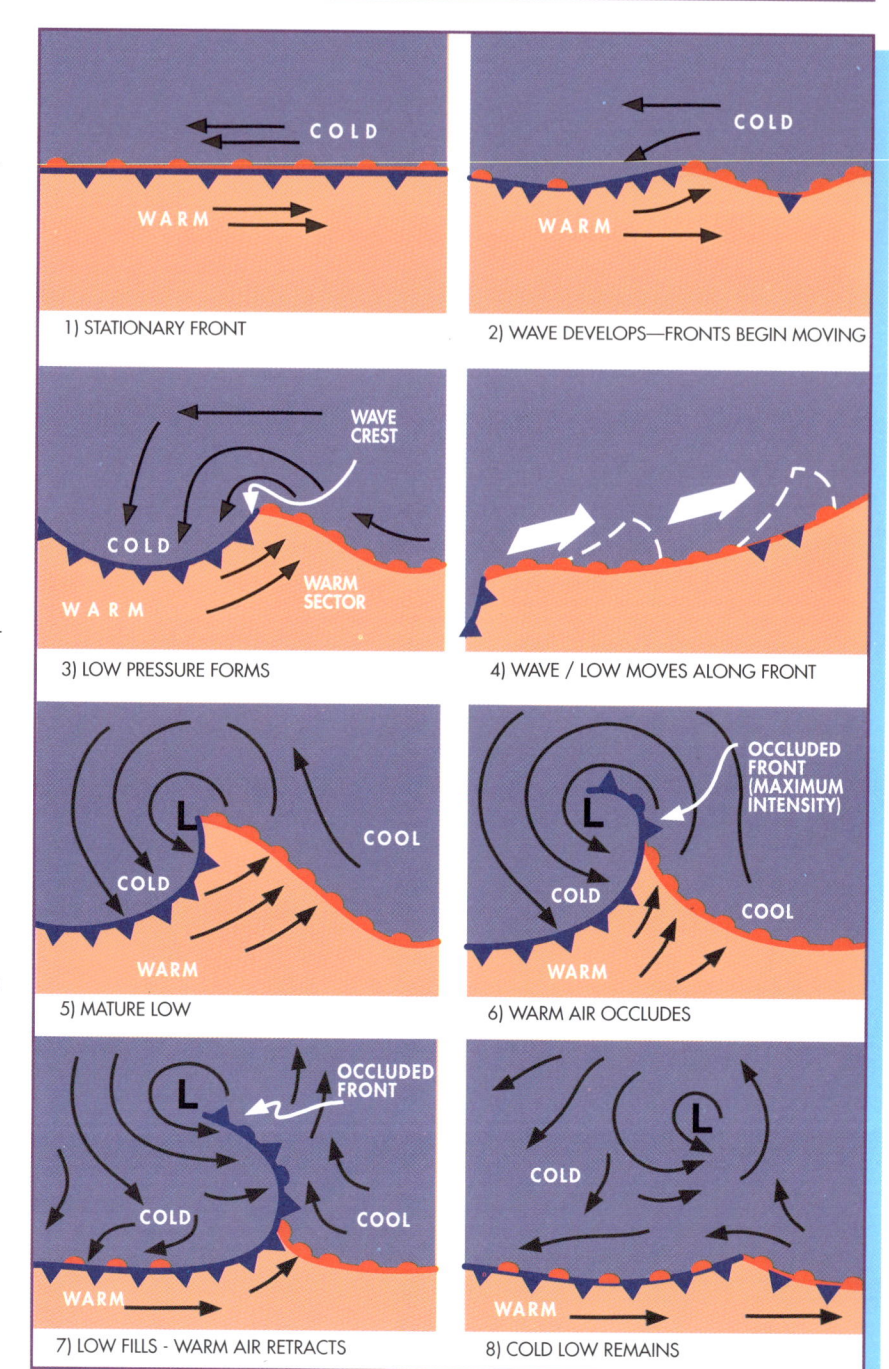

1) STATIONARY FRONT
2) WAVE DEVELOPS—FRONTS BEGIN MOVING
3) LOW PRESSURE FORMS
4) WAVE / LOW MOVES ALONG FRONT
5) MATURE LOW
6) WARM AIR OCCLUDES
7) LOW FILLS - WARM AIR RETRACTS
8) COLD LOW REMAINS

Marine Weather Tip
Smelling the Weather

Have you ever thought you could smell a change in the weather? Well, "sniffing" the weather is a valid part of observing it. High pressure that usually accompanies fair weather tends to keep scents and odours dormant. When a low-pressure system replaces the high, these scents are gently released, enabling us to "smell" a storm coming. As this verse puts it:

> If with your nose you "smell" the day,
> Stormy weather's on its way.

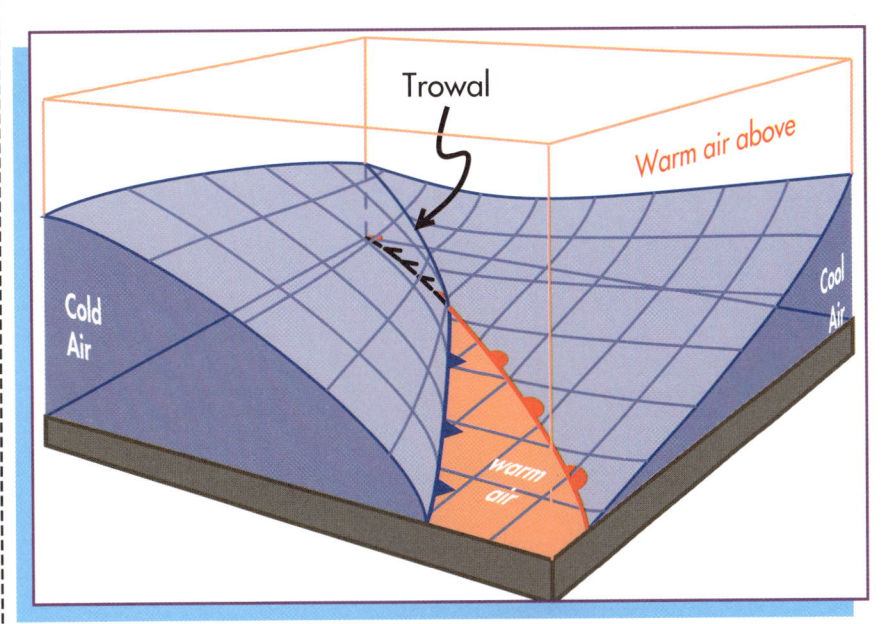

MARINE METEOROLOGY *The Basics*

TROWALS AND UPPER FRONTS— TECHNICALLY SPEAKING

3-D VIEW OF A TROWAL
A trowal (trough of warm air aloft) is a frontal structure that forms during the occlusion process of a frontal low. The warm air lifts out of the low and away from the surface. When this happens and the warm air is forced aloft, it still results in a "trough" in the warm air overhead.

In recent years, the advanced technology of satellite imagery and upper atmosphere studies have shown meteorologists that often, in the past, the "trowals" they analyzed on weather maps were in fact "upper fronts." The distinction isn't just semantics, because trowals indicate a system that is beginning to die, whereas upper fronts have quite different implications. To meteorologists and mariners alike, upper fronts are a relatively new discovery; they are seen increasingly often on weather maps as we become more skilled at diagnosing, analyzing, and predicting their existence. Mariners should recognize upper fronts and understand their implications.

An upper cold front, pushed by the higher winds aloft, moves well ahead of the surface cold front, carrying most of the significant weather with it. Meanwhile, the surface cold front, still lying in a trough of low pressure, has the normal wind shifts and pressure changes expected by the mariner. This sequence of events is seldom described in traditional meteorology "textbooks," because we were unable to identify it. New techniques and knowledge have improved our ability to "read" the weather.

A comparison of the two figures, and in particular, the section from X to Y, shows how the upper front forges ahead of the surface front—carrying the weather with it.

MARINE METEOROLOGY *The Basics*

CONVEYOR-BELT MODEL— TECHNICALLY SPEAKING

Another different way of looking at mid-latitude lows is to conceptualize the airflow through the low, rather than the fronts. This approach is called the "conveyor-belt" model. Studies have shown that these types of lows have three main airstreams, or conveyor belts. It must be noted that this model was developed by studying only slow moving frontal lows undergoing little development, and that airflows in rapidly deepening lows are far more complex. Therefore, like the frontal-low model, the conveyor-belt model is a gross oversimplification. However, despite its limitations, meteorologists have made great gains in understanding the weather using this theory.

Warm Conveyor Belt

The warm conveyor belt consists of air that originates in the south and moves northward. It rises and becomes saturated with moisture, near or north of the warm front, then continues rising until it joins the upper-level westerlies (the upper prevailing winds) northeast of the low centre.

Cold Conveyor Belt

North of the warm front, the airflow relative to the low's motion is from the east. Much of the air on the cold side of the warm front flows towards the region north of the low centre. This stream of air, called the cold conveyor belt, originates from the descending air in an earlier high-pressure system to the north.

Air in the cold conveyor belt flows westward beneath the warm conveyor belt; it draws moisture from the precipitation falling out of the warm air. The cold air then ascends as it turns around the low centre, until it, also, joins the westerlies at upper levels.

Dry Air Stream

The dry air stream originates at upper levels (10 km), to the west of the low centre. Some of this air moves eastward and subsides, reaching the surface behind the cold front.

AIRFLOW IN FRONTAL LOWS

In our example, a frontal low is over the eastern U.S. coast, with the warm front extending east and the cold front extending southwest. The cool easterly winds ahead of the warm front likely originated northeast of Newfoundland, while the southerly winds south of the warm front began over the Caribbean. The northwesterly winds behind the cold front probably began at 30,000 ft. over Ohio the day before. Meteorologists must continually track each air stream in order to predict how it will interact with other air streams over the region.

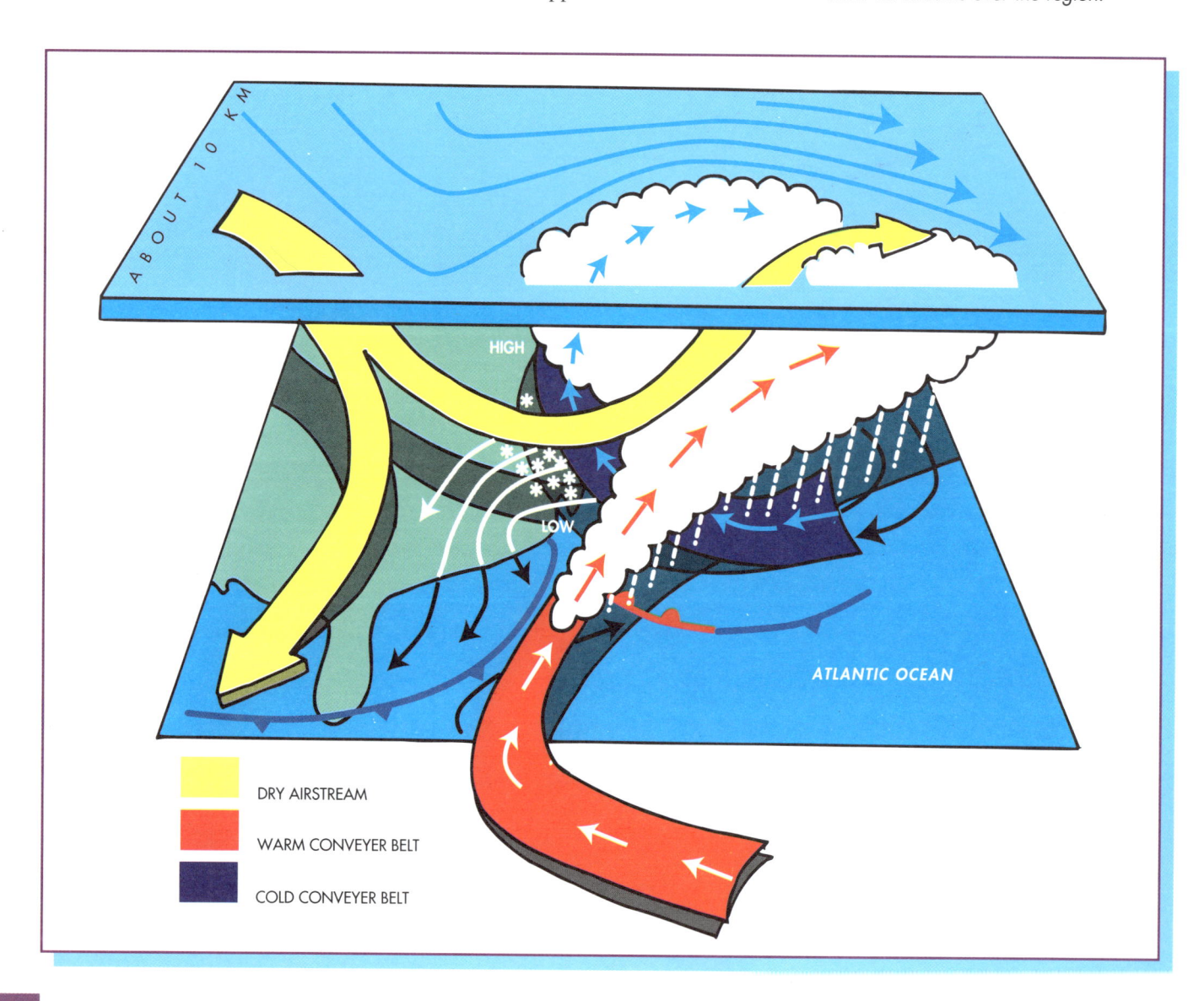

MARINE METEOROLOGY Wind

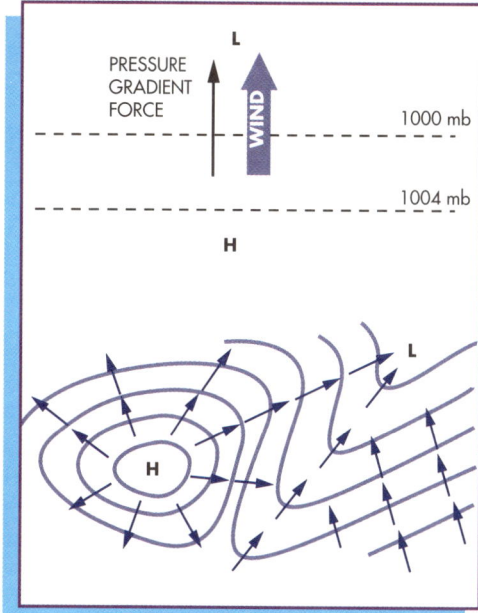

Every wind has its weather.

—Francis Bacon

OFFSHORE WINDS
The Effect of Pressure

Air is set in motion to compensate for pressure differences. This motion of air is called wind. Whether on the grand scale of the globe, or on the smaller scale of the mariner, wind results when air tries to move from a region of higher pressure to one of lower pressure, in an effort to correct these differences. The greater the imbalance, the greater the resulting wind. This driving mechanism is called the pressure gradient force (PGF).

We all know that gravity causes a ball to roll down a slope. We also know, intuitively, that it rolls down a steep grade faster than a shallow one. Similarly, the pressure gradient force causes wind to move from higher pressure to lower pressure—down the "pressure hill." As well, the air moves faster on a steep or "strong," pressure grade than on a shallow, or "weak," pressure grade. A little rhyme may help to remember:

*As a sled behaves on a hill of snow,
So blow the winds from high to low.*

We know that contours on a topographical map show ground height differences, with closely spaced contours indicating a steep grade, or "gradient." Similarly, isobar spacing on a weather map shows pressure differences, and closely spaced isobars indicate a steep pressure grade, or "strong pressure gradient." Conversely, widely spaced isobars indicate a shallow, or "weak," pressure gradient.

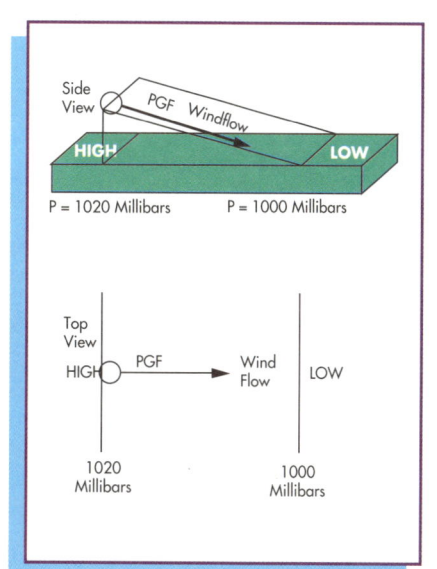

This side view shows how wind blows down a "pressure hill" from high to low pressure, and in the same direction as the PGF. The top view shows the same process, only as it would appear on a weather map.

Wind blows in the direction of the greatest pressure gradient force—just as water flowing down a hill follows the steepest slope. The arrows in the diagram above show the direction of the PGF at different spots on a map of isobars. The arrows also show the direction of the pressure gradient wind at different points.

If the earth did not rotate on its axis, the wind would blow directly "downhill" from high to low pressure. Rotation brings another force, called the Coriolis force, into play. It causes the wind to be turned to the right (in the Northern Hemisphere) by balancing against the pressure gradient force, as shown in the diagram at the top of the next page. This is hard to understand at first, because the Coriolis force is not intuitive. However, the results are too dramatic to ignore. Rather than blowing *down* the pressure hill, the wind blows *around* it, parallel to the isobars, with lower pressure on the left (looking downwind).

This wind that blows around, rather than down the pressure slopes, is called the *geostrophic* ("earth-turned") wind. Almost every book on meteorology talks about the geostrophic wind—an important term to both mariners and meteorologists. The geostrophic wind can be measured exactly just by measuring the gradient of pressure at any point on a weather map. Therefore, if you know the pressure differences over an area, you will also know the geostrophic wind. The value of this knowledge can't be exaggerated.

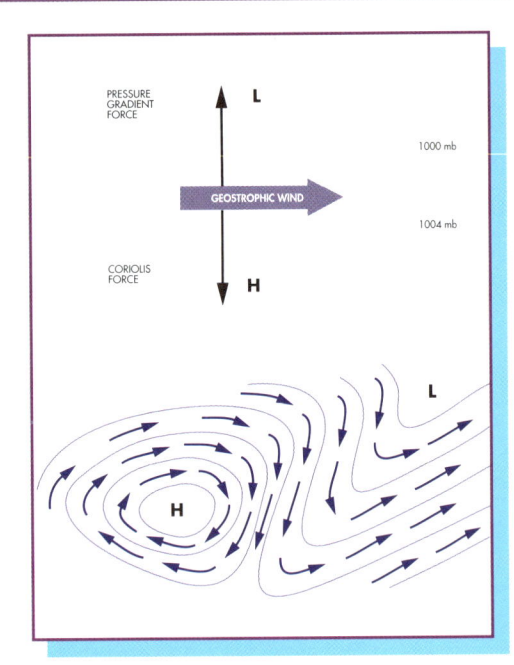

MARINE METEOROLOGY *Wind*

The Effect of Friction

A few thousand feet above the earth's surface, the wind is nearly geostrophic—it blows parallel to the isobars and is directly proportional to the gradient of pressure. Closer to the surface, however, friction between the earth and the wind creates a drag on the wind that slows it down. It no longer has enough momentum to stay parallel to the isobars, so it cuts slightly towards lower pressure—the path of least resistance. This causes the wind to spiral down the pressure hill, rather than blow around it. The rougher the surface, the slower the wind moves, and the more it spirals towards lower pressure.

An example of this friction effect is seen when comparing winds over the land and over the water. Land is a much rougher surface than open water; therefore the wind is stronger over a smooth ocean than over a rough land surface. As well, wind over the land is directed more towards lower pressure than wind over the ocean—making the land wind "backed" from the ocean wind. Because of this friction effect, wind reports from coastal land stations are not always representative of wind conditions over the water.

Some books on basic marine meteorology teach that the speed of open-water wind is simply 70 percent of the geostrophic wind, and that the direction of open-water wind is simply the geostrophic wind backed by 30°. If it were that simple, marine forecasts would be unnecessary. This simple rule can give the mariner good monthly or seasonal averages—but, it is a poor tool to use in daily forecasting.

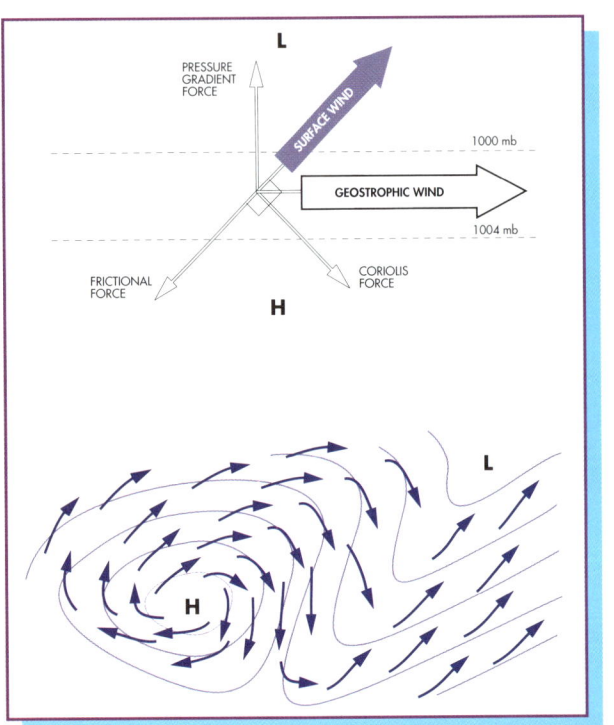

GEOSTROPHIC WIND—
Technically Speaking

A useful rule of thumb to calculate the geostrophic wind from a weather map is as follows:

WIND DIRECTION is parallel to the isobars with lower pressure to the left (looking downwind).

WIND SPEED is calculated by counting the number of isobars (analyzed at every 4 mb) that fall within a spacing of 5° latitude, and multiplying by 10. This gives the geostrophic wind speed in knots.
Example: If 3 1/2 isobars lie across Nova Scotia, from Cape North to Cape Sable (a distance of about 5° lat.), the geostrophic wind over the province is 3.5 X 10 = 35 knots.

FRICTION—Technically Speaking

In the illustration above, we see the flow of wind when a frictional force is added to the pressure-gradient and Coriolis forces. Readers familiar with basic mechanics will recognize the top figure as a force diagram showing how the three forces balance each other. The arrows are not drawn to scale and are exaggerated to illustrate the point. The resulting surface wind is directed slightly towards lower pressure and directly opposed to the frictional force. As well, the speed is lowered.

Imagine that you are swinging a ball on the end of a string. As you swing it in a circular arc about your head, you observe that a consistent rate of swinging keeps the ball at the same height. If the rate of swinging slows, gravity pulls the ball down, and the arc is now around your shoulders. Slower speed caused the ball to drop to a lower height. Similarly, wind that is slowed by friction yields to the PGF and is forced to move towards lower pressure.

Therefore, the surface wind, shown at bottom, is a cross between the pressure gradient and geostrophic winds—but slower. Ocean winds are almost twice as strong as land winds, due simply to friction.

MARINE METEOROLOGY Wind

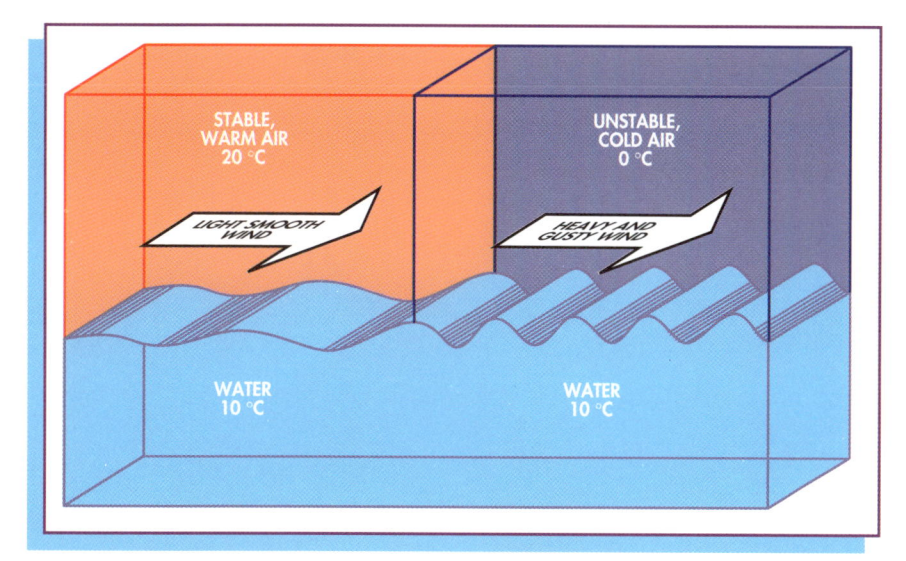

Stability over open water is largely determined by the temperature difference between water and air. If the air is colder than the water, the water warms the air near the surface, and the air becomes unstable. If the air is warmer than the water, the water cools the air near the surface, and the air becomes stable.

The Effect of Stability

When cold air sits over warmer air, the cold air, being more dense, sinks to the surface. On the other hand, when warm air lies over cooler air at the surface, they remain where they are. The air in the first case is said to be *unstable*, and in the second case, *stable*.

What does stability have to do with the wind? As noted earlier, friction makes winds near the surface slower than winds aloft. When the air is stable, the mild, "frictionless" winds aloft slide easily over the cooler blanket of air at the surface, leaving it undisturbed. When the air is unstable, updrafts and downdrafts occur as the colder air above replaces the warmer air below. Strong downdrafts reach the earth's surface as gusts; surface wind gusts are "samples" of the winds aloft that have plunged to earth. Meteorologists can predict maximum gusts at the surface from the speed of winds as high as a mile above.

*On sunny days, the land heats up air near the surface. The air becomes unstable, and gusty winds can be expected on land and very close to shore. The sea, however, does not heat up as much as the land, and the stability of the air is unchanged. References to coastal gusts in forecasts are often due to daytime heating of the land. This can be observed from offshore by noting that cumulus clouds (see **CLOUDS**) are confined to the land, leaving the offshore area cloud-free.*

11

MARINE METEOROLOGY *Wind*

STABILITY—Technically Speaking

Pressure and friction effects only partially explain the real wind experienced by mariners. Stability also plays a key role, as the accompanying diagram illustrates.

A mature low-pressure system with warm and cold fronts, is passing just south of Newfoundland. The **X**, located behind the cold front, is in air that is 10 °C colder than the water below it. The **Y**, located between the two fronts, is in air that is 10 °C warmer than the water below it. Therefore, the air at **X** is unstable, and the air at **Y** is stable. The pressure gradient at both locations is 50 knots, and frictional effects are essentially the same. The real wind at **X** is 45 knots and almost parallel to the isobars, while the real wind at **Y** is 25 knots and cuts across the isobars at an angle greater than 50 °. What is the difference between **X** and **Y**? Stability!

Meteorologists know that stability plays as important a role as pressure gradient when it comes to wind forecasting. Decades of data collection have yielded a correlation between stability, pressure gradient, and the real wind (see table). Mariners who have access to weather maps and can measure the pressure gradient (to determine the geostrophic wind), will find this information valuable.

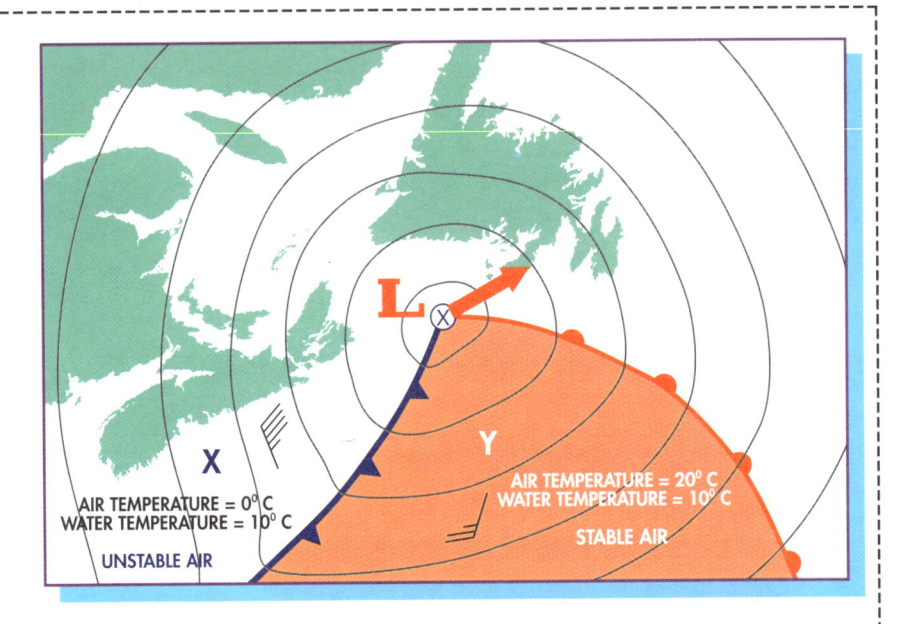

Here's a quick way to classify stability:

Air-Water Temp. Difference (°C)
Very stable   > + 10
Stable   + 4 to + 10
Neutral   - 4 to + 4
Unstable   - 4 to - 10
Very Unstable > + 10

Stability	Wind Backed By	V_g >10	V_g >20	V_g >30	V_g >40	V_g >50
Very unstable	0 °	73%	69%	65%	62%	62%
Unstable	10 °	69%	65%	62%	58%	58%
Neutral	20 °	65%	58%	54%	50%	50%
Stable	30 °	62%	54%	50%	46%	46%
Very Stable	40 °	58%	54%	50%	46%	42%

HOW TO DETERMINE STABILITY

The geostrophic wind (V_g) from a weather map measures 180 ° (south) at 40 knots. As well, the air temperature is 12 °C warmer than the water. The classification would be: "very stable." From the table, the geostrophic wind is backed 40 ° and multiplied by 46 percent—giving a real wind of 140 ° (southeast) at 18 knots. **If gusty winds are expected (as in unstable situations), add 40 percent.** In this example, gusts would be 26 knots.

The Real Marine Wind

On any given day, and within different quadrants of a storm system, real winds may range from 25 percent to 125 percent of the full geostrophic value, and may be at any angle to the isobars on the weather map. Besides pressure gradient, friction, and stability, meteorologists diagnose other factors that can dramatically influence winds at sea. These other factors (which include pressure-change effects and curving-wind effects) are quite technical, and meteorologists themselves struggle to forecast them accurately. This might lead the mariner to believe there are no general rules that work all of the time. Not so! Despite the variable factors, one rule stands as a principle to remember: Buys-Ballots Law. This law says that over open sea, if the wind is from the stern, then lower pressure will be to port (in our hemisphere). Many books state this law in slightly different terms, but the meaning is the same. **REMEMBER THIS RULE!**

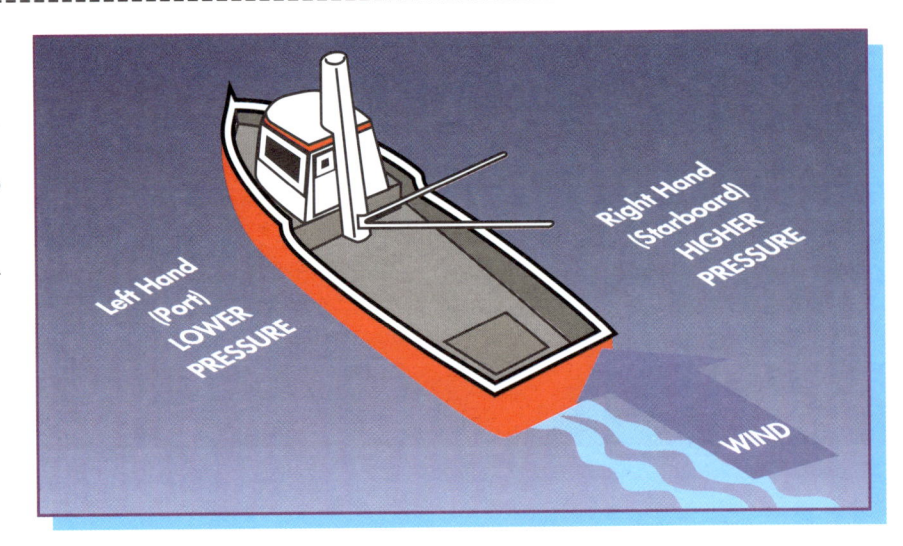

MARINE METEOROLOGY *Wind*

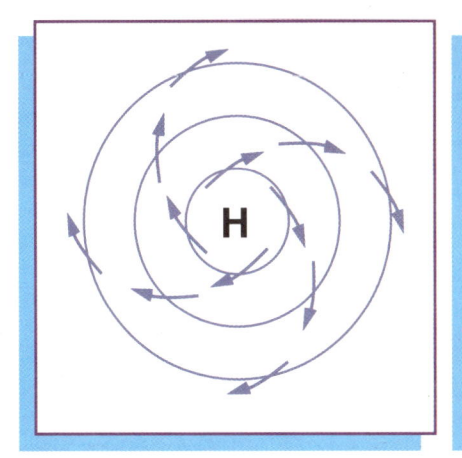

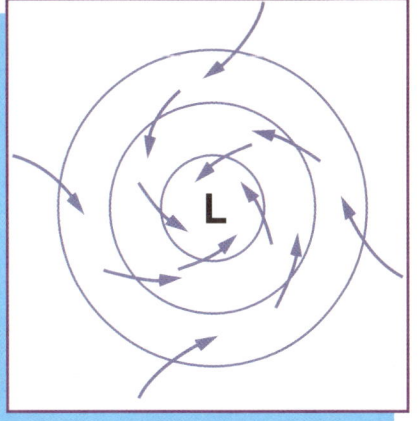

Knowing how air flows around areas of high and low pressure is critical knowledge for weather forecasters, mariners and meteorologists alike. When you tighten a bolt you do two things—increase the pressure and rotate the bolt clockwise. To loosen a bolt, you turn it counterclockwise and decrease the pressure.

Remembering this rule will be helpful; understanding it, more so. To do both, consider the following verse, while studying the diagrams above:

*Tighten a bolt; increase the pressure.
Loosen a bolt; pressure is lesser.*

*Tighten it swiftly for fair-weather wind,
Loosen it quickly; fierce storm to begin.*

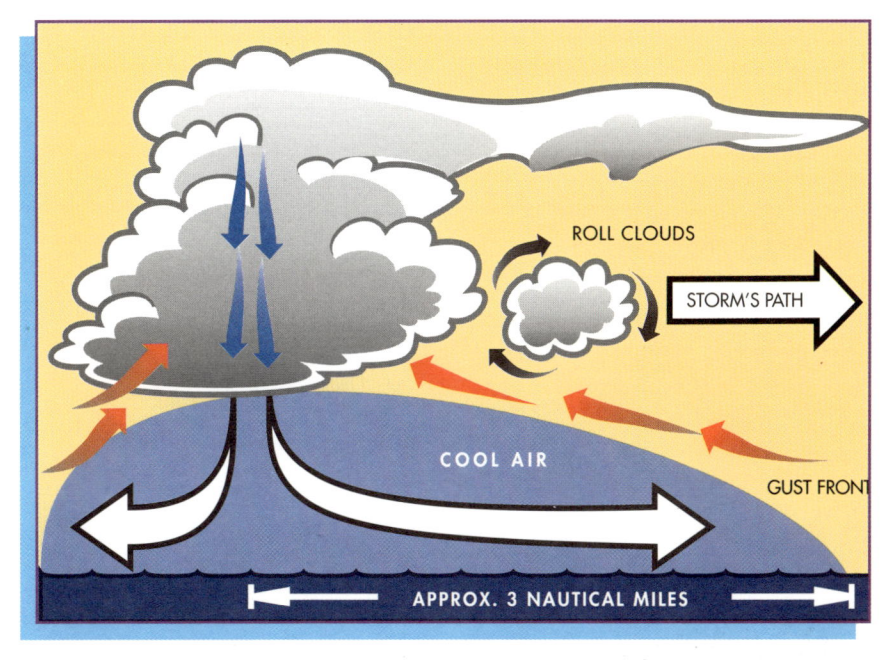

THUNDERSTORM GUST FRONT

A good rule of thumb in guessing maximum gusts in an approaching thunderstorm is to add 15 knots to the estimated speed of the approaching storm cloud; add another 10 knots if the cloud base is very low over the water. For example, assume a thunderstorm is moving in from the southwest. If the lower cloud approaches on a prevailing wind of **SW 10 knots,** *then the expected first-guess gust-speed is* **25 knots,** *or* **35 knots** *if the cloud base is low and black.*

Squalls

Thunderstorms. Individual thunderstorms are almost impossible to forecast over large marine areas. However, violent winds, called squalls, often accompany these storms and are of considerable concern to the mariner (see **STORMS: Thunderstorms**). Cold air within a thunderstorm rushes down from great heights, picking up speed and spreading out at the base of the storm cloud. The resulting gusty winds can extend 2–3 miles ahead of the cloud and rain area. These squalls or gust-fronts are less severe with isolated or air-mass thunderstorms than with cold-front thunderstorms or squall lines. Each squall is usually followed by heavy showers lasting less then 30 minutes. Absence of swell waves, a slow fall in pressure, and a lack of high cloud all suggest a short-lived squall, again less than 30 minutes.

Squall Lines and Cold-Front Thunderstorms. Thunderstorms are mainly summertime events, although they can occur in winter. Thunderstorms often form in organized lines, usually associated with cold fronts, that last for long periods. They can form either along the front, or in a separate line about a hundred miles ahead of the front. Lines of thunderstorms are called squall lines, and are often detectable on navigation radars.

Typical squall lines advance at speeds of 25–40 knots, so thunderstorms that can be seen nosing above the horizon can be expected in about an hour to an hour and a half. During these storms, gusts of 40–60 knots are common. Squalls typically are short-lived, and when one has been weathered, another one is *usually* unlikely for four to six hours. As the old saying goes, "The sharper the blast, the sooner she's past."

13

MARINE METEOROLOGY *Wind*

NEAR-SHORE WINDS

Marine forecasts are designed primarily for use in offshore waters, but mariners often operate near the shore, so they have to be aware of the effects that alter winds near the coast. The marine forecast is a good starting point when trying to gauge coastal wind effects, because local winds are influenced by open-water winds. Many effects discussed in this section are illustrated by specific local examples. If your own situation is similar to one described, you should expect similar wind or weather effects.

Winds Blowing from the Land

When wind blows from the land, it usually veers and picks up speed as it moves out over the water. This is due to the lower friction over the water. The effect is most pronounced under stable conditions, when the wind is forced to stay close to the earth's surface, "feeling the ground." Most land effects occur within 5 miles of the shore and are usually negligible beyond about 10 miles off shore.

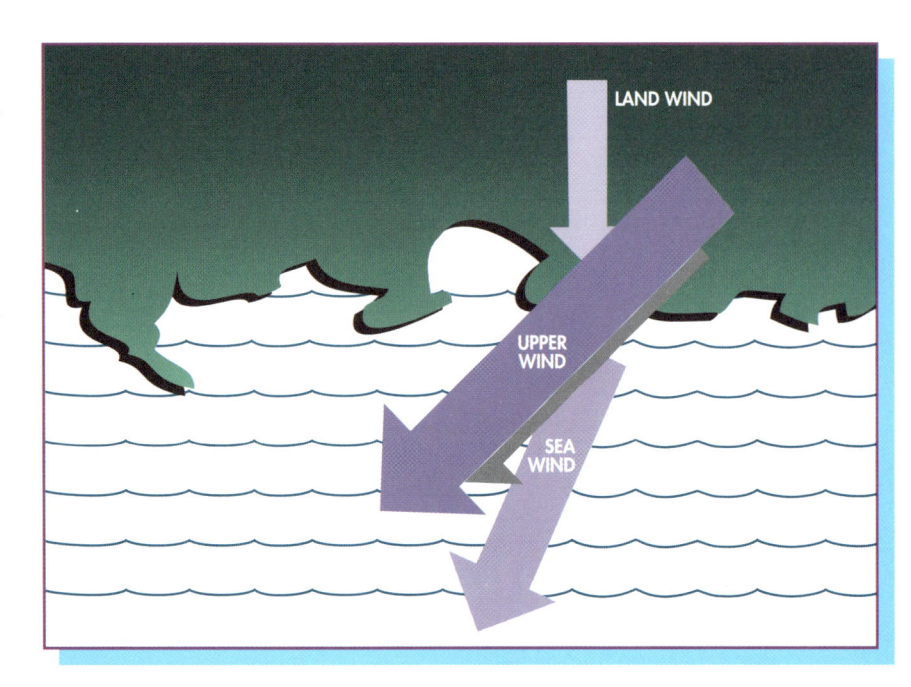

The prevailing winds in Atlantic Canada in the late spring, summer, and early fall are southwesterly. On sunny days, the sun warms the land, which in turn warms the air near the ground. This creates an unstable situation over the land areas, giving rise to very gusty winds. The warm air near the ground rises and cools, eventually falling back to the surface. The falling air pulls down stronger winds from aloft creating gusty winds inland and near the coast. Meanwhile, the winds over the water remain considerably lighter; since the water is not heated as readily as the land areas the air is more stable. On sunny summer days, light to moderate southwesterlies in the morning can often gust to strong or gale force near the coast in the afternoon due to the instability caused by this heating of the land. Reports of clear-weather squalls in the Northumberland Strait and just off northeast Newfoundland are often the result of such instability and can be dangerous to small craft. They usually occur within 5 or 6 miles of the coast and end with sunset.

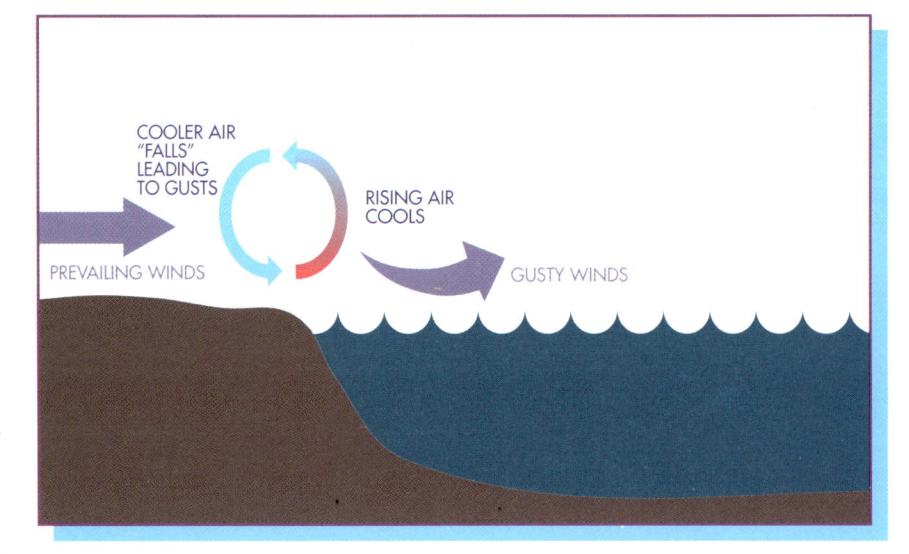

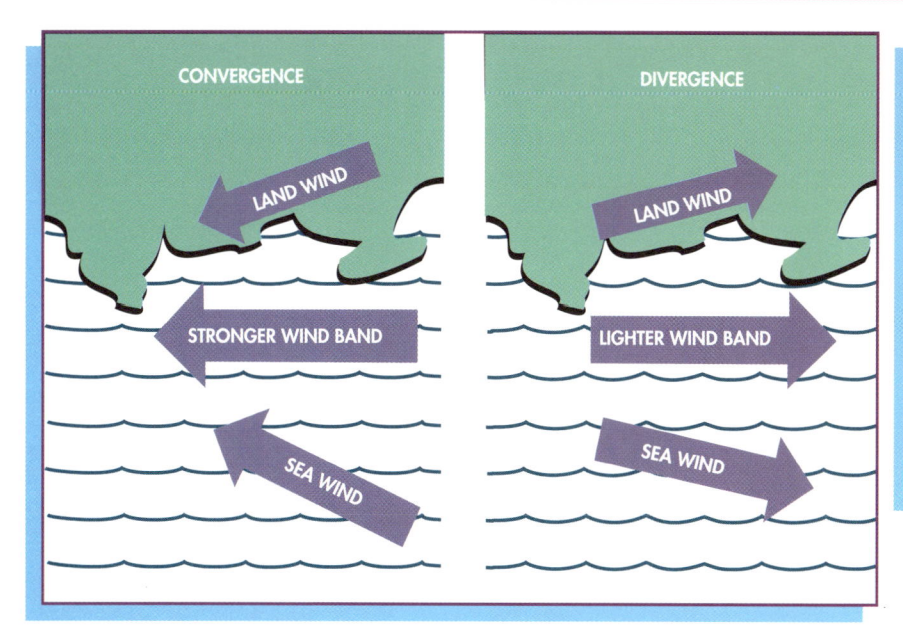

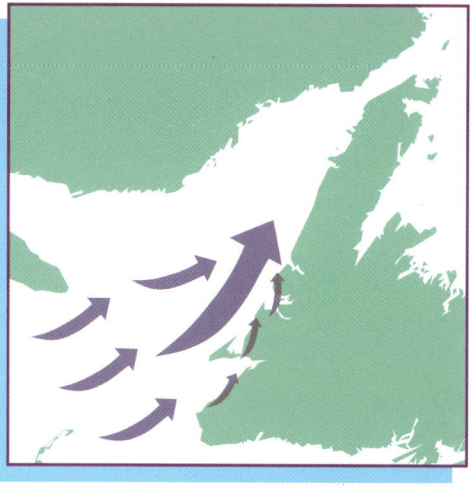

MARINE METEOROLOGY *Wind*

A well-known case of convergence occurs along the west coast of Newfoundland in southwesterly winds, associated with lows moving northwards across the Gulf of St. Lawrence.

Coastal Convergence / Divergence

When the wind is at your back and the coast on your right (coast to starboard), the different angles of surface winds over land and water (due to friction) cause the airstreams to converge; this creates a band of wind that is about 25 percent stronger within a few miles of shore. Friction along the shoreline keeps coastal wind speeds lower than those just offshore. The convergence of airstreams forces the air upwards, often causing increased cloud or a band of thicker cloud along the coast. The stronger wind just offshore is often mistaken for a sea breeze, but in fact it persists both day and night (whereas the sea breeze dies down at sunset).

When the wind is at your back and the coast on your left (coast to port), the effect is the opposite. The airstreams diverge, the wind is lighter near the shore, and there is less cloud. Note that this lack of wind near the coast in the afternoons is often dominated by a sea breeze.

Local weather effects are seldom the result of a single factor. Coastal convergence and divergence, as described here, are easily understood because friction alone is the driving mechanism for the phenomena. Normally, however, the effects of convergence and divergence are influenced by other factors such as stability, sea breeze, and channelling—often with dramatic results.

Let's look at how things can get complicated by just adding the effect of changing stability over the land during the day.

Imagine a pleasant summer day with sunny skies and a moderate breeze over the water of 15–20 knots parallel to the coast—with the coast to port. Early in the morning, the air over both land and water is stable. The wind over land is 10 knots and backed in direction away from the coast because of friction. The diverging airstreams at the coast create a band of winds that are weaker than the winds farther offshore—or about 15 knots. So far this is no different from the example of divergence previously discussed, but from here on the atmosphere takes a different turn. The sun heats up the land during the day, and by afternoon, the air over the land becomes quite unstable. The wind over offshore waters remains unchanged, but the land winds have increased substantially and veered in direction from their morning values—looking more like the geostrophic wind as the day progresses. Instead of having a divergent airstream along the coast, the winds actually converge and increase in value. What started as a band of moderate near-shore winds has turned into a band of afternoon gales along the coastline! This predictable phenomenon is experienced along parts of the eastern shore of Nova Scotia on sunny summer days.

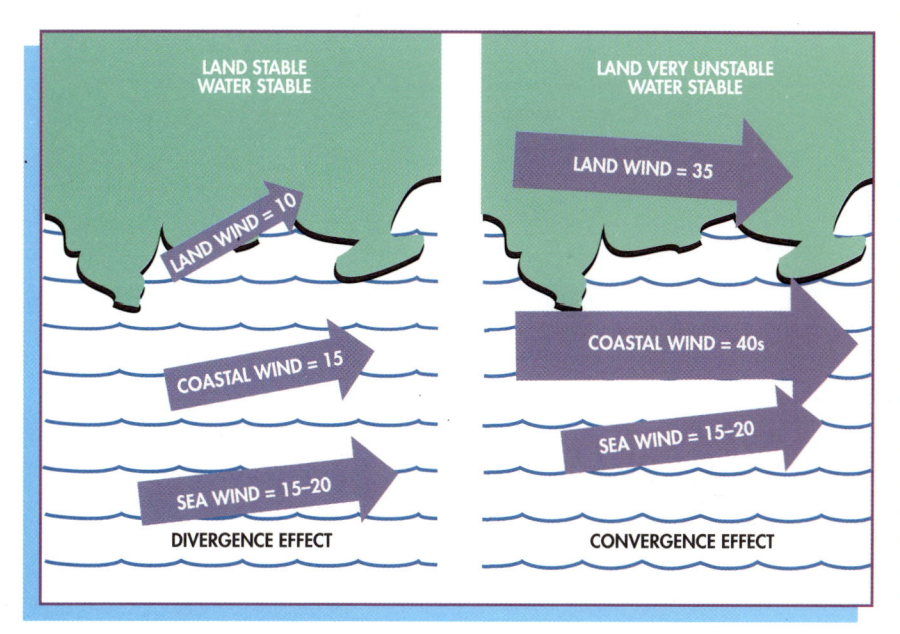

15

MARINE METEOROLOGY Wind

Cornering Effects

Coastal convergence and divergence also occur on a smaller scale, known as the "cornering effect." Looking downwind towards a land mass, one can always expect stronger winds at the left corner of the land. If the land mass is an island, and the wind can also flow past the right side, the winds will be weaker. The explanation is the same as that for convergence and divergence along the coast: friction.

These bands of stronger and lighter winds are not limited to the island shore; but they often continue downwind for tens of miles. Winds may also be turbulent and gusty to the lee of the island as eddies form downwind. Sometimes a line of cloud (parallel to the wind) or individual clouds suggest the position of the stronger wind band, while a line of blue sky or thinner cloud suggests a lighter wind band.

Sea and Land Breezes

The sea breeze is perhaps the best known and most studied local wind condition in the world. Sea breezes occur during the daytime in warm, sunny weather, when the air over a land area is heated more rapidly than the air over an adjacent water surface. The sea breeze is simply nature's way of moderating this local temperature difference. The warmer air over the land rises, while relatively cool air from the sea flows onshore to replace it. The winds aloft over the sea subside to fill the vacancy over the water, and in turn, the rising air over the land turns seaward to fill the void aloft over the water—a circulation has been established.

As the day progresses, the sea-breeze circulation strengthens and extends farther inland and seaward. The Coriolis force then takes effect, causing the sea breeze to veer. By mid-afternoon, the direction of the sea breeze shifts along the shore (a variation of 50°–60° from earlier in the afternoon) and extends from 10–20 miles seaward. The sea breeze fades around sunset, although the sea-breeze circulation may continue to drift seaward and can sometimes be found up to 40 miles from shore, in the middle of the night. Mariners sometimes refer to any onshore wind as a "sea breeze," but a true seabreeze is strongest in the afternoon and stops shortly after sunset.

Sea breezes are typically 10–20 knots but may reach 25 knots. Coastal communities will notice a considerable difference in air temperature because of sea breezes. Studies done in the metropolitan area of

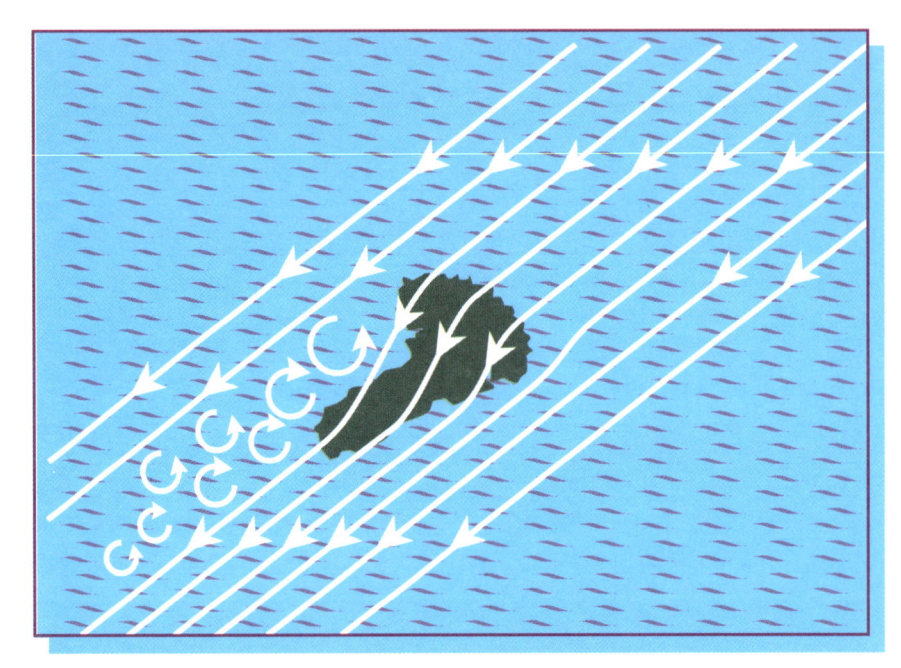

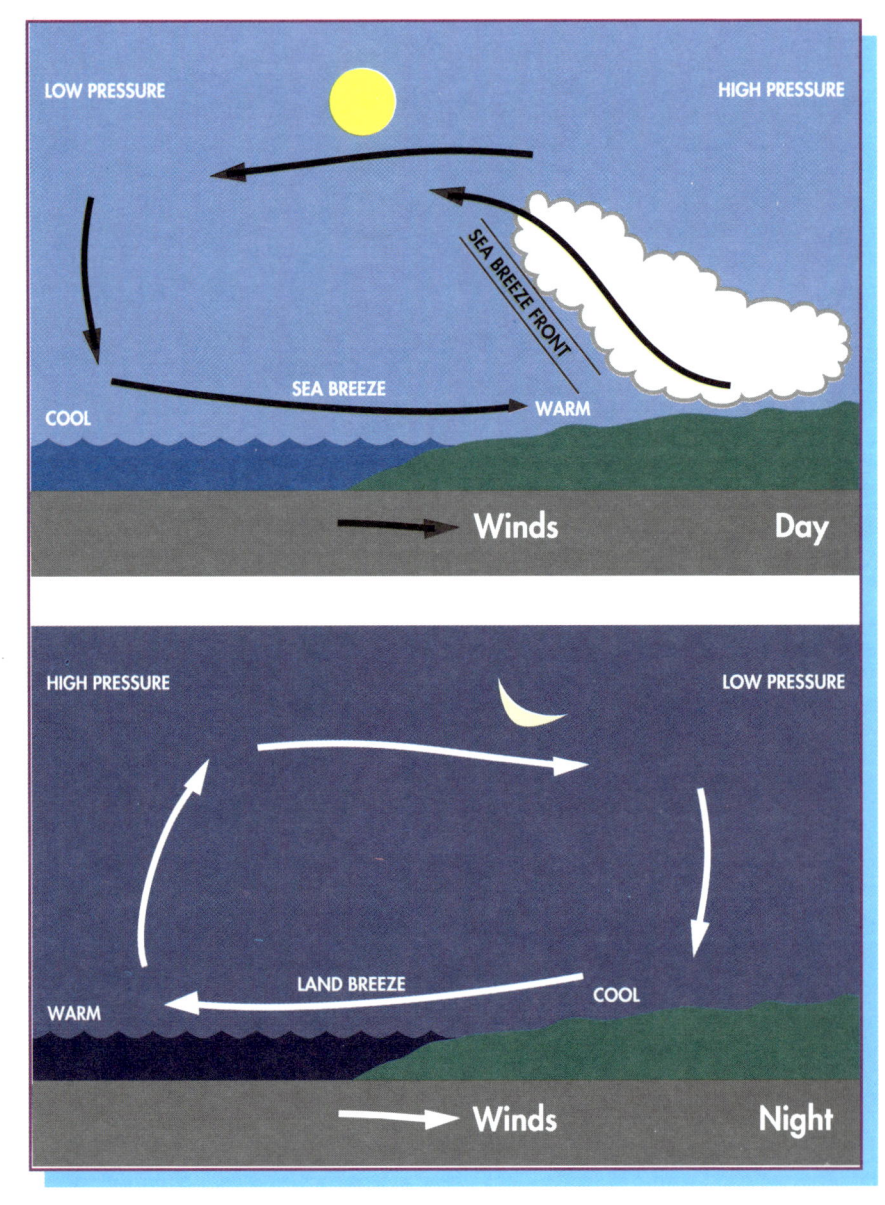

MARINE METEOROLOGY Wind

Halifax, have shown afternoon summertime temperatures to be as much as 12°C–15°C cooler at Shearwater than in Lower Sackville—just because of the sea breeze. Generally, these winds are not hazardous to mariners unless they combine with other effects. For example, northern Labrador experiences strong sea breezes where land and sea temperatures differ greatly. When they are enhanced by local funnelling effects, very strong winds result, such as those found in the fjords along the Labrador coast. Sea breezes in Atlantic Canada are generally strongest in the late spring and early summer, when water temperatures are still cold and the hours of sunlight are long.

At night, the air over land cools faster than that over the nearby ocean, causing the air to circulate in the opposite direction—a land breeze. Land breezes are usually weaker than sea breezes and have less effect on temperature. Both land and sea breezes can occur on lakes; they are, appropriately, called lake breezes.

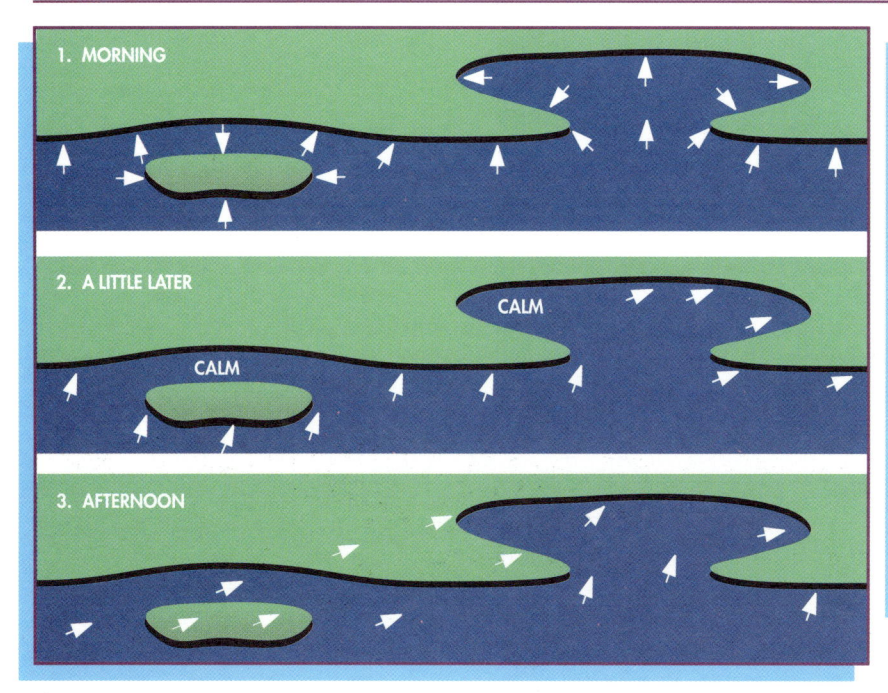

The above illustration shows whether or not a sea breeze can be expected, depending on the prevailing wind. Note that the coastline can be oriented in any direction and that the arrows on this diagram represent the prevailing wind in relation to the coastline.

Irregular Coastlines
Complicated sea breezes initially develop where the coastline is very irregular. However, as the afternoon progresses, the sea breeze expands—smoothing out and behaving as if the coastline were straight. For example, if a mariner is sailing close to the shore in a large bay, the sea breeze in the late morning will blow at right angles to the nearest shore. (figure 1) As the day progresses, the winds will veer—because of the Coriolis force—and the sea breeze will blow at more of an angle. (figure 2) If there is an initial prevailing wind offshore, a calm period will develop near the coasts of the bay and gradually drift seaward. Mariners in the bay will often notice that the winds become calm for a time in the afternoon, then increase again from a veered direction. (figure 3) This classic pattern occurs regularly in St. Margarets Bay, Nova Scotia.

With a Prevailing Wind
Since there is usually a prevailing wind in Atlantic Canada, the sea breeze cannot be fully understood without also considering the prevailing wind. If the prevailing wind is offshore, it helps the circulation to develop and allows the land to heat to its maximum. If the prevailing wind is onshore, a true sea breeze never develops, because the onshore wind prevents the land from heating up and the circulation from developing.

For prevailing winds of any direction, a true sea breeze will not develop if the wind is 20 knots or stronger.

Marine Weather Tip
One of the first clues to the onset of a sea breeze is the sudden dissolving of low cloud just offshore. This is a sign of air gently subsiding over the water—an indication that part of the sea-breeze circulation is becoming established.

MARINE METEOROLOGY *Wind*

Funnelling, Channelling, and Gap Winds

Funnelling occurs when wind is forced to flow through a narrow opening between adjacent land areas. Inside the opening, wind speed may double, much the way a pinched hose spouts water at a higher speed. The effect often occurs in straits between two islands, between an island and the coast, or in inlets and narrow bays.

Channelling is the tendency of the wind to blow along the axis of a channel or to be deflected by the land. Channelling mainly affects the direction of the wind.

When channelling and funnelling effects occur together, they can create an effect called "gap winds," which can defy the prevailing winds. Gap winds usually blow seaward out of a gap, such as a narrow cove or inlet. Gap winds often catch the inexperienced mariner by surprise.

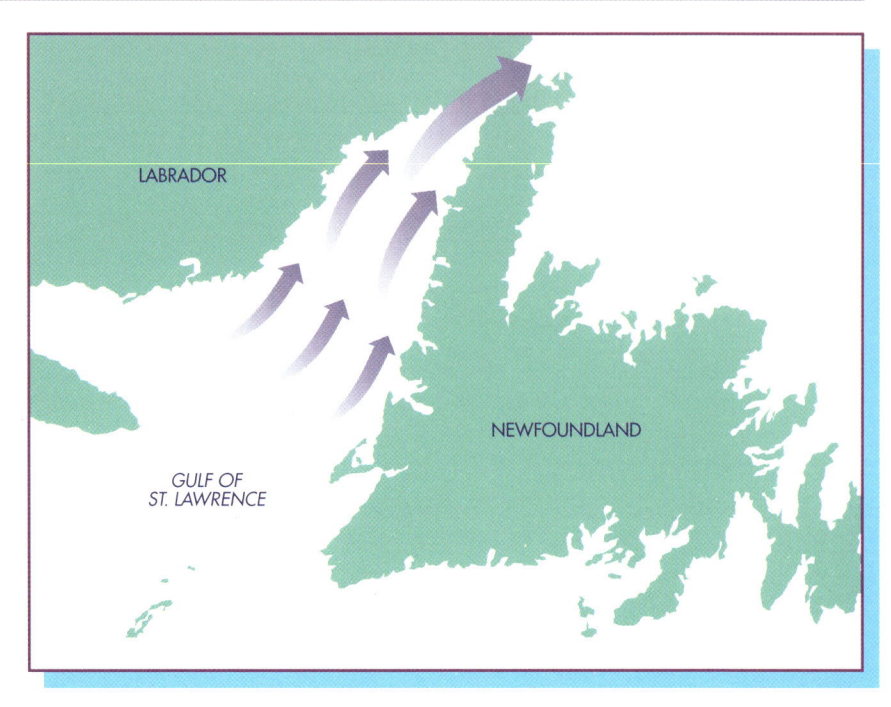

Local fishermen in the Strait of Belle Isle report that easterlies increase substantially from L'Anse au Loup to Blanc Sablon. Moving in the other direction, light southwesterlies can increase to almost gale force between these two locations. Violent, squally, easterly winds have been reported in passages and straits along the mid-Labrador coast from Hopedale to Nain. The topography and geography of this stretch of coastline allows for the development of almost every type of local wind effect possible, due to the hundreds of small islands and steep, narrow passages.

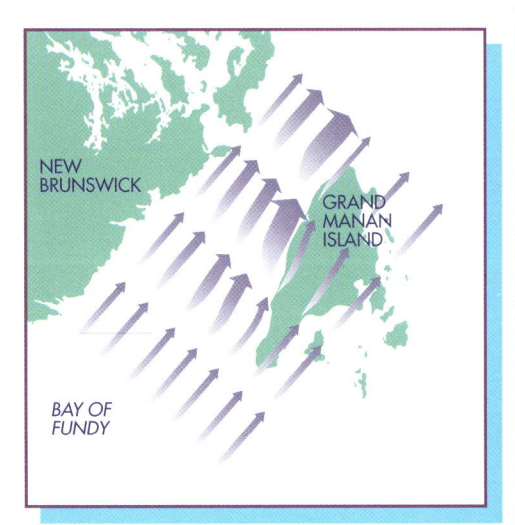

The diagram above shows how a southwesterly wind flows past Grand Manan Island in the Bay of Fundy. Note in particular how the wind varies in the passage between the island and the mainland. Channelling helps redirect the winds into the passage while funnelling increases their strength. Along the west coast of Grand Manan Island the winds are strengthened even more by a convergence effect. Wind speeds here may be more than twice that of winds upstream from the island.

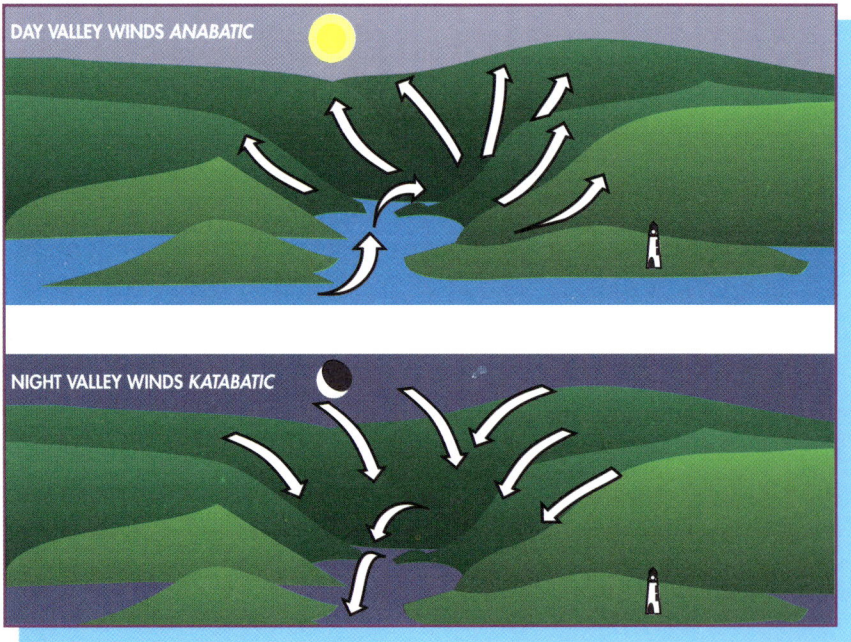

Katabatic and Anabatic Winds

When air cools over hilly land on a clear night, it becomes heavier and drains downwards early in the morning, usually following valleys until it reaches the sea. Its momentum carries it a mile or two out to sea, fanning out before it warms up and dies away. These cool night winds are called katabatic winds, or "drainage winds," and are often quite gusty. They are common throughout Newfoundland and Labrador, where local mariners call them "blow-me-downs." A mariner who takes shelter in a calm secluded cove overnight may be surprised in the early morning by the sudden onset of gusty, downslope winds from a valley at the head of the cove.

During the day, the sides of the valleys, or slopes, become warmer than the valley bottom, so the wind blows up the slope. This affects mariners because the upslope-winds cause air to be drawn up the valleys as well. These daytime, upslope winds are called anabatic winds. Katabatic and anabatic winds all contribute to stronger land and sea breezes and increased wind speeds.

In St. Georges Bay, in western Newfoundland, drainage winds cause northeasterlies during the night. These winds often counteract a moderate to strong westerly gradient wind during the later part of the night resulting in only light winds in St. Georges Bay. Fishermen listening to a marine forecast of moderate to strong westerlies may question the forecast, based on what they observe in the bay. The forecast of westerly winds will be accurate only a few miles offshore throughout the night and in the bay during the daytime hours. This is a good example of a coastal wind effect that cannot be incorporated into the forecast.

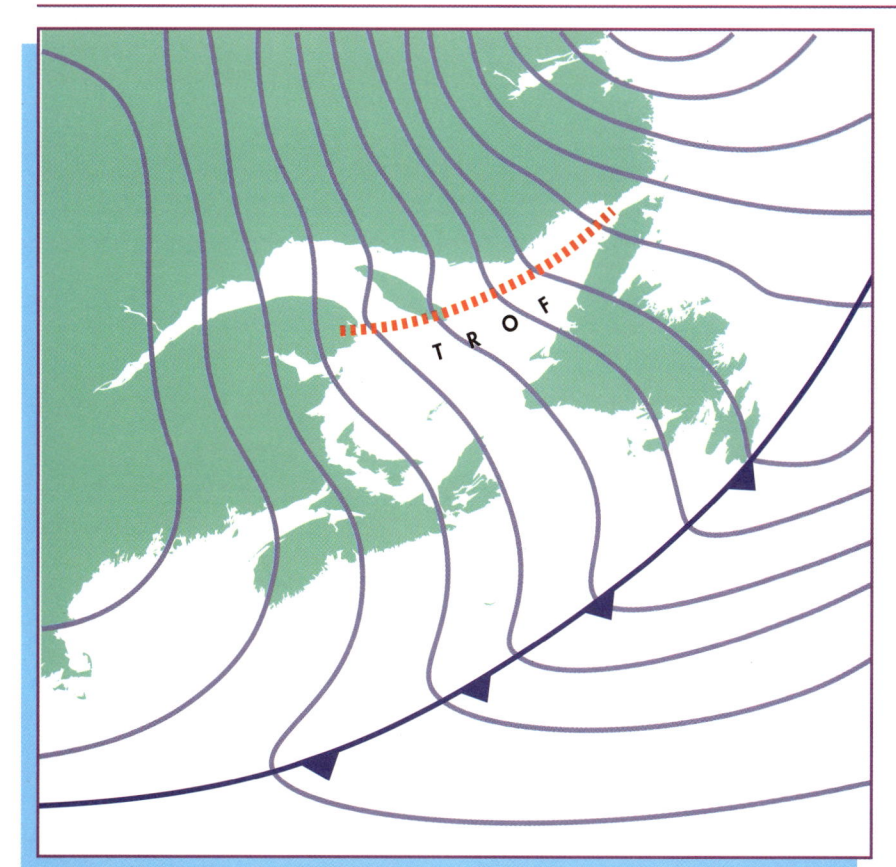

Small-scale Troughs and Lows
A pressure gradient is often disturbed by other influences in the local area, resulting in troughing, or even low pressure. This affects the winds considerably, because winds in a trough, or low, are usually much less than they would be otherwise. Here are two examples of such effects.

Thermal Troughs and Lows
When the surface is heated, the air rises, creating lower pressure at the surface. If the heating of an area is more intense than in the surrounding region, the area will develop a lower pressure. This frequently happens over islands and peninsulas in summer, when land surfaces heat up more rapidly than adjacent water surfaces. Another cause of thermal lows and troughs is warmer temperatures on inland waters than surrounding land surfaces, during the winter. The air over the water is heated more than that over adjacent colder land surfaces, creating relatively lower pressure. This is commonly seen when northwest winds blow across the Gulf of St. Lawrence in the winter. Water temperatures hover near the zero mark while adjacent land surfaces are much colder. Thermal lows and troughs do not usually have strong winds, but showery weather may occur in the rising air.

Lee Troughs and Lows
When winds blow from a westerly (southwest through northwest) direction and move over mountains or large hills, a trough of low pressure often develops on the lee side of the high terrain. The lee-troughing effect usually results in a wind direction that is backed by 60°–90° from the larger-scale wind flow. The amount of backing and the width of the band of shifted winds depend on the steepness and height of the hills. On occasion, this lee effect may even generate a small low-pressure centre. A low formed in this way is usually weak, but it can become intense if it is "picked up" by a passing frontal system and a frontal low develops. Lee troughing often occurs along the Fundy shore of New Brunswick. A moderate west-to-northwest prevailing wind results in a band of moderate southwesterlies within 10 miles of shore. Beyond 10 miles, winds return to the prevailing direction.

MARINE METEOROLOGY *Wind*

Cliff Effects

When wind flows over a sea-side cliff, it is altered. Eddies often form downwind of the cliff face, creating stationary zones of stronger and lighter winds. Strong wind zones are fairly predictable and usually remain stationary so long as wind direction and stability of the air do not change. The lighter winds, called wind shadows, vary in speed and can reverse their direction downwind of higher cliffs. Beneath the cliff the wind is usually gusty, and its direction is opposite to the wind blowing over the top of the cliff. It is reported that this effect happens in summer and early fall in Conception Bay, Newfoundland. Moderate southwesterlies can cause turbulent eddies at the head of the bay, resulting in gales. Similar, but reversed eddies may be encountered in onshore winds near cliffs.

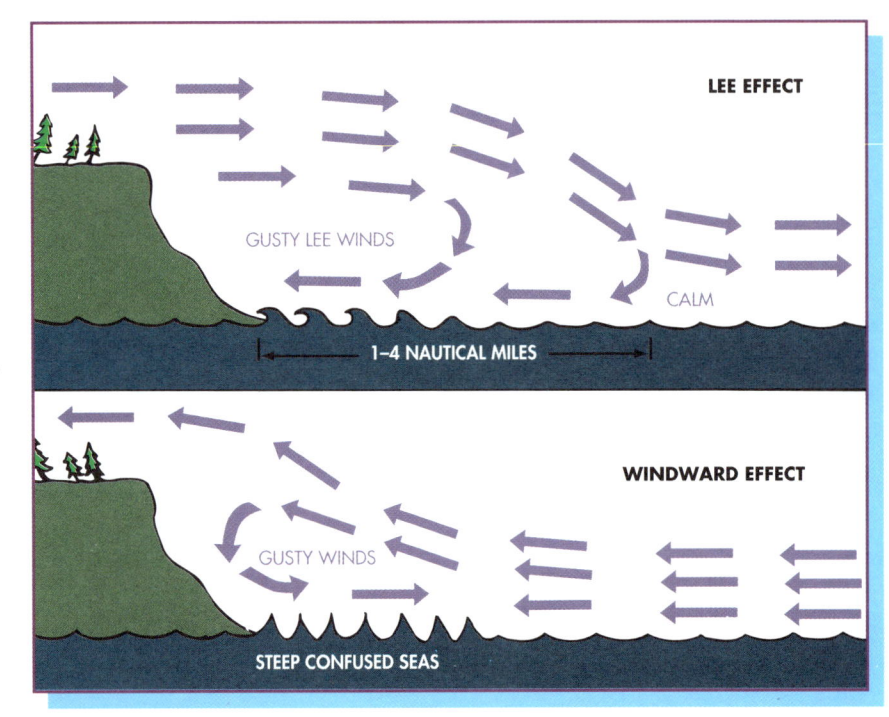

Mountain Waves

A phenomenon called "mountain waves" occurs when stable air flows over hills or mountains. This effect often combines with other effects, such as drainage winds. Mountain waves occur in many spots throughout Atlantic Canada and are only a concern to mariners when their effects reach a coastal plain or inland lake. An extreme example of this effect occurs along the west coast of Cape Breton, when southeasterly winds blow ahead of an approaching warm front. Above the surface and ahead of the front, the air is very stable. A frontal inversion (warm air over cold air) "pinches" the approaching airstream between the inversion and the surface. The airstream flowing through this narrow corridor is accelerated, creating very strong surface winds along the coastal plains, on the lee side of the hills. This effect also goes by the name *lee waves*.

In such conditions, while most Cape Breton sites are swept with strong to gale-force southeasterlies of 30–45 knots, locations along the west coast will experience storm-to hurricane-force gusts of 60–100 knots. These violent southeasterlies are well known to Chéticamp residents. Acadians refer to these winds as *les suêtes* (a corruption of the French term, *sud-est*, "southeast"). These variable, gusty winds may extend 10–15 miles out to sea, appearing in bands over the water.

Another well-known spot for mountain waves is the appropriately named "Wreckhouse" in southwestern Newfoundland. It is located between Cape Ray and St. Andrews on a stretch of coastline where winds have derailed trains and blown down power-line towers. Other effects likely combine to create very hazardous conditions. Westerly winds over the Great North Peninsula of Newfoundland also generate mountain waves—most notably at Engleé.

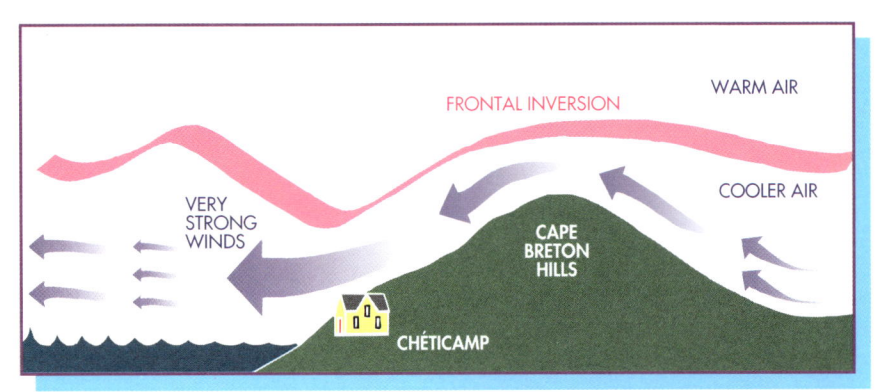

Do you remember hearing about The Storm of the Century? From March 12 to 15, 1993, a very large and intense winter storm moved through the Gulf of Mexico, up the American east coast, and through Atlantic Canada. Dozens of lives were lost. Hurricane-force winds and significant wave heights (see **SEA STATE**) of more than 10 m were widespread. When the storm reached Atlantic Canada, winds everywhere were furious, reaching their extreme along the west coast of Cape Breton. *Les Suêtes* measured a staggering 126 knots (233 km/h) at Grand Étang—more than enough to lift the roof off the nearby Chéticamp Hospital.

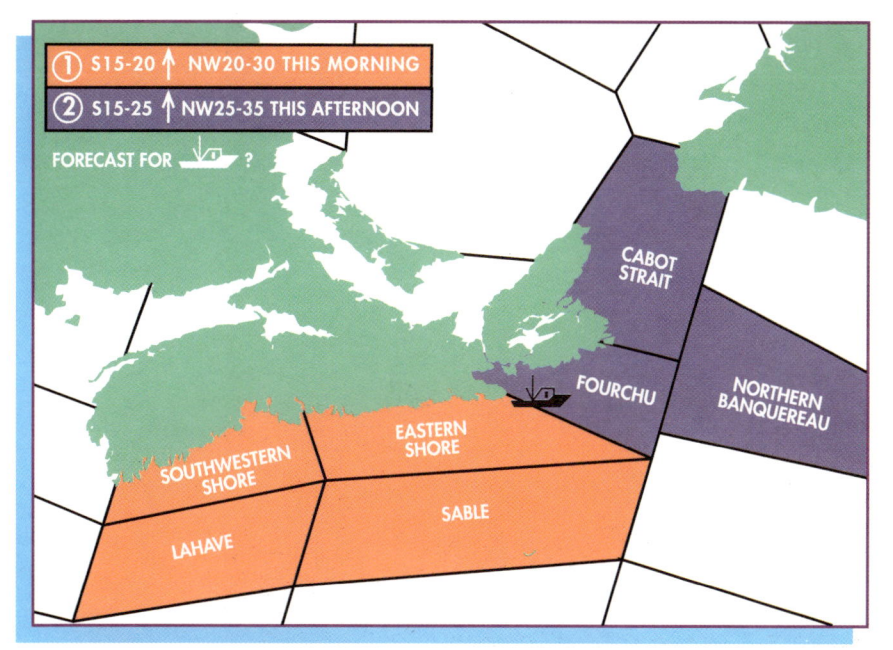

MARINE METEOROLOGY Wind

① S15-20 ↑ NW20-30 THIS MORNING
② S15-25 ↑ NW25-35 THIS AFTERNOON

FORECAST FOR ⛵ ?

CABOT STRAIT
FOURCHU
NORTHERN BANQUEREAU
SOUTHWESTERN SHORE
EASTERN SHORE
LAHAVE
SABLE

SUMMARY ON WIND FORECASTING

Using the information in this section, let's look at a specific example of how mariners arrive at the most accurate forecast for their immediate areas.

Imagine that your boat is located just north of the Derabies Islands, northeast of Canso, Nova Scotia. You are situated on the boundary between the **Eastern Shore** and **Fourchu** marine forecast areas. The marine synopsis describes a cold front moving through the Maritimes, with strong to gale-force northwesterlies in its wake.

You are listening to the 5:30 a.m. forecasts:

Southwestern Shore, Lahave Bank, Eastern Shore, Sable: Winds southerly 15–20 knots, increasing to northwesterly 20–30 this morning.

Fourchu, Cabot Strait, Northern Half of Banquereau: Gale warning continued. Winds southerly 15–25 knots, increasing to northwesterly 25–gales 35 this afternoon.

From the synopsis and forecasts, it is clear that the forecaster timed the onset of northwesterly winds with the passage of the cold front. What the mariner needs to know is, *What time will the cold front pass through my location?* The forecast says it will pass areas west of you in the morning and areas east of you in the afternoon; therefore, you can assume that the cold front will pass you about noon (give or take a couple of hours) followed soon after by the northwesterlies.

This is only your first adjustment to the forecast. Now look at the smaller scale to see what adjustments can be made for local wind effects.

Southerly winds are forecast to be 15–20 knots to the west of you and 15–25 to the east. *What will they measure for your spot?* The southerly winds ahead of the front may be slightly weaker in your location because of coastal divergence and a right-hand corner effect off Canso. Southerly winds ahead of a cold front are usually stable, and therefore not very gusty, so you can expect the southerlies to be steady near the lower range of forecast values—*southerly at 15 knots.*

The northwesterly winds are forecast to be 20–30 to your west and 25–35 to the east. *What will they be at your location?* The main effect to consider is winds funnelling down the Strait of Canso from the Northumberland Strait. A stronger band of northwesterlies will extend across Chedabucto Bay. The northwesterly winds behind the front will be stronger in your location because of a corner effect near Canso. The forecast values of 25–35 may be too low since the meteorologist is unlikely to have pinpointed these two factors: they are too detailed for the larger-scale forecast. As well, the wind will be cold and unstable leading to gustiness. Therefore, the northwest winds should be gusty and stronger than the forecast values—*northwesterly 35 knots with gusts to 45.*

The final forecast after your adjustments: *winds southerly 15 knots increasing near noon to northwesterly gales 35 gusting to 45.* This barely resembles the original forecast from the weather office, *but it will be a more accurate forecast for your location.*

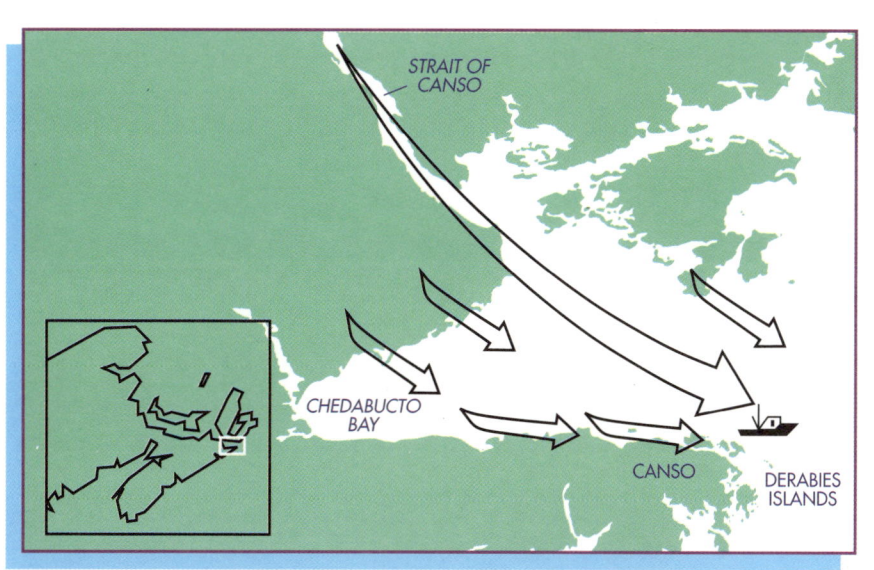

Marine Weather Tip

Once at sea, monitor Weatheradio and VHF radio continuously. Up-to-the-minute information is vital to marine safety. Don't forget to listen to the marine synopsis. It tells you where the weather systems are and where they are going. With this information you can make the adjustments just discussed.

STRAIT OF CANSO
CHEDABUCTO BAY
CANSO
DERABIES ISLANDS

21

MARINE METEOROLOGY Sea State

DEEP WATER
Wind-Waves and Swell

Traditionally, many fishermen rely on a wind forecast to predict the seas. Usually the wind provides enough information for a seasoned mariner to judge accurately, but sometimes strong currents, wind shifts, or a significant swell can greatly alter the sea state.

The following definitions will help when discussing waves:

Wave height. The vertical distance between the crest of one wave and the trough of an adjacent one.

Wavelength. The horizontal distance between consecutive crests (or troughs) in the direction they move.

Wave period. The time interval between the passage of successive crests (or troughs) at a fixed position.

Waves are created by the force of the wind on the water. Their size is determined by: wind speed; duration (the length of time the wind persists without changing direction or speed); the fetch (the distance over which winds blow from a constant direction); and the height and motion of existing swell.

Wind-waves are generated in the immediate area of the wind. They develop very quickly—within an hour or so. Subsidence time also partly depends on the wind. The period varies greatly. Wind-waves are also described as "sea."

Swells are what remain of the wind-waves after they move away from where they were generated. These long waves, or "rollers," contain a lot of energy and can take days to subside. The period of swell ranges from 5–30 seconds.

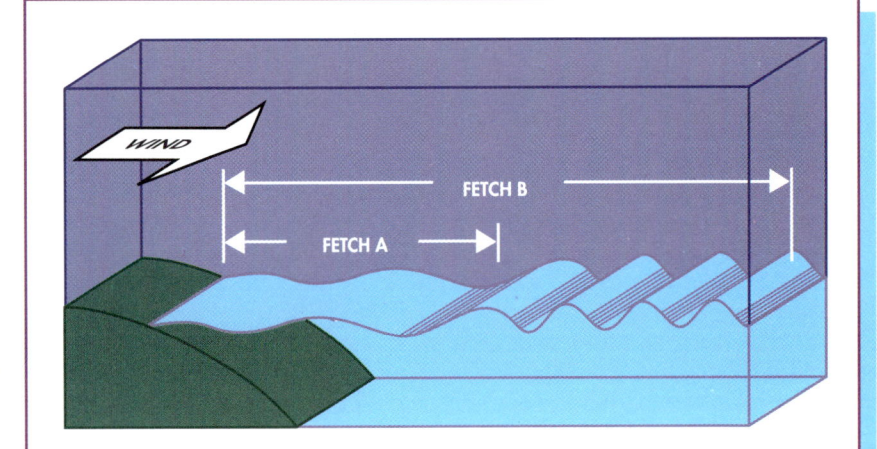

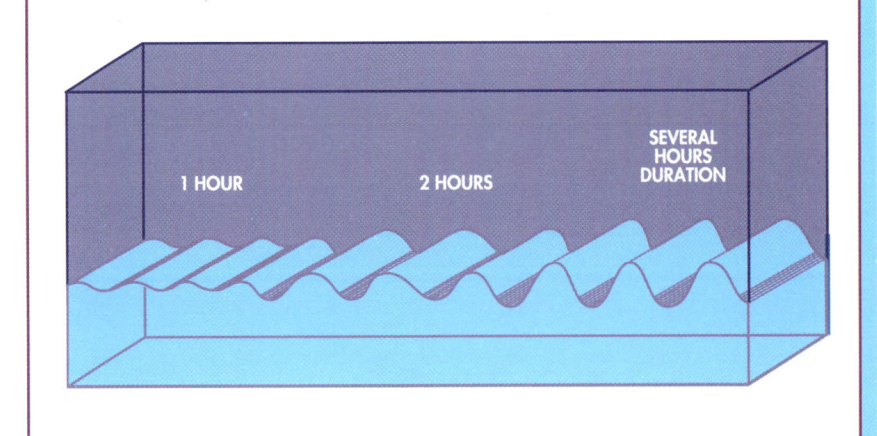

Marine Weather Tip

An approaching storm normally produces an increase in the ground swell within 24 hours before the winds hit. An increasing swell when winds are light is a very good indication that a storm is near.

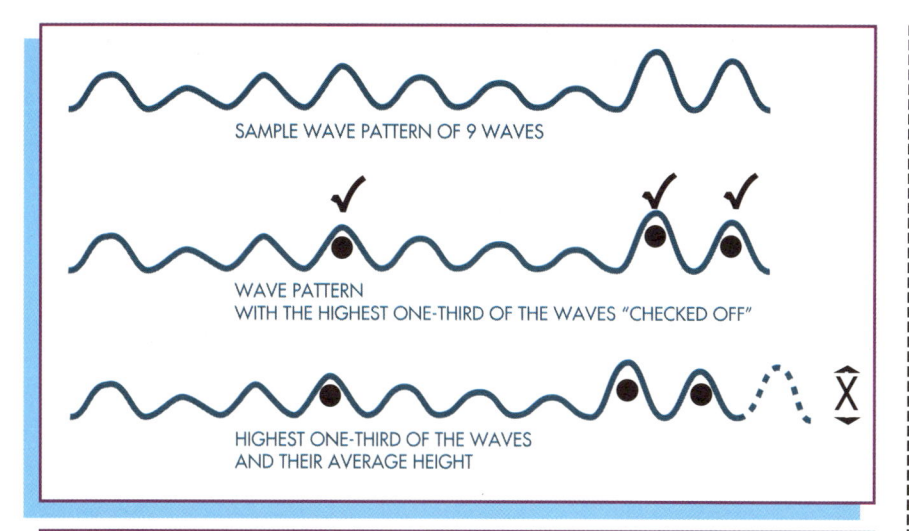

MARINE METEOROLOGY Sea State

SAMPLE WAVE PATTERN OF 9 WAVES

WAVE PATTERN WITH THE HIGHEST ONE-THIRD OF THE WAVES "CHECKED OFF"

HIGHEST ONE-THIRD OF THE WAVES AND THEIR AVERAGE HEIGHT

Average wave height	.625 X Sig Wave
Highest wave likely over a 10-minute period	1.6 X Sig Wave
Highest wave likely over a 3-hour period	2.0 X Sig Wave
Highest wave likely over a 12-hour period	2.25 X Sig Wave
Highest wave likely over a 24-hour period	2.35 X Sig Wave

This table shows the relationship between the sig-wave and other wave heights. Note that while the average wave height is only a fraction of the sig-wave, extreme wave heights can be twice that of the sig-wave.

SIGNIFICANT WAVE HEIGHT—Technically Speaking

When referring to deep-water wave heights, the term significant wave height is used. The significant height is defined as the average height of the highest one-third of all waves present.

The adjacent diagram illustrates nine waves. The three highest waves are identified (the highest one-third) and their average height is determined. This is the significant wave height, often abbreviated to "sig-wave."

The sig-wave is useful for developing a theory of wave generation based on wind force. But the sig-wave is even more useful—it corresponds to what a mariner sees when scanning the seas.

Marine Weather Tip

Away from the coast, a threatening sky with increasing black clouds and rain probably isn't part of a large-scale wind system if it is not preceded by swell; therefore, any wind should be temporary. Increasing swell from the direction of advancing storm clouds usually warns of an approaching low with a large area of strong winds.

Beaufort Scale

A very old and trusted method of estimating wind speed at sea is the Beaufort Wind Scale. This nineteenth century invention of the British Navy draws a comparison between wind speed and its effect on the sea and the ship. The scale can also be used in reverse by taking the wind forecast and determining what kind of sea can be expected. It is important to note that these descriptions of the sea surface are for fully developed seas with a given unchanging wind (i.e., unlimited fetch and duration) and that the wave-height estimates are the extreme values possible.

Force 1 (1–3 knots) LIGHT AIR
Scale-like ripples; no foam crests.

Force 2 (4–6 knotst) LIGHT BREEZE
Small wavelets; glassy; crests do not break.

Force 0 (less than 1 knot) CALM
Sea like a mirror.

ALL PHOTOS THIS PAGE: ATMOSPHERIC ENVIRONMENT SERVICE

MARINE METEOROLOGY Sea State

Force 3 (7–10) knots GENTLE BREEZE
Large wavelets; crests begin to break; foam of glassy appearance; scattered white horses; waves still less than 1 m.

Force 4 (11–16 knots) MODERATE BREEZE
small waves becoming larger; fairly frequent white horses; wave heights 1–1.5 m.

Force 5 (17–21 knots) FRESH BREEZE
Moderate waves form many white horses; chance of spray; wave heights 2–2.5 m.

Force 6 (22–27 knots) STRONG BREEZE
Large waves form; foam crest more extensive; spray; wave heights 3–4 m.

Force 7 (28–33 knots) NEAR GALE
Sea heaps up; some foam from waves blows some streaks; wave heights 4–5.5 m.

Force 8 (34–40 knots) GALE
Moderately high waves; well-marked streaks of foam. Wave heights 5.5–7.5 m. Open water very rough.

Force 9 (41–47 knots) STRONG GALE
High waves; dense foam streaks; spray affects visibility; wave heights 7–10 m.

Force 10 (48–55 knots) STORM
Very high waves; long, overhanging crests; white foam; water has white appearance; wave heights 9–12.5 m.

Force 11 (56–63 knots) VIOLENT STORM
Exceptionally high waves; sea covered with foam patches; edge of wave crests blow into froth everywhere; wave heights 11.5–16 m.

Force 12 and up (64 knots or greater) HURRICANE FORCE
Catastrophic waves; air filled with foam and spray; sea completely white with driving spray; visibility very seriously affected; wave heights phenomenal.

No photo available.

Keeping afloat was a higher priority than photography!

ALL PHOTOS THIS PAGE: ATMOSPHERIC ENVIRONMENT SERVICE

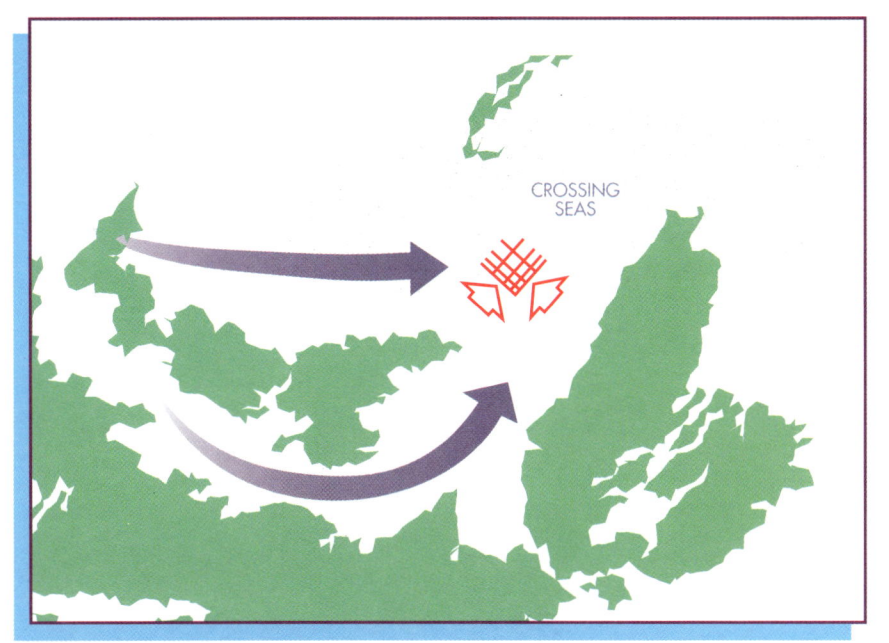

MARINE METEOROLOGY Sea State

CROSSING SEAS
In westerly winds, Wind-waves moving eastward pass to the north of P.E.I. Meanwhile, in the Northumberland Strait, winds are channelled to southwesterly, resulting in waves moving northeast. The two sets of waves meet just east of P.E.I., creating an area of crossing seas. These waves may also interact with tidal currents to produce hazardous conditions.

Crossing Seas
Crossing seas occur when one train of waves moves at an angle to another. This creates steep seas with short, sharp wave crests; mariners say the sea is "confused." Depending on the height and period of the waves, crossing sea conditions range from uncomfortable to hazardous for smaller vessels. Crossing seas combined with an underlying tidal current can be especially hazardous. Some mariners use the term, *cross seas*, which perfectly describes the "angry" nature of the waves. Wave crossing occurs when new waves are being generated over an old swell area produced by an earlier or distant storm or when storms crossing an area are accompanied by abrupt wind shifts.

Intense cold fronts moving through the Gulf of St. Lawrence are heralded by strong southerly winds and seas. Winds shifting to northwesterly behind the front cause confused and treacherous seas in the northern part of the Gulf of St. Lawrence. This is common in areas where the west or northwest winds are funnelled, as in the Gaspé Passage or at the mouth of the Bay of Chaleur.

Seiches
Every enclosed body of water sloshes around in its basin with a given frequency. These oscillations of backward and forward sloshing are called "seiches." In Atlantic Canada, only the Gulf of St. Lawrence has noticeable seiches and these are determined by weather conditions and tides.

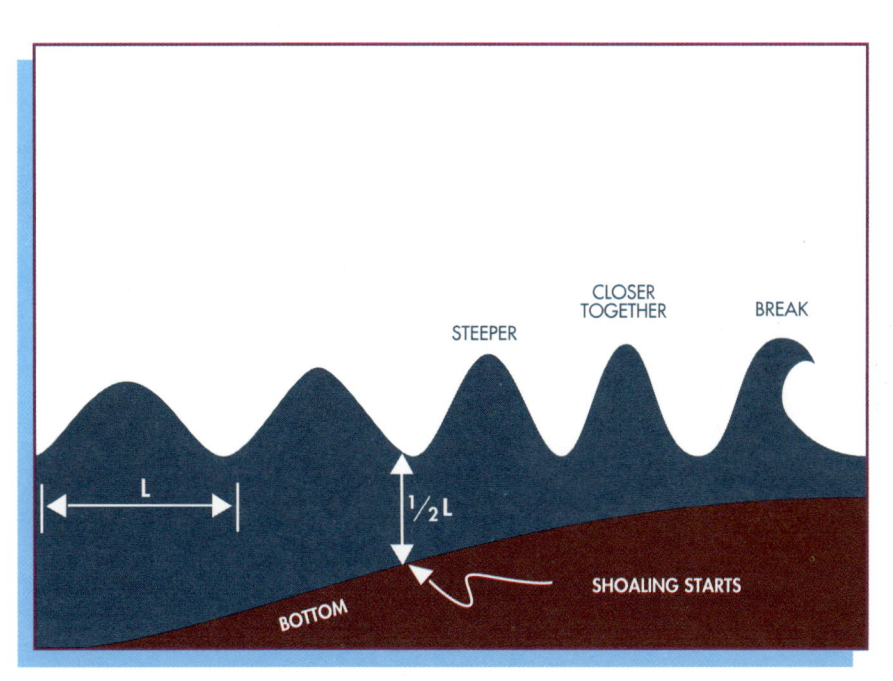

SHALLOW WATER
When waves "feel" the sea bed, the water is said to be shallow. Shallow water is defined by the waves present on a given day—not according to the absolute depth of the water.

When water depth is equal to half the wavelength, the waves begins to "feel bottom." This causes profound changes in the length, speed, and direction of the wave. Consequently, long waves begin to feel bottom sooner than shorter ones. Therefore, water that is deep with respect to wind-waves—which have short wavelengths—may be shallow with respect to swells—with their longer wavelengths.

MARINE METEOROLOGY Sea State

Shoaling: Breakers and Surf
The sea bed affects waves in two ways: "shoaling" affects the height of the waves; and "refraction" affects both their height and direction. The *Sailing Directions* for your area will describe the shape of the local sea bed and any unusual shoaling effects.

When deep-water waves reach a shoal and start to feel bottom, the energy between the crests remains the same, but the waves become higher. The wave crests move closer together making the waves steeper, until they are as high above the water as the water is deep. At this point, the wave tumbles into breakers or surf.

Refraction of Waves
When a train of waves approaches the shoreline at an angle, shoaling affects the part of the wave directly over the shallow water. This part of the wave slows and builds in height, but the part of the wave over deeper water continues at its original height and speed. As a result, the waves appear to bend and grow near the shore. This is common along the northern coast of Groswater Bay, Labrador, when strong southeasterly winds bring in fully developed seas.

Refraction happens at points, or headlands, where waves bend towards the point and "pile up." As mariners say: "Points draw waves." Frequently, refracted waves converge off capes, causing steep, confused seas.

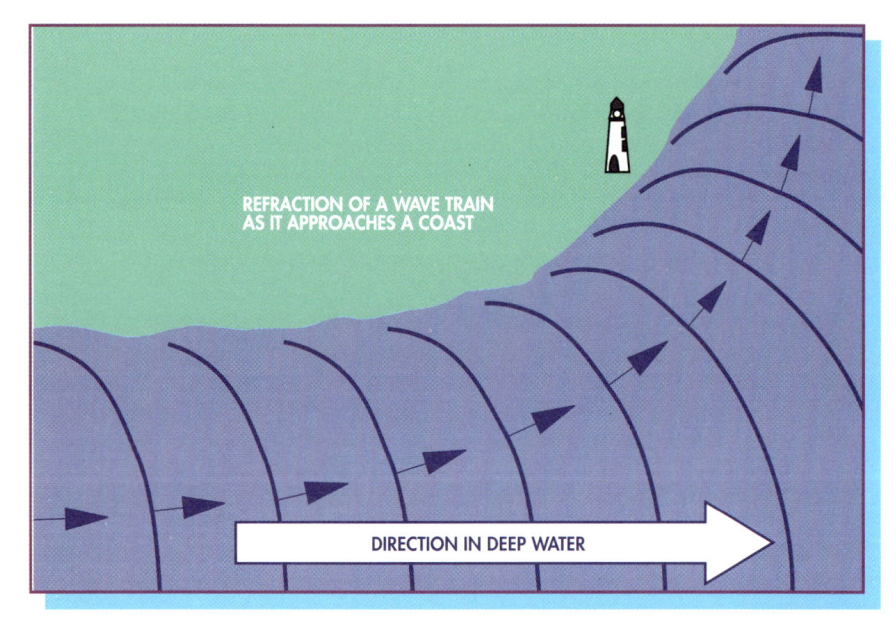

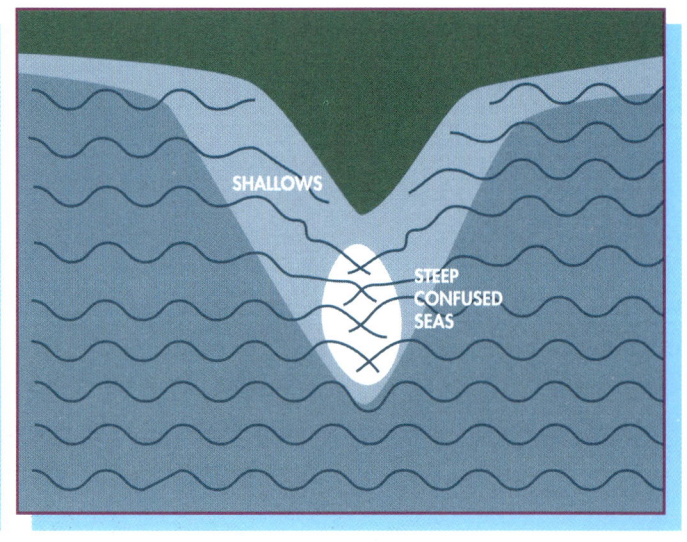

REFRACTION OF A WAVE TRAIN AS IT APPROACHES A COAST

DIRECTION IN DEEP WATER

SHALLOWS

STEEP CONFUSED SEAS

MARINE METEOROLOGY *Sea State*

Tsunamis

The most spectacular and devastating of all waves are *tsunamis*. They are popularly called "tidal waves," despite having no connection with tides. Instead, tsunamis result from submarine earthquakes, bottom-slides, or volcanic eruptions—anything causing a sudden massive displacement of water. Tsunamis can be felt at great distances—even across entire oceans. Because they are so enormous, they are not to be thought of in the same way as regular swell. Tsunamis travel at ocean depths with speeds of about 400 knots and have periods ranging from 15–60 minutes. Compare this to large ocean swells, which travel 30–60 knots and have periods of 5–30 seconds. When tsunamis reach shallower coastal waters, shoaling effects slow them down and build them to heights of 50–100 ft.—or more! Significant tsunami damage is rare in regions with a wide continental shelf—like Atlantic Canada. The shelf acts as both a wave reflector (sending much of the energy back out to sea) and as an absorber of tsunami energy through friction along the bottom.

> ***Do you remember*** *hearing about the infamous Newfoundland South Coast Disaster? On November 18, 1929, an earthquake measuring 7.2 on the Richter scale shook the ocean floor about 250 miles south of Newfoundland. In St. John's, where earth tremors were felt, some thought an explosion had occurred in the iron ore mines of Bell Island. Farther north along the coastline, people were puzzled by the mysterious, unnatural ground vibrations. But people living in settlements on the Burin Peninsula were the ones who felt the initial shocks and soon after experienced the catastrophic aftermath of the quake.*
>
> *The wrenching of the ocean floor spawned an enormous tsunami, which headed landward. Shortly after 5 p.m. on that Monday afternoon, the wave crashed into the bottom portion of the Burin Peninsula, killing nearly 30 people. The shock of the quake under the Atlantic broke undersea cables and damaged the vital telegraph system. For three days, the outside world was unaware of the disaster and the victims were isolated.*

Tides

Tides—the result of gravitational influences of the moon and sun—are an important consideration to mariners in Atlantic Canada. The pull of the moon is about twice as strong as that of the sun, so the tidal cycle is generally in tune with the moon's orbit, or the "lunar day" of 24 hours and 50 minutes. The sun's effect is usually only noticed as an increase or decrease in the lunar tides. As the earth rotates, the moon's gravitational attraction causes shifting "bulges" in the tides of the world's oceans, on opposite sides of the earth. The result is two high and two low waters every lunar day—semi-diurnal tides—at most localities. Tides with only one high and one low water per day—diurnal tides—are also quite common. The predominant tides in Atlantic Canada are semi-diurnal.

The incoming tide is called the "flood;" the retreating tide, the "ebb." When the sun, moon, and earth are in line—at new or full moon—the gravitational attractions of the moon and sun combine to produce "spring tides." These larger-than-average tides usually occur one to three days after the new or full moon (called "large tides" in the Canadian Tide and Current Tables). When sun and moon are at right angles to the earth—at first and last quarter—smaller-than-average (or "neap") tides occur.

Another factor influencing tides is the size and shape of the various basins. Each bay has its own period of oscillation, which uniquely determines the tides. In estuaries and rivers, the tide changes considerably from that observed near the entrance. In general, the low tide in such shallow areas moves slower than the high tide, with the result that the high tides catch up to the preceeding lows. Because of this, the time from low water to high water is shortened, while from high to low it is lengthened.

Water levels along coasts and inland waters are also affected by weather factors. These effects, responsible for "storm surges" (see **STORM SURGE**), can create unusually shallow water as well as flood coastal regions.

Tidal Rips

When strong currents ride over irregular shallow sea bottoms, or when two tidal streams meet, the result is a rip—a "boiling" action on the sea surface. Rips can be hazardous if they break violently, which often happens in opposing winds. Rips are frequent in Atlantic Canada, especially in Northumberland Strait and off the southwestern tip of Nova Scotia. Local *Sailing Directions* show the locations of well-known rips.

Marine Weather Tip

Mariners are advised to plan routes that take advantage of the stage of the tide (ebb-flood) and to use weather forecasts, along with local observations of wind and sea, to avoid dangerous spots. Sailing Directions *can help in figuring out these areas as well as the* Local Weather *section of this guide.*

MARINE METEOROLOGY Sea State

Longshore Currents and Rip Currents

A longshore current is created by waves breaking at an angle to the shore. If the bathymetry of the beach is irregular, then waves are concentrated in some areas due to wave refraction. The longshore currents farthest from the region of the largest breakers are strongest. The water that has accumulated in the surf-zone through the action of the breakers eventually returns seaward, often in strong narrow currents called *rip currents* (sometimes called *rip tides*).

Rip currents can reach speeds of 2–3 knots and are signposted on some beaches. A swimmer carried seaward by a rip current should not struggle against it, but swim across it, parallel to the beach. Once out of the narrow rip current, the waves will tend to carry the swimmer shoreward.

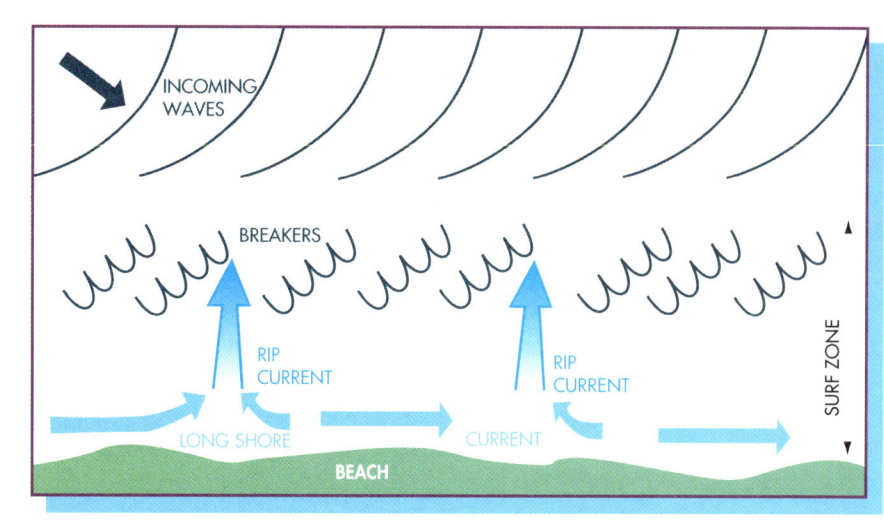

Wind-Wave-Tide-Current Interaction

Ocean currents are determined by differences in atmospheric pressure, wind, water temperature and salinity; the shape of the sea bed; the Coriolis force; and gravitational effects.

Near the coast, waves steepen and break as they run onto an opposing tidal or ocean current. When the current is strong, or the waves are large, the breaking may be vigorous. These conditions can be hazardous to vessels. The Northumberland Strait, the southern tip of Nova Scotia, and the northern edge of the Gulf Stream are well-known areas of wave-current interaction.

When tides, swells, and wind collide, and the water is shallow, conditions at sea deteriorate rapidly. For example, sea-state conditions can be hazardous just south of Yarmouth, Nova Scotia, when a southeasterly wind and waves encounter an ebb tide retreating from the Bay of Fundy. When ebb tides meet off Pointe de l'Est, Magdalen Islands, over a shallow sand bar about a mile offshore, the convergence combines with a shoaling effect to produce heavy breaking seas in strong easterly winds.

The effects of the interaction between winds, currents, and tides are not included in marine forecasts, and therefore should be seriously studied by mariners.

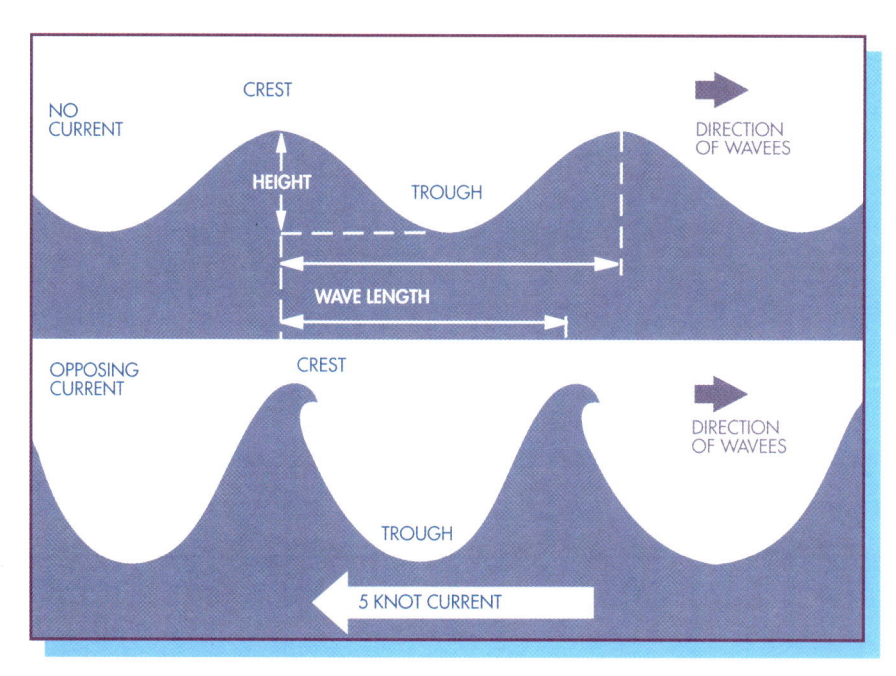

WAVES VS. CURRENT

Waves moving against a current change dramatically. The wavelength decreases, while the wave height increases. This results in a rapid steepening that may lead to breaking. A 3-m wind-wave almost doubles in height on a 5-knot opposing current and steepens to the breaking point.

MARINE METEOROLOGY Sea State

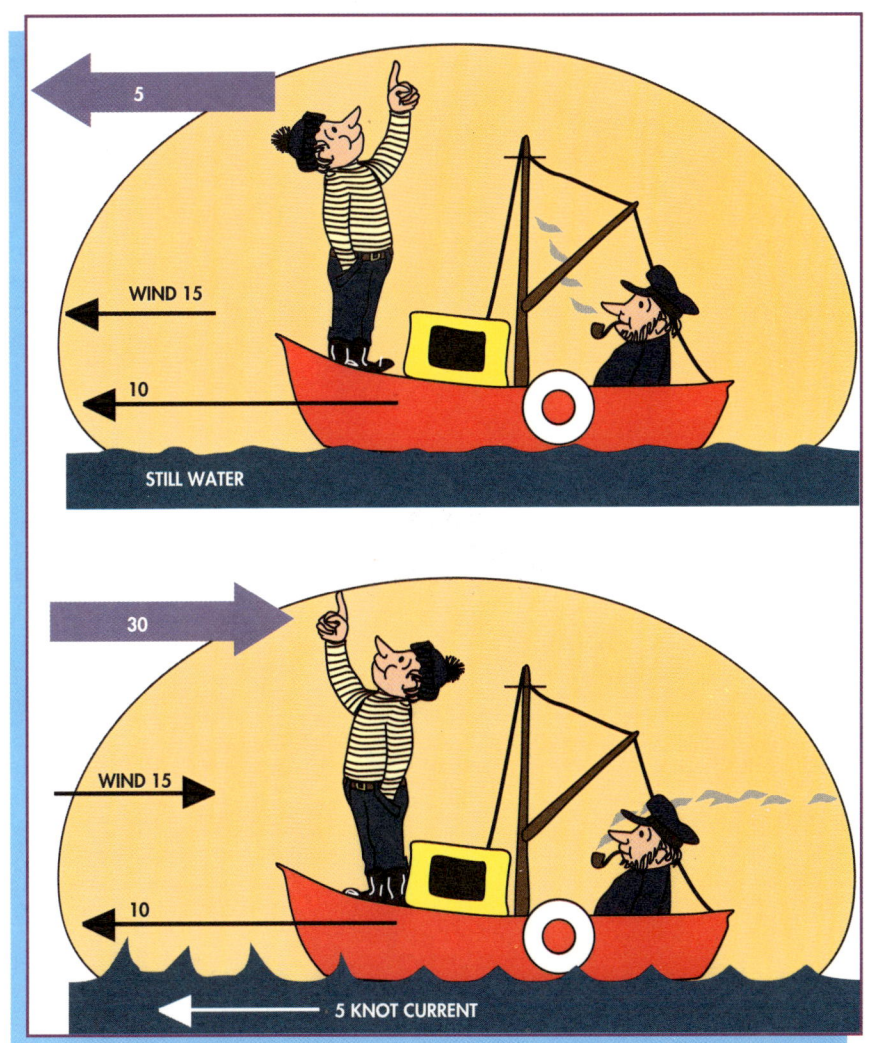

WIND VS. CURRENT

Consider the difference between the actual and apparent winds that blow across a vessel. Whenever the vessel is moving, either under its own power or on a strong current, the wind across the boat appears different from that across a nearby land station.

In the top illustration the boat is steaming at 10 knots, over still water, and there is a 15-knot tail wind. The first mate measures a wind of 5 knots from astern. In the bottom picture the boat is still steaming at 10 knots, but there is now a 15-knot headwind as well as a 5-knot tidal current running with the boat. This time, the wind measures 30 knots on the nose.

In the second case, the mate notices that the sea state is worse and may think that this is the result of the stronger wind he measured. Not so! The wind in both cases is 15 knots, but the boat's direction can either add to or subtract from the measured wind. Mariners have to remember to take their motion into account when estimating wind speed. As well, the wind opposes the current in the second case, resulting in much shorter (wavelength) and higher (wave height) seas.

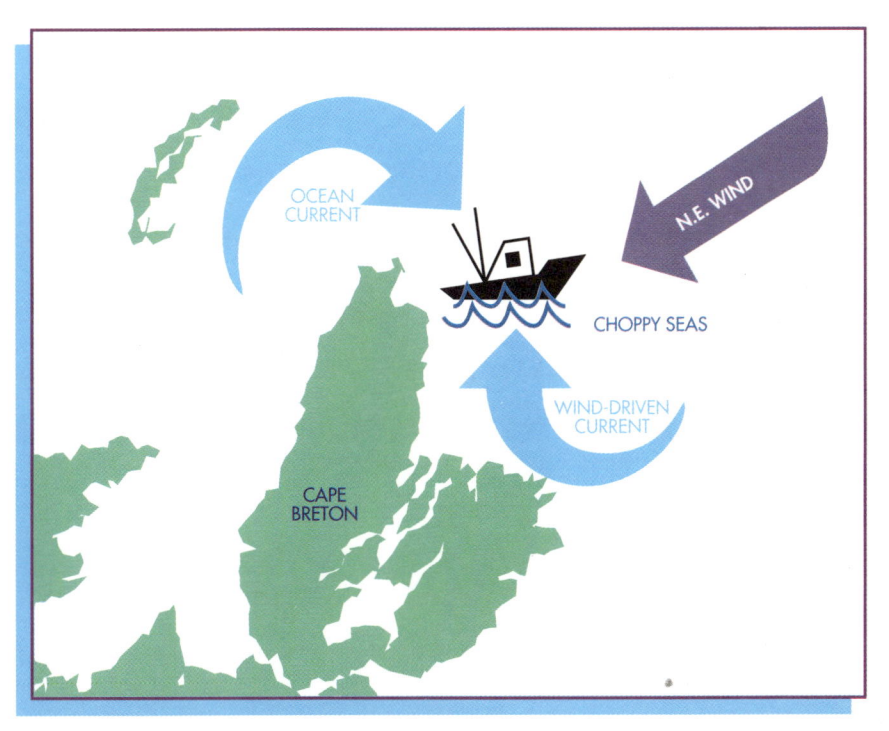

WAVES, WIND, AND CURRENT OPPOSED

Wind-driven currents can often override regular currents and tides. After persistent easterly or northeasterly winds, a north-going current with a rate of 1 knot may flow from the vicinity of St. Ann's Bay to near Cape North. There it meets the current flowing southeast from the Gulf of St. Lawrence. The direction of the currents, combined with the direction of the winds, can cause very choppy seas.

Other important factors that influence current or tidal effects are heavy rain and ice-melt. Ice-melt causes problems in Saint John, N.B. each spring when the "freshet" sends a river of fresh water far out into the saltwater harbour. The fresh water alters the currents considerably, and the change of salinity affects buoyancy. These conditions last only a few weeks, but it is one of the main factors that the harbour master and mariners must consider.

29

MARINE METEOROLOGY Sea State

Sheltering

Coastal land often shelters the mariner from the wind and the sea. A harbour with a shallow or narrow mouth prevents swell from entering. Anchoring near shore when winds blow off the land minimizes wind strengths in a storm. This is a "wind shadow."

Harbours known to provide good shelter are Pubnico Harbour in Lurcher marine area and Country Harbour in the Eastern Shore marine area. On the other hand, the bay at Point du Sud Ouest on Anticosti Island is not recommended for anchorage. Although it is sheltered from easterly winds, it can be dangerous in westerly winds, which are usually preceded by heavy swells.

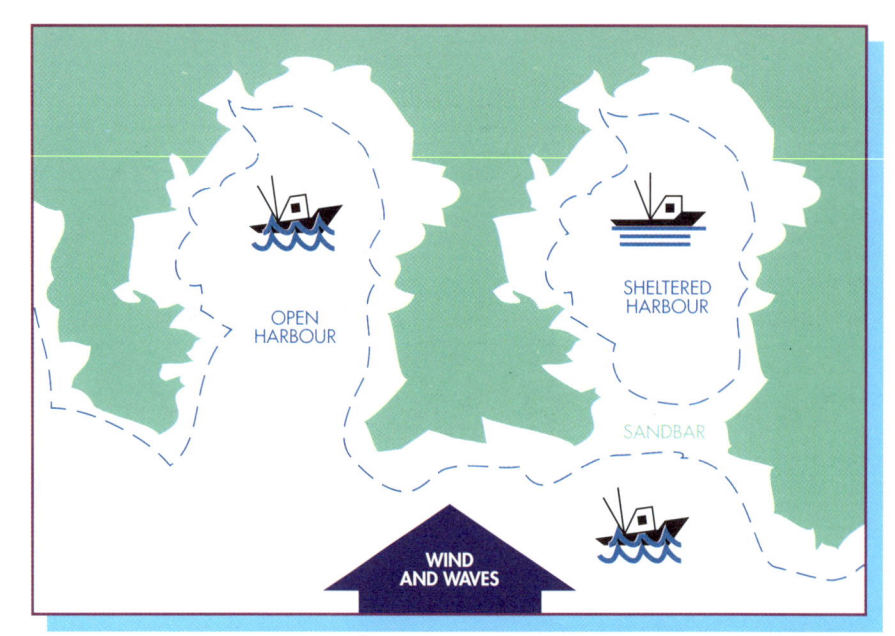

CHEDABUCTO BAY EXPOSED

Another dramatic example of the effects of sheltering is along the eastern coast of Nova Scotia. Mariners travelling close to the coastline during a lengthy west-to-northwest gale will experience only marginal gales blowing off the land and seas—generally less than a metre, due to a limited fetch. However, when they pass the exposed waters of Chedabucto Bay, the winds will often be storm force and the seas developed to 3–4 m. Visibility may be severely restricted by heavy snow-streamers, and there may be freezing spray.

Marine Weather Tip

Mariners who are sheltering in a bay or cove should always heed a marine forecast of heavier winds and waves just outside the bay. The sea state can deteriorate quickly over short distances, and mariners may unwittingly venture from a safe shelter into dangerous seas.

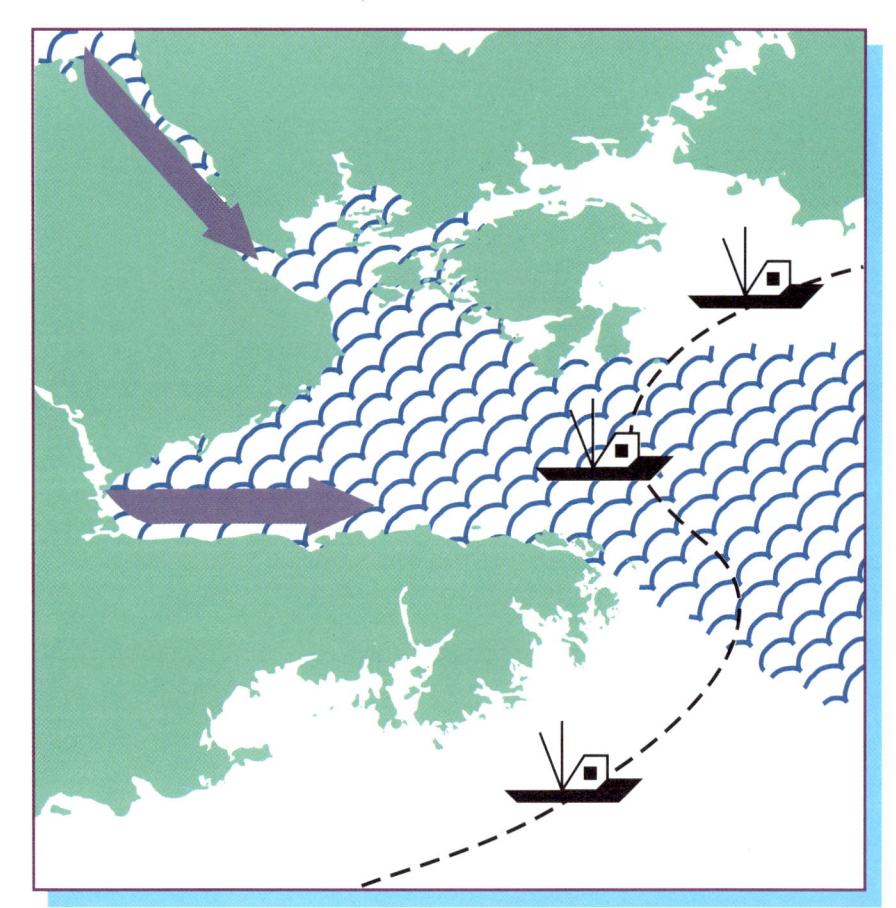

MARINE METEOROLOGY Clouds

> *Did you know* that in 1959, a new dimension was added to the study of clouds? A missile launched to 1,100 km out in space took photographs of the earth's cloud cover; at last meteorologists had a view from the top! Today, many weather satellites orbit the earth, while others remain fixed in orbit over the equator. They range from only a few hundred kilometres above the earth to tens of thousands of kilometres up, each giving meteorologists a different perspective of the clouds and weather systems that they photograph.

Mackerel sky,
*   Mackerel sky,*
Never long wet and
Never long dry.

—Anon.

Cloud activity is a key to understanding weather. By watching the clouds, as well as observing changes in temperature, wind, and air pressure, the mariner can become more aware of weather processes and can better predict how conditions will change.

HOW CLOUDS FORM

Water is present in varying amounts almost everywhere in the atmosphere—usually as an invisible vapour, but sometimes as clouds. Composed of condensed water droplets, clouds form when air is cooled, usually by being forced upwards. They also form when moisture is added to the air; for example, when air passes over a body of water.

Clouds are useful guides to future weather patterns because weather is the result of transformations in the air mass; as cloud forms change, it is likely that the weather, too will change. A variation in air mass affects the moisture content of the air and the temperature patterns at different levels of the atmosphere. Clouds take different forms only when these moisture and temperature changes occur; therefore, when a new type of cloud appears, it is reasonable to assume that a change in the weather is on the way.

TYPES OF CLOUDS

The first attempt to systematically name clouds was made by an Englishman, Luke Howard, in 1803. He classified clouds by shape into three general types: *cirrus* ("curl") clouds, *cumulus* ("heap") clouds, and *stratus* ("layer") clouds. Other types of clouds, such as **nimbus** (rain clouds), were variations on one of these three basic types.

Contemporary meteorologists try to understand clouds by classifying them according to their height above the earth's surface. The highest clouds—based 6 km and higher—have the prefix *cirro*, indicating that they are **high cloud**. They may be lumpy or smooth, as Howard noted; so we end up with names such as *cirrocumulus* and *cirrostratus*. Similarly, clouds based between 2 and 6 km are termed **middle cloud**, and carry the prefix *alto*. Cloud types such as *altocumulus* and *altostratus* are easily understood as middle cloud that is lumpy or smooth. Finally, the **low clouds**—based below 2 km—carry no prefix; simple names like *stratus* or *cumulus* are used.

CIRRUS

Cirrus clouds form in the upper regions of the sky and often precede the lower clouds of an approaching frontal low. The wispy, ethereal nature of cirrus changes into the layered **cirrostratus** or lumpier **cirrocumulus** as the low system nears. No precipitation falls from these high clouds, which are made up of ice crystals.

Cirrocumulus clouds are commonly called the "mackerel sky," because the cloud pattern often resembles the arrangement of scales on the back of a mackerel.

STRATUS

Stratus is a low, uniform, featureless layer of cloud, which is sometimes accompanied by drizzle. When it touches the ground or sea it is called **fog.**

Stratus clouds suggest that the air in which they form is stable (see **WIND**). Therefore, the wind over the sea will be lighter and steadier than if the clouds were lumpy.

MARINE METEOROLOGY Clouds

CUMULUS
Cumulus clouds have flat bases, like stratus, but build upward. Fair-weather cumulus have little build-up but these clouds can produce showers when they develop into tall towers. If the billowing occurs in layered clouds at low levels, the formation is called **stratocumulus** *—the most common cloud type observed in Atlantic Canada.*

Cumulus clouds suggest an unstable air mass, and a stronger, gustier wind than if the clouds were smooth.

NIMBUS
Nimbus is a rain cloud. It takes two forms: **nimbostratus,** *which is layered to great heights ahead of a frontal low and produces steady rain or snow; and* **cumulonimbus,** *which has grown upward from a smaller cumulus cloud and produces heavy showers of rain or snow, thunder and lightning, strong winds, sometimes hail, and in extreme cases, waterspouts.*

SIGNPOSTS IN THE SKY

We have known for thousands of years that the weather repeats itself, giving us ways to anticipate its onset. Clouds, haloes, and rainbows all tell us something about the weather. For example, the familiar rhyme: *"Red sky at night, sailor's delight; red sky in the morning, sailors take warning."* Those words are rooted in lore that predates Christ. But do they work? Sometimes, yes—sometimes, no.

European settlers came to North America from countries where weather systems move from west to east, and the rhyme holds much credibility here as well. In Canada, studies have shown that the saying about the red evening sky proves true about 70 percent of the time, while the one about the morning sky works about 60 percent of the time. However, our Caribbean friends experience weather systems moving from east to west, and the rhyme holds no value.

A red sky early in the morning suggests that many particles are present in the air. They are likely to be water droplets forming a thin veil of cloud over the sky, since early in the day there are usually fewer solid particles in the lower layers of the atmosphere than in the evening. Night-time winds are relatively light and stir up little smoke or dust; the particles that do exist are confined mostly to the surface. So a red sky at sunrise usually suggests the presence of plenty of moisture. Since the weather systems in Canada move from west to east, this condition will most likely arise when drier air is moving away to the east and the moister air of an advancing low-pressure system is approaching from the west. The mariner who uses this knowledge, along with techniques such as watching the barometer, will become a good short-range storm forecaster.

But what about the red sky at night? Again, certain conditions must exist in order for this to happen. The sun must be clearly visible; if a cloud layer associated with approaching wet weather is present, the sun will be either invisible or pale and blurred. But some cloud must show in order to be illuminated by the sun; dissipating fine-weather cumulus clouds are ideal. There should also be numerous suspended dust particles, usually associated with a summer high-pressure system. Under the quiet conditions that accompany the high pressure, the dust particles that find their way into the atmosphere during the day are trapped in the lower levels and accumulate there, "colouring" the sun's light. So the red sky at sunset tells us that, to the west, there is no heavy cloud to obscure the sun, and that the air is dry because the dust particles are smaller than if water vapour were condensed on them. We can be fairly certain that fine weather is approaching from the west.

A halo around the sun or moon is another forecasting tool for the mariner. The rays of light coming from the sun or reflected from the moon are refracted as they pass through the ice crystals of a shield of cirrostratus clouds. When the clouds are thin, the halo is dim; but as they thicken, the halo brightens, until cloud cover completely obscures the sun or moon. Canadian studies have shown that two of three times, rain or snow will arrive within 18 hours after a halo has been observed.

Why then are these signs not infallible? Several reasons. The low-pressure system causing the cloud sheet that was reddened by the rising sun may alter its course, or simply weaken and become a non-event. A red evening sky may be misleading when storm systems are too distant to be spotted in the evening, but are moving quickly enough to bring unexpectedly stormy weather the next day. As well, pollution can affect sky colour and thereby alter the effect of our rhyme.

MARINE METEOROLOGY *Vessel Icing*

FREEZING SEA SPRAY

This type of icing, by far the most serious, can produce severe structural icing. The severity of icing from freezing spray is linked to various environmental conditions, as well as vessel characteristics and activities.

Environmental Conditions

• Air Temperatures must be colder than -2°C (the freezing point of salt water) to generate freezing spray in salt water. When temperatures drop, icing conditions usually become more severe.

• Wind speed is a factor in the amount of spray produced: the stronger the wind, the heavier the spray.

• Wave heights contribute to freezing spray because the splashing of the waves generates much of the spray in the first place. Experienced mariners know that keeping to the lee of pack ice provides effective shelter from freezing spray, since the waves are dampened by the ice (although the pack ice may cause other problems).

• Water temperatures associated with freezing spray conditions are generally colder than 5°C; however, there is actually no "safe-limit." Generally, if the air is cold enough to "supercool" the spray (lower its temperature below the freezing point without turning it to ice) before it makes contact with a vessel, freezing spray is possible.

• Precipitation such as snow, while not affecting the spray itself, can add to the ice loads when freezing spray occurs. Experience has shown that icing events are frequently accompanied by snowsqualls or flurries.

It was that bad the next morning when we started to beat ice that there was four inches on the life-boat covers, aft of the wheelhouse, and the only thing that wasn't iced was the deck—because there was enough water flushing back and forth on the deck to keep it free—and the masthead. Other than that she was covered with ice: and I didn't like it one bit. I had a feeling within me that I never felt before or since, and I believe it was fear—and I hope to never see that again.

— Fisherman, Guy M. D'Entremont, Pubnico-Ouest, N.S.

Any vessel operating in eastern Canadian waters in winter has probably experienced icing. The icing of a vessel's structure can hinder shipboard activities, making the simplest tasks dangerous, exhausting, and sometimes impossible. Icing also increases a vessel's weight and draft and alters its centre of gravity. Uneven icing, along with increased wind drag, can lead to listing. A large accumulation of ice can cause a vessel to sink.

Sub-zero temperatures are required for substantial ice build-up; therefore, vessel icing is only a serious hazard from November to April. The condition can be attributed to one of three factors: freezing sea spray, freezing rain, and ice fog.

MARINE METEOROLOGY Vessel Icing

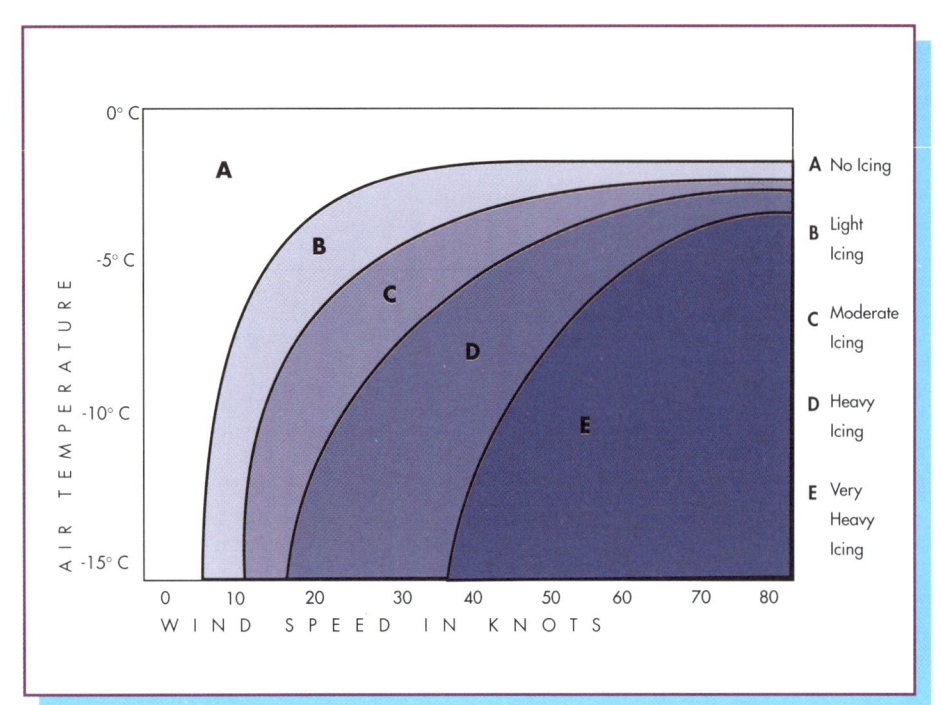

The graph shows an approximate relationship between air temperature, wind speed and vessel icing from freezing spray. Warnings are issued for moderate icing or greater.

Graph axes: AIR TEMPERATURE (0°C to -15°C) vs WIND SPEED IN KNOTS (0 to 80)
- A No Icing
- B Light Icing
- C Moderate Icing
- D Heavy Icing
- E Very Heavy Icing

Vessel characteristics

Size, weight, and hull design are critical factors in determining the amount of spray experienced by a vessel, and consequently the icing rate. Small vessels with large amounts of rigging are especially at risk, since ice build-up is most rapid on exposed surfaces with smaller diameters. Such vessels have less capacity to handle the extra ice load. When icing conditions threaten, clear deck areas of all gear and rigging that could accumulate additional ice.

Vessel activities

Speed and heading determine the amount of spray experienced by a vessel.

Marine Weather Tip

A slow-moving vessel, or one moving away from the wind, experiences far less icing than a vessel heading quickly into the wind and waves. It is also helpful to consider water temperatures in the vicinity. For example, it may be wiser for a vessel encountering freezing spray off Nova Scotia to head south to warmer water temperatures; the trip home would mean tracking through colder air and water temperatures and a head-on encounter with the northerly or northwesterly winds that are generating the icing.

FREEZING RAIN

This form of precipitation occurs when warm air rides up over cold arctic air at the surface. Rain from the warm air falls through the cold layer and becomes supercooled. Under these conditions, the rain freezes when it hits the sub-zero temperatures of a vessel's superstructure. This forms a clear glaze of ice over the decks, railings, and stairways. Less ice usually accumulates with freezing rain than with sea spray.

ICE FOG

Also referred to as *arctic sea smoke* or *steam fog* (see **FOG**), this condition can occur when light to moderate winds carry very cold air over relatively warm water. This fog is composed of minute, supercooled water droplets that freeze on contact with a vessel. It is most common in the Gulf of St. Lawrence and Labrador Sea. Only when atmospheric conditions are just right can sea smoke become thick enough to pose a serious icing problem.

Do you remember when sea smoke engulfed the bridges between Halifax and Dartmouth? For two days during the winter of 1993–94, the Halifax Bridge Commission had to sand the bridges between the two cities because arctic sea smoke rose to a height of over 100 ft.. The bridges became enveloped with this very cold ice fog, which deposited a thin film of ice on all surfaces, making for treacherous driving.

MARINE METEOROLOGY Fog

Cloud that comes in contact with the surface is called fog. The mariner caught in fog often operates without the three vital tools of navigation: sight, hearing, and radar. Fog causes obscured visibility, distorted sound, and reduced radar range; it is a phenomenon to be treated with caution and respect. When visibility is reduced to 1/2 mile or less, it is called fog. However, when visibility is greater than 1/2 mile, the condition is called mist.

Fog forms when air is unable to contain moisture, which takes the form of invisible water vapour; and warm air can hold more water vapour than cold air. There are two ways for air to become saturated: its temperature drops below its capacity to hold moisture (the "dewpoint temperature"); or it takes on more moisture than it can hold. Four basic types of fog exist; the first two when the air is cooled, and the second two when moisture is added to the air.

Sometimes out on the Bay of Fundy when the fog comes in thick you can sit on the boat's rail and lean your back up agin' it. So that's pretty thick fog out there but you gotta be careful, 'cause if the fog lifts quick, you'll fall overboard.

—A Nova Scotia sailor

RADIATION FOG

Radiation Fog forms over land early in the morning, usually under clear skies and light wind conditions. As the land surface loses heat and radiates it into space, the air also loses its ability to hold its moisture—which becomes fog. Radiation fog may drift over the water when light land-breezes (see **WIND**) develop during the night. The condition affects harbours and estuaries; it rarely spreads far out to sea and often lifts off the water surface to form low stratus clouds. After sunrise, the fog burns off over the land, then clears more slowly over the water.

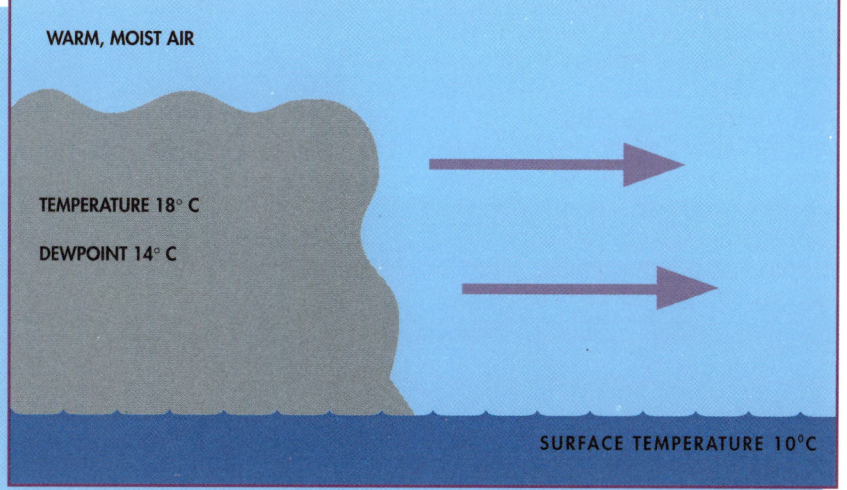

SEA FOG

Sea fog is formed when warm, moist air moves over colder sea water. The moisture in the air condenses into fog, the same way a person's warm breath condenses on a cold day. The sea-surface temperature must be a couple of degrees cooler than the dewpoint temperature for fog to form. Unlike radiation fog, which requires calm or light wind conditions, sea fog may form when winds are moderate, and may even persist as winds become strong. And unlike land fog, which usually burns off during the day, sea fog is much less affected by sunshine. As a rule, sea fog only clears by a change of air—like fresh west-to-northwest winds. Also called *advection fog,* it is of most concern to mariners in spring and summer.

MARINE METEOROLOGY Fog

SATELLITE PHOTO OF SEA FOG
This satellite picture shows how fog forms over specific areas. From the vantage point of the satellite, the strip of fog in the eastern Gulf of St. Lawrence is very narrow; however, to the mariner at sea, it is a substantial fog bank over 50 miles wide.

Sea fog indicates an area in the lower atmosphere where the air is very stable. However, stability has a direct bearing on the wind strength. (see **WIND**) Therefore, winds will be lighter in the fog than elsewhere in the less-stable or "frictionless" conditions. As a result, the fog appears to act as a barrier of sorts against stronger winds above it and at its windward edge. Hence the saying: "The thicker the fog, the lighter the wind." Some mariners believe that the fog also suppresses waves, but the real reason for decreased wave heights is stable air—giving reduced winds.

PRECIPITATION OR FRONTAL FOG
Precipitation fog, or frontal fog, forms ahead of warm fronts when warm precipitation falls through a cooler layer near the ground. The precipitation saturates the surface air and fog forms. Breaks in the precipitation usually result in the fog becoming thicker—cleared away only by drier air.

ICE FOG
Ice fog forms when very cold arctic air moves over relatively warmer water. Unlike sea fog, in this case moisture evaporates from the sea surface and saturates the air. The extremely cold air cannot hold all the evaporated moisture, so the excess condenses into fog. The result looks like steam or smoke rising from the sea surface, and is usually no more than a few dozen feet thick. Ice fog, also called *arctic sea smoke,* is normally not a hazard to mariners, but under extreme conditions the fog may be thick and cold enough to create light vessel icing.

MARINE METEOROLOGY *Storm Surge*

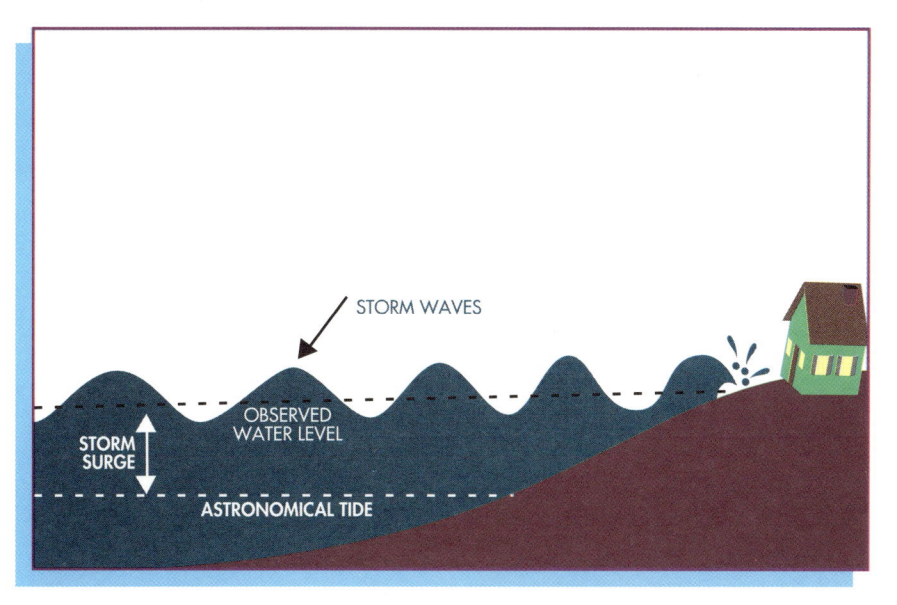

STORM SURGE

The observed tides along our coastline often differ greatly from the predicted astronomical tides published in the *Canadian Current and Tide Tables*. The discrepancy between expected and observed water levels is the result of two primary weather elements: pressure and wind. This difference in water levels is called a storm surge. A surge can be either positive or negative, increasing or decreasing the water levels from those predicted.

In shallow areas, a negative surge can cause a decrease in the depth available and therefore a risk of running aground. Higher water levels in a positive surge can cause coastal flooding and damage to piers and wharves. Small boats, whose owners thought they had been pulled "high and dry" up the beach, may become afloat. And when significant storm-surge conditions combine with high tides, the result can be catastrophic. A warning message of forecast storm surges is carried in the marine synopsis when water levels are anticipated to be more than about 2 ft. higher than normal, especially in conjunction with high tides.

The first main weather influence is barometric pressure. High pressure depresses the sea level and low pressure allows it to rise. A change in barometric pressure of 1 millibar causes a rise or fall in the sea level of about 1 cm. The result, called the *inverted barometer effect,* is not instantaneous, but is characterized by the average change over a wide area. The astronomical tide predictions in the *Canadian Current and Tide Tables* are based on average global atmospheric pressure of 1013.25 mb; departures from this pressure also mean departures from the Tide Table values. For example, imagine a deep low-pressure centre—973 mb (40 mb below the global average)—passing over the ocean. The low would act like a giant vacuum on a carpet that creates a bulge as it passes, causing a rise of 40 cm, which could create a problem in coastal zones. However, if the ocean area were under a large 1043 mb high-pressure centre, the sea level would be depressed by 30 cm (1 ft.) due to pressure considerations alone. This would mean less available draft—also a possible problem.

The influence of wind on sea level is more complicated; it depends on the shape of the sea bed as well as the strength, duration, and fetch of the wind itself. A strong wind blowing onshore will raise the sea level, which is especially noticeable at the head of long, shallow bays. Winds blowing offshore tend to have the opposite effect. Besides water "piling up" on the shore in onshore winds, there is also a movement of water to the right of the wind. An example is the storm surge along the Atlantic coast of Nova Scotia in a northeasterly wind—a wind parallel to the coast. This effect, called *Ekman transport,* is a significant factor in east-coast storm-surge events. As well, waves moving onshore travel on the elevated water level and increase the likelihood of problems for coastal residents. As a rule of thumb, meteorologists add 10 percent of the onshore significant wave heights to the water level when forecasting storm surge.

Currents are particularly sensitive to the effects of the wind. The times of slack water can be advanced or retarded considerably by strong winds. Sometimes, particularly if the following flood or ebb current is weak, the direction of current may not change and slack water may not occur.

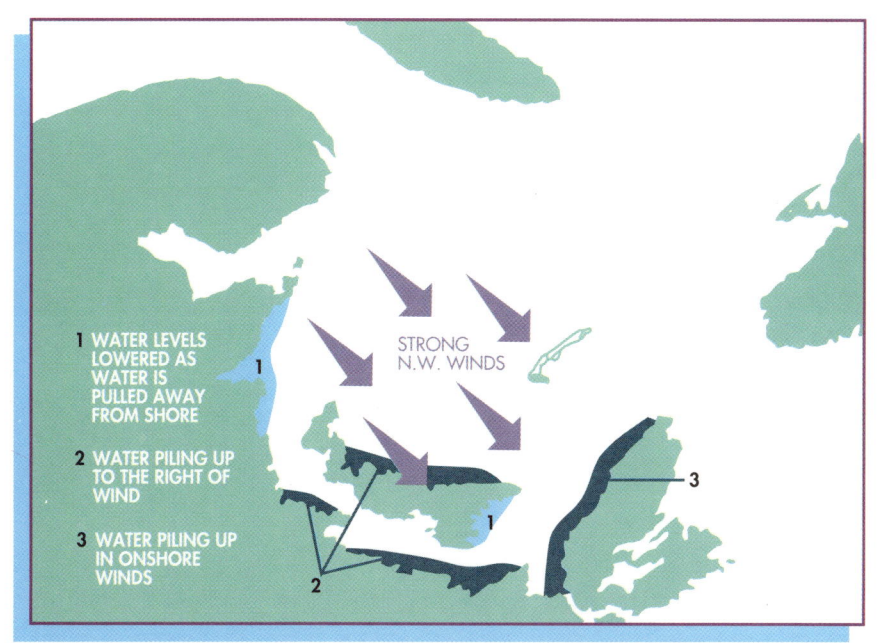

MARINE METEOROLOGY Storm Surge

Did you know that many Maritimers believe that the highest tides ever seen occurred on Groundhog Day? On February 2, 1976, an unexpectedly brutal winter storm battered the region with winds that exceeded 100 knots. Storm-surge values reached 1.5 m in the Bay of Fundy—directly under the storm centre's track. Tens of millions of dollars in damage to the fishing industry alone resulted from the combination of high winds, large waves, and abnormally high water levels.

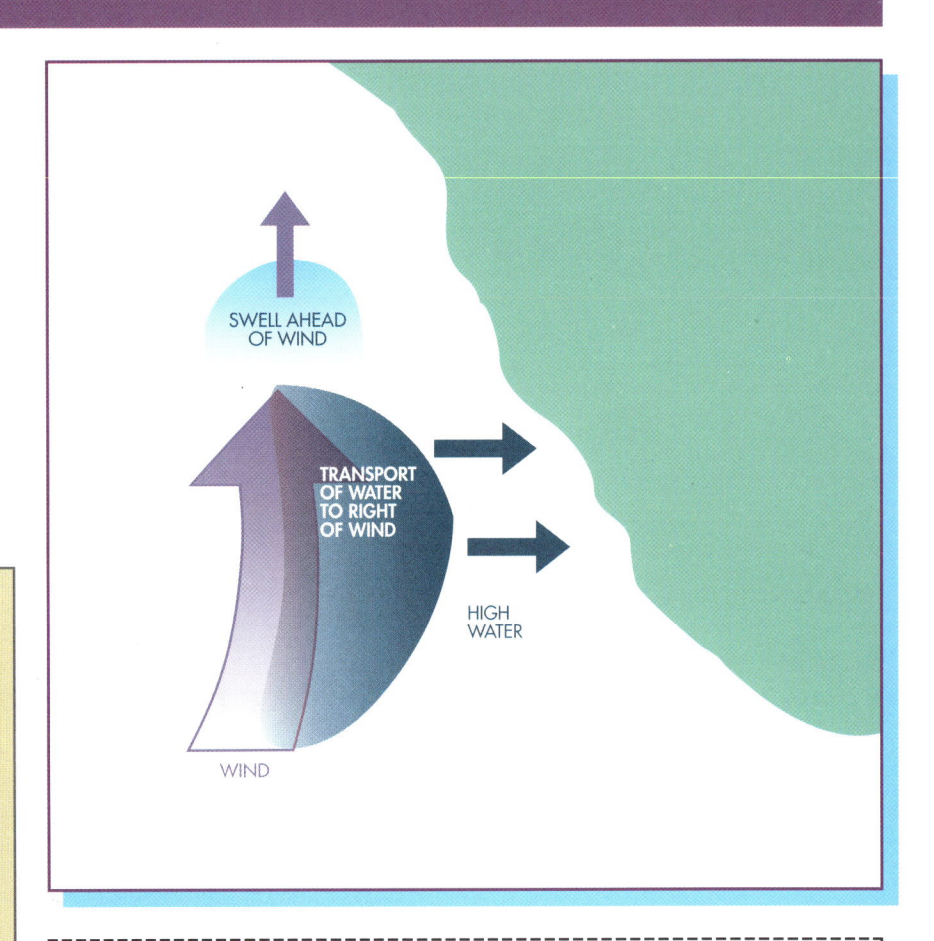

SWELL AHEAD OF WIND

TRANSPORT OF WATER TO RIGHT OF WIND

HIGH WATER

WIND

EKMAN TRANSPORT—Technically Speaking

It is easy to see how a prevailing onshore wind pushes large seas onto a coastline. However, a major source of water transport also takes place to the right of the wind direction. Friction between the wind and the sea causes the sea to move in the direction of the wind. Once the sea begins to move, it is affected by the Coriolis force, which causes objects to be deflected to the right (see **WIND**). Water is shifted to the right of the prevailing wind—Ekman transport.

In this diagram, the shore to the east is experiencing a positive surge because of the southerly wind "setting up" the water at the coast. Conversely, sea levels would "set down" if the winds were from the north. This is called a negative surge.

MARINE METEOROLOGY *Ice*

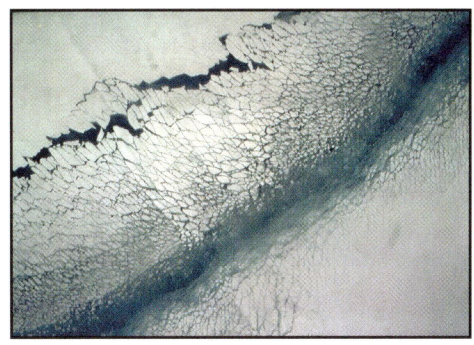

"Floating crystal castles" was the description penned by St. Brendan as he wrote about his encounter with icebergs on the high seas.

SEA ICE OR PACK ICE

Sea ice—frozen salt water—is considered an impediment to the commercial marine industry, but it can also have some benefits. A large body of sea ice inhibits waves when the wind is blowing off the ice, providing shelter to mariners in a storm (that is, when it doesn't drive towards you). Since wave heights are reduced, there is also less risk of freezing spray in strong, cold winds in the vicinity of pack ice. Sea ice reaches its maximum seaward extent in Atlantic Canada in March or April.

Formation of Sea Ice

Depending on salinity and other factors, salt water may freeze at -1°C or -2°C. Conditions must also permit the water to be layered so that warmer, sub-surface water cannot replace cooler water. Ideal areas for formation of sea ice are those where temperatures remain below the freezing point of salt water for long periods of time; where water is less saline—particularly at the surface—and where mixing, due to tidal and wave action, is inhibited. Currents transporting warm water prevent ice formation because they offset the effects of cooling. In Atlantic Canada, the waters off Labrador and Newfoundland, and the Gulf of St. Lawrence become ice-covered in winter.

Movement of Sea Ice

The complex motion of sea ice is largely determined by ocean and tidal currents, and by surface wind. Other factors include the size, thickness, shape, surface texture, and concentration of the sea ice. In general, mobile ice that has a rough surface, lower concentration, or smaller floe size will respond better to wind and currents.

Ocean and Tidal Currents

The prime movers of sea ice and icebergs over great distances are ocean currents, while fluctuating tidal currents affect the ice from day to day. Estimation of sea ice movement in harbours requires a knowledge of tides and tidal streams; navigational charts and tide tables from the Canadian Hydrographic Service are invaluable.

ICE BREAKING AWAY FROM PACK

Sea ice breaking from the main pack will often create an open lead—a passable stretch of water through the pack ice. But a vessel can become trapped when a wind shift closes the lead once again. Mariners should listen to forecasts so they can anticipate any wind shifts that might trap them in the ice.

Marine Weather Tip

Mariners experiencing smaller-than-expected waves, should suspect that pack ice is close by. Also, the sighting of marine mammals—such as seals—far from shore is another indication that pack ice may be near. Generally, water temperatures below 0°C mean that the ice edge is within 50 miles.

Wind

The wind affects day-to-day differences in ice motion and location. Ice that is deep-drafted (well below the surface) will respond much less to the wind than thin ice, although once it begins to move, its momentum will continue after the wind has died. Ice concentration is also a crucial factor to consider, since very open ice drifts with the wind about four times faster than very close ice. Concentrated ice will often spread out somewhat if it is moved for a couple of days by a persistent wind. In general, sea ice moves in response to winds in a couple of ways: *sailing* and *drifting*.

• *Sailing.* When wind blows across an ice surface, friction between wind and ice

MARINE METEOROLOGY *Ice*

results in force being applied in the direction of the wind. If the ice surface is smooth and has few topographical features, the wind will have a minimal effect. However, as the ice develops ridges and hummocks, or becomes rafted, these features can act as sails to "catch" the wind, thereby propelling the ice floe. Ice that has a rough, hummocky surface will drift with the wind about eight times faster than smooth ice.

• *Drifting.* The process of Ekman transport (see **STORM SURGE**) results in water being transported to the right of the direction that the wind is blowing. Ice that is embedded in the water will respond to the overall movement of the water as well as the wind. (Note: the effect of drifting is usually greater than the effect of sailing.) Therefore, ice floes generally move to the right of the wind direction by about 45° because of this effect.

Marine Weather Tip
The combination of wind and wind-driven currents usually results in sea ice moving at a rate of 1–2 percent of the wind speed, and in a direction that is more or less parallel to the isobars on a weather map.

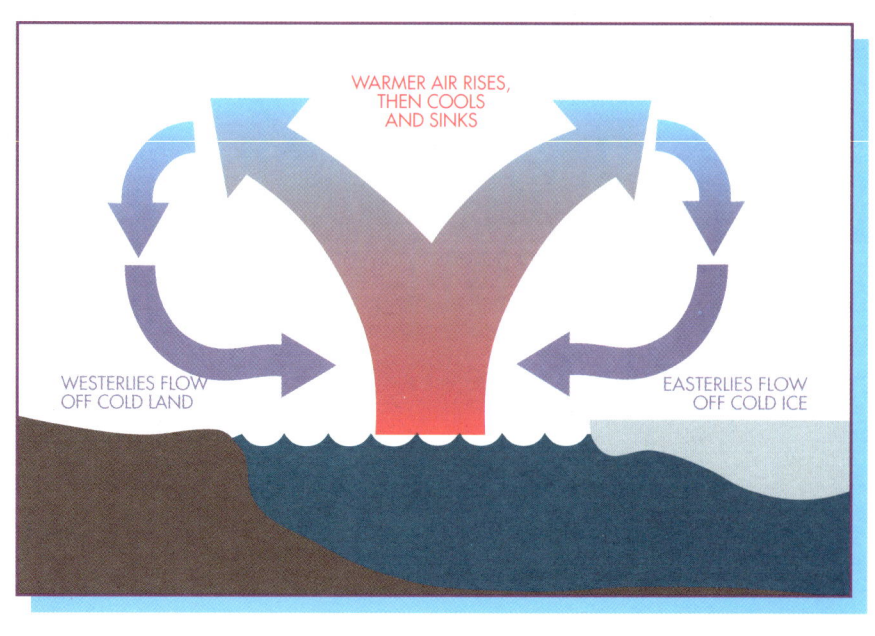

WINDS NEAR THE ICE EDGE
In winter and spring, it is common to see a few miles of open water along the ice edge. When this happens, a condition similar to a land breeze occurs. Air rises over the relatively warm open water, resulting in light to moderate winds from both the land and the ice. This process favours the formation of cumulus clouds over the open water between the land and the ice—an indication that the circulation has developed.

Do you remember when Halifax Harbour was filled with ice? That was 1987, an exceptional year for ice along the Atlantic coast. This satellite picture shows the extent of the ice on March 25. Northeasterly winds drove ice from the Cabot Strait hard ashore between Cape North and Scatarie Island. The ice also affected most of the shoreline from Scatarie Island to Chedabucto Bay. Another area of ice can be seen lying off the coast between Tor Bay and Halifax; a wind shift pushed this ice onshore two days later.

The ice shown in this picture came ashore, hampering activity in the harbour for several days. This was believed to be the first serious intrusion of ice into Halifax Harbour since 1943.

MARINE METEOROLOGY Ice

ICEBERGS

Icebergs are masses of glacial ice that have drifted seaward. Dramatic in appearance, they pose a serious local hazard to navigation; unlike sea ice, however, they do not prevent shipping activity. Icebergs are made from glaciers that formed on land areas over thousands of years. Consequently, these chunks of very old freshwater ice are much harder than the frozen saltwater floes of the Arctic Ocean and adjoining waterways. Small icebergs embedded in pack ice are often difficult to detect—a real concern for mariners. "Growlers," the "tiny" remains of icebergs, can go completely undetected in waves higher than 1–1.5 m, posing an immediate danger to neighbouring vessels.

The expression "just the tip of the iceberg" is well founded, for 'bergs are deep-drafted with most of their mass beneath the water and out of sight—which is why they are such a hazard. Almost 90 percent of an iceberg's mass is beneath the water, but its draft depth depends on its shape. For example, a flat iceberg has a draft of about five times its height, while the more famous "pinnacled" iceberg has a draft only three times its height.

Movement of Icebergs

Like sea ice, icebergs are moved around by both the wind and ocean currents, although the motion of icebergs is usually dominated by currents—ocean, tidal, and wind-driven. As with pack ice, the wind-driven currents tend to deflect the icebergs to the right of the wind direction, particularly when ocean and tidal currents are weak. Icebergs can often be seen moving against the wind—a tribute to the dominating influence of currents over wind.

Icebergs can be affected by wind, however, especially when strong, persistent winds blow. As well, the rate of wind-drift is critically linked to the height-to-draft ratio of the iceberg. Observations show that block icebergs with a 1:1 height-to-draft ratio have a drift rate of about 4 percent of the wind speed. Compare this to typical pinnacled 'bergs of 1:6 ratio, which have a drift rate of 0.4 percent of the wind speed, or $1/10$ of the rate of block icebergs.

The drift of icebergs from their point of origin on the west coast of Greenland to the coast of Newfoundland is a journey of about 1,800 miles that takes one to three years. Owing to their deep drafts of 100–200 m, larger icebergs are often slowed, either when they are grounded or caught up in the ice pack. Every spring, icebergs can be seen off the east coast of Newfoundland. Tidal currents often bring 'bergs close to shore, where they can enter harbours and become grounded in shallower water. It is not unusual to see an iceberg at the mouth of St. John's Harbour in July or August.

Extent of Iceberg Drift

In their southward travel, icebergs display drift-patterns similar to the sea-ice stream of the Arctic pack. The arrival of the winter pack along the Labrador and Newfoundland coasts usually marks the end of the season's iceberg count. This is because few icebergs survive an unseasonable drift southward into warmer water unprotected by pack ice. Wave erosion is a major factor in iceberg deterioration. Disintegration is accelerated by high waves and heavy swell, the effect of which is noticeable on icebergs that drift offshore in the Atlantic, unprotected by sea ice.

Observations by the International Ice Patrol suggest the following deterioration rate for an average-size iceberg (about 50 m high and 200 m wide):

Water Temperature (in °C)	Iceberg Melting Rate
-2–0	Nil
0–4.5	Immeasurable
4.5–7.5	Measurable but slight
7.5–10	2–3 weeks
10–15	1–2 Weeks
over 15	1 week or less

Caution: Radar May Not Help

Iceberg studies on the Grand Banks of Newfoundland have shown that radar returns from icebergs are about 60 times weaker than ships of equivalent size. These studies also show that growlers and medium ice floes cannot be detected by radar at ranges over a few miles. This means that only well-trained radar operators maintaining a keen vigil will be able to detect growlers or very small 'bergs.

Would you believe that in June of 1907, a vast discharge of icebergs into the North Atlantic sent one chunk of glacial ice south—almost to Bermuda—while another 'berg made it to the eastern Atlantic, within a few hundred miles of Ireland?

MARINE METEOROLOGY *Ice*

CAPSIZING ICEBERGS

Since most of an iceberg is underwater, the bottom tends to melt more quickly than the section above the waterline (especially in warm waters). As well, wave-action near the waterline leads to accelerated erosion of the 'berg. The result is that large chunks can break off from the bottom, making the iceberg top-heavy. When this happens, the iceberg can quickly capsize. These sudden movements often cause the icebergs to fragment into smaller pieces—these being the greatest danger to marine activities. As well, the violent and sudden overturning can pose a serious threat to mariners.

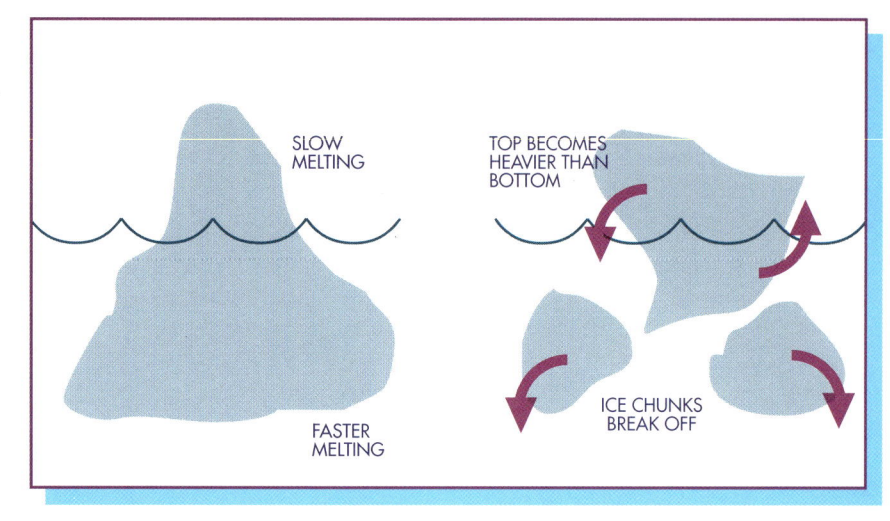

MARINE METEOROLOGY *Storms*

The term storm is used loosely by mariners to describe a weather system or event that produces strong winds, high waves, or heavy precipitation. In this context, there are a variety of storms that affect Atlantic Canada.

Four basic types of storms can be encountered in the waters off the east coast, and each is defined by the way it forms. There are the typical low-pressure centres that draw their energy from the ongoing battle between warm and cold air masses—these are *frontal storms*. *Thunderstorms* are often single "cells" of overturning air, moving independently through the atmosphere. Storms such as *cold outbreaks* and *polar lows* draw their energy from cold air. Finally, *tropical storms* and *hurricanes* draw their energy from warm ocean waters.

FRONTAL STORMS

Most of the storms experienced in Atlantic Canada are associated with frontal lows that can expand to cover the entire region. If conditions are right, some of these lows deepen and intensify explosively—hence the name "bombs" given to them by meteorologists, who must watch closely for the signs of their development.

As discussed earlier, these lows undergo a dramatic evolution. At any stage during their life cycle, gale- and storm-force winds are possible. Many mariners have found it wise to learn about the winds associated with these common storms.

When evening comes, you say, "It will be fair weather, for the sky is red," and in the morning, "Today it will be stormy, for the sky is red and overcast."

—Jesus, quoting an ancient aphorism, Matthew 16:2-3

TYPICAL WINDS WITH A MATURE FRONTAL STORM

Pressure gradient (see **WIND***) is one of the key factors in determining the wind in a given storm. However, in storms such as the one pictured here, other factors add to, or subtract from, the effect of the pressure gradient:*

(1) Storm-force winds may develop behind a cold front because strong instability, rapid pressure-rises, and clockwise-curving winds add to the effect of the pressure gradient.

(2) Storm-force winds may also develop in the warmer air and a certain distance ahead of the warm front, because rapid pressure changes add positively to the effect of the pressure gradient.

(3) Lighter winds may be experienced to the left of the low's track because counterclockwise-curving winds, rapid pressure changes (having a negative effect), and stable air combine to reduce the effect of the pressure gradient. This combination is very fortunate because the strongest pressure gradient in frontal lows is often observed to the left of the low's track—without these limiting factors, hurricane force winds would be common.

43

MARINE METEOROLOGY *Storms*

TYPICAL WINDS WITH AN OCCLUDING FRONTAL STORM

A frontal storm begins to die when the pielike wedge of warm air becomes occluded, or squeezed out, by heavy cold air pushing down behind the low. When this happens, the low centre is cut off from its supply of warm, moist air and is flooded with cold air. It then begins to weaken.

This process signals the final stages of life for the storm centre. However, it does not mean that the strong winds and other significant weather have ended. The occlusion is still an important feature, because the significant weather often moves with it as it pulls away from the low. In the case of a trowal, gale- and storm-force winds often form ahead of it, because the pressure gradient packs tightly there. Once an occlusion passes by, the winds drop dramatically. As well, heavy precipitation just ahead of the occlusion or trowal will change abruptly to fog and drizzle in its wake.

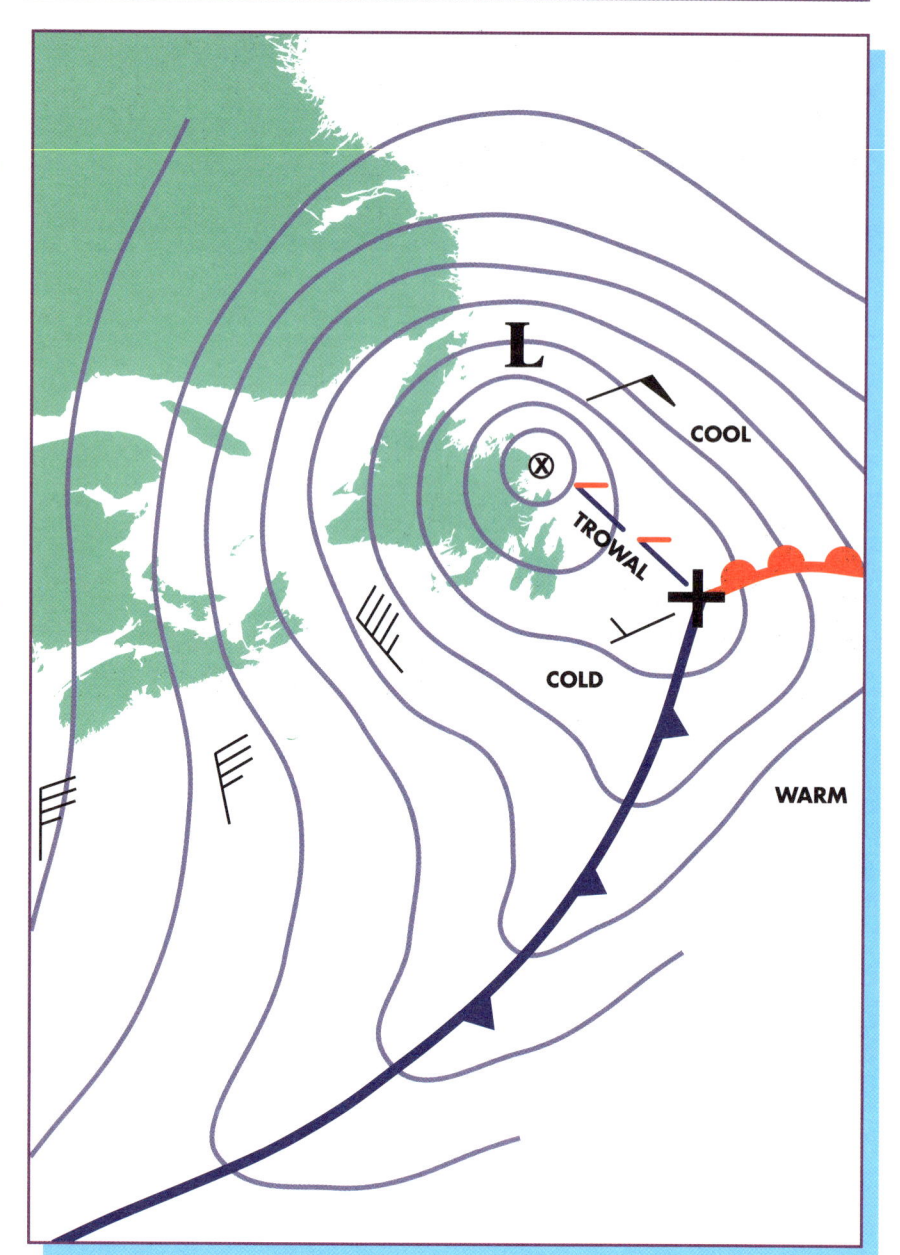

MARINE METEOROLOGY Storms

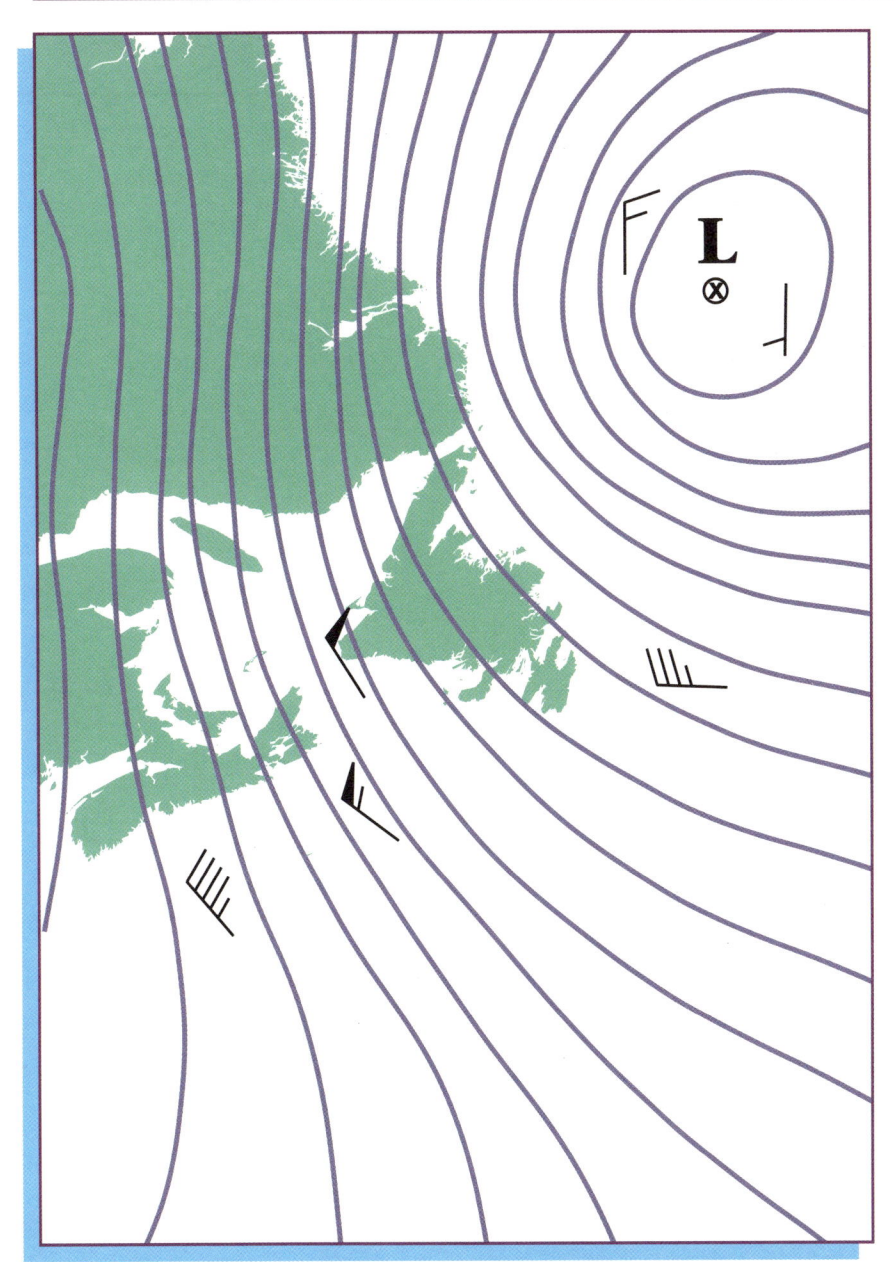

TYPICAL WINDS WITH A COLD LOW SYSTEM

Once the warm air has completely pulled out of a low, the cold air floods its core and pressure fills. As well, frictional effects of the converging winds slow the rotating mass, helping it to wind down. The low can sit in one spot, spinning slowly, sometimes for days. These systems can bring mist, drizzle, and intermittent rain or snow, with them, or shower activity can persist. Winds near the centre of a cold low are not usually very strong.

This map shows a typical early-winter pressure pattern in eastern Canada. A cold low becomes stalled somewhere east of Newfoundland or Labrador, and may persist there for many days. A high-pressure centre moving in from the west around the same time results in a "pressure squeeze" over the Atlantic provinces. Although the low continues weakening as its central pressure rises, it is far from harmless. The resulting northwesterly winds are often very cold and unstable, adding to the wind strength. In these situations, gale-force winds are usually expected over the region while storm-force and even hurricane-force winds are also possible. The waters east and south of Newfoundland, and the Labrador Sea, are most vulnerable.

Caution: Severe Winter Weather
A cold low in the Labrador Sea can signal a lengthy spell of storm-force northwesterlies—sometimes for many days. When winds persist for a few days, the seas become fully developed, and treacherous conditions of wind, waves, and freezing spray can exist. The winds can even reach hurricane force.

45

MARINE METEOROLOGY *Storms*

TYPICAL SEA STATES WITH A MATURE FRONTAL STORM

Often, wave steepness is more critical than wave height. A ship will ride a long, high wave by climbing up one side and sliding down the other. But serious difficulties arise when the ship's stern gets hung up on one steep wave crest while the bow is driven under the next one. This, and other problems, result when the length of the vessel corresponds to the distance between successive waves. Here are other dangerous situations.

In beam seas:
- excessive roll can cause cargo to shift, with the danger of listing or capsizing;
- broadside breaking waves may exert a force above the vessel's centre of gravity that is great enough to result in capsizing.

In following seas:
- there may be loss of stability on a wave crest;
- broaching can happen as a vessel is overtaken by a wave crest.

In quartering seas:
- combinations of beam and following-seas problems are possible.

The worst threat from storms is not the winds, as one might expect, but the size and ferocity of the waves that result. The following table gives a description of the sea states possible with various wind speeds, depending on duration of the wind. In these cases, it is assumed that there is no sheltering from either wind or sea, and that locations are exposed to the open ocean and the direction from which the wind and waves are coming.

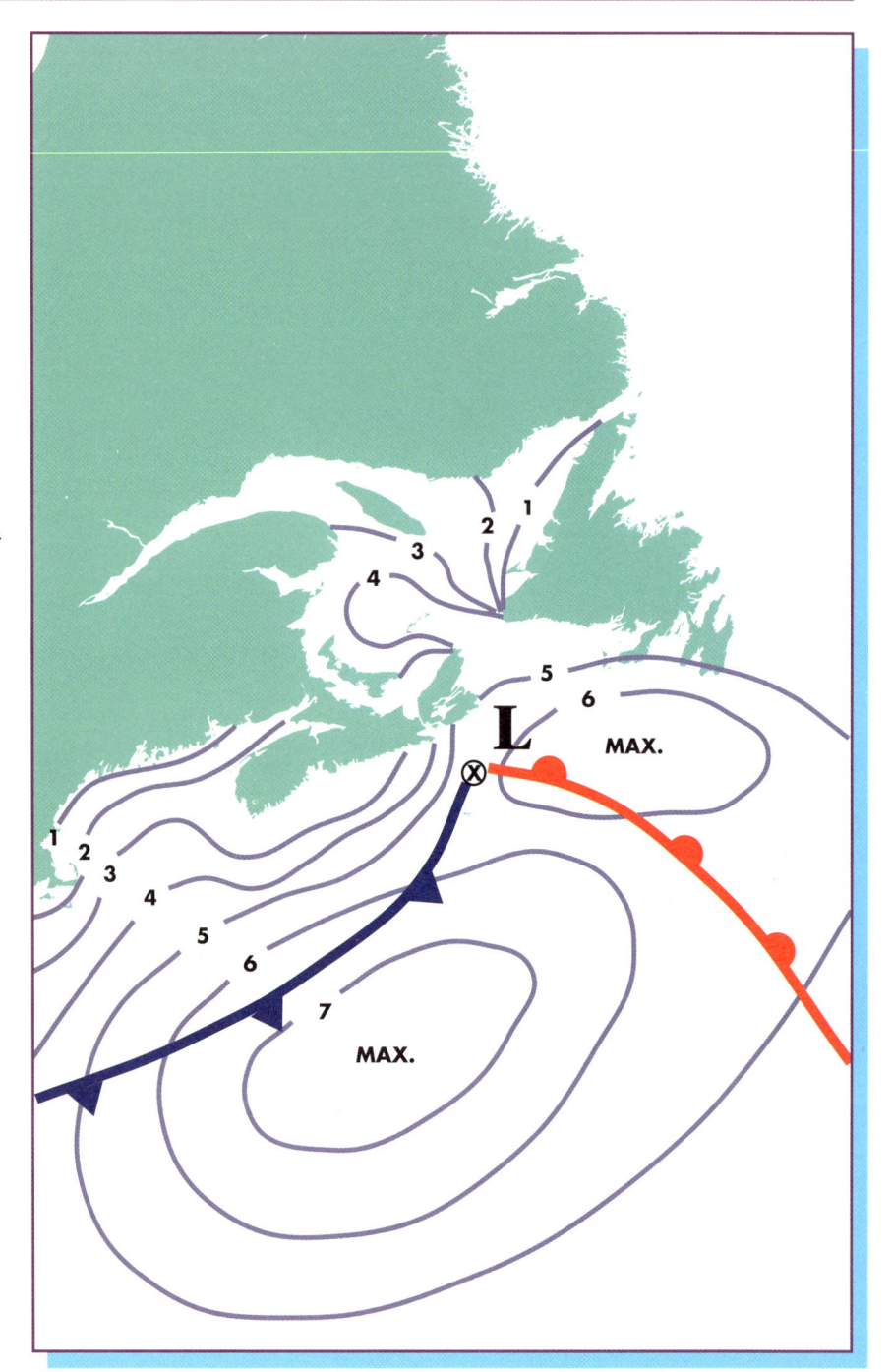

	TYPICAL WIND SPEED	SEAS AFTER 24 HOURS	MAXIMUM SEAS UNLIMITED DURATION
Strong Winds or Small Craft Warning	20–33 knots	2–5 m	3–6 m
Gale Warning	34–47 knots	5–8 m	6–9 m
Storm Warning	48–63 knots	8–12 m	9–16 m
Hurricane Force Wind Warning	over 63 knots	over 12 m	over 16 m

MARINE METEOROLOGY Storms

I saw the lightning's
  Gleaming rod
Reach forth and write
  Upon the sky
The awful autograph of God.

—Joaquin Miller,
"The Ship in the Desert"

THUNDERSTORMS

Thunderstorms concern mariners primarily because of the violent winds that can accompany them. Lightning can also be a problem at sea, since thunderstorms seek out tall, free-standing objects, such as masts, as focal points for their electrical discharge to the earth.

There are three classes of thunderstorms: *air mass thunderstorms,* which occur individually and randomly over an area; *line* or *frontal thunderstorms,* associated with a frontal system or a trough of low pressure; and *mesoscale convective complexes* (MCCs)—massive thunderstorm clusters responsible for widespread severe weather. Since only the first two are a concern in Atlantic Canada, MCCs will not be discussed.

Air Mass Thunderstorms

In summer, air mass thunderstorms usually form over land, then drift over water, which is colder than land. The storms are generally individual cloud "cells," although a few cells may combine to form a larger thunderstorm cluster. These thunderstorms commonly form in the afternoon and disperse in the evening. Many of them disperse quickly after moving over cold water; this happens frequently when thunderstorm cells move from New Brunswick or New England and pass over the Bay of Fundy or the Northumberland Strait. It is often possible to avoid them by altering course.

These storms may also form in winter when cold air rushes out over warm water, as in the case of a cold-outbreak. These thunderstorms are widespread, and altering course will seldom help the mariner to avoid them. This is a frequent problem in cold-outbreaks over the warm waters of the Gulf Stream.

STAGES OF THUNDERSTORM DEVELOPMENT

Every thunderstorm follows the same pattern of development and decay. At the start, it consists of a central core of upward-moving air; winds around the outside blow towards the centre. During the next stage, as it becomes a storm and reaches maximum intensity, a strong downdraft of cooler air develops. Rain begins, accompanied by lightning and thunder. The strong, gusty winds blow down from under the cloud and spread outwards; this is called a squall or gust front (see **WIND***). A dark menacing roll cloud often forms at the forward edge of a thunderstorm. As it reaches up, it becomes even darker and more threatening; however, the weather it brings will not be severe unless it reaches well up into the atmosphere for several miles. Cloud heights need to be well over 20,000 ft. to produce strong gusts. But it is not until the thunderheads reach up into the 40,000–60,000-ft. range that the violent squalls of 50 or 60 knots occur. In the final stage, air descends at all levels.*

MARINE METEOROLOGY *Storms*

Line or Frontal Thunderstorms
These thunderstorms often form a continuous line of activity, and there is little opportunity to avoid the storm by changing course. In addition, frontal thunderstorms are often embedded in other clouds, and the precise area of the thunderstorm activity is difficult to discern from the general cloud and rain accompanying the front.

Waterspouts
Another phenomenon frequently associated with thunderstorms off the east coast is the waterspout. Like tornadoes over water, waterspouts are vertical rotating funnels of cloud that extend down from the base of thunderstorms. The first sign that a waterspout may form comes when the cloud sags in one area. If this bulge drops towards the sea surface, forming a vortex beneath it, sea water can be carried 100 ft. or more into the air. The average diameter of a waterspout is less than 50 ft., although well-developed systems may reach a few hundred feet across. Waterspouts can often be detected on navigational radars, and unlike tornadoes, usually last less than 15 minutes. Waterspouts associated with thunderstorms are frequently reported in the Gulf of St. Lawrence and in the Northumberland Strait. Although some immature waterspouts are very small, they should be avoided because they can change to more violent systems without warning. Another type of waterspout is one that forms in the absence of thunderstorms, which is discussed in the next section.

Up there in New Brunswick the weather can change awful quick. One time I was watching the trout jump on the lake and a cold squall come down from the north. I walked out on the ice and picked up a fine mess of trout.

—A Nova Scotia fisherman

COLD-AIR STORMS
Cold-Outbreaks
One of the most difficult weather conditions for mariners is the cold-outbreak: that blast of cold arctic air that drives in behind a fierce winter storm. Strong pressure effects combined with deep instability often give rise to storm-force winds. Bitter temperatures associated with these winds can create severe freezing-spray and wind-chill conditions. The instability and wind combine to create very heavy snowsqualls in places directly under one of the "snow streamers"—a line of snow-producing convective cloud that spans tens or hundreds of miles. Winds don't have to be strong for streamers to develop, but they do need to "line up" with the winds higher in the atmosphere. This allows the cumulus and towering cumulus clouds—those responsible for the snow—to attain considerable heights without being sheered off by contrary winds aloft.

Waterspouts may even form in the absence of thunderstorms, existing simply as cold-air funnels. This is a common event in autumn cold-outbreaks over the warm Gulf Stream waters and the Gulf of St. Lawrence. It is speculated that strong gale- or storm-force conditions inhibit waterspout formation, accounting for the fact that they are more common in early fall than in winter. However, this does not preclude their formation at other times of the year.

Marine Weather Tip:
Cold Air Packs More Punch
Mariners often observe that it takes less wind to build the sea in the fall and winter, and more wind to build the same sea in summer. This is partly because the air is more dense, or heavier, when it is cold and can give more momentum or energy to the water as it blows over the surface. Sea states that grow quickly, reaching up to 10 m, are not uncommon in the region in cold-outbreak conditions.

MARINE METEOROLOGY *Storms*

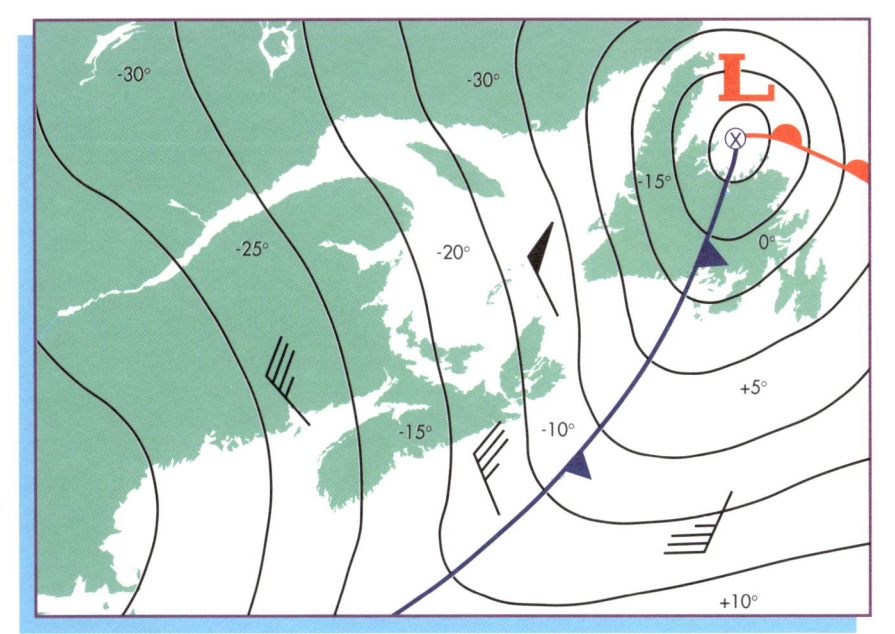

COLD OUTBREAK OVER ATLANTIC CANADA
This map shows a fresh outbreak of very cold arctic air. Temperatures change quickly, from +10°C in the warm sector, east of the cold front, to -20°C in the area a few hundred miles behind the cold front. The accompanying storm-force northwesterlies bring bitterly cold conditions with heavy seas and freezing spray.

Polar Lows
Polar lows or *arctic-instability lows* are examples of small-scale storms that can pack a wallop. They are low-pressure areas that form when cold arctic air spills out over relatively warm water. A favoured location for these storms is just off the ice edge along the coast of Labrador in late fall and winter. They have also been observed off the east and south coasts of Newfoundland.

Although they are small in diameter, usually less than 60 miles across, polar lows can bear winds of hurricane force. It is nearly impossible to predict their formation; however, once they are visible on satellite pictures, they can be forecast to some extent. Forecasters have discovered, through satellite photography, that these lows form more frequently than was previously thought. They can easily go undetected unless they come into contact with a reporting station or vessel, or show up clearly on a satellite picture.

Hurricane —
the evil wind

—From the Carib Indian word *huracan*

HURRICANES AND TROPICAL STORMS
Hurricanes are atmospheric heat-engines. These storms, arguably the most powerful in the world, transform the quiet stored energy of warm, moist tropical oceans into vicious winds, raging seas, torrential rains, and widespread flooding. Hurricanes can pack winds well above 100 knots and are accompanied by confused and mountainous seas of 8 m or more. If a hurricane nears a shoreline, the combination of storm surge and high seas can cause coastal flooding. As well, hurricanes are usually accompanied by rainfalls of 100–200 mm in a matter of hours.

Did you know that the energy released by the condensation process (when invisible water vapour condenses into water droplets) of a hurricane in one day can equal the energy released by fusion of 400, 20-megaton hydrogen bombs? More simply put, if the released heat energy of one day were converted to electricity, Atlantic Canada's electrical needs would be met for decades.

49

MARINE METEOROLOGY *Storms*

Stages Of Development
Before a hurricane is born, it first goes through a process of growth and development that can take days or weeks.

Tropical Disturbances
When a moving area of thunderstorms in the tropics maintains its identity for 24 hours or more, the U.S. National Hurricane Centre (NHC) in Florida classifies the weather system as a **tropical disturbance.** Meteorologists watch for further development.

Tropical Depressions
If the area of thunderstorm activity organizes so that a definite rotation develops and winds become strong (20 knots or greater), the system is upgraded to a **tropical depression.** At this point, a surface low pressure can be analyzed, and it is given a number. A serious vigil is maintained by meteorologists, and air reconnaissance flights may be dispatched by the NHC to get a closer look if the system is close to land.

Tropical Storms
If the winds continue to increase, reaching a sustained gale force (34 knots or greater), the system is upgraded to a **tropical storm.** The numbering system is dispensed with and the storm is given a name (see **APPENDICES**). This stage is often misleading to mariners, who understand the normal terminology of "storm" to mean winds in excess of 47 knots. Detailed routine bulletins are issued regarding the track and development of the storm, as it is now a threat to life and property. Tropical storms have winds that are tame in comparison to a hurricane; however, rainfalls of 100–200 mm are quite common—and flooding very possible.

Hurricanes
Should the winds reach a strength of 64 knots or more, it becomes a *hurricane.* At any stage, these systems are characterized by gusty winds, with the gusts up to 50 percent stronger than the steady winds. In the case of a hurricane, the sustained winds are very dangerous, while the gusts are often devastating. Hurricanes are ranked by strength into five categories:

Category 1. Wind strength 64 to 82 knots; storm surge over 1.2 m; damage ***minimal.***
Category 2. Wind strength 83 to 95 knots; surge over 1.8 m; damage ***moderate.***
Category 3. Wind strength 96 to 113 knots; surge over 2.7 m; damage ***extensive.***
Category 4. Wind strength 114 to 135 knots; surge over 4 m; damage ***extreme.***
Category 5. Wind strength more than 135 knots; surge over 5.5 m; damage ***catastrophic .***

How Hurricanes Develop
A hurricane will survive as long as it remains over warm water; however, its movement is controlled by the forces that drive the storm either ashore or over colder water beyond the tropics, where it will die. This thrust away from the tropics is the clockwise curve that takes a hurricane into the eastern United States and Canada.

On average, only two or three tropical storms affect Atlantic Canada each year. At middle latitudes, such as Atlantic Canada, the end usually comes swiftly. Colder air penetrates the swirling vortex; the warm core of the storm cools and acts as a "thermal brake" on further intensification. Decades of observations have shown that it takes water temperatures above 26°C to create a hurricane. Even though some large hurricanes may travel for days over cold North Atlantic water, all storms are doomed once they leave the warm tropical waters that sustain them. The farther they venture into higher latitudes, the less fuel they receive from the sea, unless they receive a new source of energy such as a merging frontal system. The lack of fuel finally kills the storms.

Over land, hurricanes break up rapidly. Cut off from their oceanic source of energy, and with the added effect of frictional drag, their circulation rapidly weakens and becomes more disorganized. Torrential rains, however, may continue well after the winds are diminished.

Hurricanes are often resurrected into **extratropical cyclones** at higher latitudes by combining with existing frontal systems. Many storms moving up the east coast are in the throes of this transformation when they reach Atlantic Canada. In such cases, large continental lows are often invigorated by the remnants of storms born over the tropical sea. During this shift from tropical to extratropical, the inner region of hurricane-force winds will diminish to storm force or lower, while the extent of gale force winds expands considerably. In some instances, this transformation can be rapid and dangerous; the resulting extratropical storm can develop into a powerful storm with winds and seas similar to those experienced in winter. In 1954, for example, Hurricane Hazel transformed from a tropical storm to an extratropical storm as it moved over land. Although no longer a hurricane, the storm remained destructive, and dozens of lives were lost because of intense flooding.

MARINE METEOROLOGY *Storms*

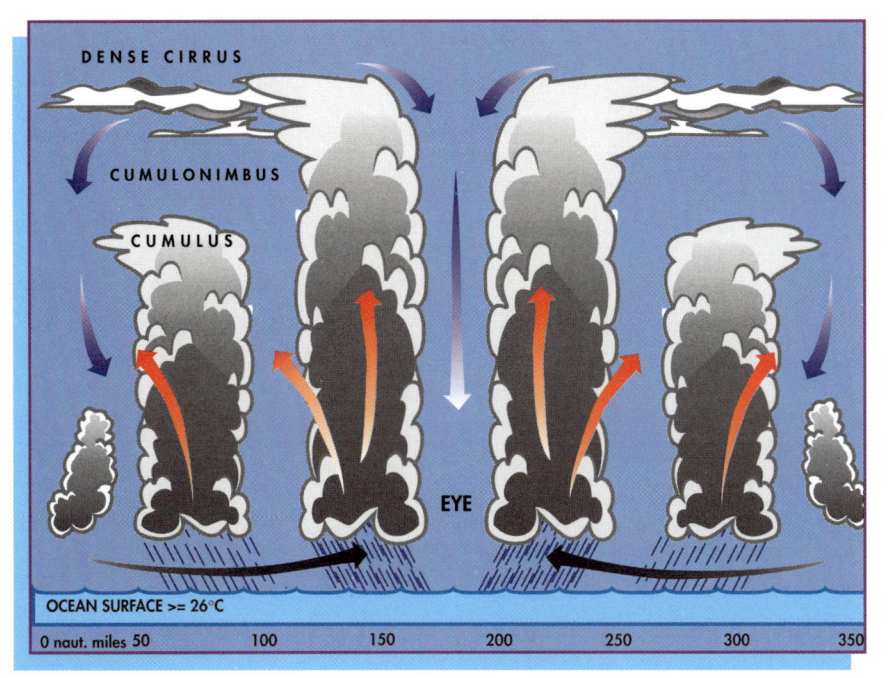

HURRICANE CROSS-SECTION

The thunderstorms that were involved in the initial stages of development are still present, but in greater number and intensity. At the centre of the storm is the famous "eye," in which winds go calm.

Winds at the surface feed into the interior of the hurricane and are sent rocketing skyward through the thunderstorms at the eyewall, the ring of clouds around the eye. At high altitudes, the winds reverse direction and flow away from the centre. In the centre itself, a downward airflow produces clear skies. As well, the pressure gradient becomes very flat in the eye, resulting in calm winds. On average, the eye is 30–60 miles in diameter. However, things change dramatically in the eyewall; here, the greatest threat of wind damage exists, with winds of 100 knots or more, rotating violently counterclockwise around the calm eye.

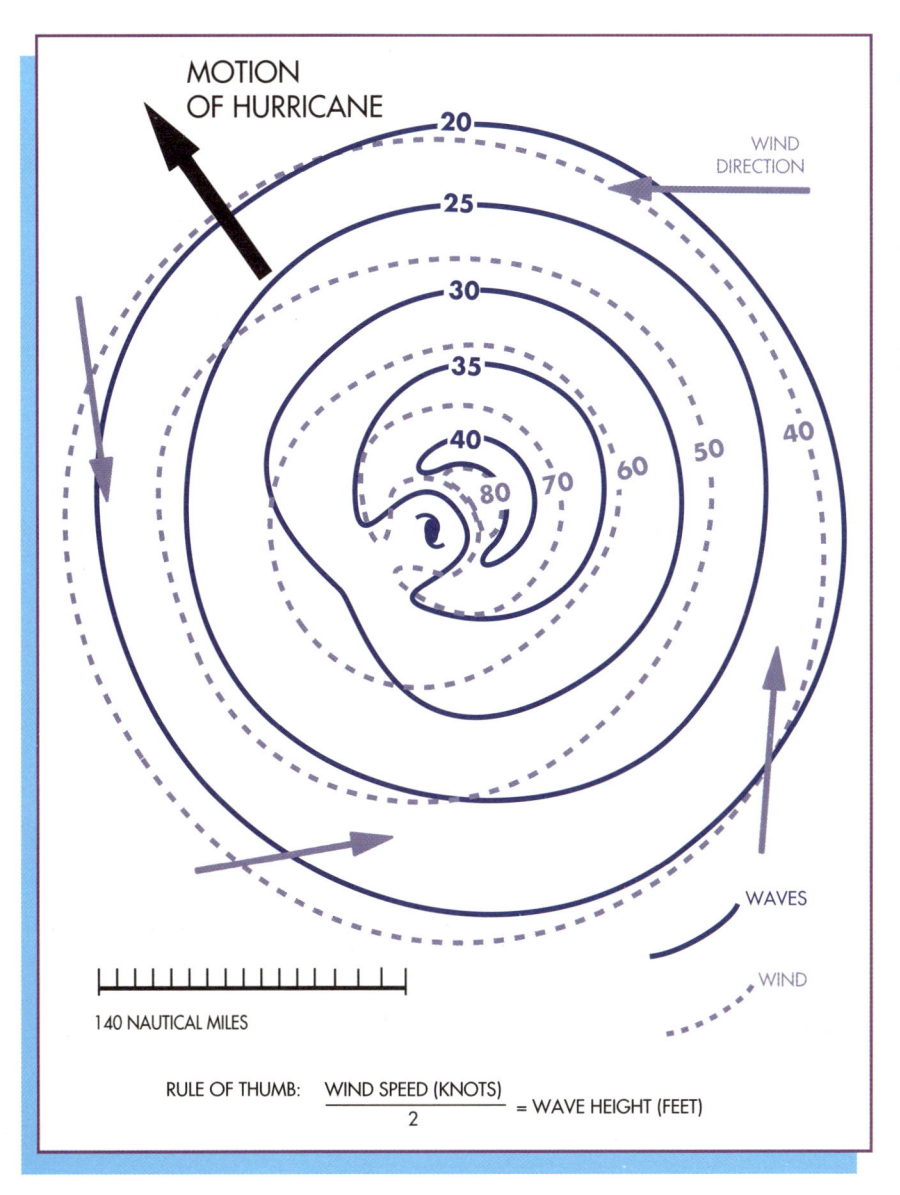

TYPICAL WINDS AND WAVES WITH A SLOW-MOVING HURRICANE

A reliable rule of thumb for estimating the wave heights with a slow-moving hurricane is derived by a simple formula: wind speed (in knots), divided by 2, equals wave height (in ft.). This relationship, while an empirical one, accounts for the increasing wave heights with wind speed. For example, a wind speed of 80 knots would result in seas of 13 m (40 ft.).

The diagram also shows how both winds and waves are higher to the right of the hurricane's track. Many books on basic seamanship teach that the right semicircle (to the right of track) is unnavigable, to be avoided at all costs. However, since hurricanes seldom sneak up on us any more, weather forecasting and warning systems in Atlantic Canada should make any encounter with a hurricane an avoidable experience.

RULE OF THUMB: $\dfrac{\text{WIND SPEED (KNOTS)}}{2}$ = WAVE HEIGHT (FEET)

BE PREPARED—CHECKLIST

In case you missed it earlier, here is a valuable checklist that can help make forecasts more useful, anywhere marine forecasts are available:

What is the present weather?
Listen to reports from along the route you are planning. Keep a "weather eye" open.

What is the forecast trend—worse, the same, or better?
Consider how long you will be at sea.

What marine warnings are in effect or forecast?
Interpret the warnings as they apply to you:
- Are forecast conditions beyond my limits?
- Will local effects create conditions beyond my limits, even if no warning is in effect?

What is the weather summary?
Consider the location and forecast movement of fronts and pressure systems described in the synopsis.

What forecast areas are important to you?
Where are you?
- Make sure you listen to the right forecast.
- Also listen to the forecast for adjacent areas.
- If you are near one end of the area, you may need to adjust the time when the weather is going to affect you, depending on where it's coming from.

Where are you going?
The reports and forecasts for all areas through which you are going to travel should be monitored.

Where is the weather coming from?
Listen to reports from areas where the significant weather is now.

Are you offshore or near shore?
- If offshore, you can probably use the forecast with only a few minor adjustments.
- If near shore, you may need to make your own adjustments to the forecast.

Marine Weather Tip: What Do the Warnings Mean?

Each warning has the following basic interpretation:

Small Craft Warning — *Be cautious.*

Gale Warning — *Expect rough weather. Don't get caught in open water unless your boat can handle rough weather.*

Storm Warning / Hurricane Force Wind Warning — *Stay ashore or try to avoid the heavy weather.*

MARINE WEATHER CLIMATOLOGY

Climate is a description of the average weather conditions in a region over many years. The "averages," "frequencies," and "extremes" referred to in this section, are determined by studying and recording day-to-day weather systems for long periods. The average conditions vary considerably from month to month and even from year to year.

The following profile illustrates the diversity—and potential hostility—of our marine environment, even before local weather effects are taken into consideration.

WIND

The prevailing winds over the region are westerly to northwesterly in winter and southwesterly in summer. In winter, wind speeds average around 20 knots, with gales occurring 10–20 percent of the time and storm force winds 1–2 percent of the time. In summer, wind speeds are much lower averaging 10–15 knots; storms are rare, and gales occur less than 2 percent of the time. Extreme wind gusts of over 100 knots have been recorded both in winter and in association with tropical systems.

Many gale and storm systems are still intensifying as they pass through the region or develop over the western Atlantic. Consequently, winds over northeastern regions are, on average, stronger than those over the southwest.

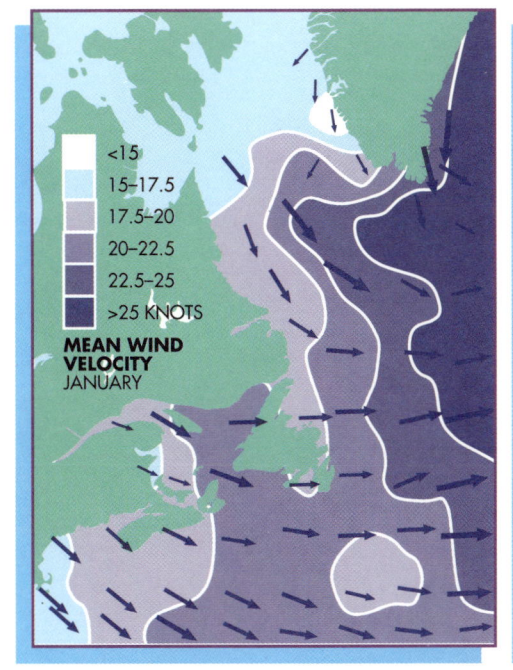

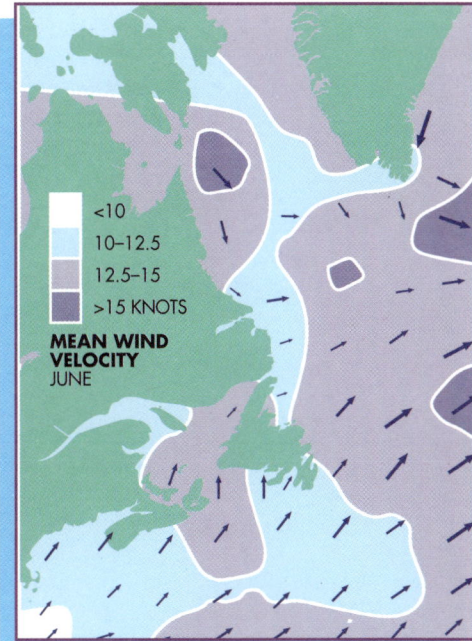

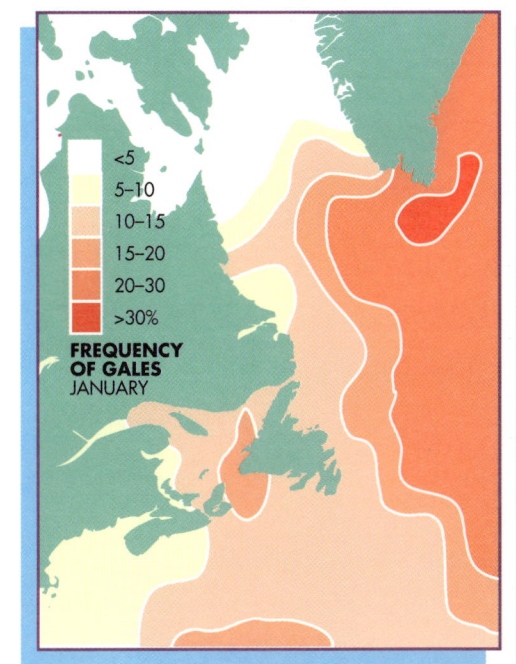

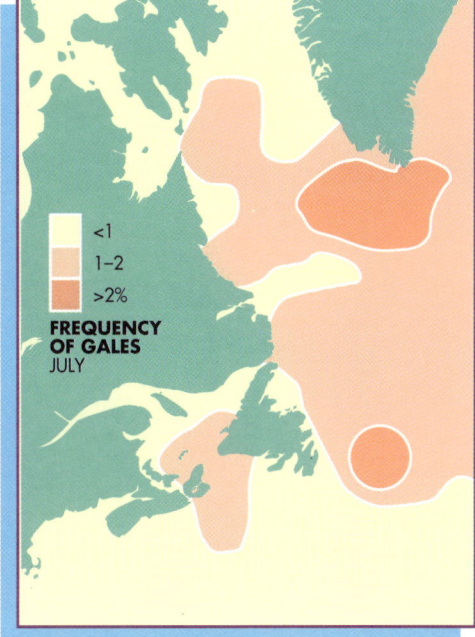

MEAN WIND VELOCITY JANUARY
<15
15–17.5
17.5–20
20–22.5
22.5–25
>25 KNOTS

MEAN WIND VELOCITY JUNE
<10
10–12.5
12.5–15
>15 KNOTS

FREQUENCY OF GALES JANUARY
<5
5–10
10–15
15–20
20–30
>30%

FREQUENCY OF GALES JULY
<1
1–2
>2%

53

MARINE WEATHER CLIMATOLOGY

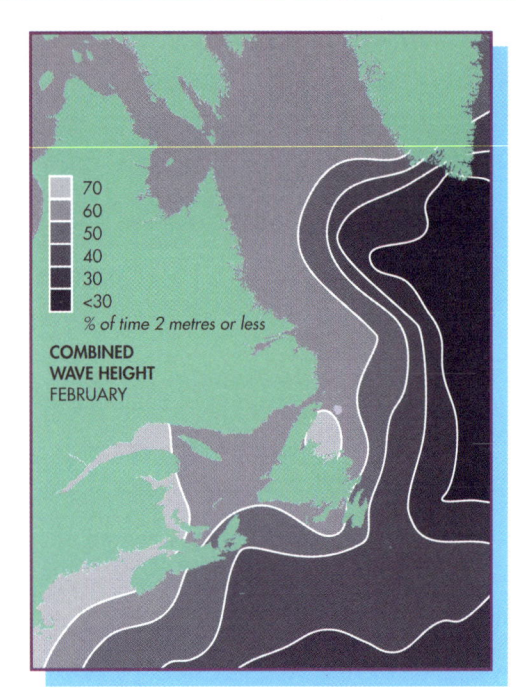

WAVE HEIGHTS

Wave heights are determined by the wind. Consequently, the highest waves usually occur in the coldest months, when storms are strongest. As well, mariners observe that winter winds pack a greater "punch" than summer winds, likely due to the greater momentum of cold air.

In winter, wave heights on offshore waters are greater than 2 m more than half the time; in summer, wave heights exceed 2 m only 10–20 percent of the time. Wave heights over 6 m, while rarely observed in summer, are recorded 5–10 percent of the time in offshore waters in winter. Because wind strength is greater in the northeast, wave heights are generally higher as well in those areas.

VESSEL ICING

The main cause of icing on a ship's superstructure is freezing sea spray; it can be a hazard during winter months—especially to the operation of smaller vessels.

Freezing spray accompanies strong winds, low temperatures, and high waves. The potential for hazardous ice accretion on a vessel is quite low in warm Scotian Slope waters, but in the colder waters of the Labrador Sea and the Gulf of St. Lawrence, the possibility of icing is 30–50 percent during January. Freezing spray generally occurs between November and April and most commonly in February—the coldest month. An exception is the Labrador coast and the Gulf of St. Lawrence, where sea-ice formation inhibits wave development—and decreases freezing spray potential. In these areas, December is normally the worst period. By contrast, the cold, ice-free waters south of Newfoundland are subject to freezing spray throughout the whole risk period.

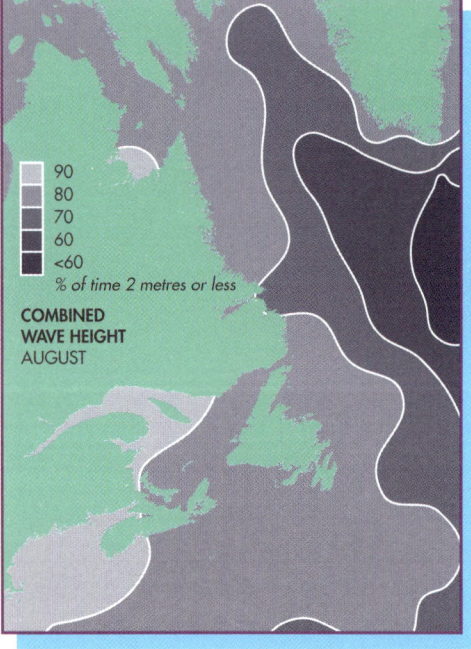

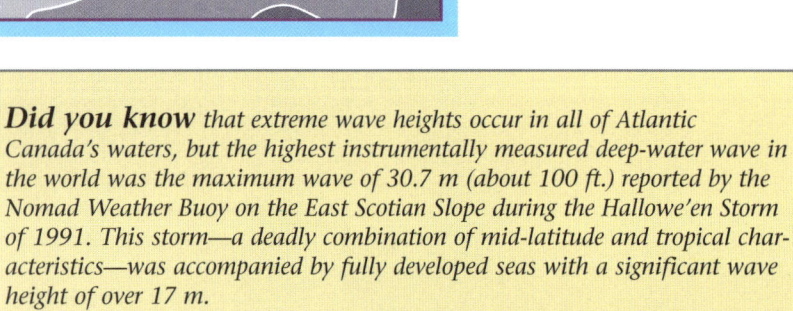

Did you know that extreme wave heights occur in all of Atlantic Canada's waters, but the highest instrumentally measured deep-water wave in the world was the maximum wave of 30.7 m (about 100 ft.) reported by the Nomad Weather Buoy on the East Scotian Slope during the Hallowe'en Storm of 1991. This storm—a deadly combination of mid-latitude and tropical characteristics—was accompanied by fully developed seas with a significant wave height of over 17 m.

Less than a year and a half later, in March 1993, a monstrous frontal storm moved through the Gulf of Mexico, up the American coast, and through Atlantic Canada. Wave heights near those of the Hallowe'en Storm were reported once again from the slope waters south of Nova Scotia. At least eight vessels sank in the storm—from the Gulf of Mexico to Atlantic Canada. This storm was appropriately dubbed "the storm of the century."

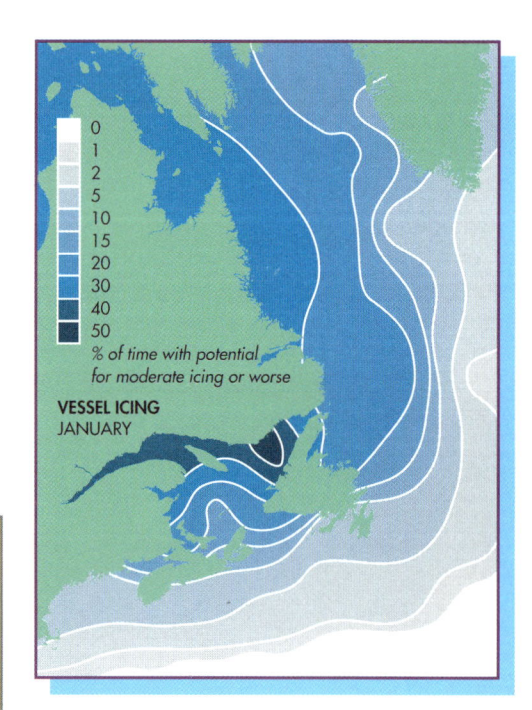

MARINE WEATHER CLIMATOLOGY

FOG

Water droplets in the air reduce visibility. When visibility is reduced to 6 miles or less, it is called mist. Visibility of 1/2 mile or less is called fog.

Atlantic Canada experiences some of the thickest and longest-lasting fogs in the world. Fog is most prevalent in late spring or early summer, when warm, moist air from the south flows over the relatively cold waters. The highest frequency occurs over the Grand Banks, in July, with visibility below 1/2 mile more than 40 percent of the time. The pool of cold water that lingers around southwestern Nova Scotia causes frequent and persistent fogs in that area. The southwestern Gulf of St. Lawrence, by contrast, remains relatively fog-free because of milder water temperatures and dry air coming off the land.

In early fall, fog decreases markedly as cooler, drier air moves into the region, while sea-surface temperatures are at their warmest.

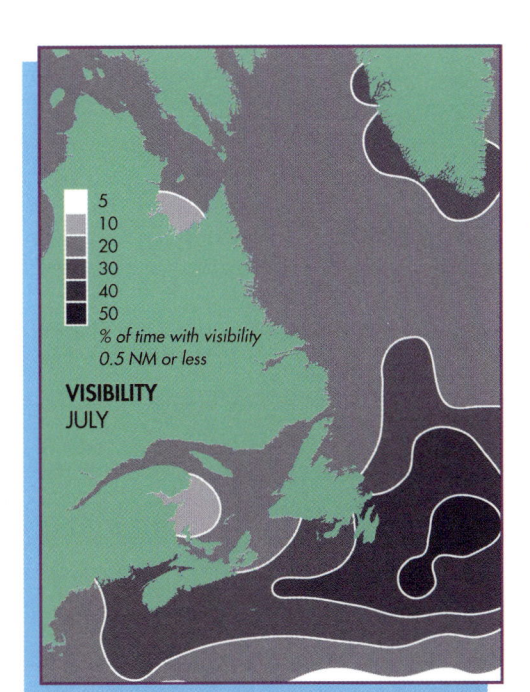

PRECIPITATION

Precipitation is 3–4 times more frequent in winter than in summer, because intense cyclonic systems are more numerous. Storm systems close to Greenland often stall over the Labrador Sea and dissipate slowly—causing precipitation that lasts for days.

Many mariners rely on the old adage, "if you know the wind, you know the weather," when speculating about precipitation. And they're right. While rain can occur any time of the year throughout the region, this rule of thumb is most useful from October to May, when any type of precipitation is possible. Snow can accompany winds of almost any direction; rain usually occurs with a south or southwest wind; and freezing rain is typically observed with east or northeast winds. In spring, freezing drizzle and northeasterly winds can persist along the coastlines of Labrador and eastern Newfoundland for days on end. West-to-northwest winds are notorious for bringing snow streamers and very poor visibility to their facing coastlines. Such areas may experience twice as many "snow days" as other localities. Along the western coast of Newfoundland, for example, there are roughly 25 days of snow in January—dumped by cold northwesterly winds that pick up moisture from the warm waters of the Gulf of St. Lawrence.

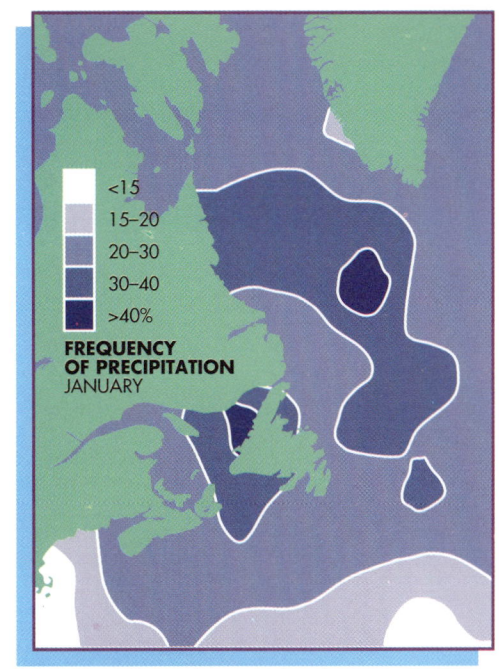

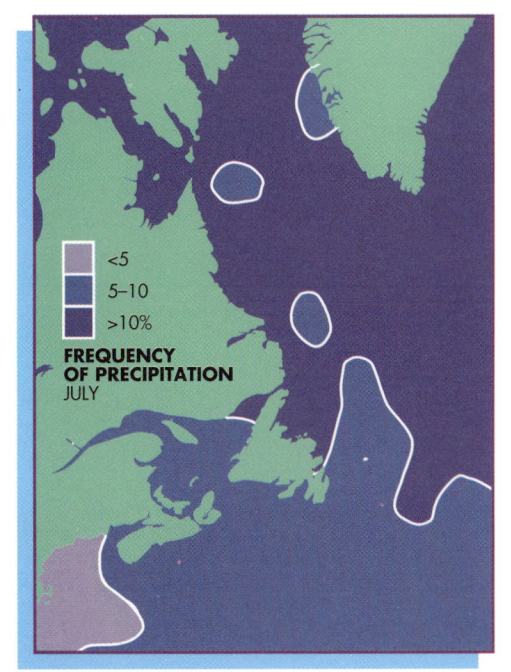

MARINE WEATHER CLIMATOLOGY

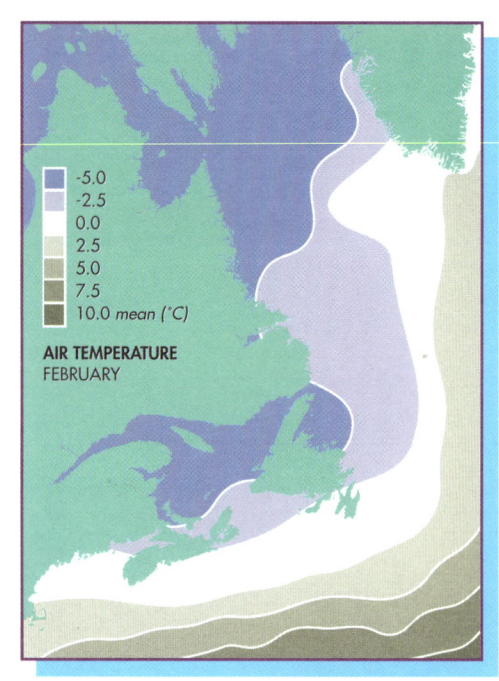

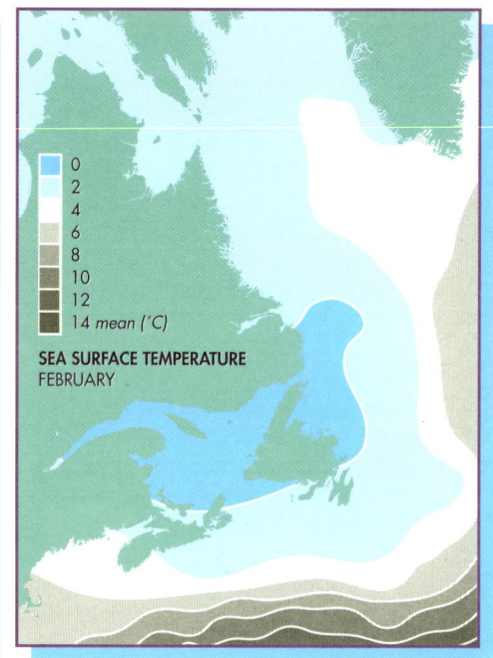

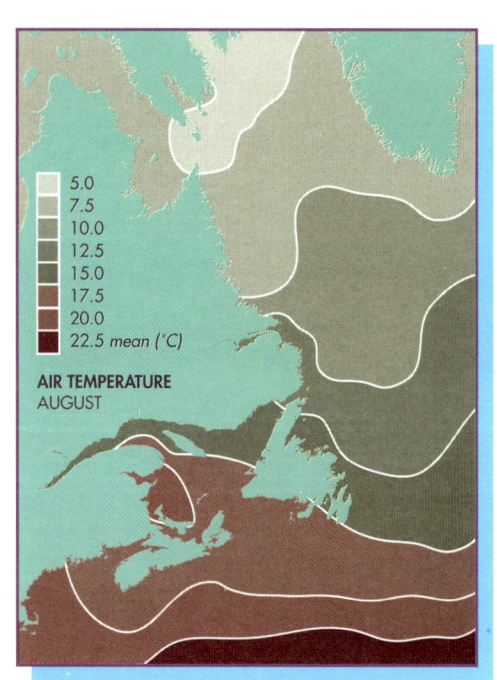

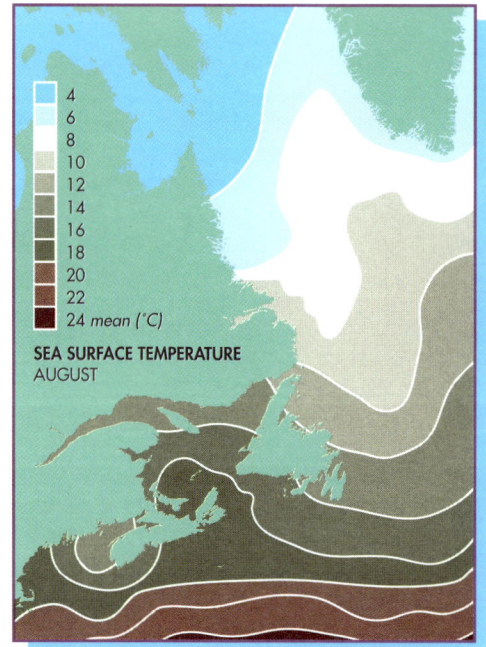

AIR TEMPERATURES

Air temperatures at sea are strongly influenced by the moderating effects of the water temperature. Away from the coast, the daily and seasonal variations are much smaller than on land. Average air temperatures range from -8°C in the north in winter, to 20°C offshore in summer.

SEA SURFACE TEMPERATURES

Sea surface temperatures greatly influence the climate of Atlantic Canada. Along the Labrador coast and the east coast of Newfoundland sea surface temperatures average 0°C in winter and rise slightly in summer to a range of 3°C to 7°C. These temperatures can also drop to -2°C—the freezing point of salt water. Greater seasonal change occurs in the Scotian Slope waters, where average winter temperatures hover near 8°C, rising to 20°C in summer.

MARINE WEATHER CLIMATOLOGY

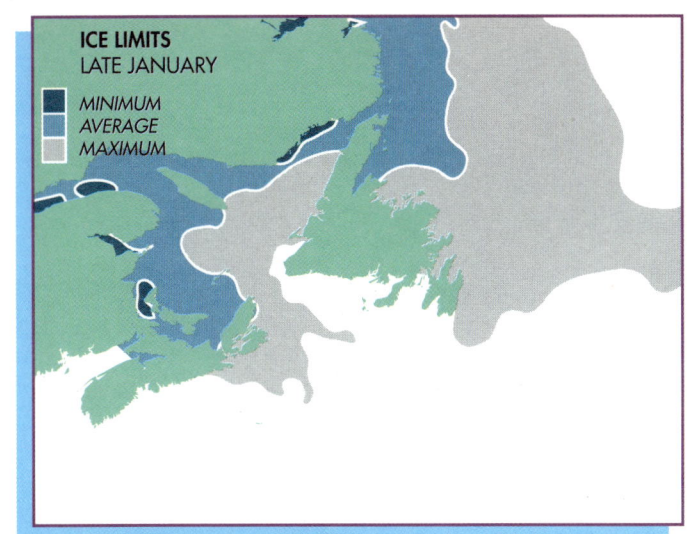

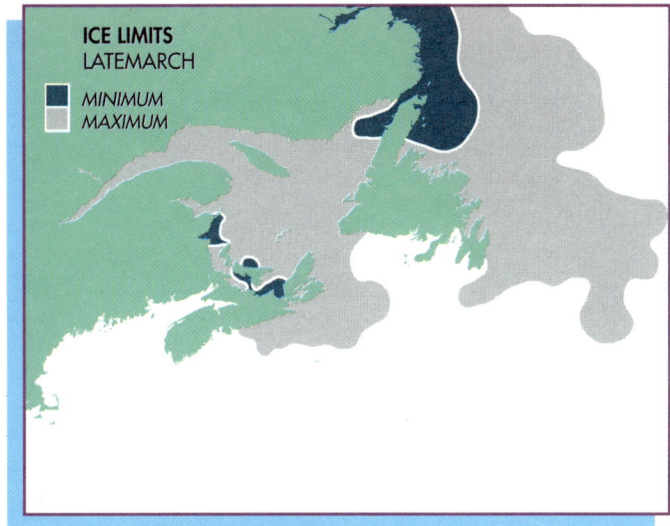

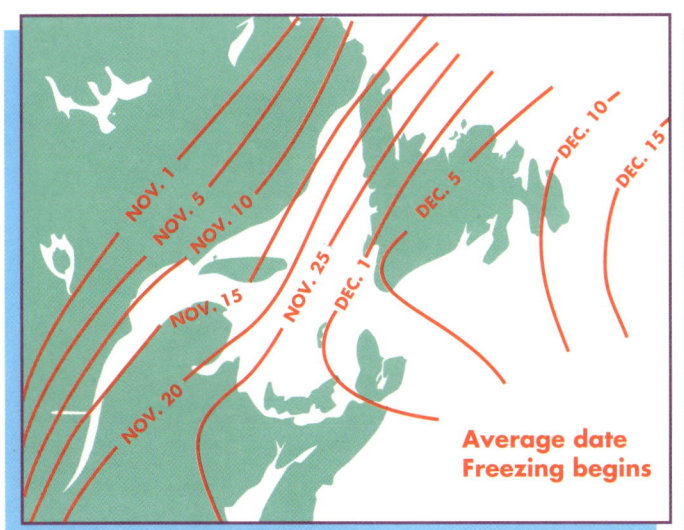

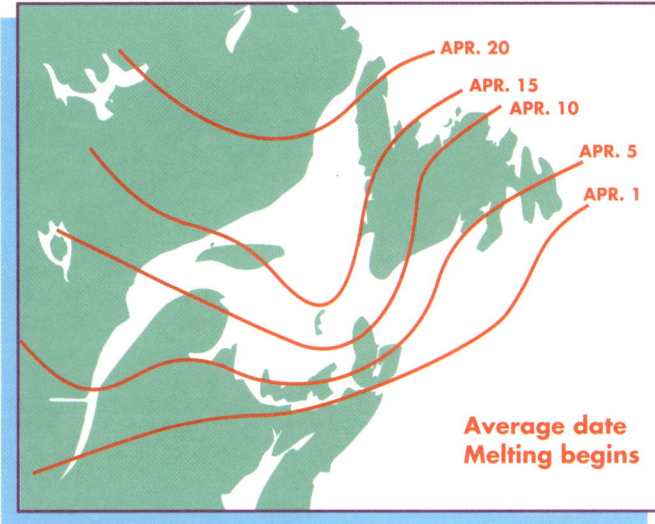

ICE LIMITS — LATE JANUARY
- MINIMUM
- AVERAGE
- MAXIMUM

ICE LIMITS — LATE MARCH
- MINIMUM
- MAXIMUM

Average date Freezing begins (NOV. 1, NOV. 5, NOV. 10, NOV. 15, NOV. 20, NOV. 25, DEC. 1, DEC. 5, DEC. 10, DEC. 15)

Average date Melting begins (APR. 1, APR. 5, APR. 10, APR. 15, APR. 20)

SEA ICE

Sea ice is a fact of winter in most waters off Labrador and Newfoundland, and in the Gulf of St. Lawrence. Ice inhibits the fishing industry and is therefore of great concern to mariners and forecasters. Its extent varies greatly from year to year, typically peaking at the end of March, then retreating northward. In the Gulf of St. Lawrence, however, where the ice break-up begins in the northwestern gulf, remnant ice is still pushing out through the Cabot Strait in late spring. By September, sea ice generally exists only in the far north; by November it begins to drift down the coast of Labrador, and the ice season resumes.

The shorter days of autumn bring cold air temperatures to Atlantic Canada. Freezing conditions develop first along the northern Labrador coast and the north shore of the Gulf of St. Lawrence—usually by early November. A large heat reserve in the sea slows the southward spread of colder conditions, so average daily temperatures don't fall below 0°C in Prince Edward Island and the Magdalen Islands until the end of November. Average sub-zero temperatures do not begin until the second week of December on Cape Breton Island and Newfoundland's Avalon Peninsula.

MARINE WEATHER CLIMATOLOGY

ICEBERGS

Icebergs are by far the most dangerous form of ice. These blocks of frozen fresh water slowly make their way south each year after being calved from the glaciers of Greenland or Baffin Island. They may take from one to three years to reach the Grand Banks; an average of 400 arrive each year. Icebergs are much harder than saltwater ice and come in a vast array of shapes and sizes—each one a hazard to navigation.

Glaciers fracture and produce icebergs more frequently when temperatures are mild. Mild temperatures also reduce sea ice that can dock icebergs—especially south of 45°N. In colder years, fewer icebergs are formed, and many become trapped in sea ice. A small iceberg embedded in floes of sea ice may be hazardous because it's hard to detect. When the sea ice begins to melt, or retreat, the icebergs resume drifting into southern waters.

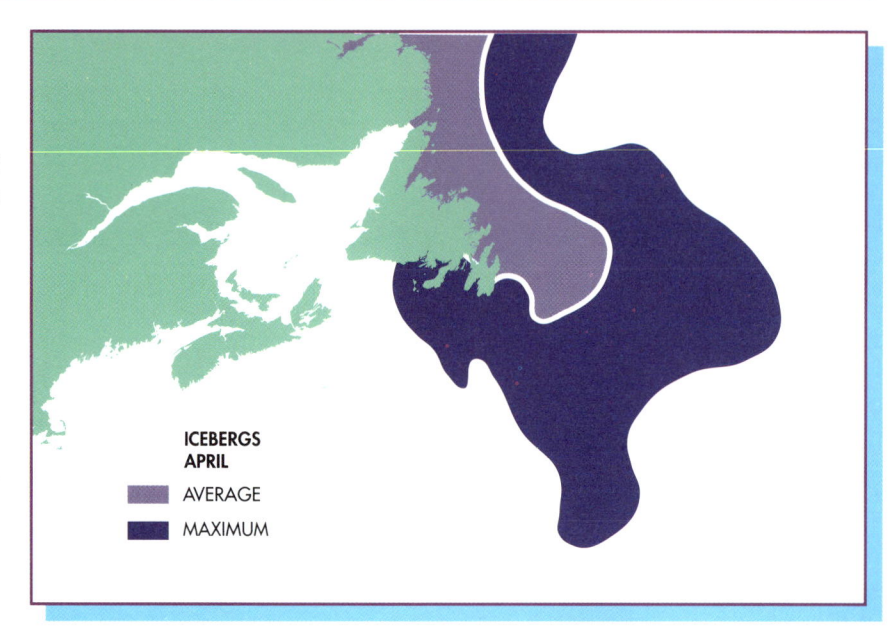

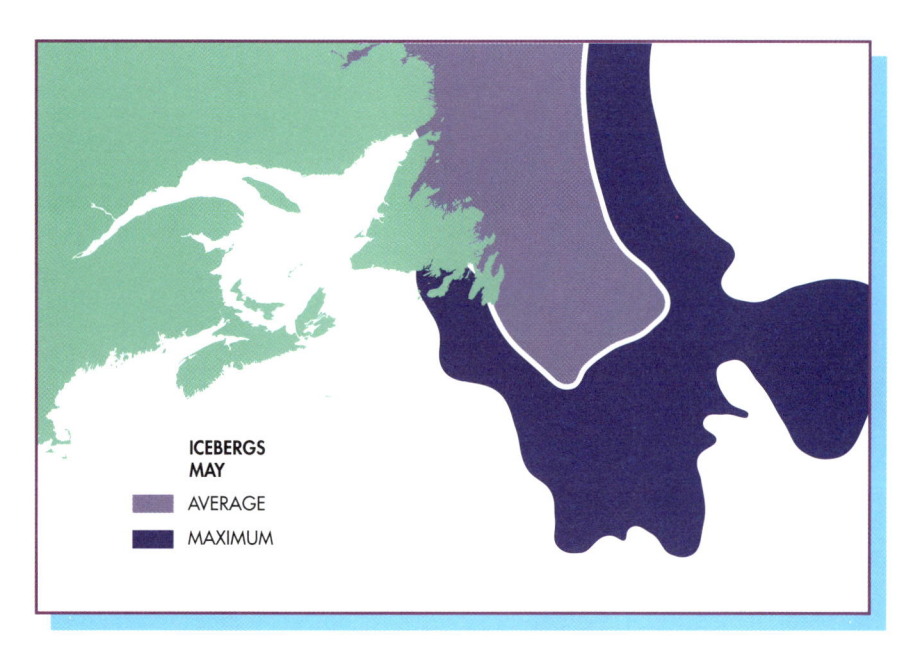

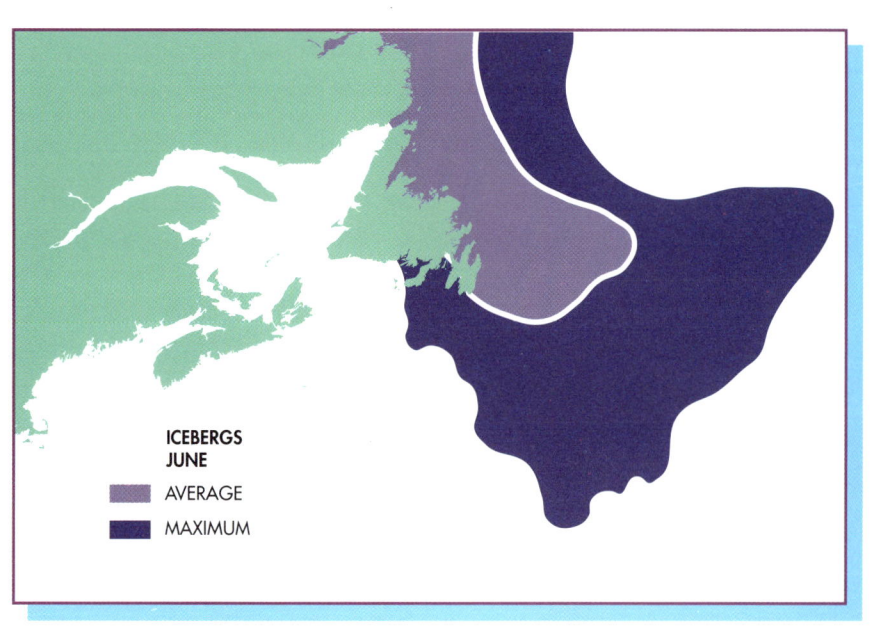

ICEBERGS
APRIL
AVERAGE
MAXIMUM

ICEBERGS
MAY
AVERAGE
MAXIMUM

ICEBERGS
JUNE
AVERAGE
MAXIMUM

MARINE WEATHER CLIMATOLOGY

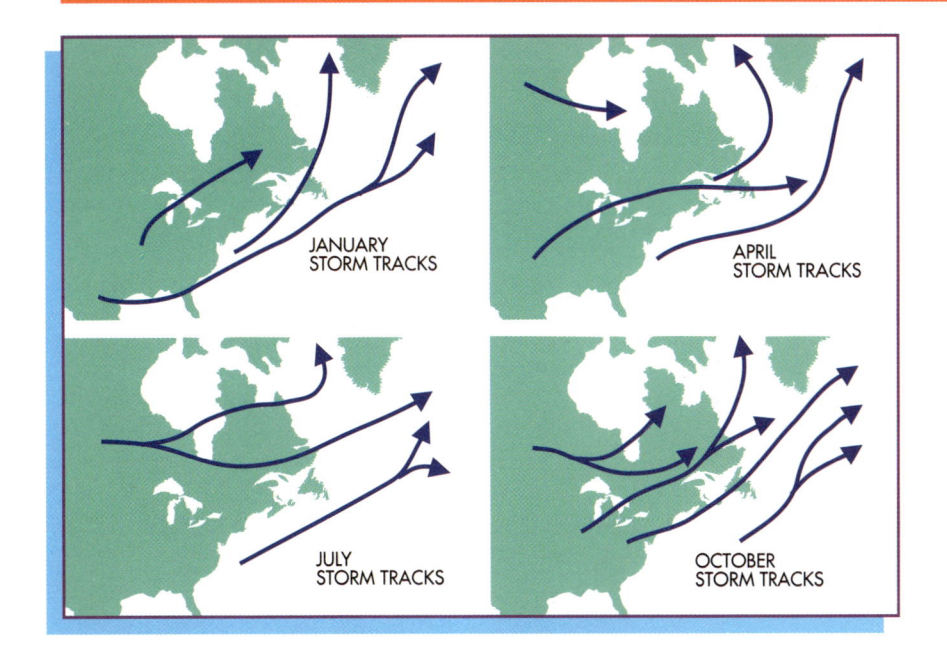

JANUARY STORM TRACKS

APRIL STORM TRACKS

JULY STORM TRACKS

OCTOBER STORM TRACKS

FRONTAL LOWS

The strength of a frontal low depends in part on the time of year; winter lows are more severe than those in summer. Yet they develop similarly, drawing strength from the contrast between cold and warm air (with this difference being greatest in winter. See **THE BASICS**) For example, gale-force winds are 10 times more likely to accompany these systems in the winter than in the summer. Storm-force winds with frontal lows, while rare in summer, are not uncommon in winter and occur from 1–4 percent of the time.

The North Atlantic is well known for the sudden development of frontal lows. In the waters of Atlantic Canada, a low-pressure centre can intensify with little notice. Meteorologists have studied this phenomenon for a long time; intense lows that develop explosively are, appropriately, called "bombs." Most bombs occur in winter, but some years they're rare, while other years experience storm after storm.

The track of frontal lows depends on the season. In winter, cold arctic air pushes south of Atlantic Canada, so frontal lows track farther south than during the summer, when the cold air has retreated to the north. It should be noted that these seasonal variations only provide a general pattern; each low tracks according to the daily location of air masses.

MARINE WEATHER CLIMATOLOGY

TROPICAL CYCLONES

Hurricanes and tropical storms—known generically as *tropical cyclones*—are among the most dangerous of all storms faced by the mariner. Vastly different from the frontal lows typically experienced in eastern Canada, they are also relatively rare in northern waters. Tropical cyclones only develop over very warm tropical waters; consequently, Atlantic Canada's hurricane season is from June through November. But there can be exceptions. Most tropical cyclones experienced in Atlantic Canada are spawned off the west African coast, making their way across the Atlantic, where they usually turn northward and weaken.

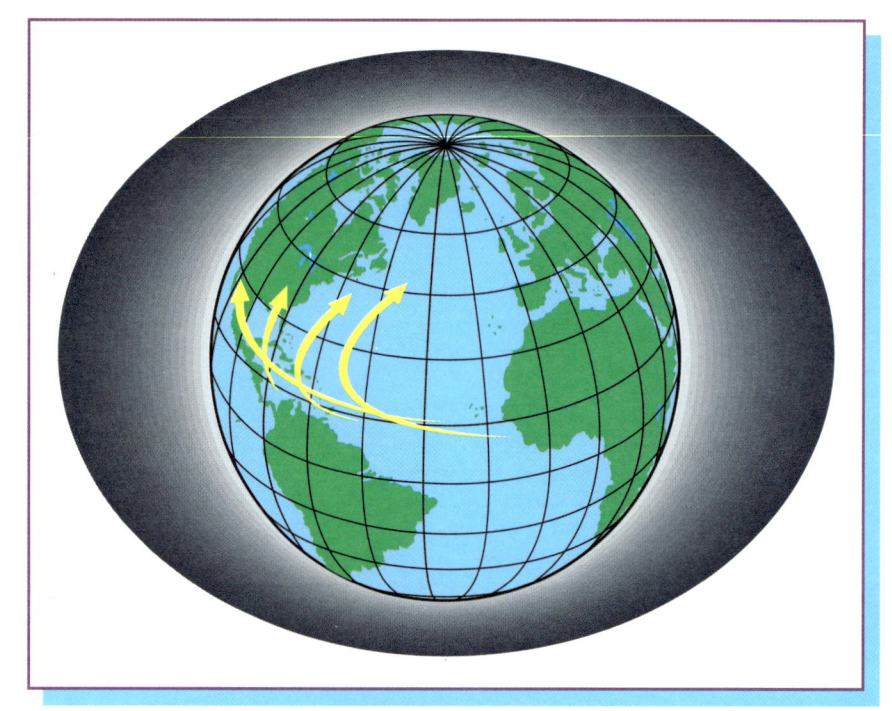

This diagram shows the primary and secondary tracks of tropical cyclones through Atlantic Canada's waters. Also shown is the average number of tropical cyclones per year (from 1949 to 1983) that brought gale-force winds to some part of the region. While these storms are rare, their frequency is unpredictable. In 1969, five hurricanes and three tropical depressions hit our area. "Major" hurricanes (sustained winds over 100 knots) are extremely rare, with only one even approaching the region in the last three decades.

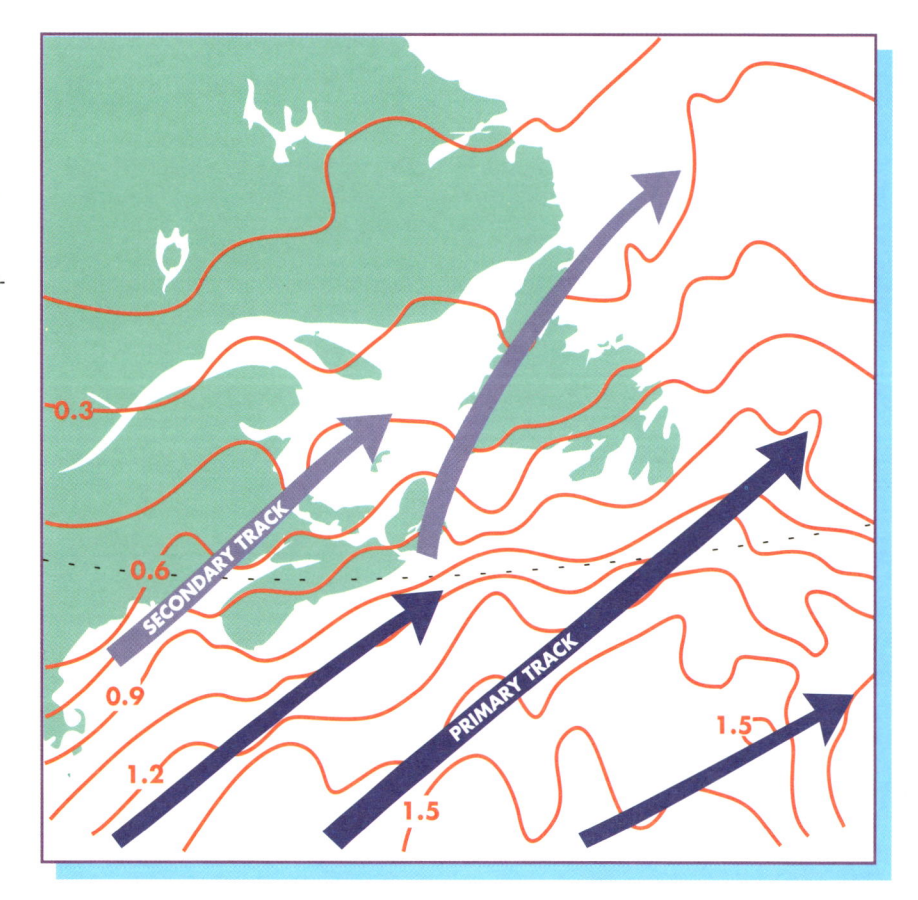

MARINE WEATHER CLIMATOLOGY

OCEAN CURRENTS

Ocean currents are like rivers of water flowing through the ocean. Atlantic Canada is influenced by many of these currents—most significantly the Gulf Stream and the Labrador Current. The Gulf Stream is a very warm current that originates in the Sargasso Sea and passes south of the slope waters. The cold Labrador Current begins in the Arctic and moves along the coast of Labrador and the east coast of Newfoundland. It then branches into smaller currents: one passes south of the Avalon Peninsula and moves west along the south coast of Newfoundland; the other flows through the Strait of Belle Isle into the northern Gulf of St. Lawrence.

Ocean currents have a huge impact on Atlantic Canada's weather. The proximity of cold Labrador Current and the Gulf Stream create dynamic weather patterns unique to this region. The weather in turn has an effect on the currents. The predicted currents published in the *Canadian Tide and Current Tables* consist of average ocean currents plus tidal streams, but do not include wind-driven currents that change continuously with the passage of weather systems. This map shows the long-term averages of the region's currents.

TIDES

Although tides are not a weather phenomenon, they affect meteorological and oceanographic conditions. The largest tides in the world occur in the Bay of Fundy, and coastal areas of Atlantic Nova Scotia and the Gulf of St. Lawrence experience significant tidal rips. Although the predominant tides in Atlantic Canada are

MARINE WEATHER CLIMATOLOGY

semi-diurnal, each area experiences unique tidal conditions. For detailed discussion about tides, consult the *Sailing Directions* for your area.

Bay of Fundy

The tides in the Gulf of Maine move into the Bay of Fundy. The narrower width of the bay, towards its head, is one factor that increases the range of both the semi-diurnal and diurnal tides. The most important factors however, are the length and depth of the bay, which give it a natural period of oscillation that closely corresponds to that of the semi-diurnal forces. Consequently, spring tides in the upper parts of Chignecto Bay and Minas Channel have a range of about 11.3 m, as compared to about 3 m in the Gulf of Maine.

The highest tidal range in the Minas Basin is 16.4 m, and in Cobequid Bay 16.8 m—the highest recorded tides in the world.

The top map shows average heights and relative times for spring tides in the Bay of Fundy.

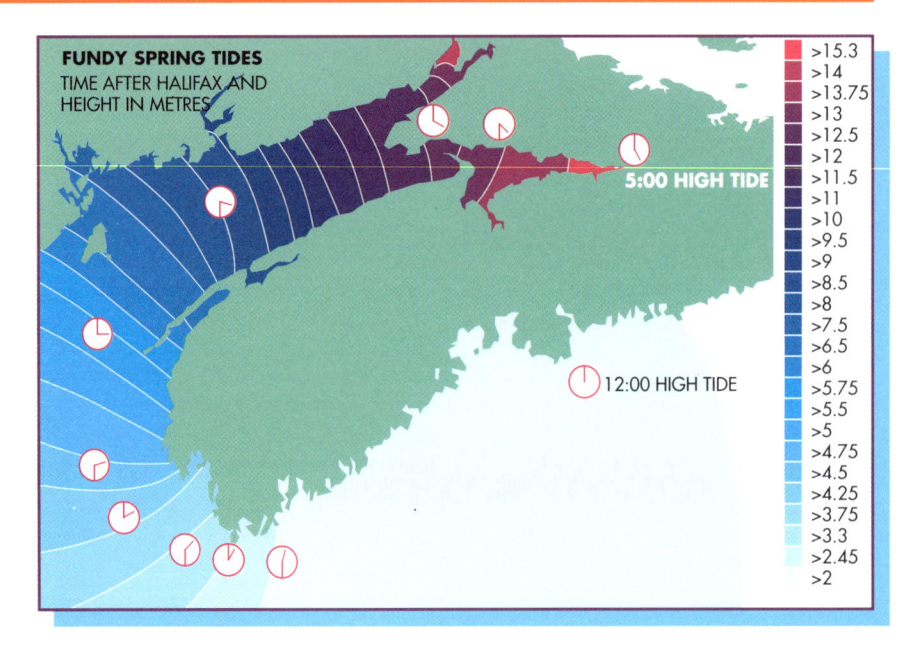

Atlantic Coasts of Nova Scotia and Newfoundland

The tide along the south-facing coastlines are semi-diurnal. High water occurs almost simultaneously along all points from Placentia Bay, Nfld., to Shelburne, N.S. The tidal range is not very great; the difference between high and low water seldom exceeds 1.8 m. Along the east coast of Newfoundland the tide is mixed but mainly semi-diurnal. High water occurs simultaneously along the coast, and the tidal range is about 0.9 m.

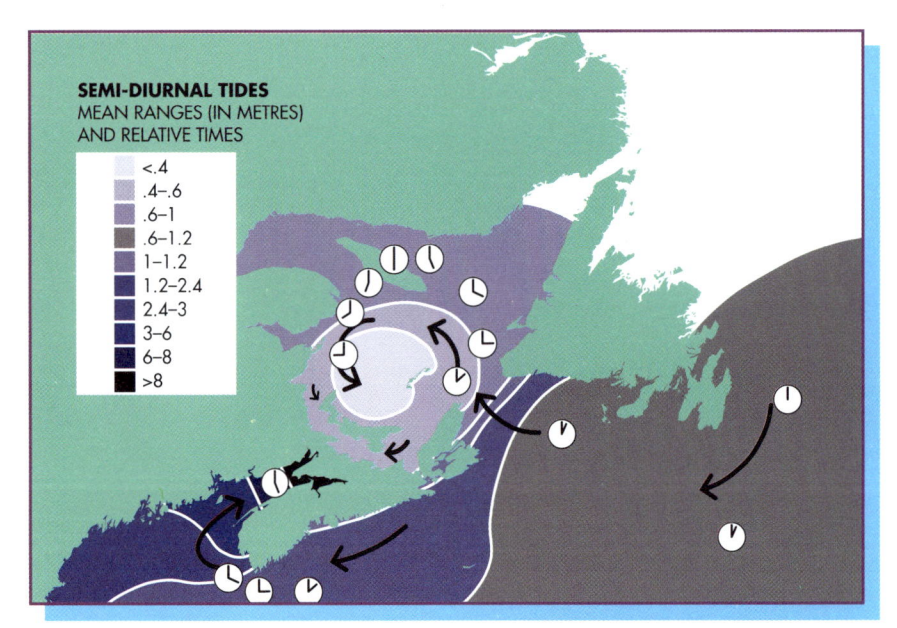

Gulf of St. Lawrence

The tide moving through the Cabot Strait and the Strait of Belle Isle into the gulf is of a mixed type, but mainly semi-diurnal (except along the coast between Cape Tormentine and Richibucto, New Brunswick; and near Savage Harbour, Prince Edward Island, where the diurnal tide dominates). At the southern tip of the Magdalen Islands and near Crossman Point, New Brunswick, the tide is entirely diurnal, with only one high and one low water every day. The range of the tide throughout the gulf is less than 2.7 m.

The semi-diurnal tide moves as a counter-clockwise circulation round the gulf. High water in Cabot Strait coincides with low water in the estuary of the St. Lawrence River. Three hours later, it is high water in the northeast gulf and low water in the southwest gulf. The pivot point of this circulation lies near the southwest coast of the Magdalen Islands. The range of the semi-diurnal tide is zero at this pivot point and increases outwardly towards the perimeter of the gulf.

The bottom map shows mean ranges and relative times of the semi-diurnal tides.

Labrador Coast

The tide along this coast is very uniform, both in the time of high water and in its range; it's only towards the heads of inlets that any great changes occur. Near the coast, the flood tide generally runs northward, while the ebb flows southward, rarely reaching 0.5 knots, except around headlands. Because of the intricacies of the coastline—fringed with innumerable inlets and small islands—currents inshore must remain a matter of local knowledge. Strong, dangerous currents up to 7 knots flow into the fjords and through the tickles in this region.

LOCAL WEATHER

The effect of large-scale weather systems on local weather depends on where you're located. In offshore waters, forecasting wind and sea is challenging, but possible. In nearshore waters, the complexities make detailed forecasts almost impossible. For example, a large frontal low passing south of Nova Scotia may bring hurricane-force southeasterlies to Chéticamp, storm-force easterlies to Burgeo, and moderate northeasterlies to Saint John Harbour. The same storm may cause abnormally low water levels along one stretch of coast, while another coastline is inundated. Each bay, peninsula, inlet, and island can dramatically change the local effect of the large weather systems that come our way.

This section describes some of the better-known local marine weather effects in Atlantic Canada.

LOCAL WEATHER *Fundy*

Fundy Northwest

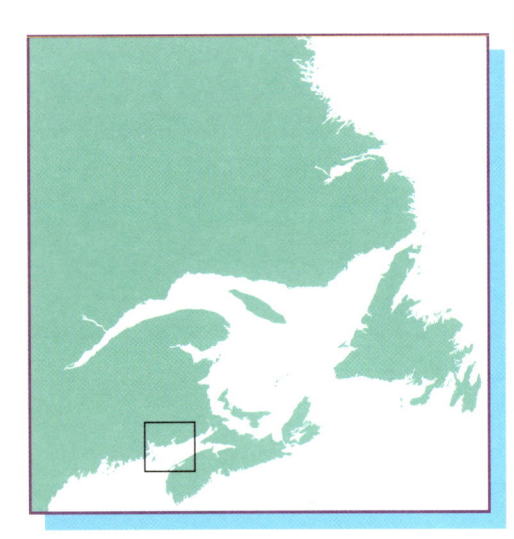

GENERAL CONDITIONS

High tides and strong currents bring cold water and fog to the New Brunswick shore. Currents running with or against the wind greatly affect wave and weather hazards. Passamaquoddy Bay differs from the rest of the coast, due to its sheltered inland position and limited water exchange with the Bay of Fundy. On the other hand, Grand Manan has an exposed location, and the "microclimates" of its shores vary considerably.

For easier reading, this coastline has been divided into five sections.

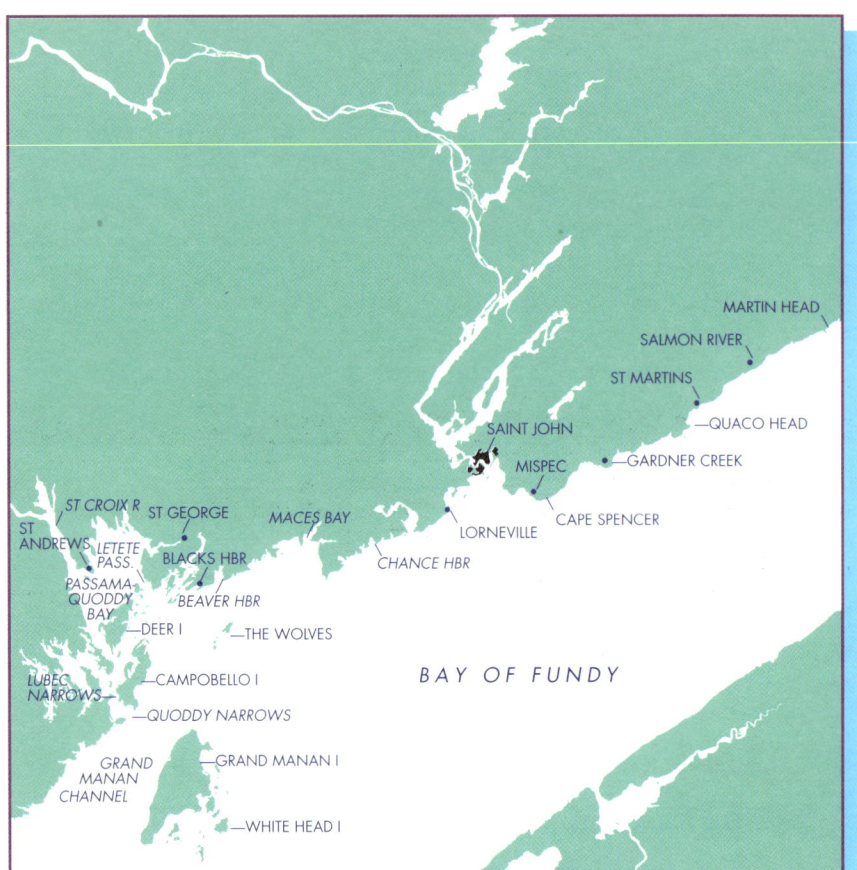

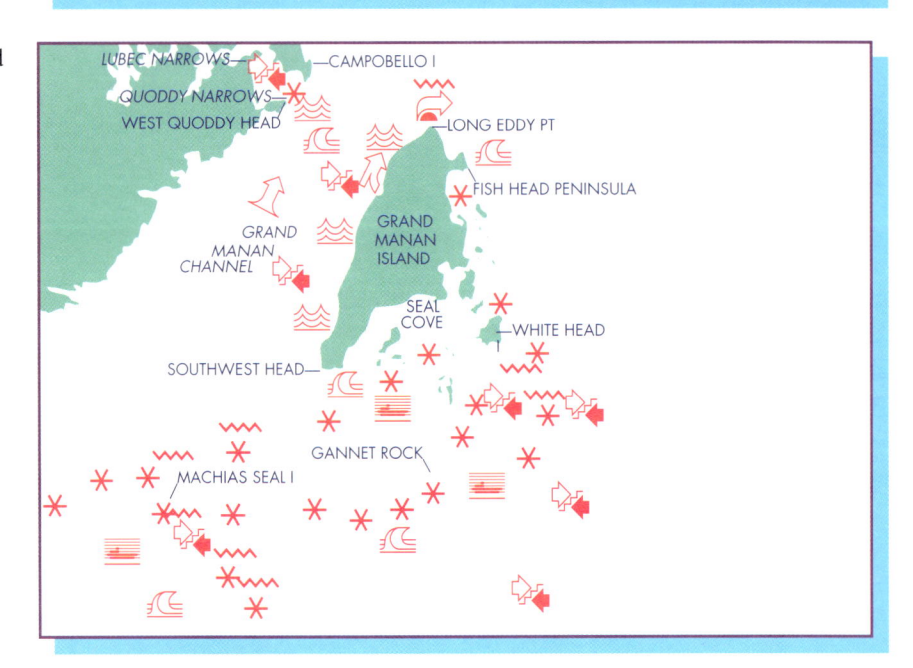

GRAND MANAN

Grand Manan is about 13 miles long and 6 miles across at its widest point. Steep, rocky cliffs on the west side of the island rise from 200 ft. near Southwest Head to about 400 ft. near Long Eddy Point. From this high ridge, the island slopes gradually down to its eastern shores.

Strong winds and currents occur in the Grand Manan Channel; these often oppose one another, causing rough seas.

Islands, rocks, and shoals extend about 8 miles southeast and 10 1/2 miles southwest from Grand Manan. Strong currents, spawning numerous rips, run in this foggy,

LOCAL WEATHER Fundy

hazardous area. Some unusually steep waves are found in places, as a result of shoaling and wind-opposing-current effects. In contrast, there are no outlying shoals off the northeast coast. The area in the immediate lee of the land is often clear of fog, but elsewhere it shrouds the island.

Tidal currents through the deep Grand Manan Channel run at 1.5–2.5 knots, but close to Grand Manan they attain rates of 3 knots. Strong southwesterly winds opposing the ebb current create rough conditions, especially near the island, where both wind and current are stronger. Crossing, choppy wave patterns occur close to the shoreline, due to backwash from the cliffs.

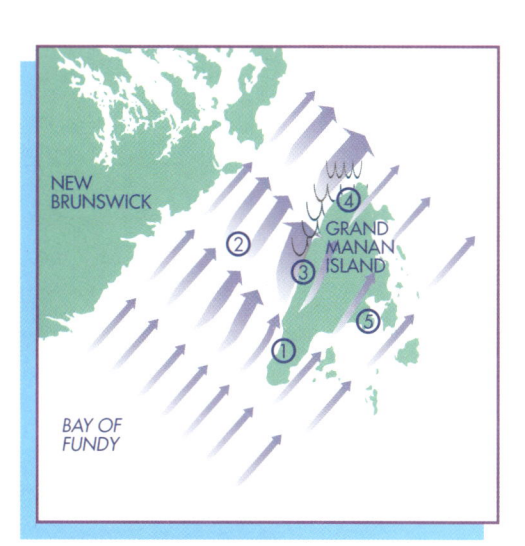

LONG EDDY POINT
Northeasterly gales are perhaps the worst winds in the Bay of Fundy. They bring large seas to Grand Manan's northeastern shores, particularly off the Fish Head Peninsula. A tidal rip, created by converging tidal streams, lies off its namesake, Long Eddy Point. This area is especially rough, with northeasterly winds on the flood tide.

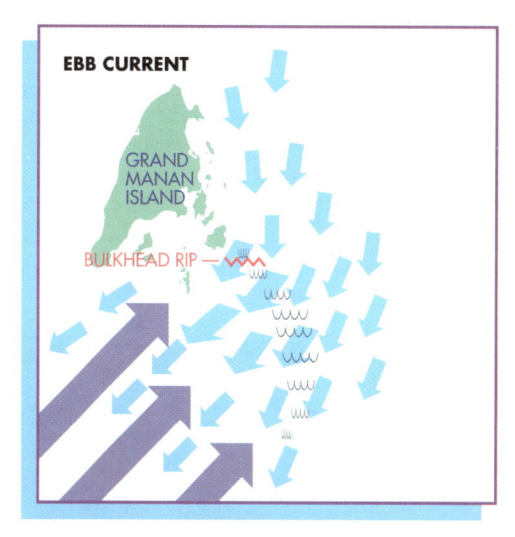

GRAND MANAN CHANNEL

(1) Channelling
Southwesterly winds are common in the Grand Manan Channel and are directed along the shoreline by the cliffs on Grand Manan's west coast.

(2) Funnelling
The coastal channelling (1) strengthens the wind where the Grand Manan Channel gradually funnels towards its northeastern end.

(3) Convergence
Coastal convergence also contributes to these strong shoreline winds and is enhanced off northwestern sections by cornering.

(4) Cornering
This is where the strongest winds and highest seas occur.

(5) Divergence
Coastal divergence over the south coast of the island makes for much lighter winds off northeastern shores.

BULKHEAD RIP
The Bulkhead Rip southeast of Grand Manan, and the area south of it where the sea bed shoals rapidly, is another treacherous location. Very strong currents flow here, particularly on the ebb tide. The area is described by one local fisherman as "a place to be avoided, with strong winds from the southwest quadrant."

Caution: Wind Opposing Tide
A 20-knot southwesterly through the Grand Manan Channel on the ebb tide is reported to give worse wave conditions than a 40-knot southwesterly in the Bay of Fundy on the flood tide.

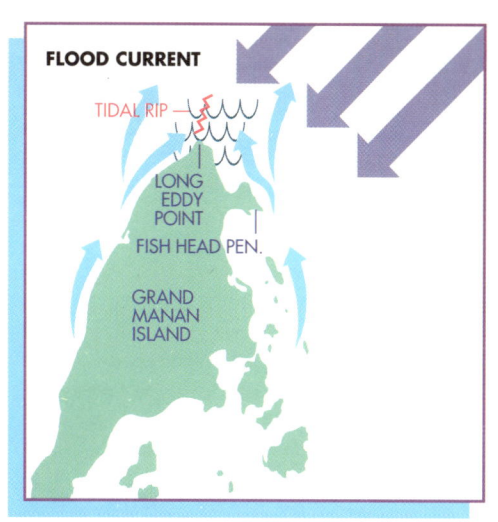

LOCAL WEATHER *Fundy*

QUODDY NARROWS TO MUSQUASH HARBOUR

Tidal rips occur south of Point Lepreau and in the exposed area just south of The Wolves. Point Lepreau should be given a wide berth when the wind there opposes the current. Rough, choppy water is often found near The Wolves, especially with easterly winds on the flood tide.

Sea breezes are common along this coastline on warm sunny days. They are southwesterly and relatively strong, due to the large temperature contrast between land and sea. Strong southwesterlies are often found in the waters east of Campobello Island, blowing from the Grand Manan Channel towards The Wolves.

PASSAMAQUODDY BAY AND APPROACHES

The Approaches

Very strong currents flow between the islands that stretch across the entrance to Passamaquoddy Bay. The strongest of these currents is through the Lubec Narrows, where 8 knots has been recorded on the ebb tide. The flood stream passes on each side of Indian Island, then turns sharply into Western Passage; this forms a whirlpool in the narrows between Deer Island and Eastport, known as the Old Sow. Reputed to be the largest whirlpool in the world, the Old Sow is most active about three hours before high water—and it is dangerous at times for small boats. The roughest waters in this area are found where currents are exposed to high winds and seas. The following seven trouble spots are identified with numbers on the two maps:

1. Letete Passage
Currents can run at 5 knots and are strongest three hours before and after high tide. The passage is encumbered with rocks and ledges, with many tidal swirls and eddies, particularly on the ebb flow. The area is fairly sheltered, except from easterlies and southeasterlies. When strong or gale-force southeasterlies oppose the ebb tide, it gets very rough as swells enter the passage and becomes impassable for small boats. The outside islands are also dangerous under these conditions, since waves break heavily around them.

2. Letete Passage
Northwesterly winds on the flood tide also create rough conditions in Letete Passage, but these are not so serious.

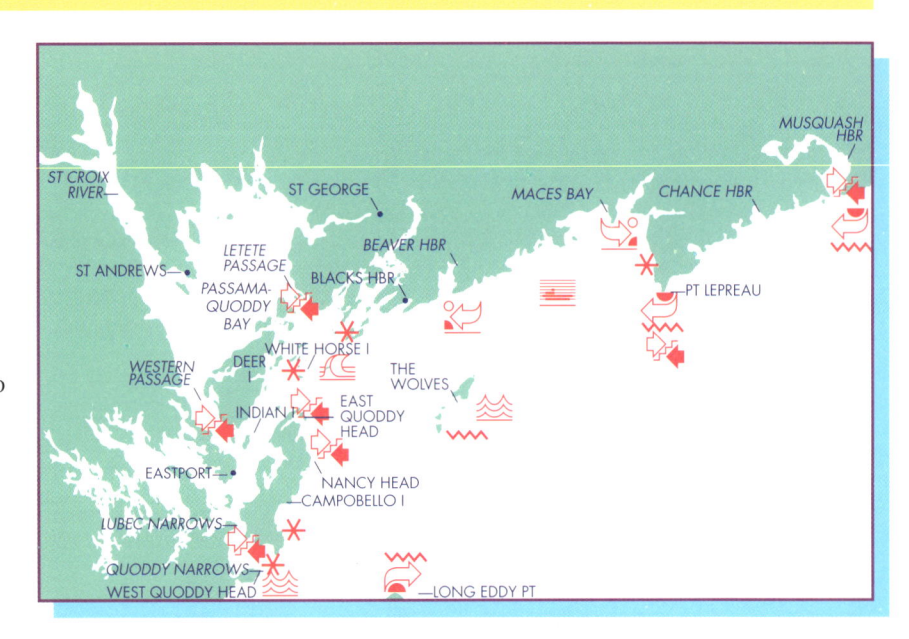

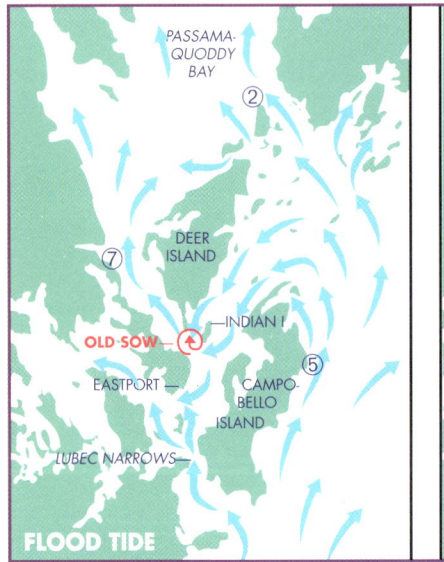

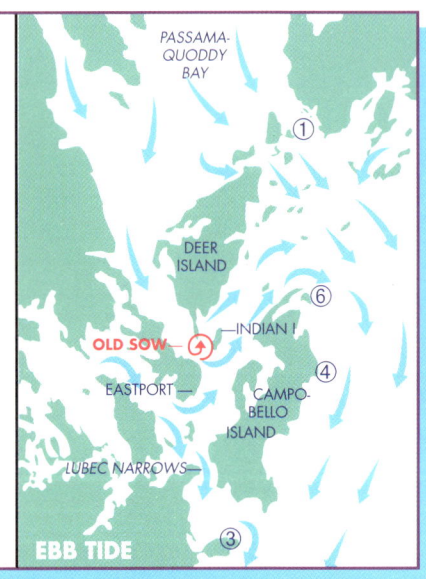

3. Quoddy Narrows
Strong winds and large seas from the south can pass up through the Grand Manan Channel. These create a rough breaking sea in the approaches to Quoddy Narrows, especially on the opposing ebb tide.

4. Nancy Head
Very rough conditions are found off Nancy Head on Campobello Island with an opposing ebb tide.

5. Nancy Head
Rough conditions, but not as pronounced, also occur off Nancy Head with a northeasterly on the flood tide.

6. East Quoddy Head
Strong easterly or northeasterly winds create a rough breaking sea off East Quoddy Head on the ebb tide.

7. Western Passage
The roughest seas at the northern entrance to Western Passage are found when northerly gales oppose the flood current.

Passamaquoddy Bay

Except near its entrance passages and at the mouth of the St. Croix River, tidal currents in Passamaquoddy Bay are weak. This bay is completely sheltered from the seas in the Bay of Fundy, and winds from the south pose little difficulty. The worst wind is a northerly or northwesterly gale that creates short,

LOCAL WEATHER *Fundy*

choppy seas—especially over southern sections—that in turn produce freezing spray in winter.

The northeast portion of the bay freezes over on calm, cold winter nights, but this ice is usually short-lived. During the spring freshet, however, blocks of ice exit the rivers and caution must be exercised, particularly at night or in fog.

In summer, air and sea temperatures in the bay are considerably warmer than elsewhere along this coastline and the incidence of fog and strong sea breezes is much lower. On a typical summer day, any fog will gradually clear out of the bay and continue out in the afternoon to just past White Horse Island. Due to its inland location, Passamaquoddy Bay is subject to some heavy summer thundershowers, which move across from Maine.

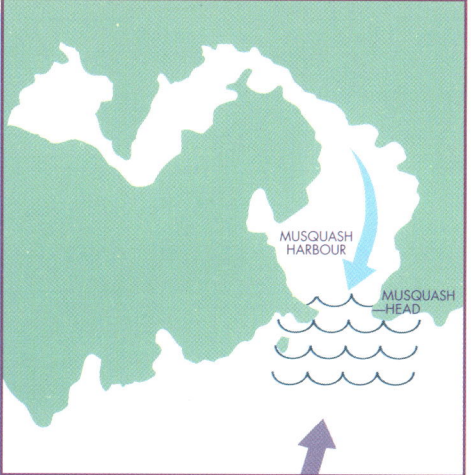

MUSQUASH HARBOUR
This harbour is the estuary of the Musquash River. An area of choppy, breaking seas develops at the harbour entrance when strong winds oppose the ebb current. This current is much enhanced during the spring freshet and after heavy rainfall.

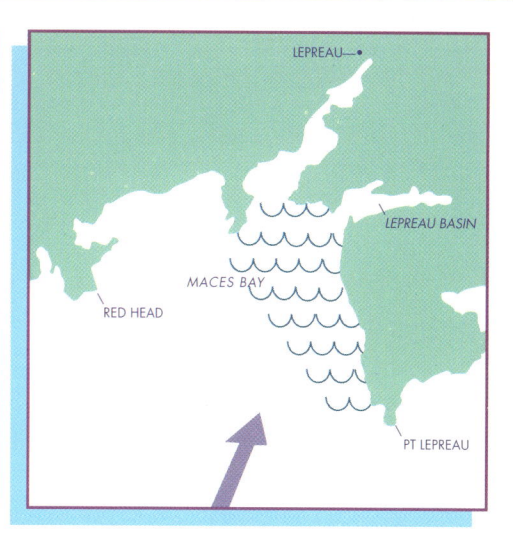

MACES BAY
Considerable shoaling occurs over the ledges on the eastern side of Maces Bay. This area is exposed to gales and swells from the southwest, and heavy breaking waves are frequently found there.

Marine Weather Tip: Fresh Water Deteriorates First

Fresh water from the rivers entering Passamaquoddy Bay gets rougher much faster than the salt water. With a rapid shift or increase to strong northwesterlies, choppy white water can be seen over the fresh water before the same conditions develop over the salt water.

SAINT JOHN HARBOUR

This major harbour is completely sheltered from northwesterly winds and protected from easterly winds by Cape Spencer—out to about 3 miles. The currents and eddies within Saint John Harbour are extremely complex. Large tides occur here, and there is a strong outflow of fresh water from the Saint John River.

Under the influence of the tide, the denser, heavier salt water advances and retreats like a wedge beneath the fresh water. After low tide there is a strong influx of salt water at depth, while at the surface there is a strong outflow of fresh water. When water levels in the harbour exceed those in the river, there is a change in current at the famous Reversing Falls; subsequently, salt water floods upriver and the flow in the harbour is entirely inward. After high water, the salt water continues upstream until there is a change in flow once again at the Reversing Falls. The current is then entirely outward and fresh water floods out into the harbour.

The duration of the various phases of the current-cycle depends on the height of the tide and on the water levels within the river. For instance, during the peak of the spring freshet, there is an almost continuous outgoing current, and the water in the harbour is mostly fresh. The boundary between the fresh water and the salt water is marked by a foam line, which often shows up on ships' radar. Outside the foam line, the colour of the salt water is greenish-blue. Inside the foam line, the fresher water is brown. Experienced mariners report that the worst weather conditions in the harbour occur with south-southwesterly gales, and that waves are rougher in the fresh water.

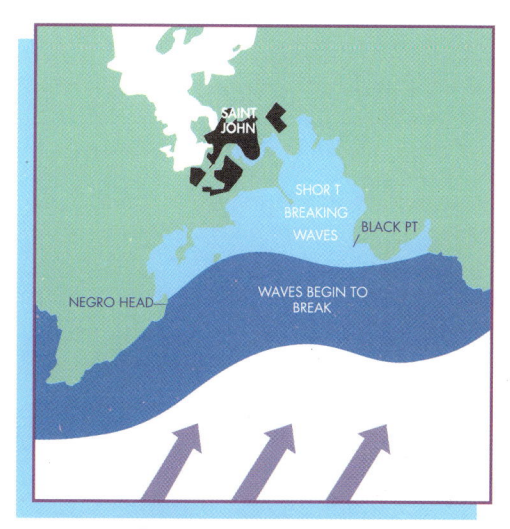

SAINT JOHN HARBOUR
With south-southwesterly winds, seas become progressively shorter and rougher towards the head of the harbour, due to shoaling. These wave conditions further deteriorate with an opposing surface current.

LOCAL WEATHER *Fundy*

OUTGOING TIDE
When there is a salt wedge in Saint John Harbour, rougher seas can occur in the fresh water. This happens because the denser salt water creates a "false bottom," which then enhances shoaling. Wave conditions worsen when salt and fresh water currents oppose the wind—as when a falling tide combines with an outward flow from the Reversing Falls.

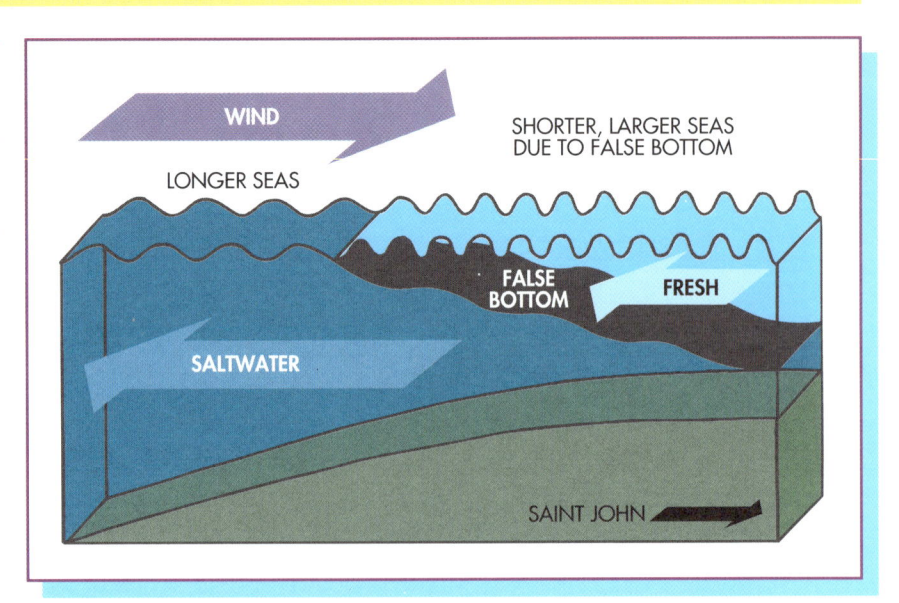

[Diagram: WIND blowing left over water; LONGER SEAS on left transitioning to SHORTER, LARGER SEAS DUE TO FALSE BOTTOM on right; FRESH water flowing right over FALSE BOTTOM; SALTWATER flowing left below; SAINT JOHN labeled at right.]

INCOMING TIDE
Contrasting wave conditions across the salt wedge may be more noticeable when the tide in the harbour is rising, and the flow is outward at the Reversing Falls. In this case, only the current within the fresh water opposes the wind.

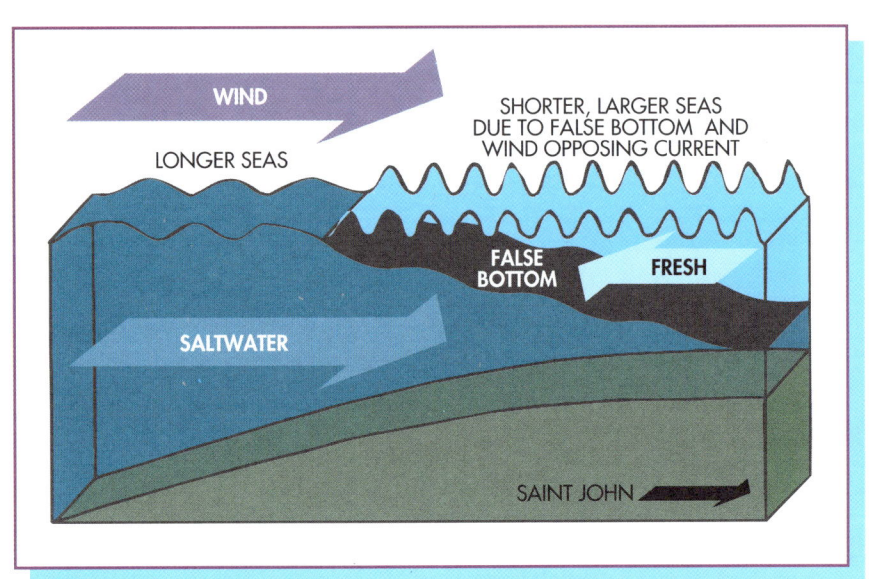

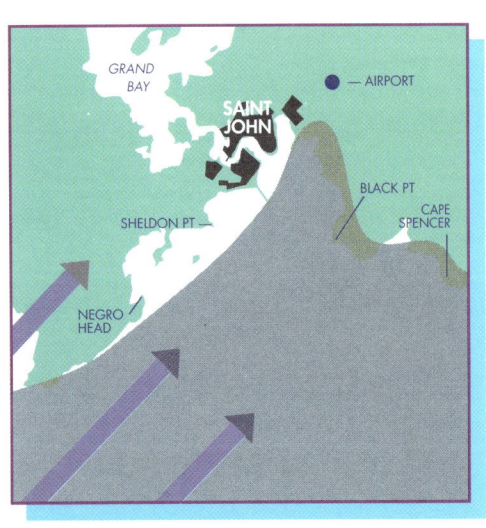

[Diagram: WIND blowing left; LONGER SEAS on left, SHORTER, LARGER SEAS DUE TO FALSE BOTTOM AND WIND OPPOSING CURRENT on right; FRESH water flowing right over FALSE BOTTOM; SALTWATER flowing right below; SAINT JOHN labeled at right.]

[Map: Saint John area showing GRAND BAY, AIRPORT, SAINT JOHN, SHELDON PT, BLACK PT, CAPE SPENCER, NEGRO HEAD, with arrows indicating southerly wind coming onshore.]

SAINT JOHN FOG
Fog in Saint John is associated with a southerly wind. If the wind is more southwesterly, fog usually clears in the city and on the western side of the harbour.

Fog is common in Saint John, as is the sea breeze on warm, sunny days. In summer, fog is influenced by the tide and often coincides with, or follows, the arrival of the relatively cold salt water. The sea breeze is a southwesterly of 15–25 knots and is reported to extend about 5 miles offshore, giving some chop and whitecaps. Both the fog and the sea breeze result in considerable cooling at the waterfront. A temperature difference of 20°C has been recorded between the downtown area and the airport, about 10 miles inland.

LOCAL WEATHER *Fundy*

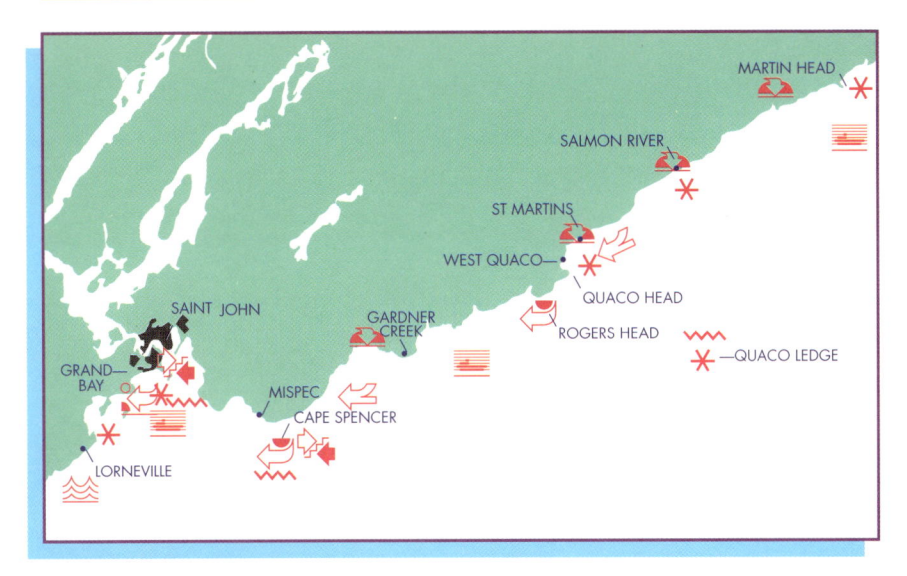

CAPE SPENCER TO MARTIN HEAD

The shoreline from Cape Spencer to Martin Head is generally high and is intersected by numerous rivers entering the Bay of Fundy. Except at the river mouths, coastal waters within 0.5–1 mile of shore are generally protected from north-to-northwesterly winds. With such winds, seas build up gradually away from the coast. Katabatic winds have been reported from some river valleys. They develop during the evening and are strongest at night, reaching 15–20 knots. During the spring freshet, ice from the rivers can be hazardous at night and in fog. Blocks of ice also can be found close to the river mouths in winter, when a high run of tides lifts them from the riverbanks.

Coastal convergence occurs along this shoreline with an easterly wind and is enhanced by cornering off the prominent headlands. These effects are most pronounced in the St. Martins–West Quaco area, and off Rogers Head and Cape Spencer.

Tidal streams averaging 2 knots run parallel to the shore, forming rips off the headlands. Wave conditions deteriorate everywhere when strong winds oppose these currents. This effect is particularly hazardous south of Cape Spencer, especially with a strong southwesterly on the ebb tide. Local fishermen advise that, under such circumstances, small boats should stay 3–4 miles south of this headland.

Summer thunderstorms along this coast are mainly associated with the passage of cold fronts from New Brunswick, and are most frequent in late afternoon and evening. Thunderstorms often weaken or dissipate completely as they move out over the cold waters of the Bay of Fundy.

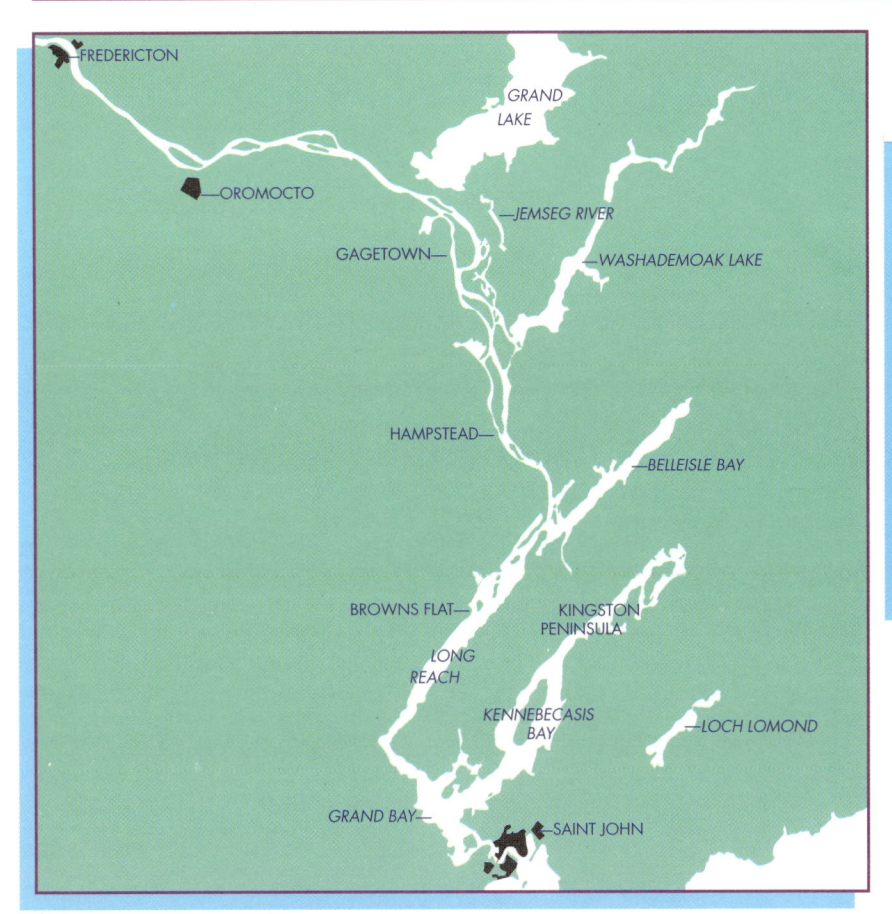

Saint John River

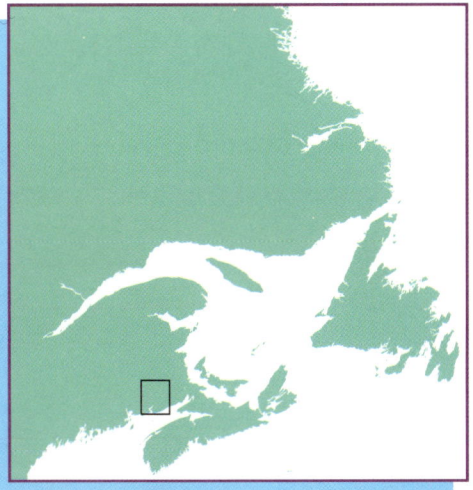

The Saint John River is a popular area for recreational sailors. The major marine weather conditions yachters can expect to encounter along the river are outlined in two sections: the Lower Saint John River and the Upper Saint John River.

LOCAL WEATHER Fundy

LOWER SAINT JOHN RIVER

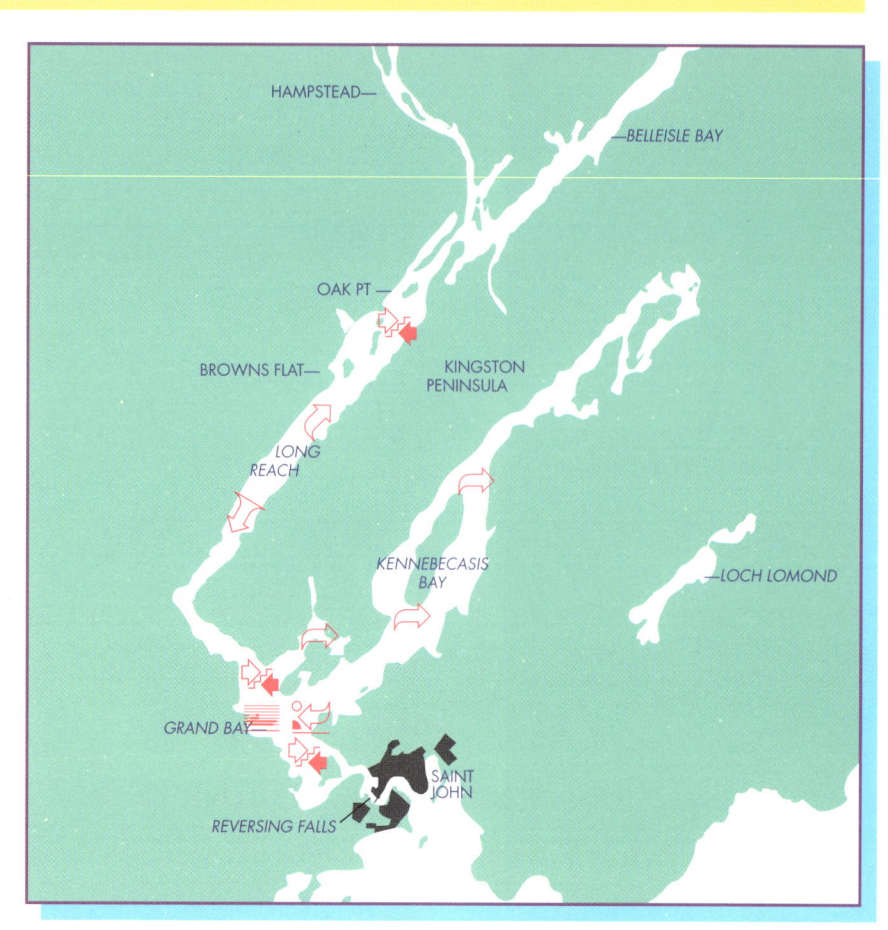

The Reversing Falls
Vessels can only pass through the Reversing Falls when the waters in the Saint John River and in Saint John Harbour are near level. Ordinarily, the slack water period lasts for 10 minutes, occurring about 2 hours and 25 minutes after high water at Saint John, and 3 hours and 50 minutes after low water. The falls can be navigated for about half an hour before and after this time. During the spring freshet, from early April to the middle of May, water levels in the river are extremely high. This makes the falls impassable to vessels going up-river, since the tide usually does not rise to the river level. During the freshet, a 7-knot current has been reported at the Reversing Falls. Heavy rainfall also raises the water level in the river, although to a much lesser degree than the freshet. A heavy rainfall at Fredericton is reported to raise the river level downstream by several feet; if replenished by still more rain, these abnormally high river levels may take up to two weeks to subside. A high run of tides at Saint John acts to delay the runoff. Recent heavy rainfall tends to advance the time of slack water after high tide in Saint John, while delaying it after low tide. Extreme drought conditions have the opposite effect. A study of storm surges in the Bay of Fundy suggests that strong southwesterlies slightly advance the phase of the tide, while strong northeasterlies delay it.

Grand Bay and Kennebecasis Bay

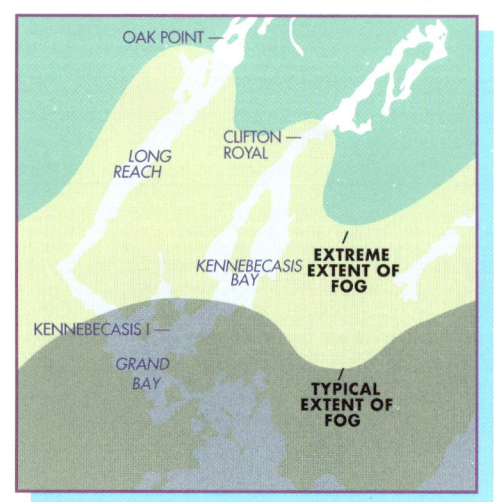

SEA FOG
Sea fog is common in Grand Bay. Its usual position is as shown, but sea fog has been reported in Long Reach as far as Oak Point, and in Kennebecasis Bay as far as Clifton. On otherwise fine summer days, it usually clears between 9:00 a.m. and 10:00 a.m.

SEA BREEZE
If the wind is calm in the morning, southerly sea breezes often blow in from the coast in the afternoon. The sea breeze is about 10–12 knots and typically reaches Long Island in Kennebecasis Bay and Harding Point in the approach to Long Reach. Once the sea breeze goes down with the sun, yachters are usually left becalmed.

LOCAL WEATHER Fundy

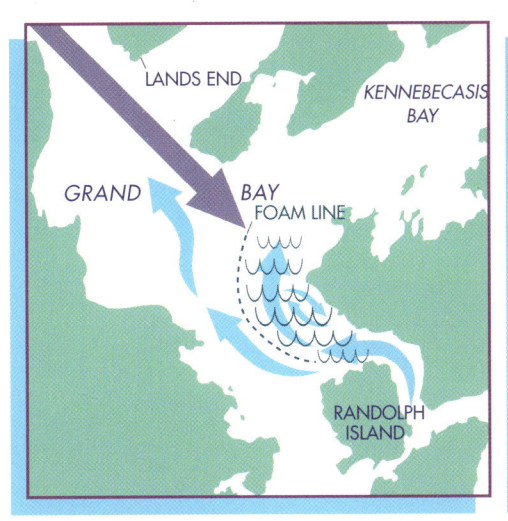

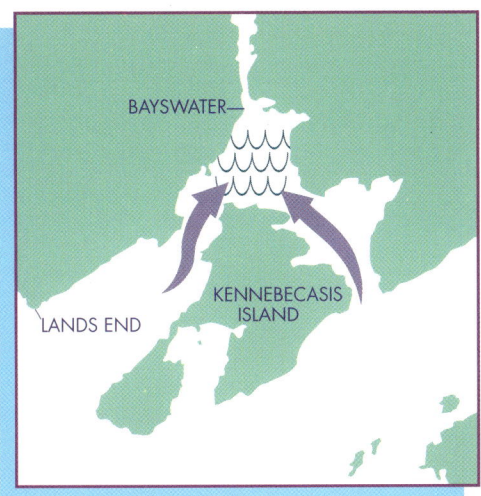

GRAND BAY
On the flood stream, the current in Grand Bay divides into Long Reach and Kennebecasis Bay; at ebb, currents from Long Reach and Kennebecasis Bay converge in Grand Bay. A foam line often marks this division. When strong northwesterlies blow through Grand Bay, an area of small, choppy waves (less than 1 m) is found near the stronger currents of the flood stream. One hour after high tide, the current diminishes and waves in this area flatten out.

KENNEBECASIS ISLAND
Channelling occurs around Kennebecasis Island with a southerly wind. The convergent airflows here create an area of confused, gusty winds to the north of the island. Under such circumstances, yachters will notice a change from a tailwind to a headwind when sailing around Kennebecasis Island.

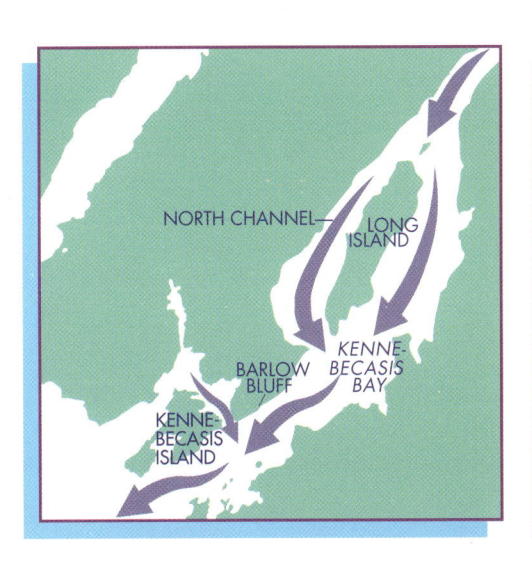

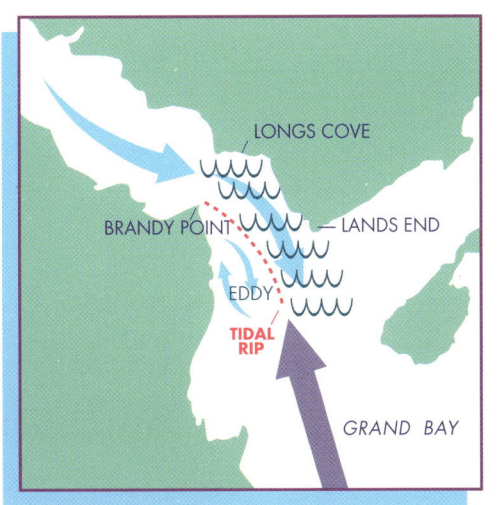

LONG ISLAND
With a northeasterly wind, the airflow is channelled on either side of Long Island. Sailing down Kennebecasis Bay, stronger gusty winds blow out from North Channel; when sailing around the southern tip of Long Island, one finds that a tailwind changes to a headwind. The channelled wind blowing out between Barlow Bluff and Kennebecasis Island is not very strong. With a southwesterly, channelling around Long Island is hardly noticeable.

LANDS END
Because of shallows off Brandy Point, the current sets strongly onto the shores between Longs Cove and Lands End. A choppy, 0.5–1 m sea is experienced here when there is a strong opposing southerly or southeasterly wind.

71

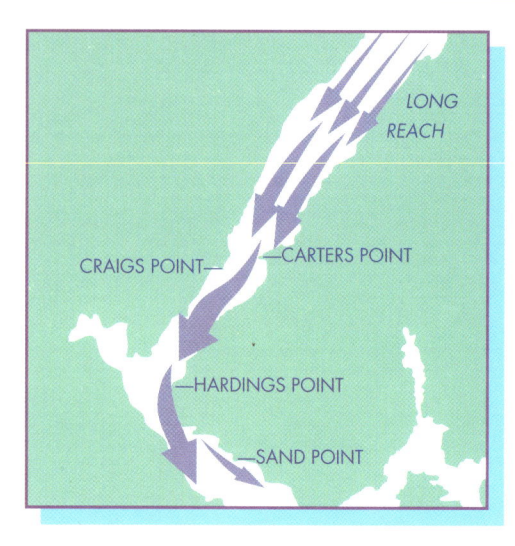

LOCAL WEATHER Fundy

Long Reach
Channelling is significant in Long Reach, which is surrounded by high ground. The wind often blows along its entire length either from the southwest or the northeast.

Salt water often reaches up to Oak Point, and the air temperature on the river can suddenly get colder there. Consistently warmer weather is found up-river from Oak Point.

Thunderstorms tend to be more frequent over Long Reach than Kennebecasis Bay, due to uplift from the high ground.

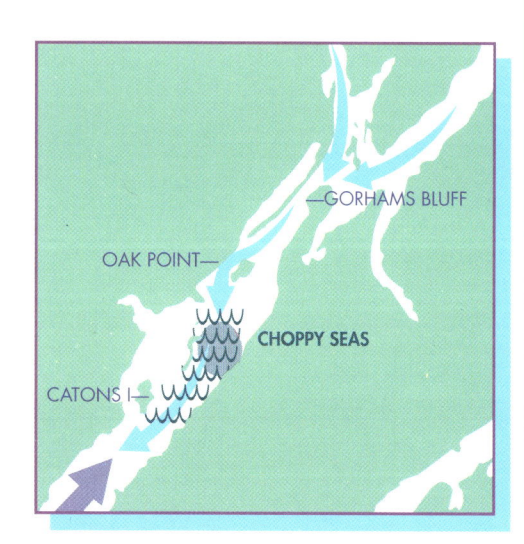

LONG REACH
With northeasterlies, slightly stronger winds are experienced near Carters Point and Craigs Point, where Long Reach narrows. After the river bend at Harding Point, light winds are found in the lee of land at Sand Point, with stronger, gusty winds on the opposite shore. Waves don't build up significantly with a northeasterly wind in Long Reach, because opposing currents are not that strong.

OAK POINT
A strong current flows southward past Oak Point and Catons Island. When this is opposed by strong southwesterlies blowing up Long Reach, a short, steep, breaking sea develops. With gale force winds, seas of 1.5–2.5 m have been reported here.

A southeasterly wind against the current also gives choppy seas here (see blue shaded spot on map).

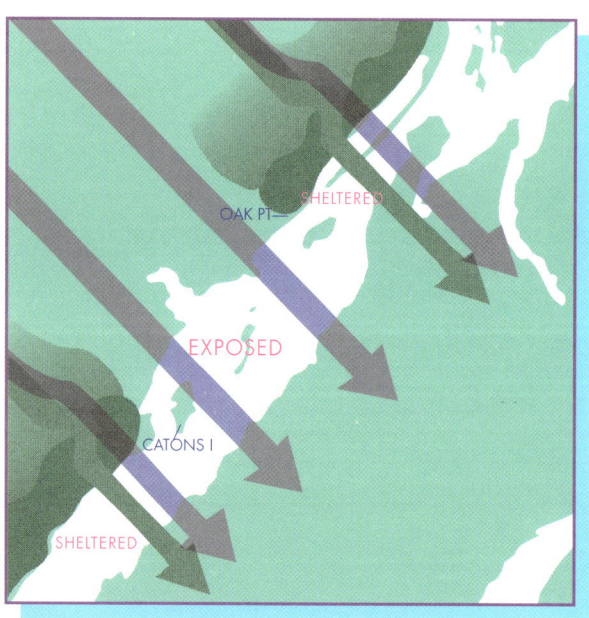

OAK POINT–CATONS ISLAND
Northwesterlies are sheltered in Long Reach as far as Catons Island, but from there to Oak Point, northwesterlies blow strongly, until yachters reach the lee of the hills again. These winds can reach gale force.

LOCAL WEATHER *Fundy*

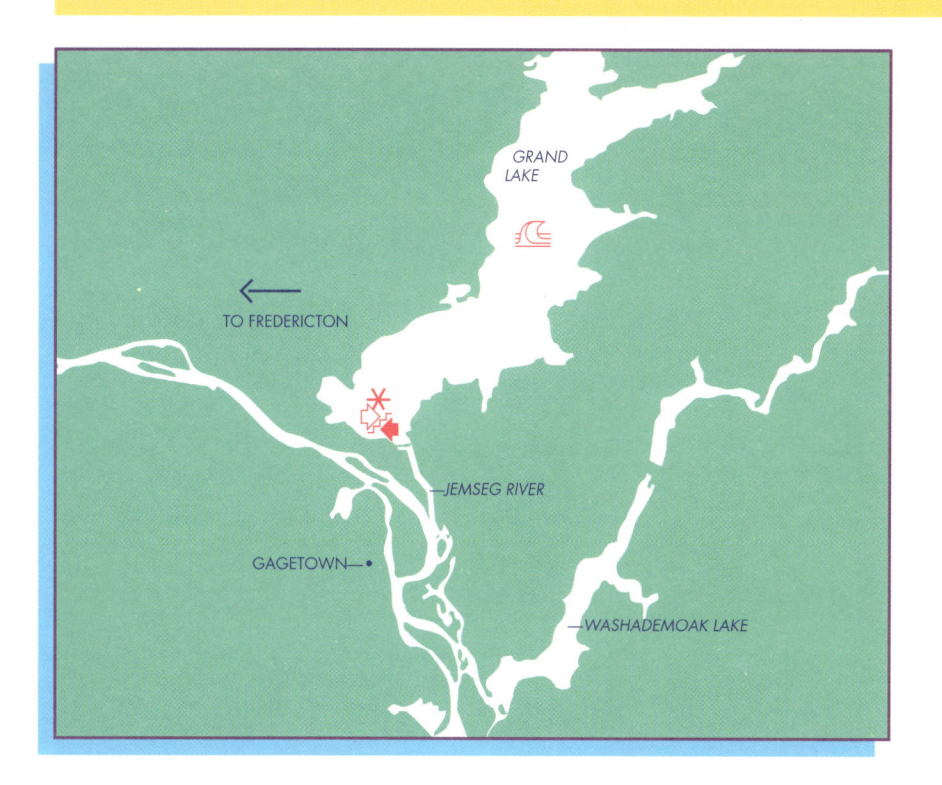

UPPER SAINT JOHN RIVER AND GRAND LAKE

Grand Lake, the largest in New Brunswick, is connected to the Saint John River by the Jemseg River. The southern part of the lake is shallow, while relatively large seas of 2 m can build up anywhere within the main body of Grand Lake.

Northeasterly gales in Grand Lake give large seas, which break to the bottom in the shallow waters leading to the Jemseg River. Local mariners agree that it is not a good idea, at such times, to try to enter the Jemseg River from Grand Lake, or vice versa. Conditions are very sheltered on the river and give no warning of what awaits on the lake. Several yachts coming from the river are reported to have gone aground.

Southwesterly winds are also bad in this area, since they blow strongly across the low marshlands south of the lake. These winds build up a steep chop as they oppose the current, which drains the lake into the Jemseg River. This condition is worse after a heavy rainfall.

Thunderstorms are frequently reported in summer over Grand Lake, and a large waterspout has also been seen there. Climatological statistics show that there are, on average, 11 days per year when thunderstorms occur at Saint John, increasing inland to 15 per year at Fredericton. Eighty percent of these thunderstorms occur during June, July, and August.

Upstream from Gagetown, the Saint John River is relatively narrow, and the surrounding terrain is low. Thunderstorms affect the area, but there are no other known local weather effects.

Marine Weather Tip: Thunderstorm Watches/Warnings

Heavy thunderstorms affecting Grand Lake and the Saint John River are monitored by the public forecast service as part of Environment Canada's Summer Severe Weather Program. Severe weather watches and warnings for the area are broadcast on Weatheradio and by local radio stations.

LOCAL WEATHER *Fundy*

Upper Fundy

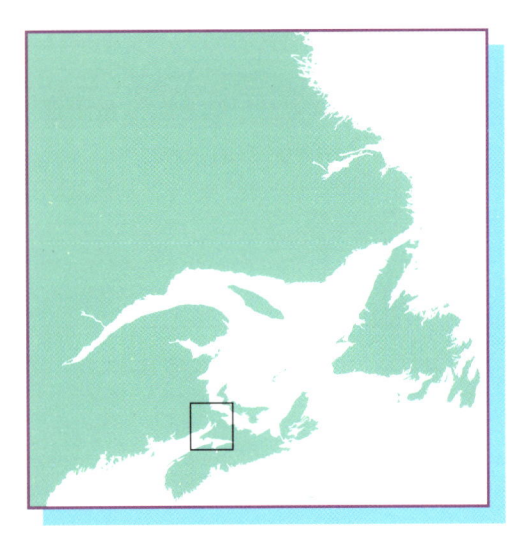

GENERAL CONDITIONS

Extremely high tides and strong currents dominate the local weather effects in this area. Most weather-related hazards occur when the wind and current are opposed. Currents range from 2 knots in the Bay of Fundy to reportedly more than 10 knots through the Minas Channel. From January to March, the Minas Basin and the northern parts of Chignecto Bay fill with blocks of ice which move with the currents and the wind. Harbours within the Minas Basin are generally closed, from January until early April.

For easier reading, this coastline has been divided into two sections.

CHIGNECTO BAY, CUMBERLAND BASIN, AND SHEPODY BAY

In Chignecto Bay, the tidal currents set parallel to the shore at an average rate of about 2 knots, increasing towards the head of the bay. In Cumberland Basin the currents set at 4–5 knots, and in Shepody Bay, 3–4 knots. Tidal rips and eddies are common off major headlands and over shallow water. The worst weather conditions occur with southwesterly and northeasterly winds, especially when these oppose the tidal currents. The area tends to be well sheltered from other wind directions. Southwesterlies are funnelled in Chignecto Bay and blow strongly into Cumberland Basin, which is surrounded by marshy flats—where they are intensified on summer afternoons by decreased stability.

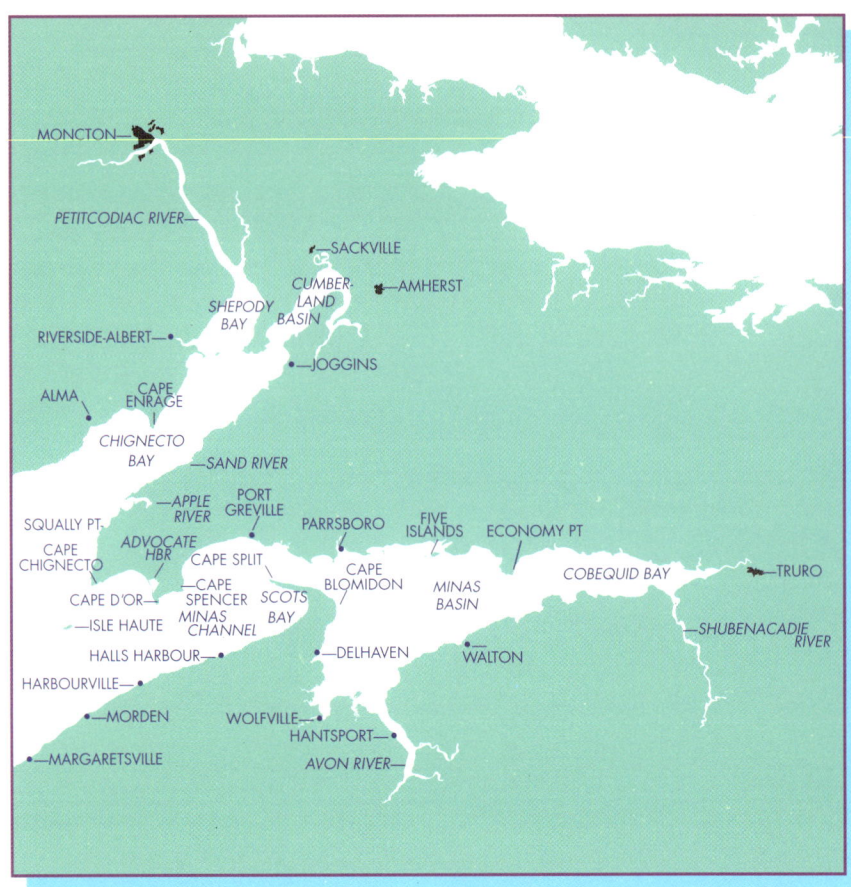

Southwesterlies in Cumberland Basin can gust to gale force or storm force, producing rough waves, the largest of which are off Pecks Point; meanwhile, winds are often light in Shepody Bay. With southwesterlies, seas are choppy everywhere on the ebb tide, but they are particularly rough in the following areas: off Cape Enrage, due to the sharp headland and strong currents; off Ragged Reef Point, where larger seas are found due to shoaling; southwest of Cape Maringouin, in the turbulent area where currents flowing from Cumberland Basin and Shepody Bay

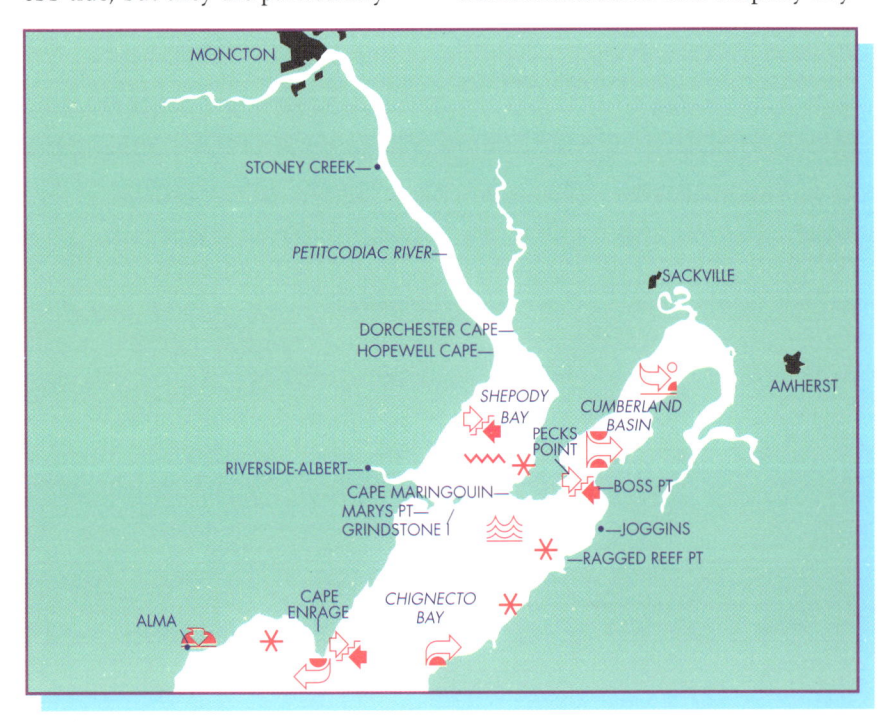

LOCAL WEATHER Fundy

converge; and between Boss Point and Pecks Point, in the entrance to the Cumberland Basin, where both wind and current are particularly strong. In these areas, strong winds opposing the tide can produce waves over 3 m, and even light to moderate winds produce choppy seas. Northeasterlies also blow strongly through the area and create choppy seas with the flood tide, especially in Cumberland Basin; however, these seas are smaller than those associated with the southwesterlies, because they are limited by fetch.

Tidal rips extend north-northeast from Grindstone Island for about 5 miles into Shepody Bay. Conditions here worsen with a strong opposing wind. On summer days, fog is reported to burn off quickly, north of the narrows between Hopewell Cape and Dorchester Cape. The Petitcodiac River is noted for its tidal bore, which occurs between Stoney Creek and Moncton.

Marine Weather Tip
Many coastal communities were originally settled because they were sheltered from the worst of the wind. Mariners should remember that wind and other marine conditions reported from inhabited coastal sites may be significantly different from those occurring over open water.

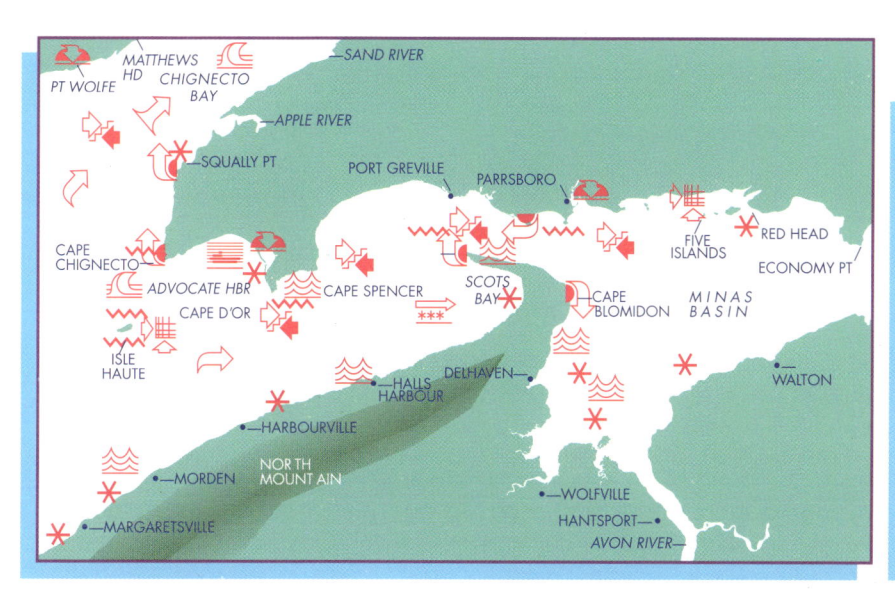

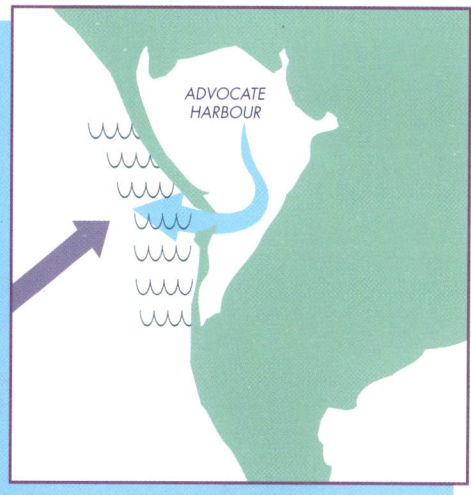

FUNDY EAST AND MINAS BASIN

Large swells that move up the Bay of Fundy do not generally penetrate much past Cape d'Or, although they do get into Scots Bay on occasion, where they are amplified by shoaling. Similarly, fog, common in spring and summer, becomes less frequent east of Cape d'Or.

Weather phenomena in this area are strongly dependent on the phase and strength of the tide. From Cape Chignecto eastward, tidal rips and eddies occur off virtually every point or cape. When the wind opposes these currents, conditions can become dangerous for even the most experienced mariner.

The flood stream in this area is reportedly more dangerous than the ebb stream, especially during spring tides. Two potentially dangerous, and highly respected areas are Advocate Harbour and Cape Split.

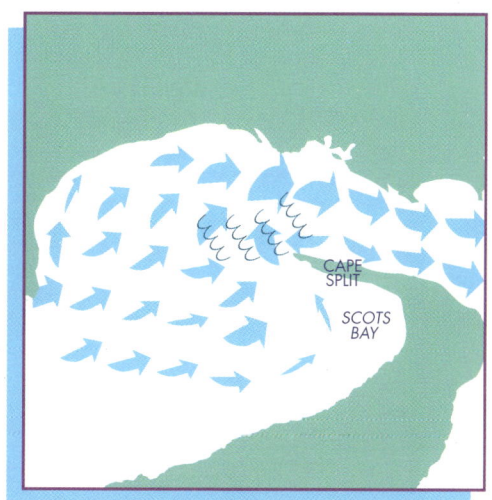

CAPE SPLIT
Near Cape Split, the tidal stream first fills Scots Bay, then floods past the cape. This chart of tidal flood currents shows that opposing currents meet off Cape Split, creating what one local fisherman has called "a wall of water" and "whirlpools as big as my house."

ADVOCATE HARBOUR
Shoals off the entrance to Advocate Harbour, combined with a continually shifting gravel bar, make this a hazardous place. When a strong wind opposes the tidal stream, even the most experienced fishermen avoid the area.

LOCAL WEATHER Fundy

TIDES
The world's highest tides are found in the Minas Basin, and extensive mud flats appear at low water. Most wharfs, like the one shown here at Delhaven, become completely dry. High and low water in the Minas Basin is about one hour later than at Saint John.

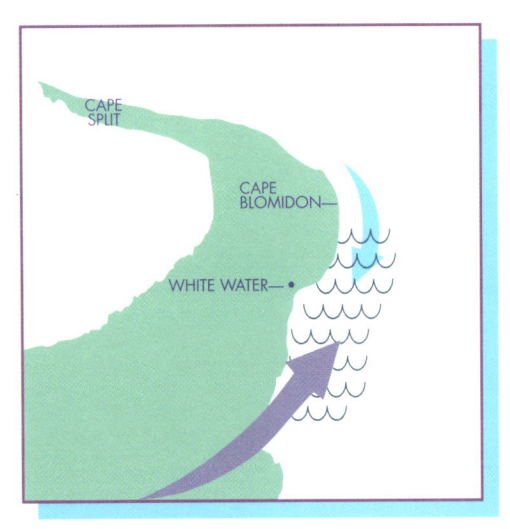

WHITE WATER
Channelled southwesterlies from the Annapolis Valley blow strongly south of Cape Blomidon, over an area known locally as White Waters. Choppy, white water is indeed found here, especially during the first four hours of the flood stream.

Marine Weather Tip
The place names on a map often tell a lot about the nature of the area. Squally Point, White Water, and Cape Enrage describe the dangers that can be found along this coast. Cape Blomidon was once known as Cape-Blow-Me-Down, and Wolfville was once named Mud Creek.

The largest seas in the Minas Basin develop over western sections, with easterly gales on the flood tide. This can produce a short, steep sea, of 3–3.5 m. Although strong coastal winds do occur from Economy Point to Cape Chignecto, particularly in easterlies, this stretch of coastline is very well sheltered from northerlies and northwesterlies.

In summer, air and sea temperatures in the Minas Basin are considerably higher than in waters west of Cape Split. This is due to the warming influence of the mud flats and the surrounding land. There are no sea breezes to speak of, and fog is infrequent and usually limited to the early morning hours. Summer thunderstorms moving from the Annapolis Valley sometimes cross Minas Basin, reaching the coast again near Economy Point. These storms can be accompanied by heavy squalls and large hailstones.

In winter, blocks of ice from the Minas Basin sometimes move out through the Minas Channel towards Cape Spencer. This ice is mainly current-driven, rather than wind-driven, and currents here are very strong. In the Minas Basin itself, open water can fill in with ice very quickly.

Cobequid Bay lies east of Economy Point, and there is no marine activity here. The area is famous, however, for having the world's highest tides; extensive mud flats develop at low water.

The coastline from Margaretsville to Scots Bay is relatively straight and free of outlying shoals. The Margaretsville Bank is the most significant shoal in the area. A ridge of hills, known as North Mountain, runs parallel to the coast. In southwesterlies, stronger winds are found close to the shoreline, due to coastal convergence. Experienced mariners report that these stronger winds, often accompanied by breaking waves, occur within 1–1.5 miles of shore. In these cases, the roughest wave conditions are found over the shallower waters within $1/2$ mile of the coast, especially when the ebb current is running.

Caution: Headland Winds
Cornering causes northwesterly winds to be especially strong off Cape Blomidon. With a northwesterly wind of 25–30 knots in the Minas Basin, a 40-knot wind is experienced off this headland.

LOCAL WEATHER *Fundy*

Fundy Southeast

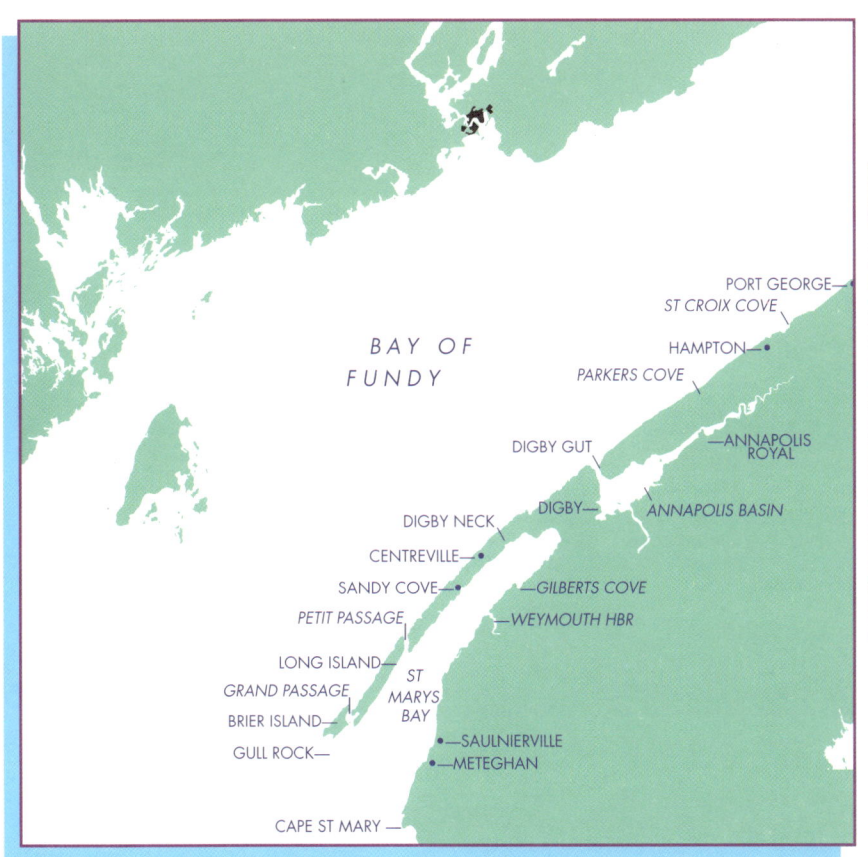

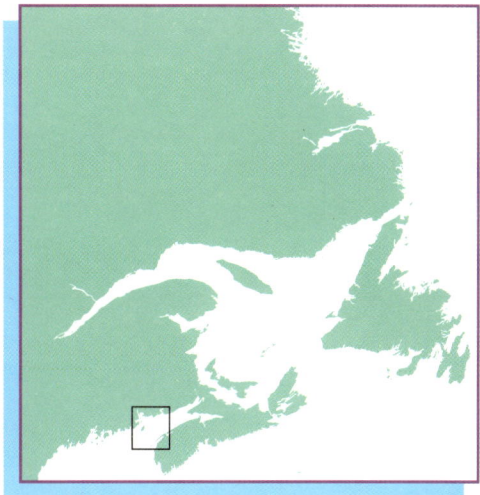

Brier Island. Wave conditions deteriorate everywhere on an opposing wind—especially in and over the above-noted passages and shoals. Shallows are also found in the eastern shores and head of St. Marys Bay, but elsewhere waters deepen rapidly.

Fog is less frequent along this coastline, than south of Cape St. Marys, since southerly winds here blow offshore. In winter, the area is affected by considerable flurry activity in a northwest or westerly airflow.

For easier reading, this coastline has been divided into two sections.

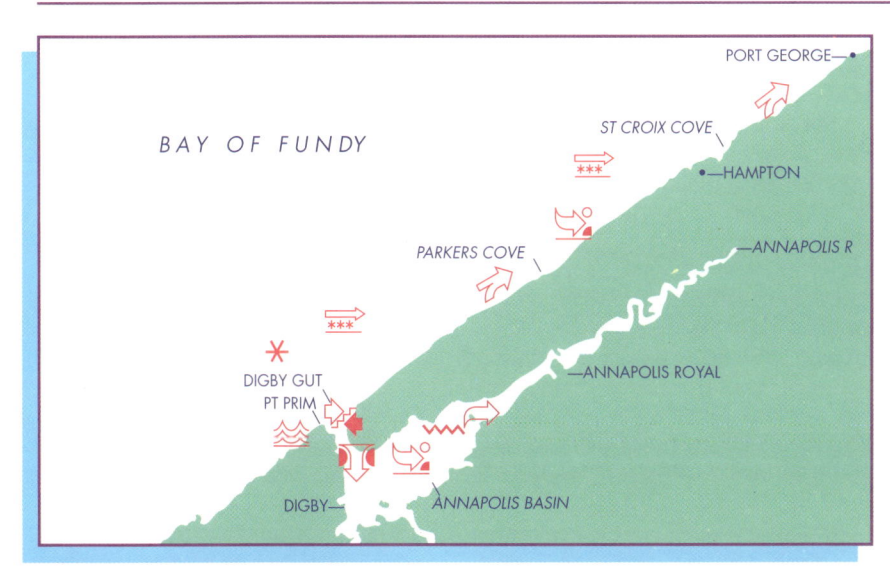

GENERAL CONDITIONS

The marine weather conditions in this area are largely influenced by high tides and strong currents. Currents here generally set parallel to the shoreline at a rate of 1.5–2.5 knots. They are considerably stronger through Digby Gut, Petit Passage, and Grand Passage, and over the dangerous shoals around

PORT GEORGE TO PRIM POINT AND ANNAPOLIS BASIN

From Port George, the coast running southwest to Digby Gut is free of outlying shoals. Coastal convergence strengthens southwesterly winds near the shoreline. The sea breeze is a moderate northwesterly wind. Tidal currents run parallel to the shore at a rate of 1.5–2.5 knots, and wave conditions deteriorate when currents set into an opposing wind.

Digby Gut is a steep-sided deep-water passage, 0.4 miles wide, which leads into the Annapolis Basin. Strong currents flow through this passage, reaching a maximum rate of about 5 knots. The times of high-water slack and low-water slack are almost the same as the times of high and low water at Saint John. Northwesterlies blow straight through Digby Gut, and with an opposing (ebb) current, choppy conditions develop at its entrance, just off Prim Point. This effect is noticeable even with a wind of only 15 knots. A southwesterly swell in the Bay of Fundy will move into the entrance of Digby Gut, and large seas are experienced there with a strong ebb current.

77

LOCAL WEATHER *Fundy*

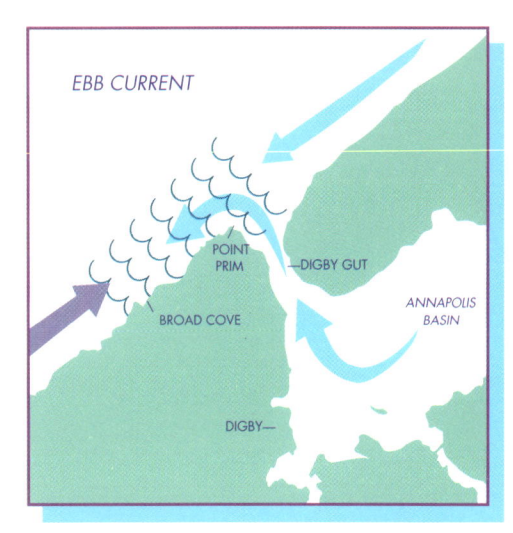

DIGBY GUT
The strong currents moving in and out of Digby Gut can extend along the coast as far as Broad Cove. An opposing southwesterly wind encourages choppy conditions to develop along this stretch of shoreline.

Although mainly landlocked, the Annapolis Basin is subject to strong winds due to channelling. Southwesterlies blow in over the low land, separating it from St. Marys Bay, and northeasterlies blow in from along the Annapolis Valley. A northeasterly gale is the worst wind here, creating breaking seas at Digby. Southwesterly winds of 15–25 knots are commonly found on summer afternoons in the Annapolis Basin, creating whitecaps. Under these circumstances, conditions outside Digby Gut are often calm.

In exceptionally cold weather, ice develops on the tidal flats in the Annapolis Basin and can then be carried to lee shores by the wind and tide.

The Annapolis River is navigable as far as Annapolis Royal. Changes in currents in the river may occur without notice, due to operation of the sluice gates at the hydroelectric power station.

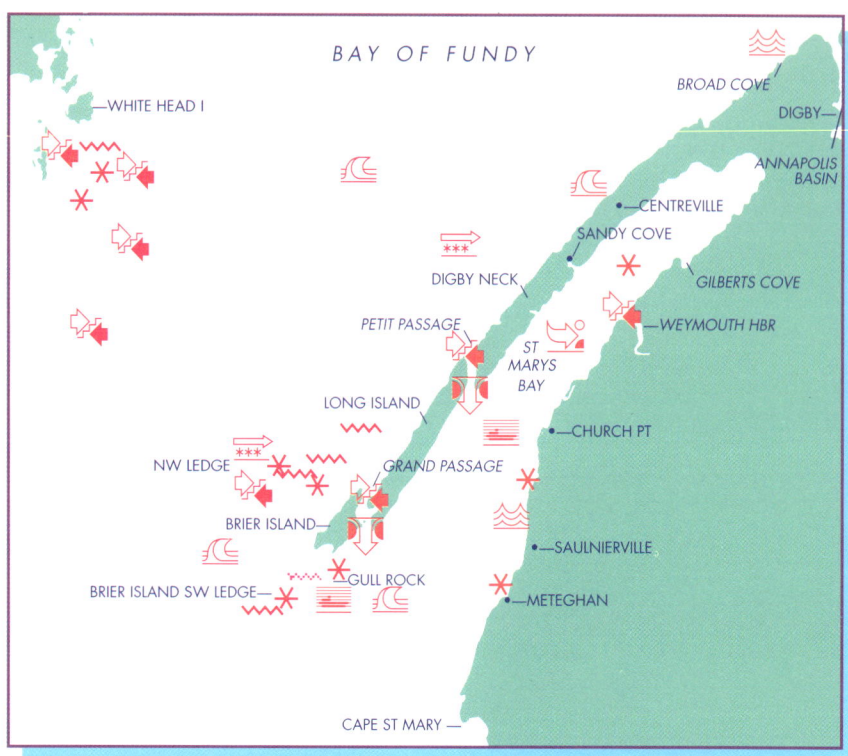

BROAD COVE TO BRIER ISLAND AND ST. MARYS BAY

The tidal streams along the bold shoreline of Digby Neck and Long Island run parallel to the shore at a rate of 2–2.5 knots. The roughest conditions here are experienced when these currents oppose southwesterly or northeasterly gales, both of which can bring large seas. Fog is more frequent over Brier Island, Long Island, and Digby Neck (especially southern shores) than over coastal sections northeast of Centreville.

The Gull Rock Bars, most of which are dry at low tide, extend south of Brier Island to Gull Rock. Heavy tidal rips extend about 3 1/2 miles southwest from Gull Rock, to beyond Brier Island Southwest Ledge. This exposed area has strong currents. Very dangerous conditions—with heavy breaking seas—develop there in rough weather.

Northwest Ledge and its neighbouring shoals are also dangerous. Currents here set to the north on the flood tide, and to the south on the ebb tide, with both streams reaching a maximum of about 4 knots. Seas can break to the bottom here when gales and currents are opposed.

St. Marys Bay is exposed to gales and swells from the southwest, during which rough conditions prevail close to shore between Meteghan and Saulnierville, due to shoaling. Beyond Church Point, the waves diminish markedly; the bay is largely protected to the north and northwest by Digby Neck, Long Island, and Brier Island. However, gales from the north create short, steep waves over southeastern sections of the bay, making Saulnierville Harbour very choppy.

The sea breeze in St. Marys Bay is a westerly wind of 15–20 knots, which usually begins around noon. Although it blows through the whole bay, it is strongest over the eastern shores, where it creates whitecaps. Southwesterly winds blow over the low land at the head of the bay and into the Annapolis Basin.

Southwesterly winds are known to raise the water level in St. Marys Bay, while northeasterly winds lower it. Tidal currents in the bay set parallel to the shore at a rate of about 1 knot. However, much stronger currents are found in the approaches to Grand Passage and Petit Passage, and very rough conditions develop there when strong or gale-force winds oppose the south-going ebb stream.

LOCAL WEATHER *Fundy*

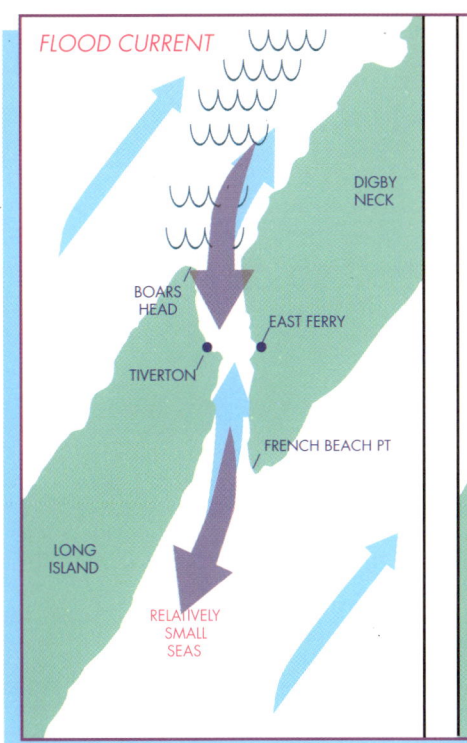

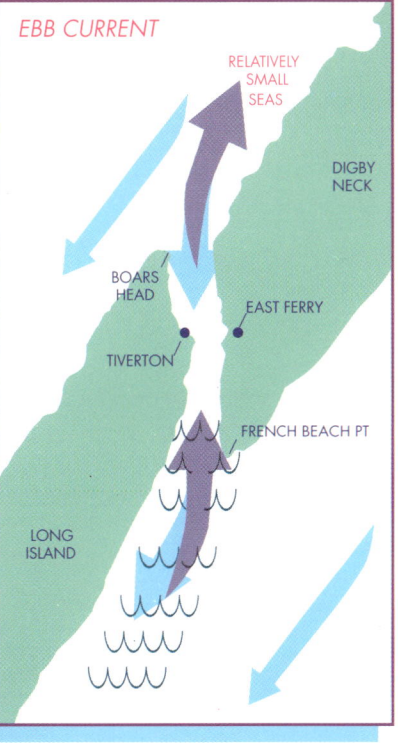

PETIT PASSAGE

This passage lies between Long Island and Digby Neck; it is narrower and deeper than Grand Passage. The land on each side is high, and channelling and funnelling contribute to the strong winds often found there. Extremely strong currents flow through the passage, attaining a maximum rate of 8 knots on the north-going flood stream and 7 knots on the south-going ebb stream. When strong, or gale-force, winds oppose these currents, heavy breaking waves develop within the passage and in its windward approaches. Like Grand Passage, northerly winds on the flood stream give the worst conditions; when rough waves prevail at one entrance, relatively small seas are found at the other. High-water slack occurs 1 hour before the time of high water at Saint John. Low-water slack occurs 1 hour and 3 minutes before low water at Saint John.

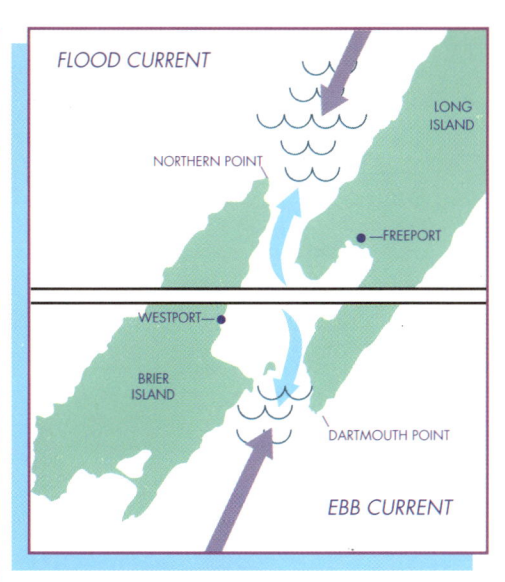

GRAND PASSAGE

This passage lies between Brier Island and Long Island. Very strong currents flow here, reaching a maximum rate of 6 knots on the north-going flood stream and 5 knots on the south-going ebb stream. When a strong (or gale-force) northerly or northeasterly opposes the flood current, a heavy breaking sea develops north of the passage. Similarly, a strong southerly or southwesterly wind on the ebb current gives rough conditions south of the passage, but the seas are not nearly as large. Mariners get little warning of these rough wave conditions when entering the passage from the other side, where relatively small seas are found. The passage is shallow in places and is subject to channelling and funnelling, especially with a northerly wind. High-water slack occurs 57 minutes before the time of high water at Saint John. Low-water slack occurs 1 hour 18 minutes before low water at Saint John.

WEYMOUTH HARBOUR

Rough, breaking seas are experienced for about 1/2 mile from the mouth of Weymouth Harbour when a northwesterly or westerly wind of 25 knots or more opposes the area's strong ebb current. This current is enhanced after heavy rainfall by outflow from the Sissiboo River.

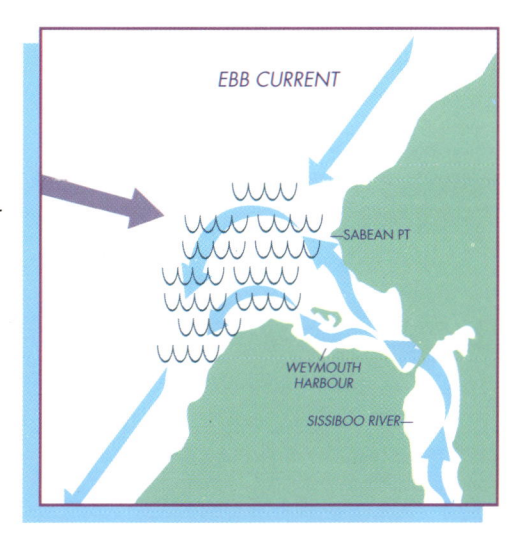

LOCAL WEATHER Atlantic Nova Scotia

Southwest Nova Scotia

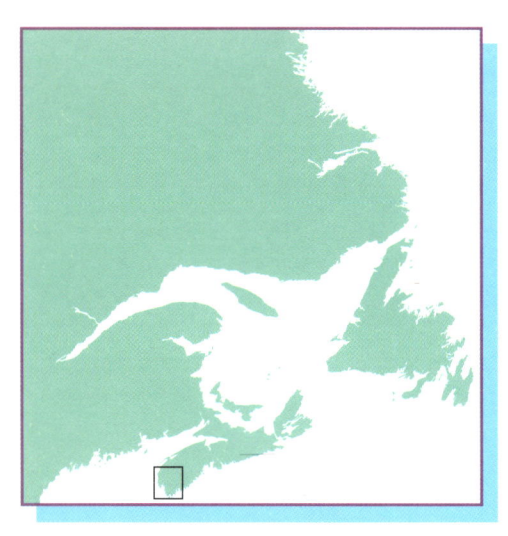

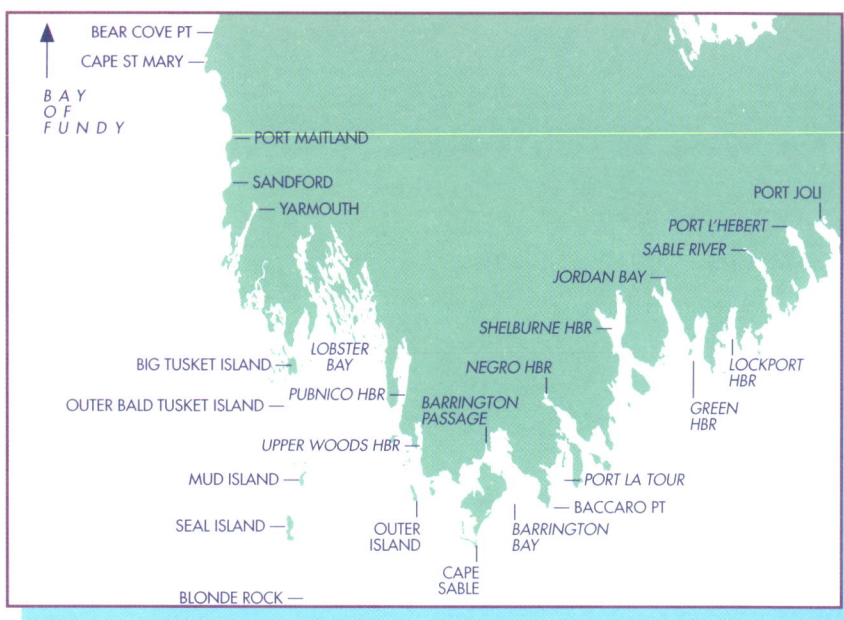

GENERAL CONDITIONS

From Cape St Marys to Cape Sable, strong tidal currents are common, due to the high tides in the Bay of Fundy. There are numerous shoals and islands off this stretch of coast and many associated tidal rips. The sea state deteriorates markedly when the tide runs against a strong or gale-force wind, and dangerous conditions can develop. Sea-surface temperatures along this coast are relatively cool in the warmer months due to the mixing action of the tides, so fog is very common. During winter, cold northwesterly outbreaks bring snow flurries and reduced visibility.

The bays along the coastline from Cape Sable to Port Joli generally have a north to south or north-northwest to south-southeast orientation and cut deeply inland. Many of them are exposed to southerly gales and protected from northeasterlies. Friction over land makes easterly sea winds back to northeasterlies across these bays. They increase in strength across the entrances due to coastal convergence and past the headlands, due to cornering. Within the bays, winds lose strength, due to sheltering by the land. The sea breeze along this coast is a southerly and sets more strongly into the various bays than over the headlands between them.

For easier reading, this coastline has been divided into two sections.

Did you know that in 1967, Yarmouth had its foggiest summer on record? The Yarmouth Weather Office reported fog on 85 of the 92 days of June, July, and August. Sea-surface temperatures along the coast of southwestern Nova Scotia are relatively cold during the warmer months, when the water is churned up by strong currents over the local shallows. This cold-water pool creates frequent, dense, and persistent fog.

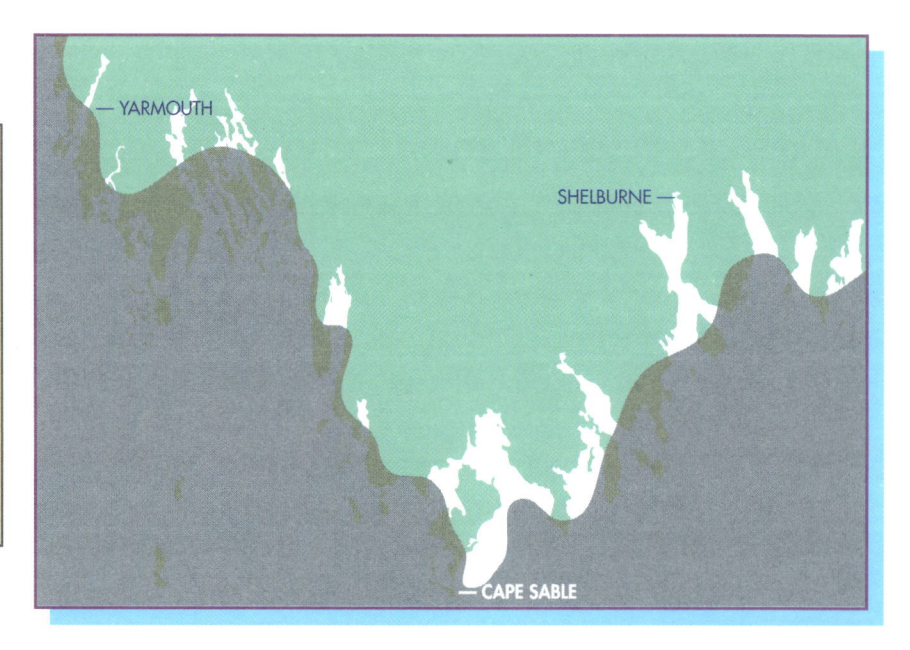

FOG ON A TYPICAL SUMMER'S DAY

This map shows where fog usually lies by early afternoon on a summer day that starts out foggy everywhere. Note that east of Cape Sable, the fog has retreated to the headlands, while west of the Cape, it remains farther inland.

LOCAL WEATHER Atlantic Nova Scotia

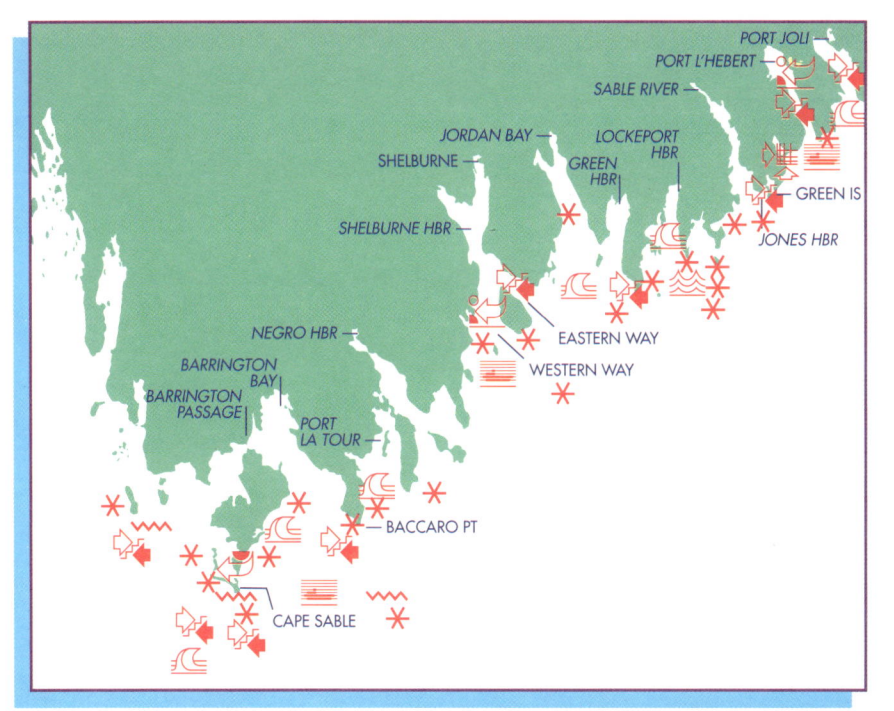

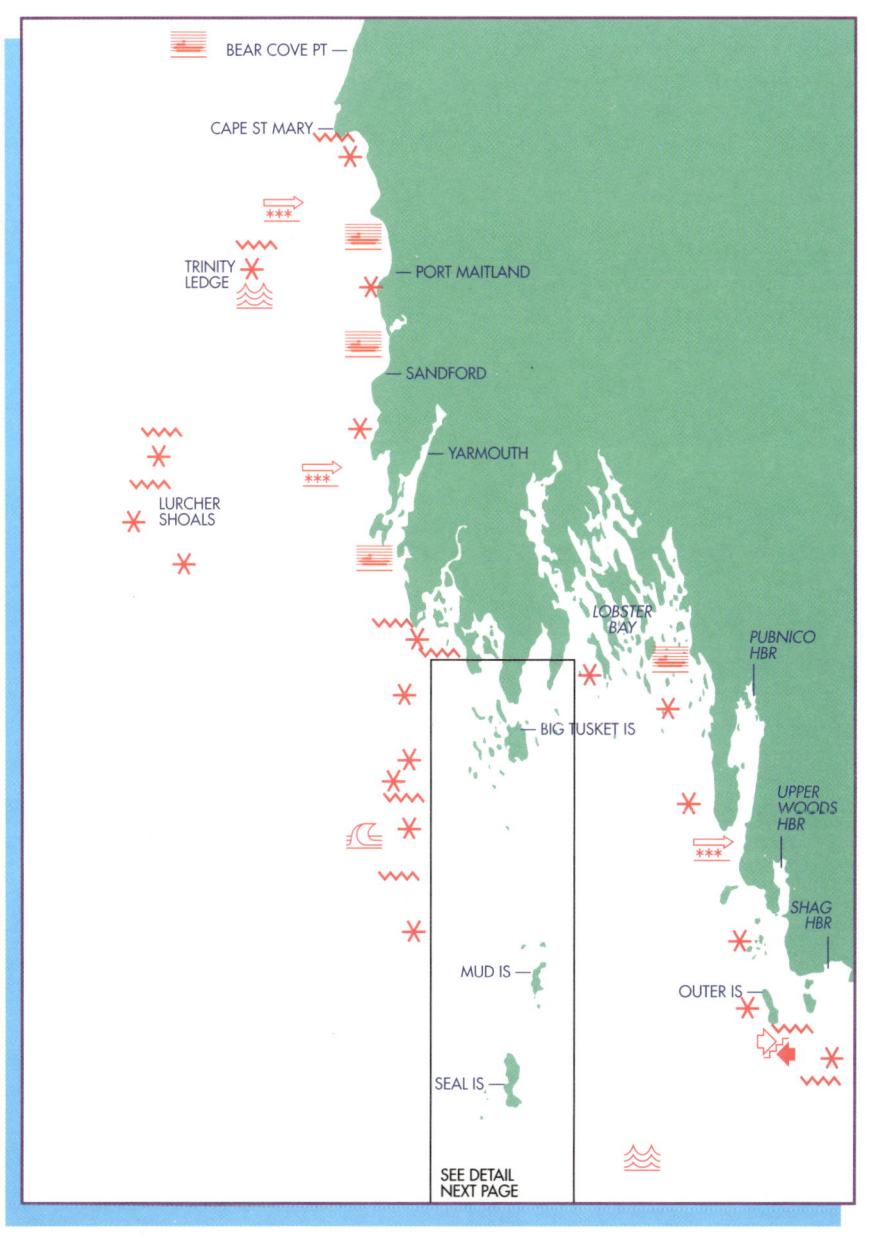

CAPE SABLE TO PORT JOLI

Gales from the south send large seas into several bays along this coast; notably, Barrington Bay, Port la Tour, Jordan Bay, Green Harbour, Lockeport Harbour (seas break across its entrance), and Port Joli. Choppy waves are reported to develop when strong winds oppose the ebb current in the Eastern Way to Shelburne Harbour, in the entrance to Port L'Hébert, and in Port Joli. Strong current—up to 5 knots—occur in the narrow entrance channel to Jones Harbour, just outside Sable River. This entrance is difficult to navigate when a southerly wind or swell opposes the ebb current. A heavy sea from the east or southeast causing crossing seas in the lee of Green Island.

Considerable shoaling occurs over the shallows around Cape Sable, which are exposed to swells from many directions. Strong tidal currents of up to 4 knots run south of this headland, along with heavy tidal rips. Very rough and dangerous conditions develop when these currents are opposed by strong or gale-force winds. A southeasterly gale on the ebb current is reported to be worse than a northwesterly gale on the flood current. Conditions are aggravated by crossing seas, due to ground swell or wind shifts. Extreme caution is essential in this area; the coastline is often foggy, and Cape Sable can present a poor radar image.

A heavy tidal rip is found over Trinity Ledge, and the waters in this area, are reportedly "always unsettled." The roughest conditions develop when strong winds or heavy swells from the southeast oppose the ebb tide—producing choppy, breaking waves.

BEAR COVE POINT TO SHAG HARBOUR

A series of islands and shoals extends south of the Yarmouth Peninsula for about 18 miles, to Seal Island and Blonde Rock (see details on next page).

Rough conditions similar to those farther down the coast at Cape Sable occur between 0.5–1.5 miles south of Bon Potage Island, in an area known as the Shag Harbour Rip.

LOCAL WEATHER Atlantic Nova Scotia

Marine Weather Tip: Wind Opposing Current

Tidal currents are strong everywhere along this coastline; even away from shallow water, wave conditions deteriorate when the current runs into a strong or gale-force wind. Fishermen seldom measure wind speed directly, but estimate it visually from the sea state. In this region, a northwest wind is said to increase on the flood tide; this local adage helps fishermen predict the deterioration in sea state that occurs when the wind opposes the current. Indeed, the relative wind over the bow of a ship does increase under these circumstances, because the current and the movement of the vessel—which usually motors with the current. The real wind, however, stays the same in comparison to a fixed reference point such as the land.

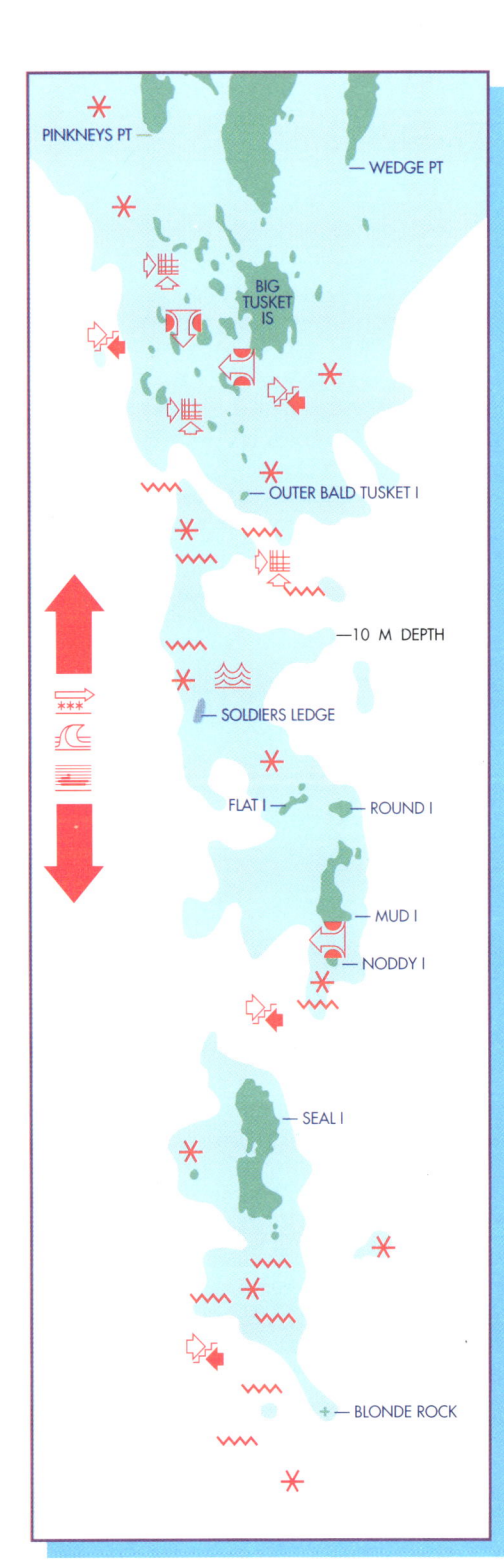

TUSKET ISLANDS

Strong currents flow between the Tusket Islands, creating many heavy tidal rips and eddies. Strong gap winds are also found here, because of the combined effects of channelling and funnelling. When these winds and currents are opposed, short, steep waves develop— particularly with a northwesterly wind against the flood stream. These conditions, and crossing seas, contribute to the unusual, confused, "square" wave patterns that have been reported in this area. Heavy tidal rips occur over several shoal patches, extending from Outer Bald Tusket Island to Soldiers Ledge.

SEAL ISLAND

The area from Flat Island to Blonde Rock is completely exposed to gales and swells, and is subject to considerable shoaling. Strong tidal currents flow here, running mostly southeastward (ebb stream) and northwestward (flood stream). Both these streams reach about 4 knots in the relatively deep channel between Noddy Island and Seal Island; they are also quite strong south of Seal Island, near Blonde Rock. The strong currents spawn several tidal rips in the area, and those west of Blonde Rock resemble breakers, even in fair weather. Wave conditions deteriorate everywhere when the wind opposes the current, notably between Mud Island and Noddy Island, between Noddy Island and Seal Island, and near Blonde Rock. Some unusual, steep, "square" standing waves have also been observed in these areas.

LOCAL WEATHER *Atlantic Nova Scotia*

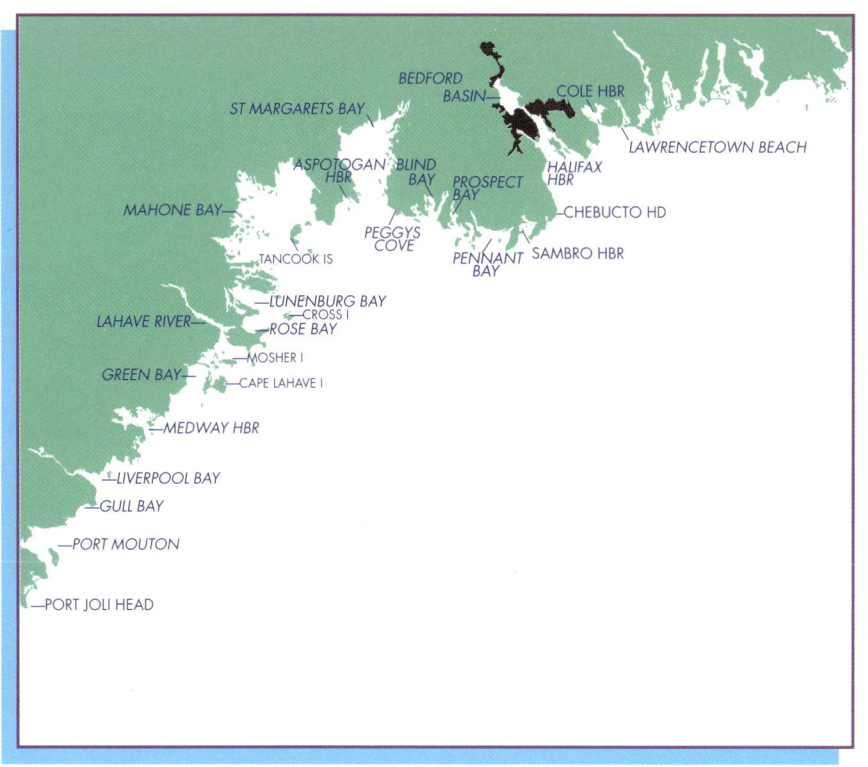

Southeast Nova Scotia

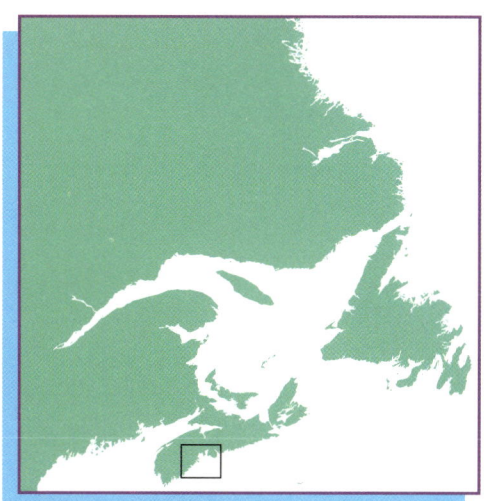

GENERAL CONDITIONS
This coast is affected by Atlantic swells, considerable fog, and south-southwesterly sea breezes. Except for some constricted entrances, tidal currents are weak and irregular and the general flow is towards the southwest.

For easier reading, this coastline has been divided into three sections.

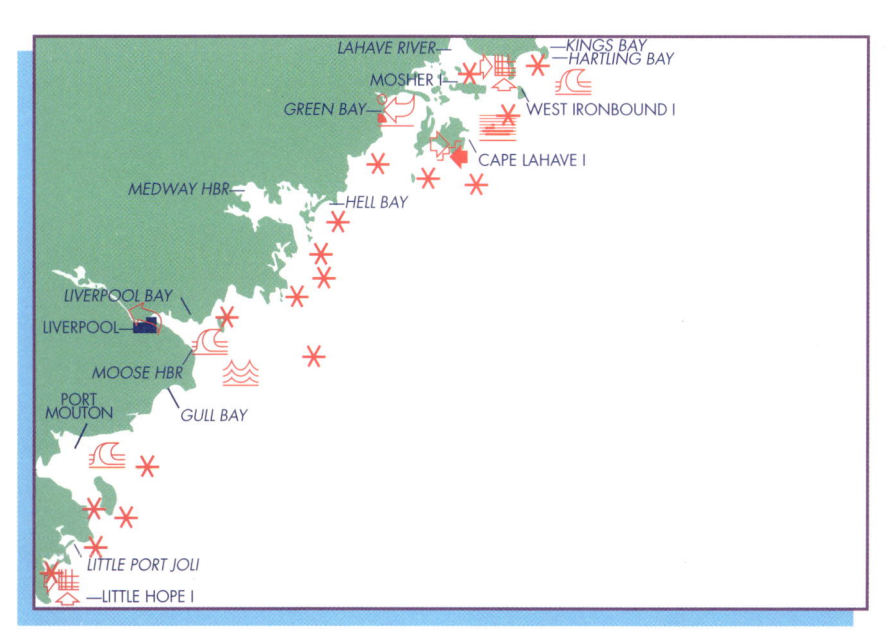

LITTLE HOPE ISLAND TO KINGS BAY
With onshore swells, crossing seas are found in the lee of Little Hope Island; these sea conditions worsen with an opposing wind and current between the island and mainland.

Winds in Liverpool Bay are often southeasterly or northwesterly, due to channelling. The bay is exposed to southeasterly gales, which send in large seas. With an onshore wind of 25 knots or more, the seas break right across the entrance of nearby Moose Harbour. Similarly, easterly gales send large seas into Port Mouton; these waves break across the entrance to Port Mouton Harbour, sometimes making it impossible for boats to enter or leave.

Medway Harbour and its entrance are lined with rocks and shoals. Breaking waves are common over the shoals just east of the harbour entrance and in nearby Hell Bay.

Kings Bay and Hartling Bay are entirely exposed to wind and swells from the southeast. These conditions create crossing seas in the lee of West Ironbound Island.

83

LOCAL WEATHER Atlantic Nova Scotia

LAHAVE RIVER TO SHAD BAY

Large seas are often found southeast of Cross Island, which lies in the approaches to Lunenburg Bay. Choppy seas often occur over the shallow water between Cross Island and East Point Island, especially when a southwesterly wind sets against an opposing current. The deeper passage between Rose Point and Cross Island is exposed to gales and seas from the southeast quadrant, and choppy conditions are often experienced around Rose Point.

The coastline changes its orientation west of Mahone Bay and St. Margarets Bay; these large bays lie well inland, which makes them subject to the strong, gusty, southwesterly winds that sometimes occur over land on summer afternoons because of increased instability from daytime heating. Summer thunderstorms develop over interior southwestern Nova Scotia and often track east-northeastward. Usually they pass well inland, but sometimes they move across the bays bringing hail, lightning, and heavy squalls.

Mahone Bay, in contrast to neighbouring St. Margarets Bay, is relatively shallow, and the islands and shoals across its entrance tend to buffer the waves. The tidal currents between the Tancook Islands, and between Little Tancook Island and the mainland, are strong enough to give choppy seas when opposed by strong winds. Nearby Dares Point is known to be a windy headland. Fog in Mahone Bay tends to burn off to seaward of the Tancook Islands, especially with a southwesterly wind.

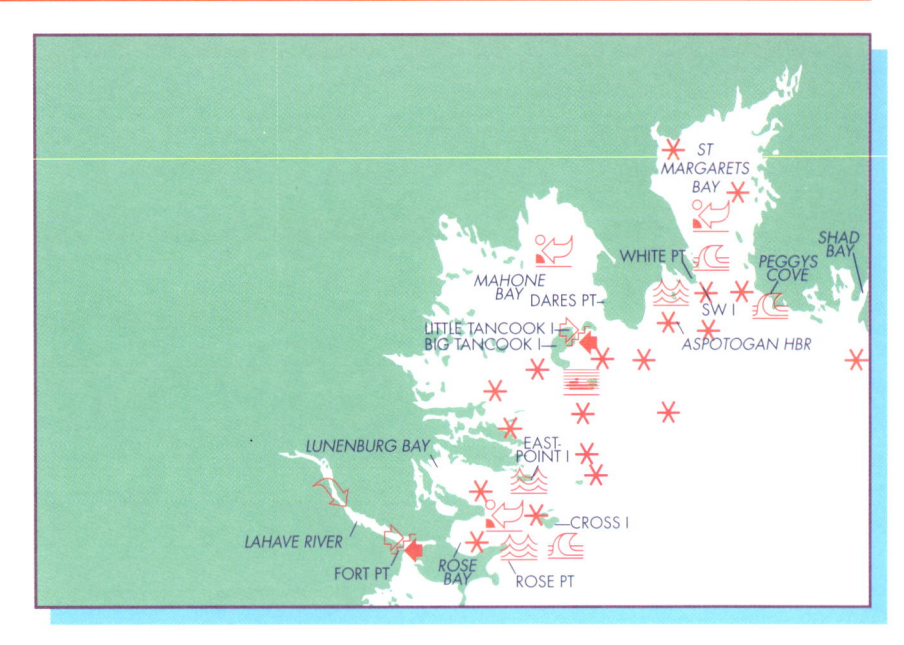

Large seas from the south affect Peggys Cove and can move into the relatively deep St. Margarets Bay. Under such conditions, considerable breaking waves can make the eastern shore of this bay a rugged and dangerous place. With a southerly wind or swell, choppy seas, due to backwash, occur just south of White Point on the Aspotogan Peninsula; shoaling causes choppy seas between White Point and Southwest Island. Sea breezes in St. Margarets Bay often blow at right angles to the shore in the late morning; by early afternoon, the sea breeze drops off then picks up again from the southwest in the late afternoon.

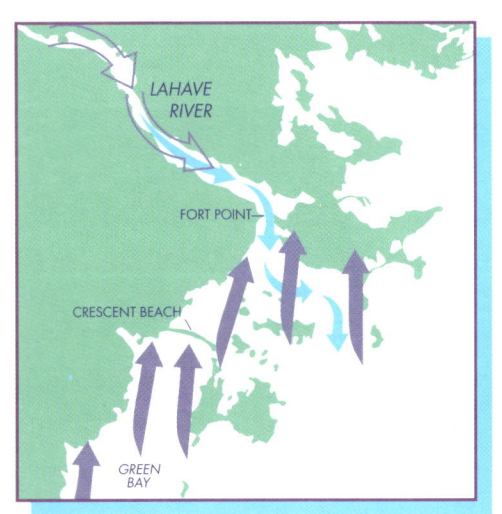

LAHAVE RIVER

A strong south-southwesterly sea breeze blows over Green Bay and Crescent Beach and into the approaches to the Lahave River. When sailing up this long river—which is subject to some channelling—this cool wind can become light and turn into warm and gusty west-northwesterlies farther up the river. The current in the narrow entrance to the river near Fort Point can reach 3–4 knots, and choppy seas occur there with an opposing southerly wind. Although fog is common in the area during the spring and summer, it usually burns off over the Lahave River during the day.

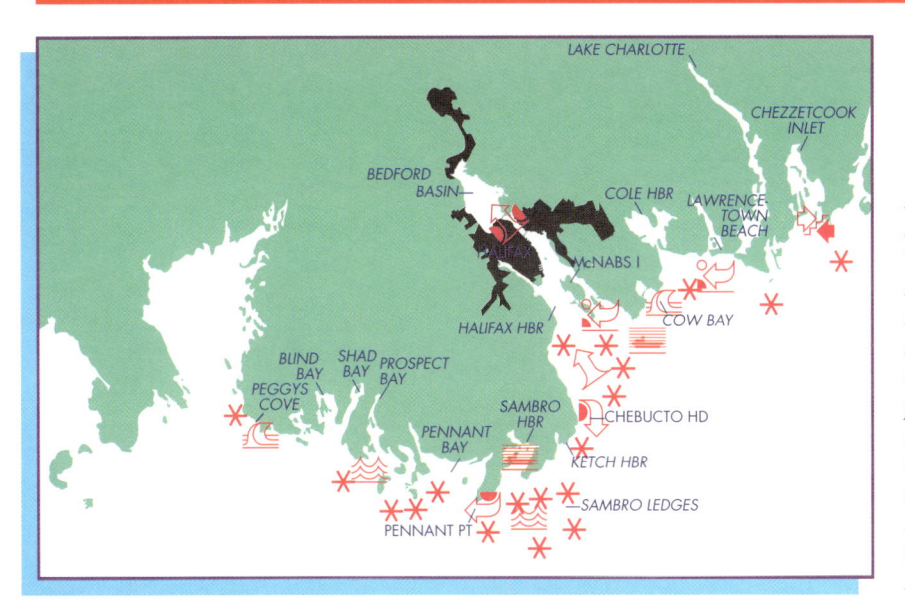

LOCAL WEATHER Atlantic Nova Scotia

Marine Weather Tip: Sea Breeze With Fog

The sea breeze at Halifax and over the Sambro Peninsula starts as a southerly and tends to veer more southwesterly through the afternoon. Fog sometimes burns completely clear of the headlands but can be seen lingering offshore and over the Sambro Ledges. When the sea breeze sets in during the afternoon, fog often returns to Sambro Harbour and Ketch Harbour, then moves across the approaches of Halifax Harbour.

HALIFAX HARBOUR AND VICINITY

Shoaling is a significant problem over the foggy Sambro Ledges. Choppy seas often occur over the deeper waters there, particularly after a wind shift. Cornering contributes to the strong winds often found off Chebucto Head and Pennant Point. In winter, when snow is falling in Halifax, easterly winds from the relatively warm ocean can modify temperatures enough to change the precipitation to rain over the southern sections of Sambro Peninsula.

A strong sea breeze of 20–25 knots blows at Lawrencetown Beach, due to the local topography and to the marshy flats inland. This cool breeze is a delight for windsurfers, but less popular with sunbathers. Large seas also come ashore here and farther west, at Cow Bay.

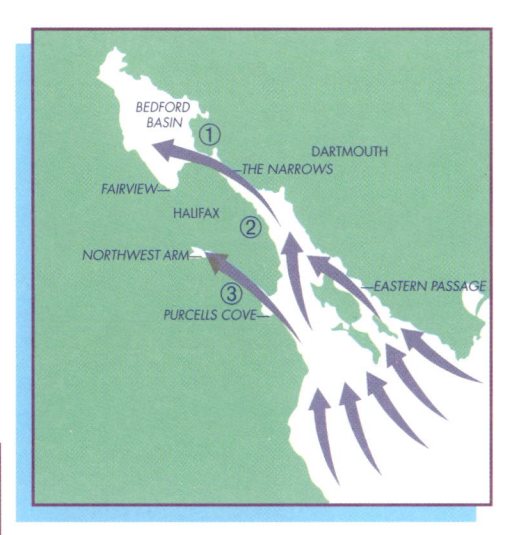

HALIFAX HARBOUR

Southeasterly winds are funnelled somewhat in Halifax Harbour and blow strongly through the Narrows and into Bedford Basin. Southeasterlies are also channelled strongly into the Northwest Arm.

Other points of interest:

1. Northwesterly winds are gusty at the head of Bedford Basin and are funnelled from Bedford Basin into the Narrows.
2. When sailing close to the Halifax water front, yachters may experience strong gusts with westerly winds; this is due to wind channelling down some of the downtown streets.
3. Channelling is very noticeable with a southwesterly wind from the land at Purcells Cove and, to a lesser extent, near Fairview.

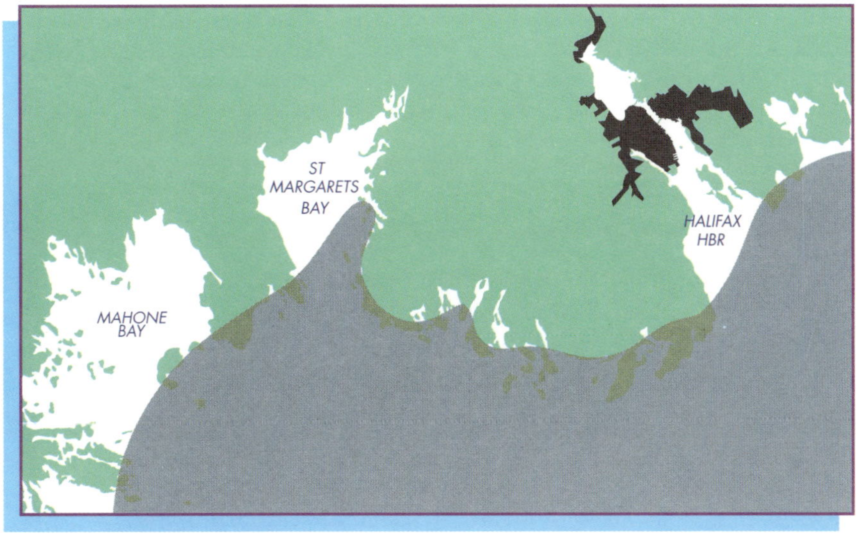

RETREAT OF THE FOG

This illustration shows the areas where fog usually retreats by early afternoon on a summer day that begins foggy over land and sea.

LOCAL WEATHER Atlantic Nova Scotia

Eastern Shore

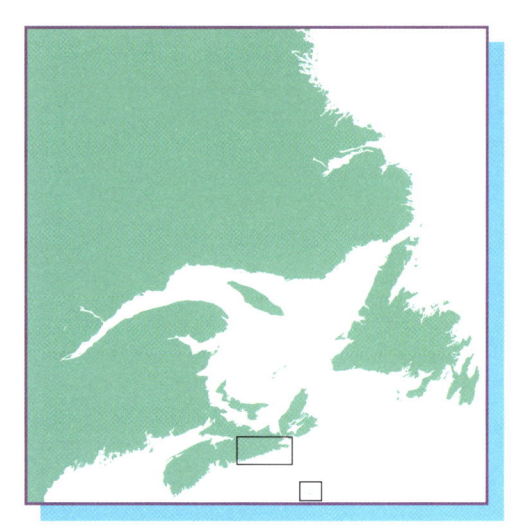

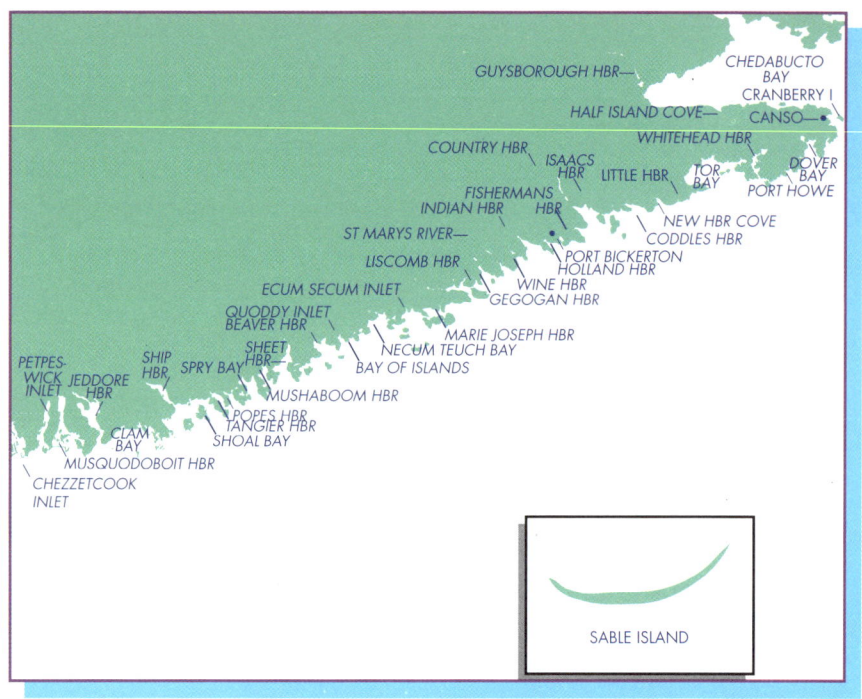

GENERAL CONDITIONS

This stretch of coastline has many interesting, and often challenging, wind effects. An east-to-northeast wind is generally boosted along the coast due to coastal convergence; however, in the bays and inlets the frictional effects of the land reduce the winds markedly. The diminishing effect of coastal divergence should be seen in southwesterly winds—but there is an exception. In summer southwest winds prevail, and sunny afternoons create unstable conditions over the land. The unstable land winds (which become more westerly) converge with offshore southwesterlies in a zone of strong to gale-force west-southwesterlies along the coast.

Nova Scotia's Eastern Shore—especially sections southwestward from Liscomb Harbour—is fringed with islands, rocks, and shoals that shelter many harbours and coves from the full force of Atlantic swells.

The southern sections of Chedabucto Bay contain few outlying shoals. The bay is open to easterly gales that bring large waves ashore. Since southerly winds blow offshore, the southern shores of the bay are relatively clear of fog, especially during the afternoon. This shoreline is affected by flurries in a northwesterly airflow.

Fog is common in the late spring and summer along this coast, and it is often dense and persistent.

Persistent east and northeast gale or storm-force winds can bring storm-surge conditions to this coastline.

The sea breeze generally starts as a southerly, then tends to veer more southwesterly by mid-afternoon. Because harbours and inlets along this coast are generally oriented northwest to southeast, the sea breeze blows across the entrances to the harbours, and by afternoon the fog often retreats to that point, moving back into the harbours at night.

Tidal currents along this shoreline are irregular and weak. Except in a few restricted entrances, the strongest currents flow towards the southwest; choppy conditions can develop offshore when these currents are opposed by a southwesterly wind—especially after a wind shift from the northeast.

For easier reading, this coastline has been divided into two sections. A separate section deals with Sable Island.

Caution: Stay Offshore

Mariners plying this coast are advised to stay well offshore. Indeed, Sailing Directions recommends that vessels stick to at least the 40-fathom line between Cape Canso and Halifax.

CHEZZETCOOK INLET TO ECUM SECUM

This coastline is strewn with islands, rocks and shoals; steep, breaking seas can develop several miles from the mainland. Large seas sometimes occur between the islands in the approaches to Shoal Bay, Spry Bay, and Necum Teuch Bay, but, most mainland harbours and coves are quite sheltered.

Strong tidal currents of 2–3 knots flow through the narrow entrances to Chezzetcook Inlet, Petpeswick Inlet and Musquodoboit Harbour. Heavy rains and melting snow can increase the rate of the ebb flow to 4 knots or more. These inlets are shallow, and breaking waves are found at their entrances

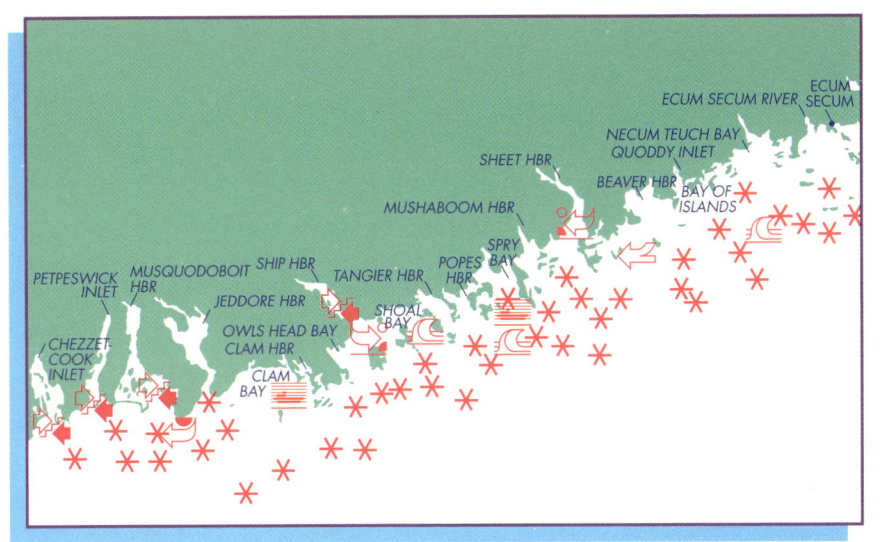

LOCAL WEATHER *Atlantic Nova Scotia*

during strong or gale-force southerlies—especially when these winds oppose the ebb current.

The normal tidal currents in the entrance to Ship Harbour are modest, but the ebb current is greatly increased after heavy rainfall or snow melt. Under these conditions, choppy seas are experienced when the current is opposed by a southeasterly wind.

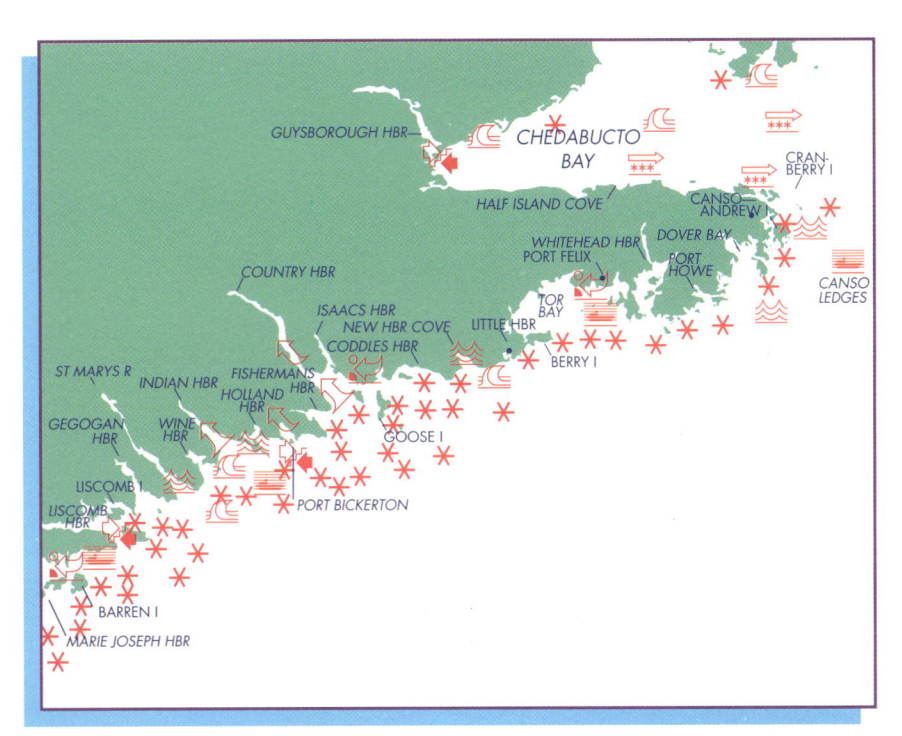

many islands and shoals, which buffer the sea. This fine harbour is 13 miles long, and the shores are steep on both sides, rising from 200 ft. near the entrance to over 400 ft. near its head. Channelling occurs here, and the harbour is subject to funnelling with a southeasterly wind.

Marine Weather Tip: Wind Shift

When sailing up Country Harbour in summer, yachters will find that a cool southwesterly sea breeze at the harbour entrance often turns into a warm northwesterly headwind en route.

Large waves come ashore along the coast from New Harbour Cove to Little Harbour. These seas break right across the entrance to Little Harbour, and backwash causes them to become choppy off the east side of New Harbour Cove.

Tor Bay is largely protected by a series of islands and shoals across its entrance, upon which the sea breaks heavily. The southwesterly sea breeze is stronger over the eastern sections of the bay, where it can raise some chop and whitecaps, and contribute to often persistent fog in the area.

The currents in the narrow entrance to Guysborough Harbour are strong, especially after a heavy rainfall. The shallow outer sandbar at the harbour entrance is often impassable due to heavy breakers—particularly when easterly winds and swells oppose the ebb current, which can reach 4–5 knots.

MARIE JOSEPH HARBOUR TO CHEDABUCTO BAY

Strong southwesterly gusts have been reported on summer afternoons in the lee of Liscomb and Barren islands, when only moderate local winds prevailed elsewhere. These gusts are likely due to the significant size of the islands and are a result of daytime heating of the land.

Strong tidal currents run south of Liscomb Island in the deep-water channel to Liscomb Harbour. Very rough conditions develop there when a strong or gale force southeasterly opposes the ebb current.

The entrances to St. Marys River, Wine Harbour, and Indian Harbour Bay are not protected by offshore shoals and are thus fully exposed to Atlantic swells. The eastern shore of Indian Cove deepens rapidly, and backwash produces choppy seas within a quarter-mile of the coast. The shallow heads of these bays become a mass of breakers during southeasterly gales. In the entrance to the St. Marys River, this condition is aggravated by a strong outflow current, especially after a heavy rainfall.

Country Harbour is protected by

LOCAL WEATHER *Atlantic Nova Scotia*

RETREAT OF THE FOG
Fog is mainly associated with southerly winds and often burns off the land during the morning; retreating to the coast. This map shows where the fog typically lies by early afternoon on a summer day that starts foggy inland. Note that the inner reaches of the bays and inlets are clear of fog.

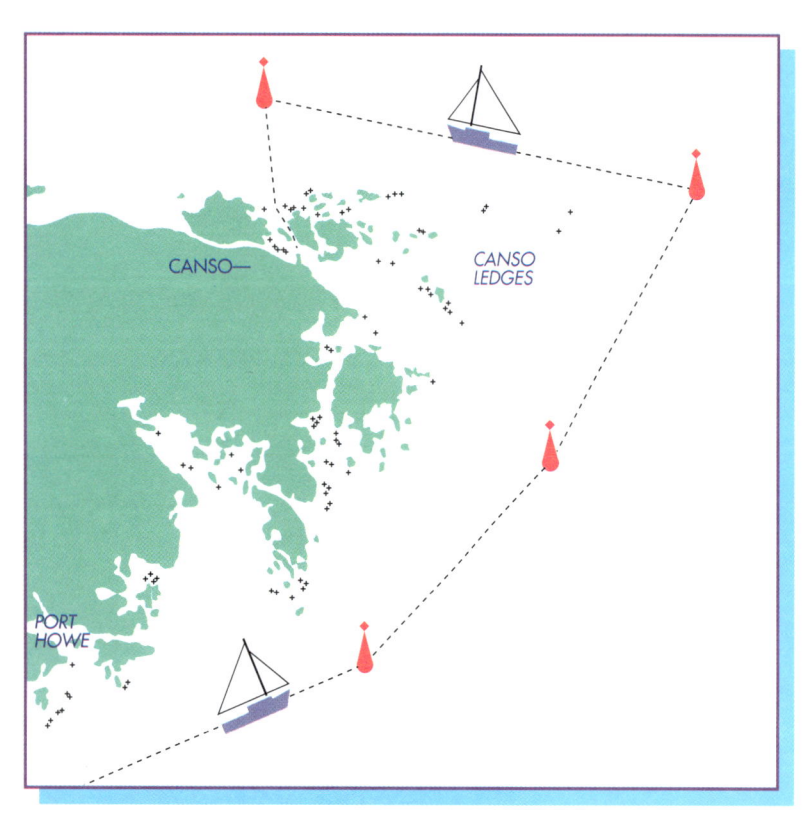

PORT HOWE–CANSO
When sailing from the southwest, there are many hazards along the island routes between Port Howe and Canso. This area, as well as the Canso Ledges, is often foggy—and the irregular shallows there can cause confused, steep waves. If fog prevails, or if the seas are heavy from the south, experienced yachters recommend staying outside the fairway buoys and entering Canso from the northwest.

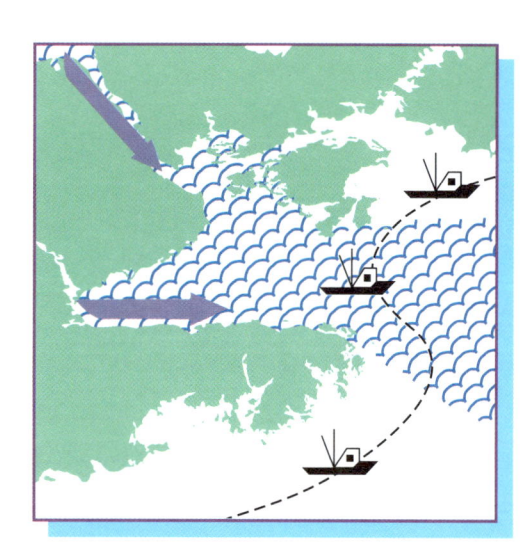

CHEDABUCTO BAY
Mariners travelling close to this coastline during a west or northwesterly blow may experience a significant deterioration in the weather when passing the exposed waters of Chedabucto Bay. Winds there are stronger and seas higher than along the coast—4 m seas have been reported with storm-force winds. Snowsqualls may severely reduce visibility, and freezing spray may be encountered, even when these conditions are absent elsewhere along the route

LOCAL WEATHER Atlantic Nova Scotia

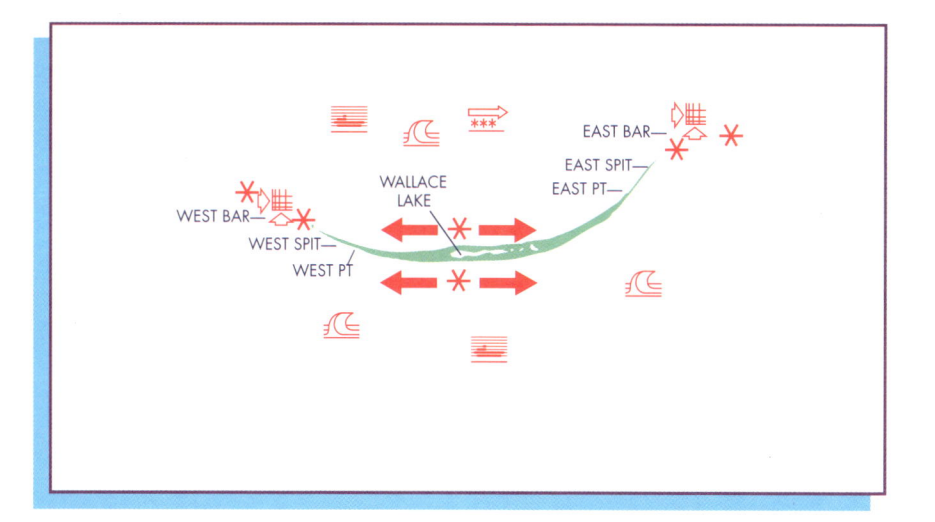

SABLE ISLAND

Sable Island is a restricted, dangerous area. Except for emergencies, no boat may land there without the permission of the Canadian Coast Guard. From time to time, vessels shelter from gales in the lee of the island; for that reason, some local weather information is presented below.

Sable Island is completely exposed to the full force of the Atlantic and is affected by gales and large seas from all directions. The island's beaches and sand bars are known to shift occasionally. Depths of less than 33 ft., on which the sea breaks heavily, extend about 8 miles northeast of East Spit and about 5 miles west-northwest of West Spit. The waters off the north coast of the island shoal seaward in a regular pattern, and sandy ridges run parallel to the coast, and close to shore. The sea breaks heavily on these ridges, and during strong northerly winds, organized rows of breakers, often in continuous lines, occur within about 1/4 mile of the shore.

Waters deepen more slowly off the south coast of the island, and depths vary irregularly. During strong southerly winds, breakers lie within about 1 mile of the shore, but these are generally disorganized. Crossing seas, due to the shoaling effect of the bars, occur within 1 mile of East and West spits, particularly when the wind blows parallel to the island.

Sable Island is very foggy, especially in spring and summer. During June and July, fog prevails about one-third of the time, and it has been known to persist for nearly a week without clearing. During periods of fog, which can persist even in high winds, visibility is slightly better to the lee of the island.

On those rare occasions when the wind is nearly calm, sudden temperature changes can occur. In summer, the island can heat up by 5°C in one hour, causing light sea breezes of 5 knots. Cumulus clouds may then develop, but dissipate as they drift seaward. At night, under clear skies and calm winds, temperatures sometimes fall at this same rate, and radiation fog forms, but it is seldom more than 20 ft. thick and it breaks up as it drifts seaward on the slightest breeze.

During very cold outbreaks in winter, freezing spray and snow streamers forming off the coast of Nova Scotia can affect the area.

Caution: Open Sea Conditions
Vessels near Sable Island should pay close attention to the weather forecast since rapid weather changes can occur there, and wind shifts can quickly change a sheltered coast into an exposed one. Add to that the complexities of many coastal effects and the conditions can be very dangerous!

LOCAL WEATHER Cape Breton

Cape Breton East

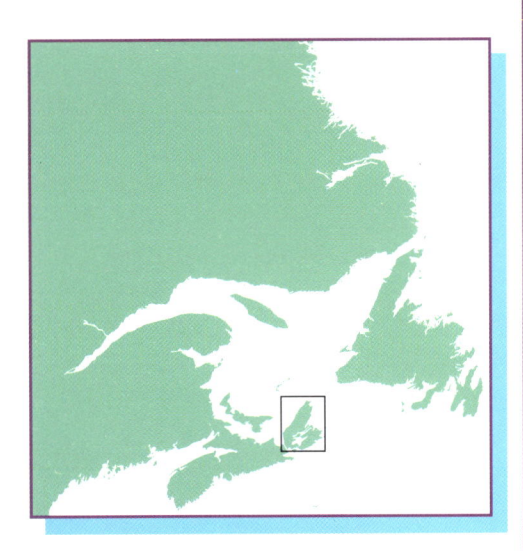

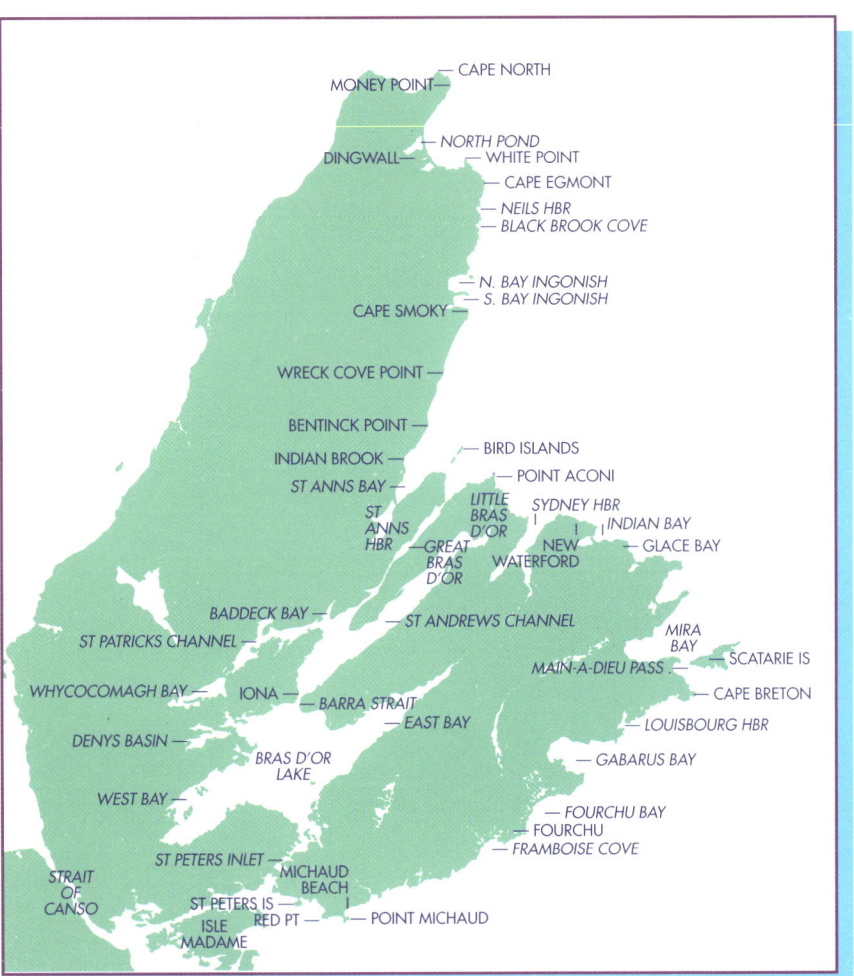

GENERAL CONDITIONS

Local weather in this area is as varied as the shoreline itself. Mountainous terrain and deep coastal waters characterize the north, while there are gentle hills and shallow bays in the south.

For easier reading, this coastline has been divided into four sections.

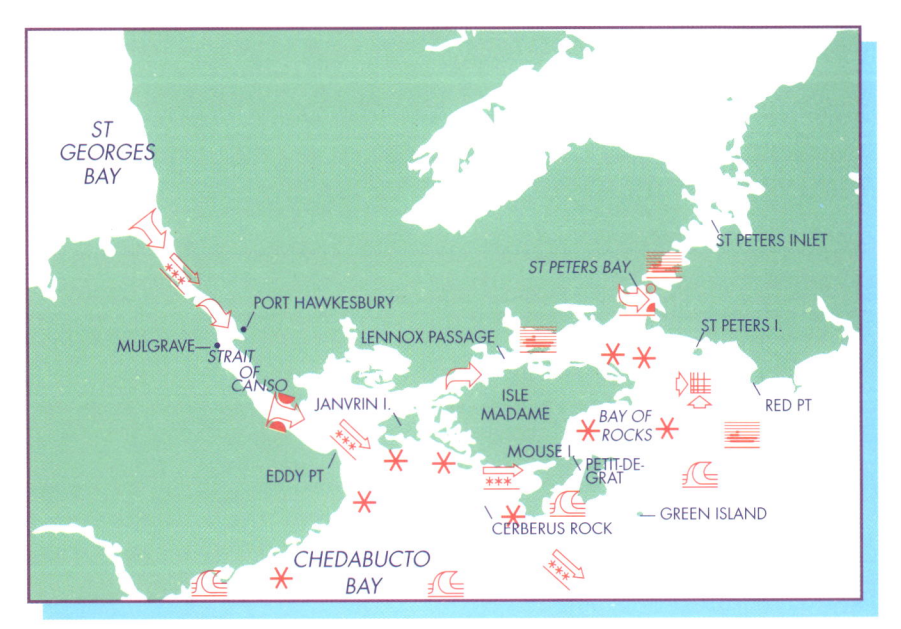

STRAIT OF CANSO TO POINT MICHAUD

Channelling and funnelling occur in the Strait of Canso with both a northwesterly and a southeasterly. This effect is enhanced with a northwesterly, when a gap wind blowing out of the strait may be felt over the northern sections of Chedabucto Bay, as far east as Cerberus Rock. In late fall and winter, snow streamers can accompany these northwesterlies until St. Georges Bay freezes over. The resulting flurries affect the Strait of Canso, Janvrin Island, and southern sections of Isle Madame to Green Island. On the south shore of Chedabucto Bay, these flurries can affect the coast from Half Island Cove eastward to Cranberry Island.

Lennox Passage separates Isle Madame from Cape Breton Island. The passage is full of shoals, and currents can be strong. Southerly sea breezes affect the area, and on fine summer days, when mariners are en route from the passage into the Strait of Canso, they will notice that a southerly wind on the beam often turns into a northwesterly headwind.

Large seas from the Atlantic affect the southeast coast of Isle Madame. In strong southerly winds, the sea usually breaks across the entrance to Petit-de-Grat Harbour, near Mouse Island.

LOCAL WEATHER Cape Breton

POINT MICHAUD TO LOUISBOURG

This coastline, which dips gradually down below the Atlantic, is characterized by shallow, rocky, and exposed bays—such as Framboise Cove and Fourchu Bay. Most sections of this coast are exposed to the full brunt of Atlantic swells, and shoaling effects are common.

Fog, which is usually associated with southerly winds, is a major problem; in late spring and early summer, fog is frequent, dense, and persistent. Sea breezes along this coastline are southerly, and average 15–20 knots. Coastal convergence can accompany a northeasterly wind.

Gabarus Bay is open to bad weather from the east and southeast. Its north shore is steep, with cliffs rising abruptly to 200 ft.; some backwash occurs in these seas.

The entrance to the fine, historic harbour of Louisbourg is well protected by islands and shoals, upon which the sea breaks heavily. The sea breeze blows the length of the harbour and can be as strong as 25 knots, giving some chop and whitecaps towards the village end.

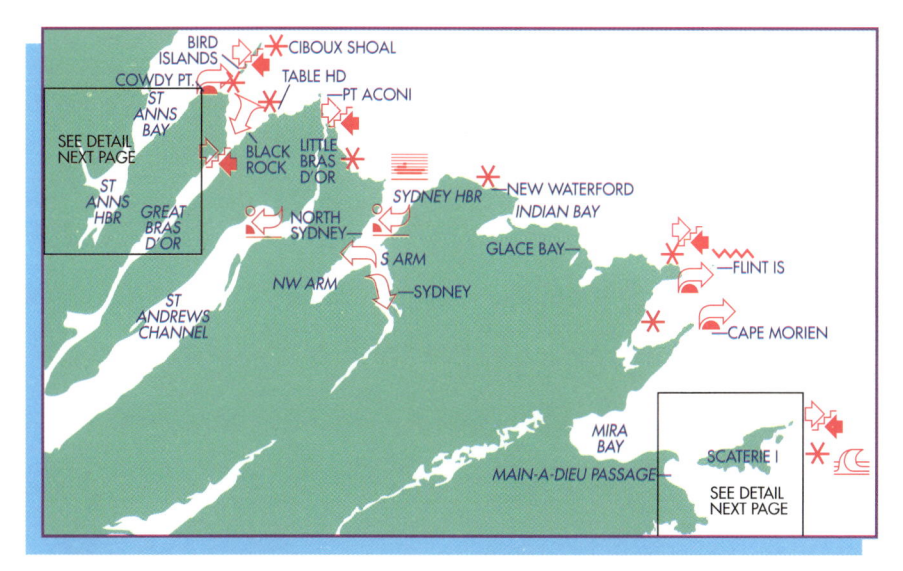

SCATARIE ISLAND TO ST. ANNS BAY

The character of the coast changes considerably along this shoreline, as mountains in the northwest give way to moderate elevations in the southeast. The coast is exposed to gales from the northeast quadrant, which send heavy seas into Mira Bay, Morien Bay, Glace Bay, and Indian Bay. Morien Bay becomes particularly rough, since it has a large area of shallow water at its head. Cornering is experienced with a westerly wind off Cape Morien and Wreck Cove. Northeasterly sea breezes, averaging 15 knots, develop on this coast. These breezes are stronger in the various channel entrances and can be accompanied by fog.

In Sydney Harbour, a northeasterly wind is channelled into the North West Arm and the South Arm. Conversely, channelled winds blowing seaward through the two arms converge in the harbour. The sea breeze here is a northeasterly of 15–20 knots. In late spring and early summer, this cold wind is sometimes accompanied by fog; in winter and spring, northeasterly winds can bring ice into Sydney Harbour.

Currents flowing from the Great Bras d'Or channel can be felt as far seaward as Table Head, and turbulent, chaotic seas are experienced with an opposing wind. The entrance to the Little Bras d'Or is closed by breakers when there is a heavy sea, especially when the strong tidal stream sets against an onshore wind. The Bird Islands consist of Hertford Island and Ciboux Island. Strong currents flow between the two islands and over Ciboux Shoal, and choppy seas develop there with an opposing wind.

LOCAL WEATHER Cape Breton

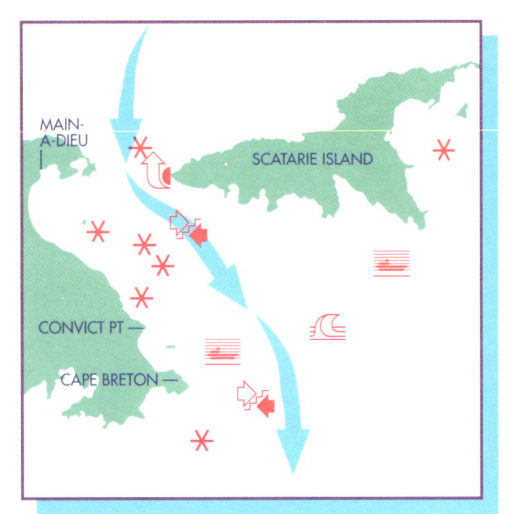

MAIN-A-DIEU PASSAGE
This passage is complicated by several shoals, especially on the western side where, even in fair weather, white water can often be seen. This is a dangerous place in bad weather. Strong currents flow here, and the passage is exposed to gales and swell from the southeast. In addition, the area is often shrouded in fog.

ST ANNS BAY AND HARBOUR
This wedge-shaped bay lies between Kelly Mountain to the east and Murray Mountain to the west. Winds prevail from the southwest or northeast, due to channelling. Northeasterlies are also funnelled and can be violent. It is common to find southwesterlies inside the harbour when southeasterlies blow over the open water beyond the approaches to the bay.

Sea breezes are northeasterly and can be as strong as 25 knots; although they raise some chop and give whitecaps, they produce little sea. Cornering is experienced off Cowdy Point with a southwesterly.

Strong tidal currents run through the narrow entrance to the harbour where the Englishtown ferry crosses. The normal tidal current here has a maximum strength of 4 knots, but the seaward current can be considerably stronger after heavy rainfall and during the spring freshet. When a northeasterly wind opposes a seaward current, rough conditions may be found near the ferry crossing and $3/4$ of a mile seaward of it.

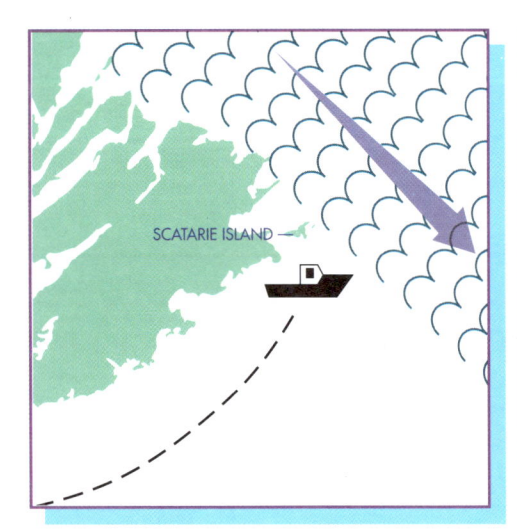

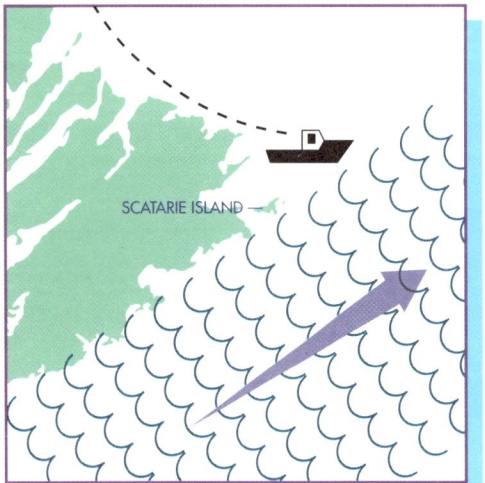

SCATARIE ISLAND
A change in weather is often experienced in the waters east of Scatarie Island. The mariner coming from the southwest is exposed at this point to gales and swells that may be running from the north and northwest. A mariner approaching from the northwest is exposed to bad weather from the south and southwest.

LOCAL WEATHER Cape Breton

INDIAN BROOK TO CAPE NORTH

This dramatic and mountainous coastline is free of outlying shoals, except near the Bird Islands. Peaks just inland reach elevations of more than 1,400 ft. which greatly influences winds near the coast. Strong winds, enhanced by mountain-wave effects, can occur after a cold front passes, producing violent gusts in areas such as North Bay Ingonish and South Bay Ingonish. During summer evenings, katabatic winds can flow from the river valleys leading into Ingonish Harbour, South Pond Dingwall, and North Pond Dingwall. These are generally only light breezes, but in Ingonish Harbour they can be strong enough to raise whitecaps.

This coast is exposed to gales from the east, which send heavy seas into the Ingonish bays and Aspy Bay often preventing entry into Dingwall Harbour. Cornering causes northwesterly winds to be particularly strong off the steep headlands of Cape North, Money Point, Cape Egmont, and Cape Smokey. Choppy seas occur off steeper sections of this coastline due to backwash, particularly when the waves hit at an angle to the cliffs. Flurries over the western highlands in a northwesterly airflow can spill over North Mountain into Aspy Bay and Cape Egmont; however, they seldom reach Neils Harbour. This mountainous coastline is generally not influenced by strong sea breezes.

Caution: Lee Effects

In a northwesterly airflow, wind eddies often form in the lee of steep cliffs, from Money Point to just south of Blue Point. Under such conditions, small waves and moderate, gusty, southeasterly winds may be expected within 1/2 mile of shore. Beyond that point, the winds become strong, gusty, and northwesterly, and waves begin to build.

LOCAL WEATHER Cape Breton

The Bras D'or Lakes

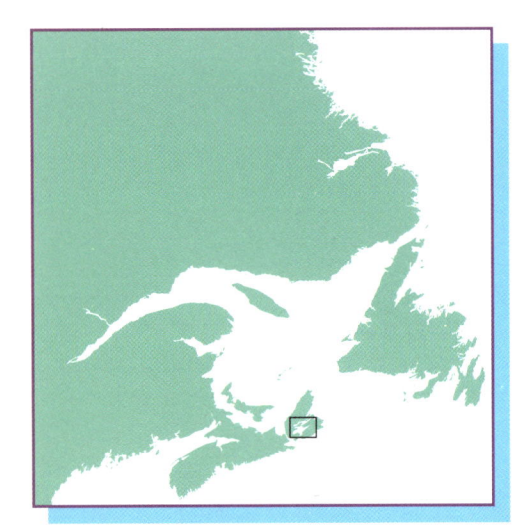

GENERAL CONDITIONS

This section is written with the yachter in mind.

The Bras d'Or Lakes consist of two enclosed bodies of water, known locally as the "small lake" (Great Bras d'Or Lake)—to the north of Iona—and the "large lake" (Bras d'Or Lake), to the south. The small lake consists of three major channels, with a southwest-northeast orientation. The surrounding mountains and hills influence the wind patterns on the water, frequently causing channelling and funnelling, and sometimes setting up mountain waves.

The lakes are considerably less salty than the surrounding ocean waters, due to the influx of fresh water from many streams. The tidal range is small, but there are strong tidal currents in the constricted passages leading to the sea and in the Barra Strait. These currents, and the water levels within the lakes, are affected by rainfall, snow melt, and strong winds.

The weather on the lakes is greatly influenced by the water temperature and the surrounding topography. In summer, the prevailing wind is southwesterly at 10–15 knots; gusts to 25 knots often develop in the afternoon, but die out by early evening. Warm water temperatures in summer inhibit fog formation, but early-morning radiation fog develops occasionally in coves and along the shoreline, dissipating shortly after sunrise. Mountainous terrain generally protects the area from sea fog, except for the Great Bras d'Or and the St. Peters areas. Summer sea breezes can bring fog partway up the channels. Thunderstorms and showers occur more frequently over the Bras d'Or Lakes than at Sydney, likely because of warm water temperatures and local topography.

Ice forms on the Bras d'Or Lakes early in January and lasts until late March or early April. Sea ice often fills the Great Bras d'Or channel as far south as Seal Island.

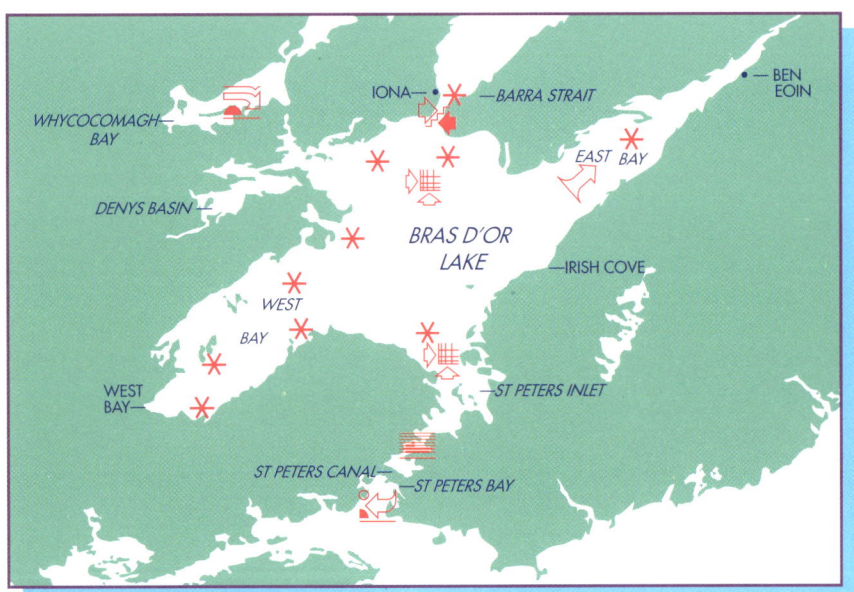

BRAS D'OR LAKE

Bras d'Or Lake is entered from the north through Barra Strait. Normal tidal currents there have a maximum flow of about 3 knots; when these are opposed by high winds, large irregular waves develop. All yacht races are stopped and restarted on either side of the train bridge here, and auxiliary power is recommended when passing through the strait.

The larger reaches of Bras d'Or Lake allow for considerable sea formation during high winds; short, steep waves may develop over the shallower waters. Gale-force northwesterly winds can bring large waves to the southern shores during the fall and early winter. Crossing seas, often breaking, occur where wave trains leaving the various bays and inlets intersect. Smaller crossing seas have been reported to the lee of some islands in West Bay. The narrow, steep-sided St. Peters Canal—the southern entry point to this lake—is sheltered from all wind directions except southwesterly and northeasterly. South-to-southwesterly sea breezes from the Atlantic affect St. Peters inlet and are often accompanied by fog.

LOCAL WEATHER Cape Breton

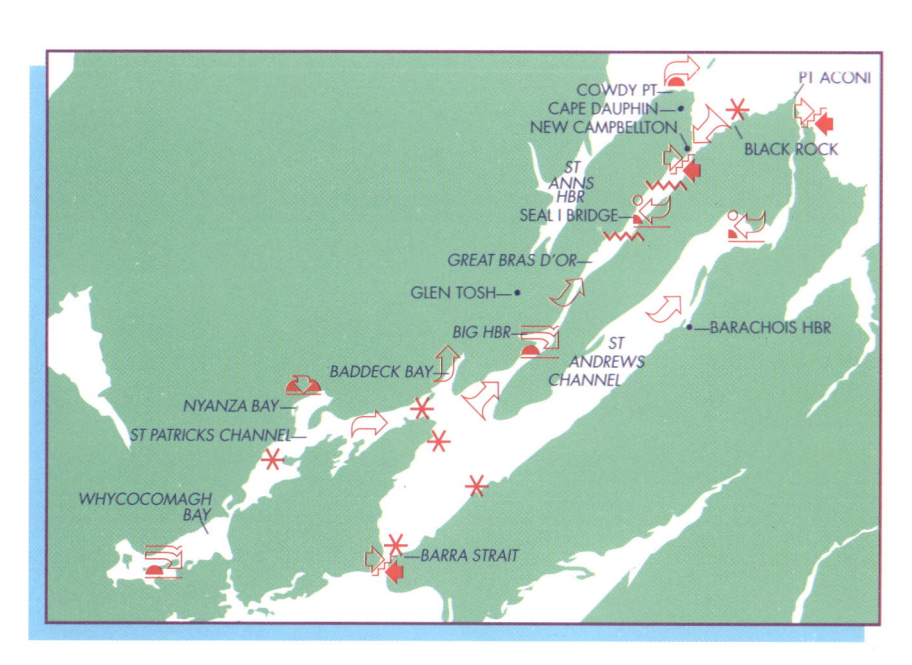

GREAT BRAS D'OR LAKE

The Great Bras d'Or channel is the main passage into the lakes from the north. It is narrow and surrounded by high ground; the predominant winds are southwest or northeast. Winds are funnelled somewhat at both entrances to the channel. Normal tidal currents in the narrows near New Campbellton are 4–5 knots, and runoff is reported to increase the seaward current to as much as 8 knots. These strong currents cause tidal rips and eddies, particularly near the narrows and seaward to Black Rock. Steep, choppy seas can be hazardous in this area when the wind opposes the current.

On fine summer afternoons, a northeasterly sea breeze of 20–25 knots often blows into the Bras d'Or channel. These breezes are strongest over the northeastern sections, up to Seal Island Bridge, but sometimes reach Big Harbour, where they become noticeably weaker. These winds are cold and sometimes bring fog up to Seal Island Bridge.

Channelling also occur to a lesser degree in St. Andrews Channel and St. Patricks Channel. St. Andrews Channel experiences some sea formation and shoaling in bad weather. Violent westerly and northwesterly winds can develop in the farther reaches of St. Patricks Channel due to mountain waves from the high ground to the north; some knockdowns have been reported there. In the evenings, gentle katabatic winds can flow through the river valleys leading into Nyanza Bay. A northeasterly wind blowing through St. Anns Harbour continues through the valley past Glen Tosh and into Baddeck Bay. The winds seldom exceed 25 knots, but can cause sleepless nights on yachts moored in Baddeck Bay.

LOCAL WEATHER Cape Breton

Cape Breton West

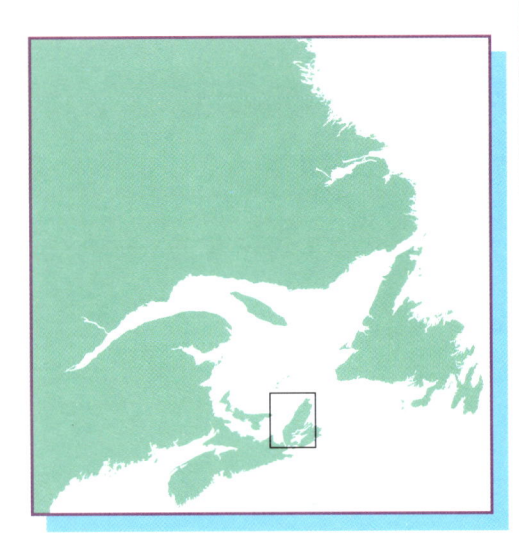

GENERAL CONDITIONS

Most of this picturesque stretch of coastline is exposed to strong northwesterlies that bring large seas and swell onshore. In winter, as long as there is enough open water, these winds also bring snow streamers off the gulf. The heaviest snowfalls occur from Inverness northward.

Sea breezes along this coast are mainly west or northwest. Where river valleys open to the sea, local sea breezes are often enhanced by anabatic winds moving up the mountainsides.

The steep terrain along this coastline makes for drainage winds and arctic sea smoke at many places, notably: Pleasant Bay, and at the mouths of Sailor Brook (in Sailor Cove), Blair River (in Polletts Cove), Fishing Cove River, and Corney Brook.

For easier reading, this coastline has been divided into two sections.

CAPE NORTH TO MARGAREE ISLAND

Along most of this coastline, westerly winds are redirected to southwesterly by the high terrain. Seas become confused when sea and swell from the west meet these southwesterlies near the coast.

Coastal convergence and cornering create a significant effect at Cape St. Lawrence. Southwest winds are never light off this Cape and are often twice as strong as over the Gulf. This convergence of southwesterlies should be noticeable along the coast, as far south as Presqu'ile.

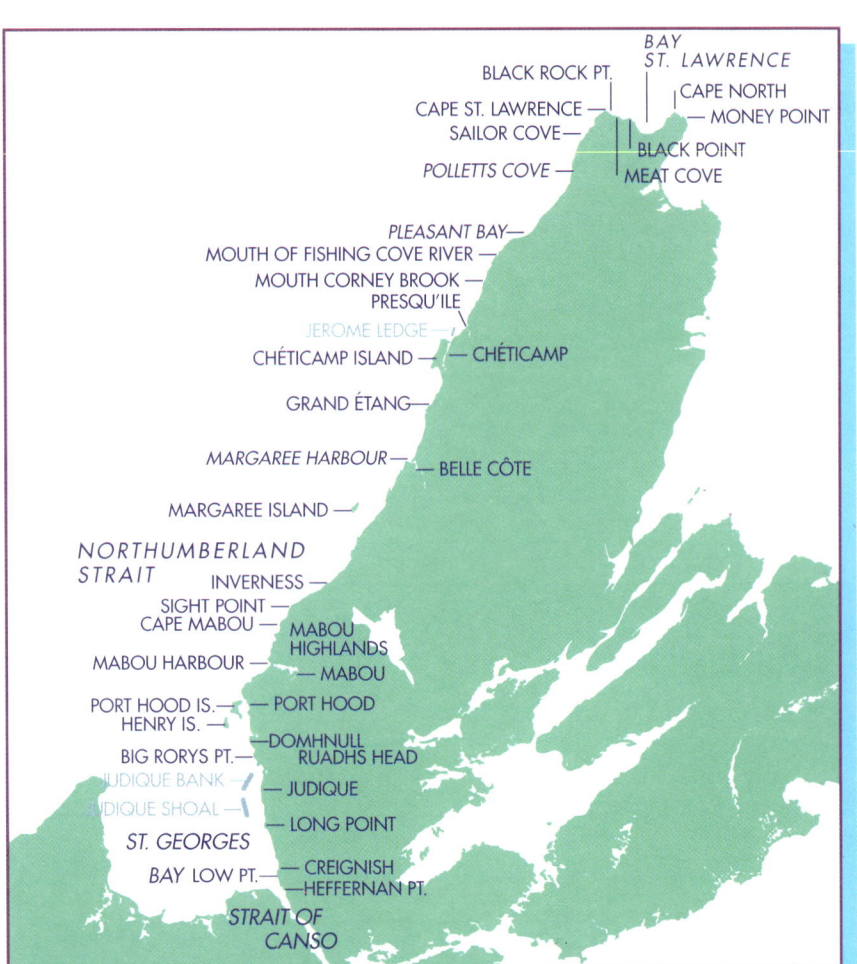

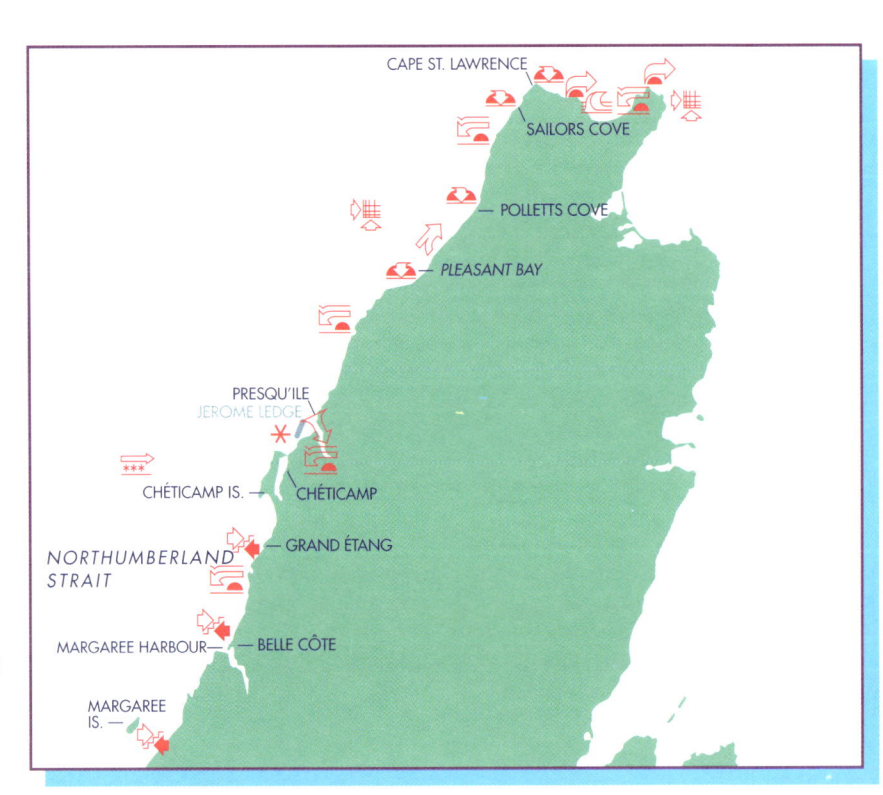

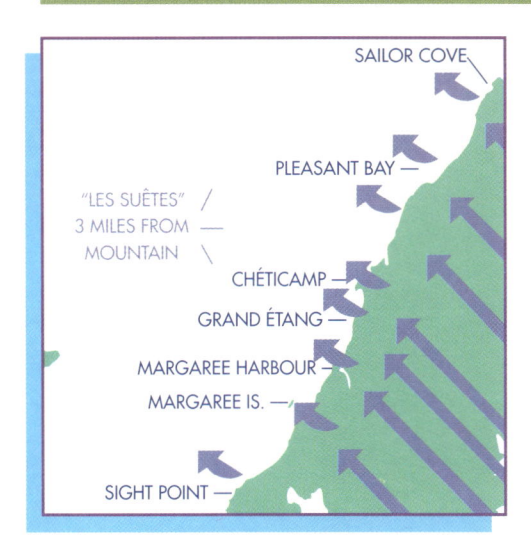

LOCAL WEATHER Cape Breton

LES SUÊTES
Perhaps the best-known and most significant local effect in the Maritimes is the violent southeasterly winds near Chéticamp, les suêtes. They are caused by mountain waves developing off the highlands of Cape Breton. On average, it is about 3 miles from the mountain peak to the strongest surface wind. Under these conditions, wind speeds along the west coast of Cape Breton are about twice that of other locations.

Did you know that the Maritimes Weather Centre in Bedford, N.S., began issuing special inland and marine warnings for les suêtes in 1992? Since the early 1990s, meteorologists have come to recognize signs of these violent winds and can forecast them accurately and well in advance.

In the March 1993 Storm of the Century, les suêtes at Grand Étang exceeded 125 knots and the ripped the roof off the Chéticamp hospital.

MARGAREE ISLAND TO PORT HASTINGS

Along this coastline, westerly winds are redirected to southwesterly by the high terrain.

Port Hood is sheltered from the west by Port Hood Island, Henry Island, and the reefs between them. It is partially sheltered from the northwest by a breakwater but is exposed to the south, and sustained southerly or southwesterly gales will send in heavy seas.

Northwesterlies are channelled between Port Hood Island and Henry Island, creating steep and confused seas in the shallow water between the islands.

Southerlies are strengthened by coastal convergence along most of the coast, from Port Hood to Low Point. Cornering increases this effect off some prominent headlands, such as Domhnull Ruadhs Head, Big Rory's Point, and Long Point.

Caution: Wind Opposing Current
It is reported that a nasty sea develops in Margaree Harbour when winds oppose the current, especially during a run-off when freshwater currents in the harbour are significant.

LOCAL WEATHER *Northumberland Strait*

Northumberland East

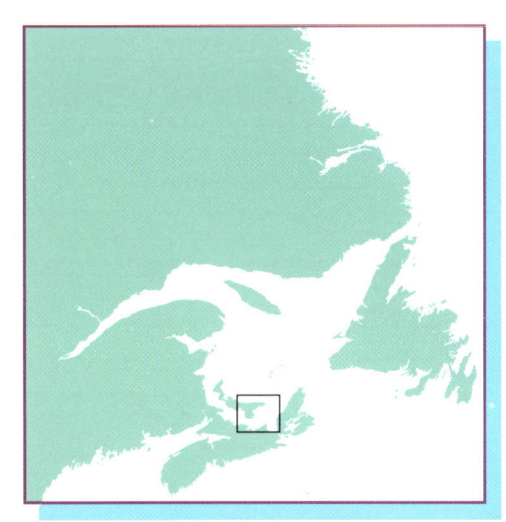

GENERAL CONDITIONS

Warm water temperatures along this coast can lead to marine hazards in late summer and fall. Squall lines sometimes occur, and waterspouts are often sighted.

Fog is not so common here as in other Canadian Atlantic waters, since the air brought by southerly winds dries out somewhat as it crosses Nova Scotia.

Sea breezes along the north shore of Nova Scotia tend be northeasterly and are limited to otherwise calm, sunny days. They occur from about midday to near dusk.

St. Georges Bay and the eastern part of Northumberland Strait are open to a long fetch from the northeast, since there is no land to block wind or sea all the way to the Strait of Belle Isle. Sustained northeasterly winds bring heavy seas. Fishermen report that northeasterlies also reduce the lobster catch; swells may become large enough to disturb lobsters on the sea floor.

For easier reading, these coastlines have been divided into three sections.

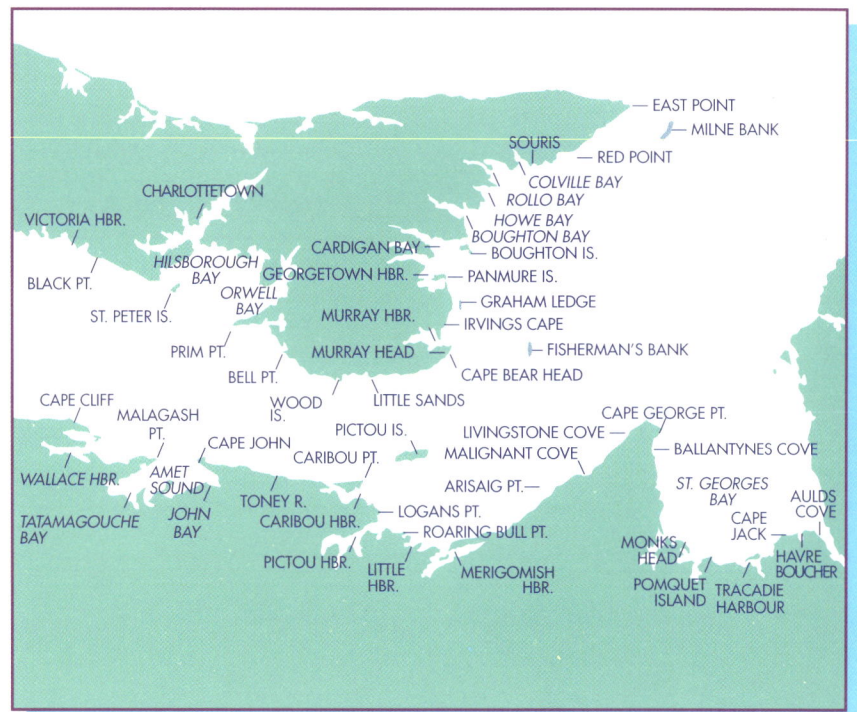

EAST POINT TO CAPE BEAR HEAD, P.E.I.

There are many harbours and bays along this stretch, with narrow, shallow entrances. They provide shelter from seaward-blowing winds, but little protection from onshore winds, which also make them difficult to enter. Nearly all these harbours are subject to rapid silting and shifting of their channels. Mariners should note that navigational aids marking the best channels may be moved without advance notice.

LOCAL WEATHER Northumberland Strait

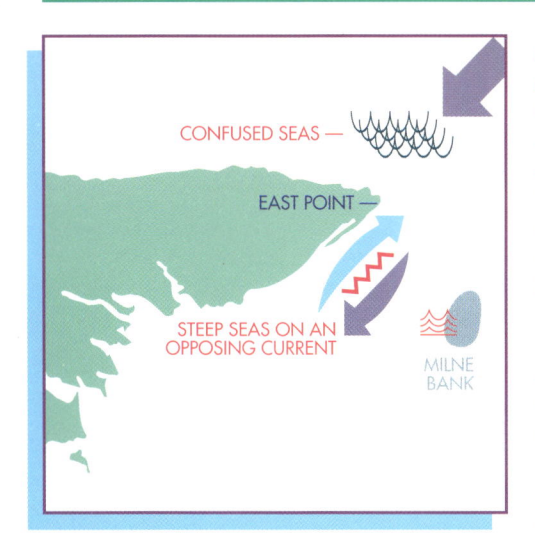

PROBLEMS AT EAST POINT

East Point is possibly the most dangerous coastal location around Prince Edward Island. Winds are strengthened by cornering effects near the point, when they blow from anywhere between northwest and northeast. The effect is greatest within about 5 miles of the point, but may extend halfway across Northumberland Strait. These winds frequently blow against the tidal stream, increasing the seas. The worst combination is northeast winds against an ebbing (northeast-going) tide, particularly over the shoal water, which extends about 1 mile eastward from the point.

Haven of Rest: Souris Harbour
Souris Harbour, with its deep entrance, is easy to enter under almost all weather conditions.

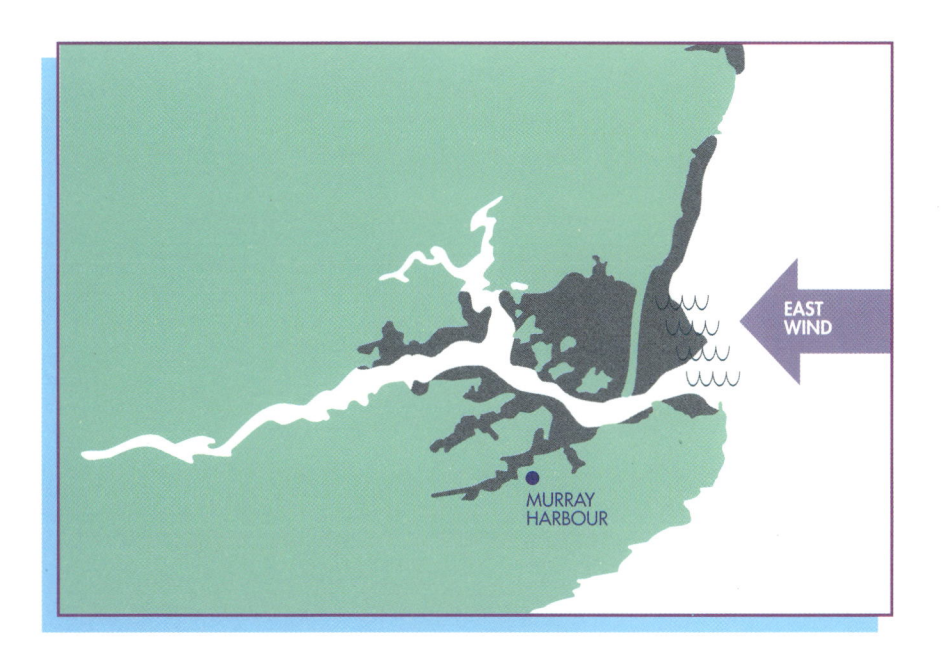

EASTERLIES IN MURRAY HARBOUR

The channel into Murray Harbour, P.E.I., is sometimes impassable in easterly winds because a line of breakers sets up across the mouth of the harbour over shallow water.

LOCAL WEATHER Northumberland Strait

AULDS COVE TO MERIGOMISH HARBOUR

The Strait of Canso is surrounded by high terrain, which causes considerable funnelling and channelling. These effects are most pronounced in northwesterlies which can blow much stronger in the Strait than in St. Georges Bay. This effect occurs as far as 2–3 miles out from the North Canso Light, but it is strongest south of the light.

Prevailing southwesterlies on summer afternoons blow very heavily off the land along this stretch of coastline. Instability from daytime heating creates strong, gusty land-winds that carry offshore for a few miles before diminishing to lighter, steadier values.

The eastern localities of northern Nova Scotia are more vulnerable to large waves than anywhere else along the Northumberland Strait. A long fetch to the north and northeast allows the fully developed seas of the Gulf of St. Lawrence to enter the strait. Mariners in this area note that "nor'easters" make for "awful conditions."

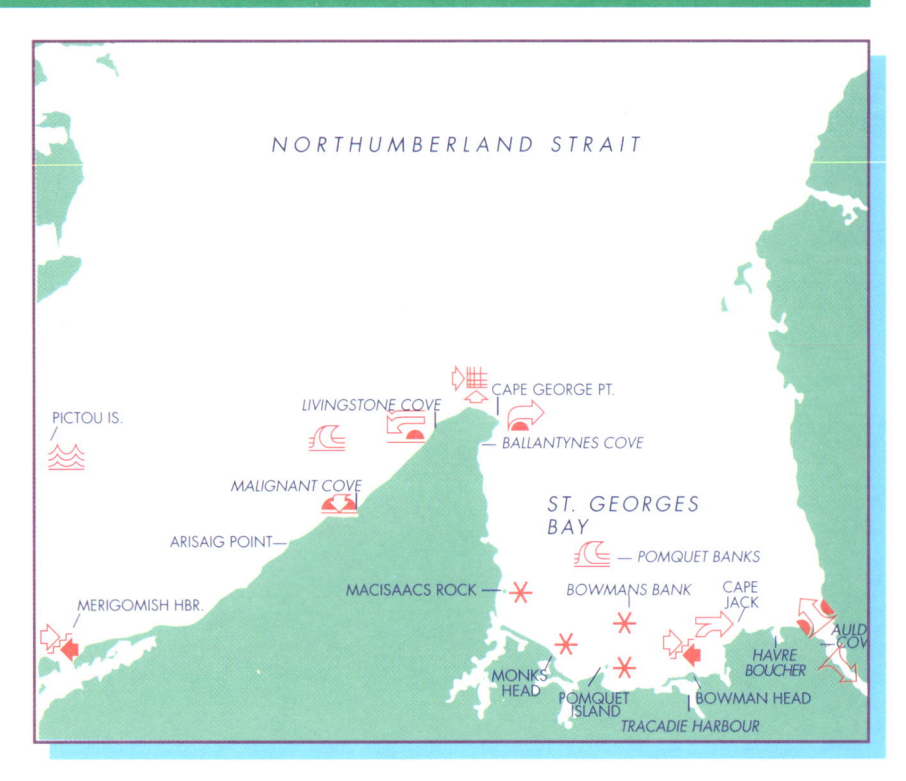

Marine Weather Tip: Look Upstream

Northwesterly winds can develop very quickly in the wake of a passing storm. The winds start in the west and spread east, so mariners can forecast their arrival by heeding observations from locations upstream, such as Caribou Point. When winds increase in Arisaig Harbour (about 40 km due east of Caribou), the boats fishing farther east (in St. Georges Bay) are warned by radio. This gives them time to retrieve their gear.

PICTOU ISLAND TO VICTORIA HARBOUR

In summer, westerly winds are often much weaker along the south shore of Prince Edward Island than near the coast of Nova Scotia. The island's coast may be calm, while moderate to strong westerlies are blowing along the southern side of the Strait. This discrepancy is caused by coastal divergence along the P.E.I. coast.

The area around Pictou Island is well known for poor sea conditions.

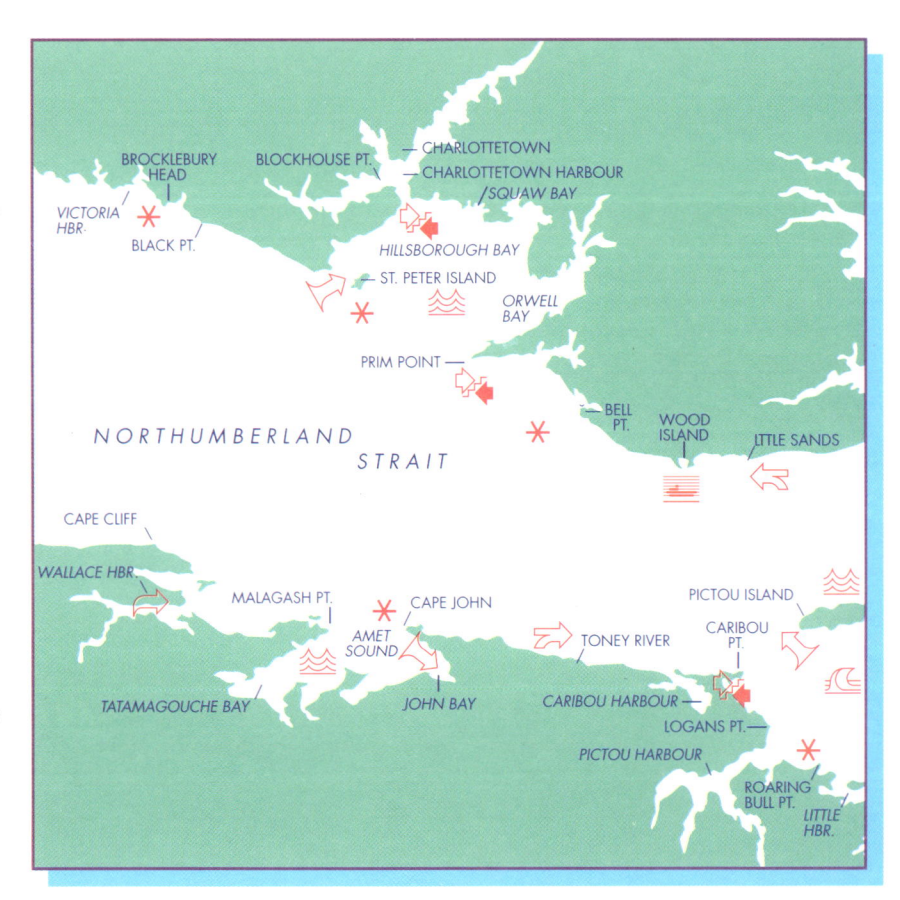

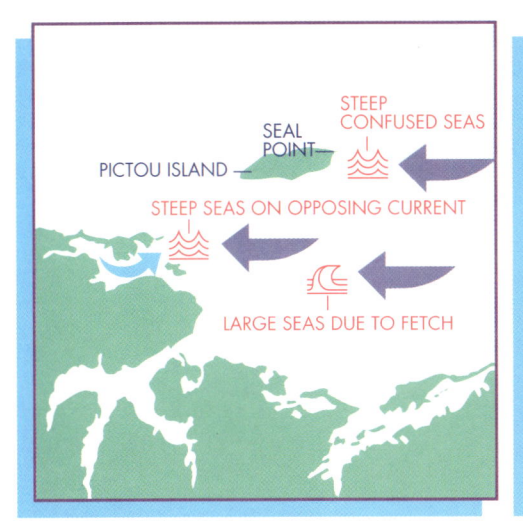

LOCAL WEATHER Northumberland Strait

EASTERLIES
The eastern end of Pictou Island becomes rough in easterlies. Although shoaling is not severe, the waves tend to be larger, due to a lengthy fetch. A reef extends from Seal Point, with deep water on either side.

WESTERLIES
Westerlies funnel between Caribou Point and Pictou Island, strengthening the wind, while the shallow water causes steep, confused seas, further complicated by tidal currents around the island. Currents generally flow from the west and split into two branches along either side of the island.

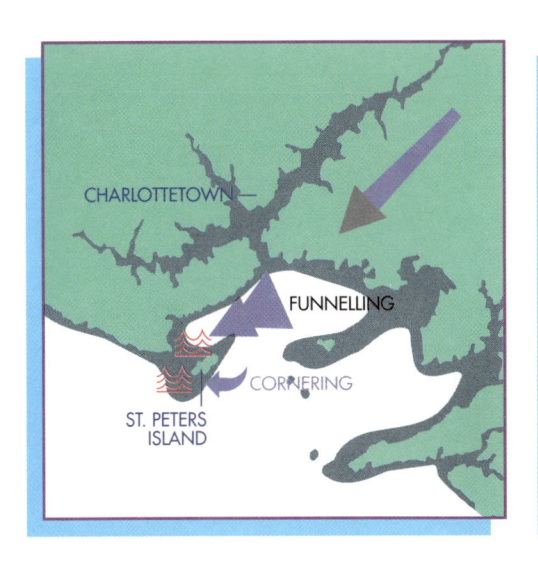

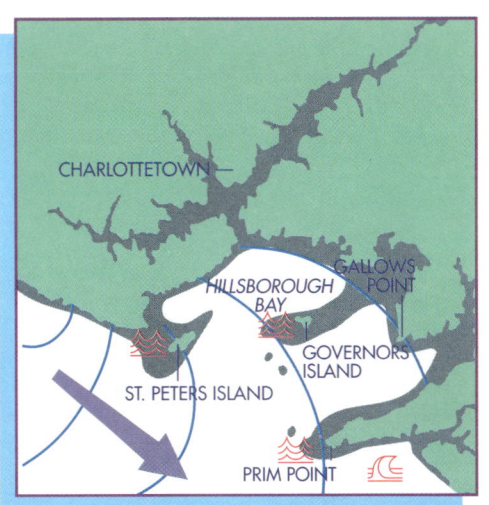

CHARLOTTETOWN HARBOUR: NORTHEASTERLIES
Northeasterly winds are stronger along the southeastern side of St. Peters Island, due to cornering effects.

CHARLOTTETOWN HARBOUR: NORTHWESTERLIES
West-to-southwest winds blow over a substantial fetch from Baie Verte and can bring heavy seas into the eastern part of Hillsborough Bay. These seas affect the coast from Gallows Point to Prim Point and the Bay seaward of Governors Island. When northwesterlies are blowing the full length of Northumberland Strait, swell will turn, or "refract," into these sections of coast. Conditions can become hazardous, because there are many shoals and reefs in Hillsborough Bay.

LOCAL WEATHER *Northumberland Strait*

Northumberland West

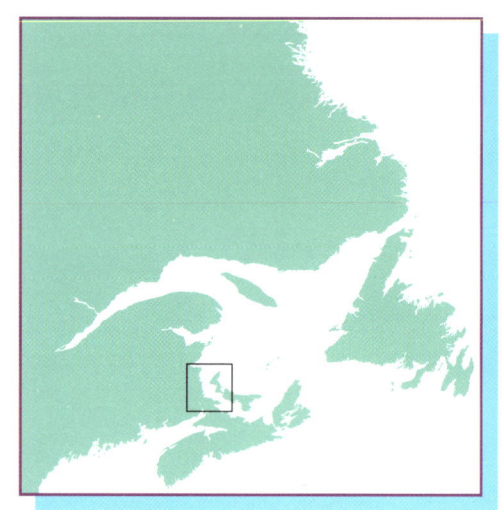

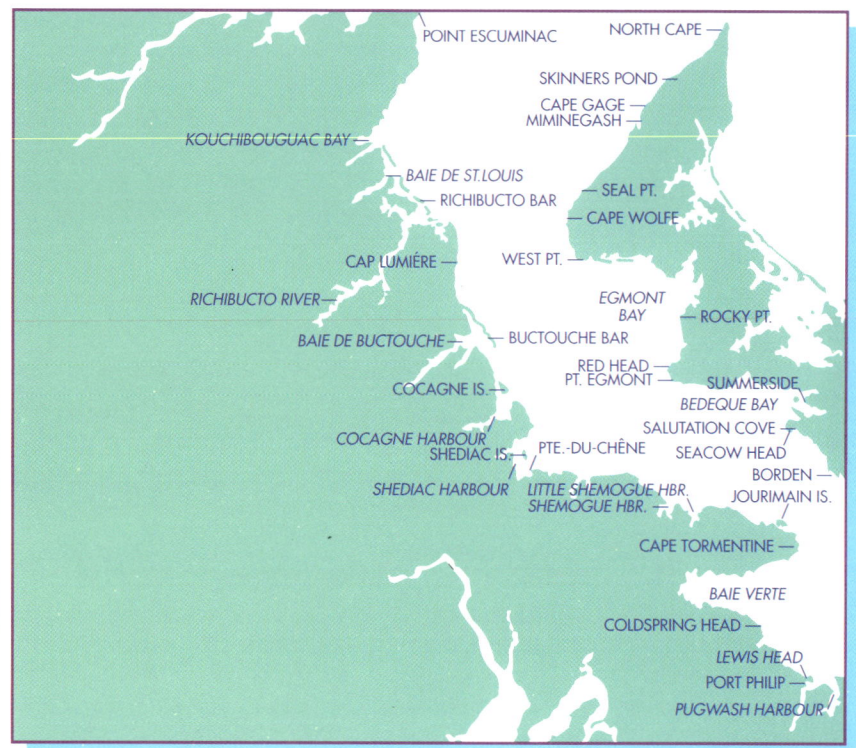

GENERAL CONDITIONS

These waters enjoy some of the warmest summertime sea-surface temperatures in the Maritimes. Consequently, the area gets little fog. But warm water has its drawbacks. Summer thunderstorms moving from New Brunswick often die out when they reach the cold water in the Bay of Fundy or the Gulf of St. Lawrence, but in the Northumberland Strait, the warm water keeps them active. Two ships were hit by lightning in August and September of 1990.

For easier reading, these coastlines have been divided into four short sections.

BORDEN TO CAPE EGMONT

Northumberland Strait narrows in Abegweit Passage, between Borden and Cape Tormentine. Northwest and southeast winds are funnelled and channelled through this gap, where wind speed can be 30 knots faster than over the rest of the strait.

PUGWASH HARBOUR TO COCAGNE ISLAND

Baie Verte experiences strong southwesterly winds that blow in from the Tantramar Marshes and cause very choppy conditions along the shore. Easterly winds can also bring rough seas into the bay. These effects are compounded by shoal water in locations such as Aggermore Rock, Laurent Shoal, Spear Shoal, and Heart Shoal.

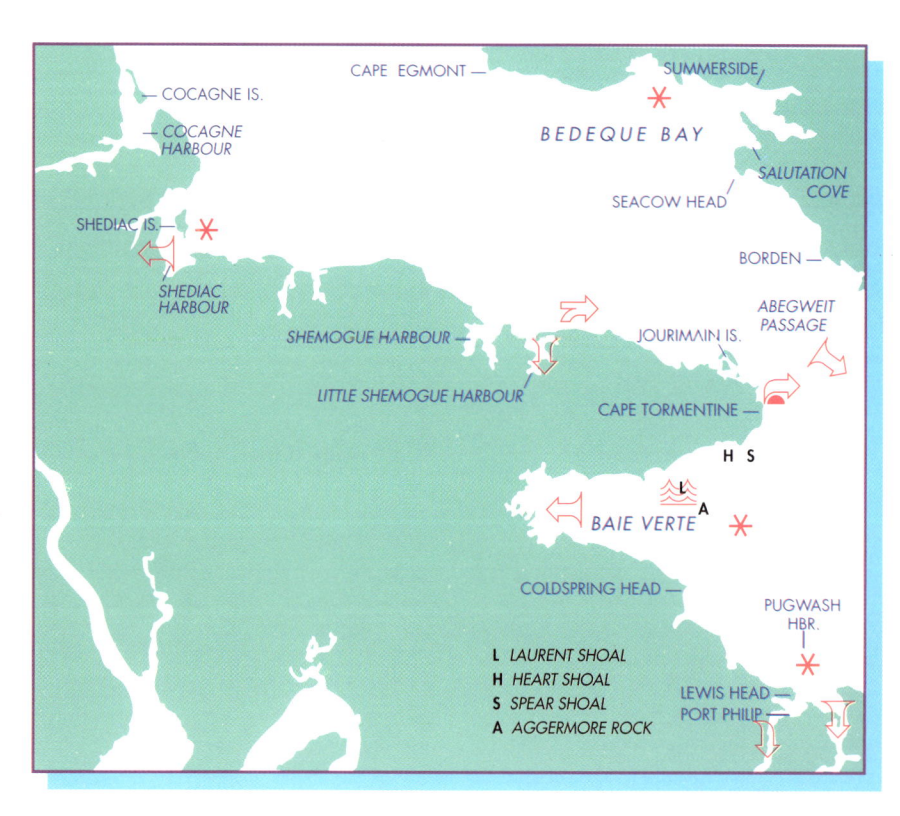

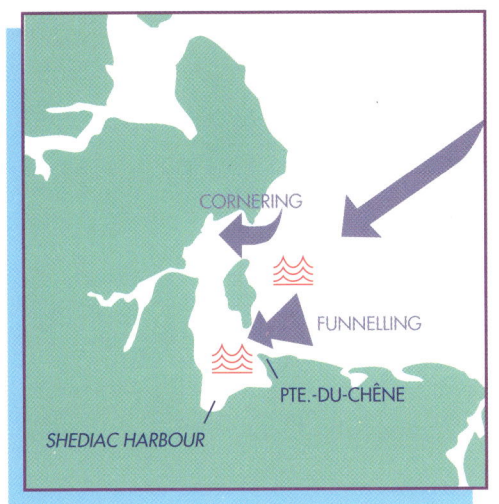

LOCAL WEATHER *Northumberland Strait*

SHEDIAC
Very shallow water makes the approach to Shediac Harbour from the east dangerous, except for small craft. Northeast winds are funnelled as they enter Shediac Bay and bring particularly rough seas to the shoals around Pointe-du-Chêne.

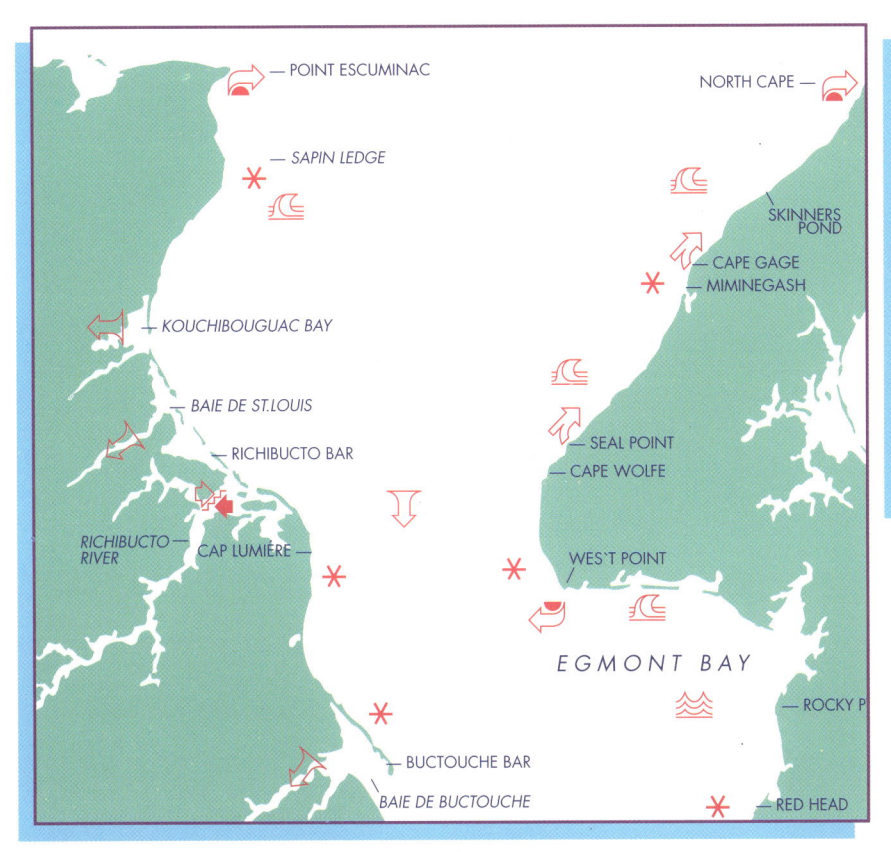

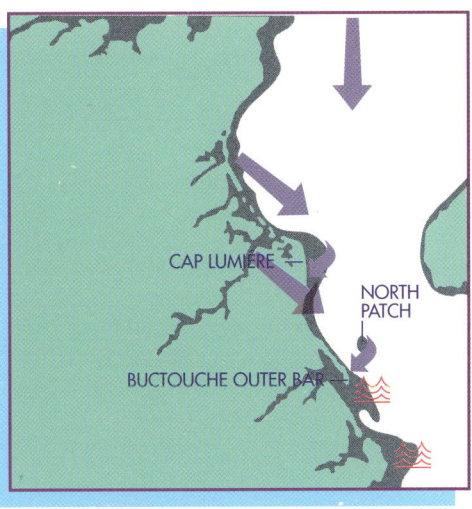

NORTHERLY WIND
The funnelling of northerly winds at the northern entrance to the Northumberland Strait is felt most strongly just east of Cap Lumière, where the winds create breaking seas in the shallow waters to the south.

BAIE DE BUCTOUCHE TO POINT ESCUMINAC
The coastline from Richibucto to Point Escuminac is exposed to northeast winds. Conditions can become dangerous due to shallow water and irregular seas. The highest seas are at Sapin Ledge.

RED HEAD TO NORTH CAPE
Egmont Bay, between West Point and Cape Egmont, provides good anchorage with offshore winds. Maximum fetch is with southwesterly winds, which can create choppy conditions. Southerly winds may be stronger near Red Head and Rocky Point due to cornering and coastal convergence.

LOCAL WEATHER New Brunswick and P.E.I. North

New Brunswick North and Gaspé

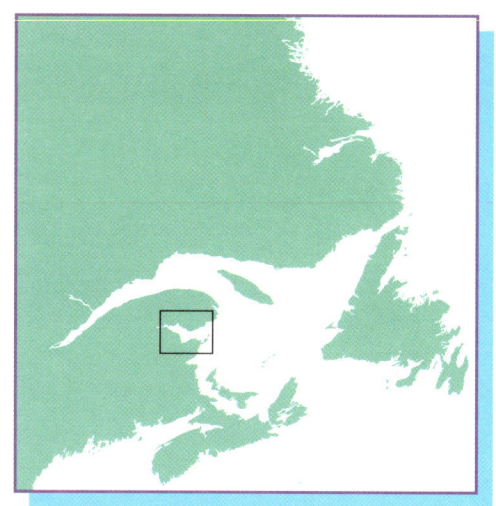

GENERAL CONDITIONS

The Bay of Chaleur is the largest bay in the Gulf of St. Lawrence. It is deep and has no detached shoals, except near the coast. The water gradually becomes shallow towards the head of the bay.

West of Cape D'Espoir, the area is sheltered from most winds. In fall, however, west or northwest winds can be a problem in the bay. Cold air moving over relatively warm water can very quickly bring storms from the west or northwest. What look like squalls at first may last for 12–48 hours.

For easier reading, this coastline has been divided into three sections.

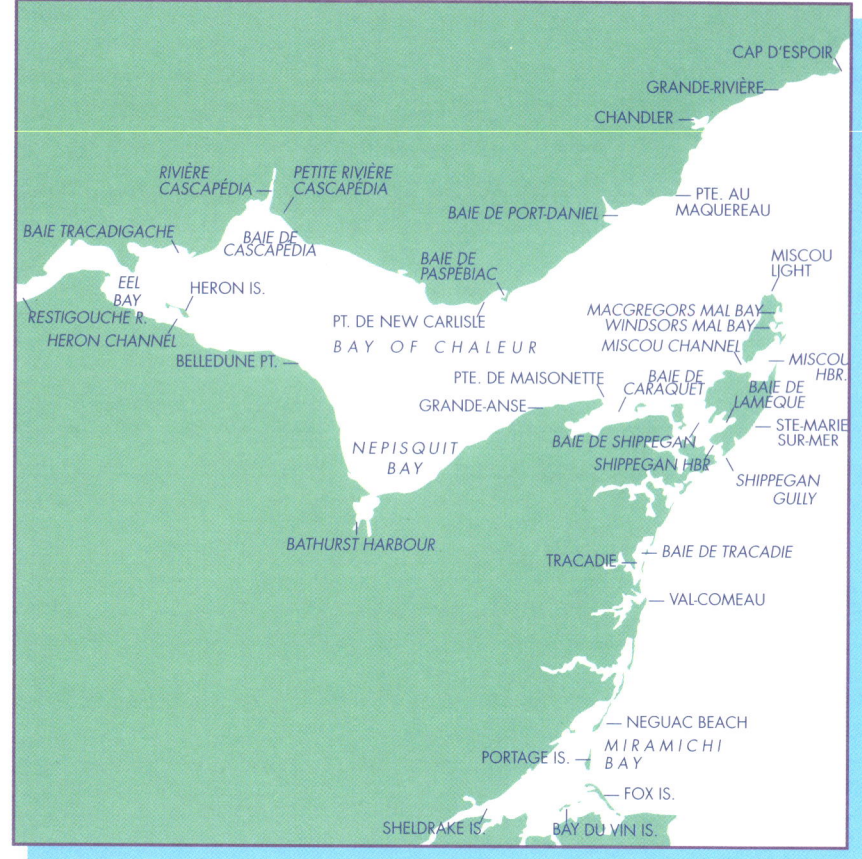

Do you remember when tragedy struck Miramichi Bay? On June 20, 1959, a fearsome storm brought northeasterly winds that whipped up huge waves and a storm surge, causing coastal flooding and damage on land. The fishing fleet was out that night, and many ships were destroyed. Thirty-five lives were lost. Some ships survived by sailing into deeper water and facing into the waves.

LOCAL WEATHER New Brunswick and P.E.I. North

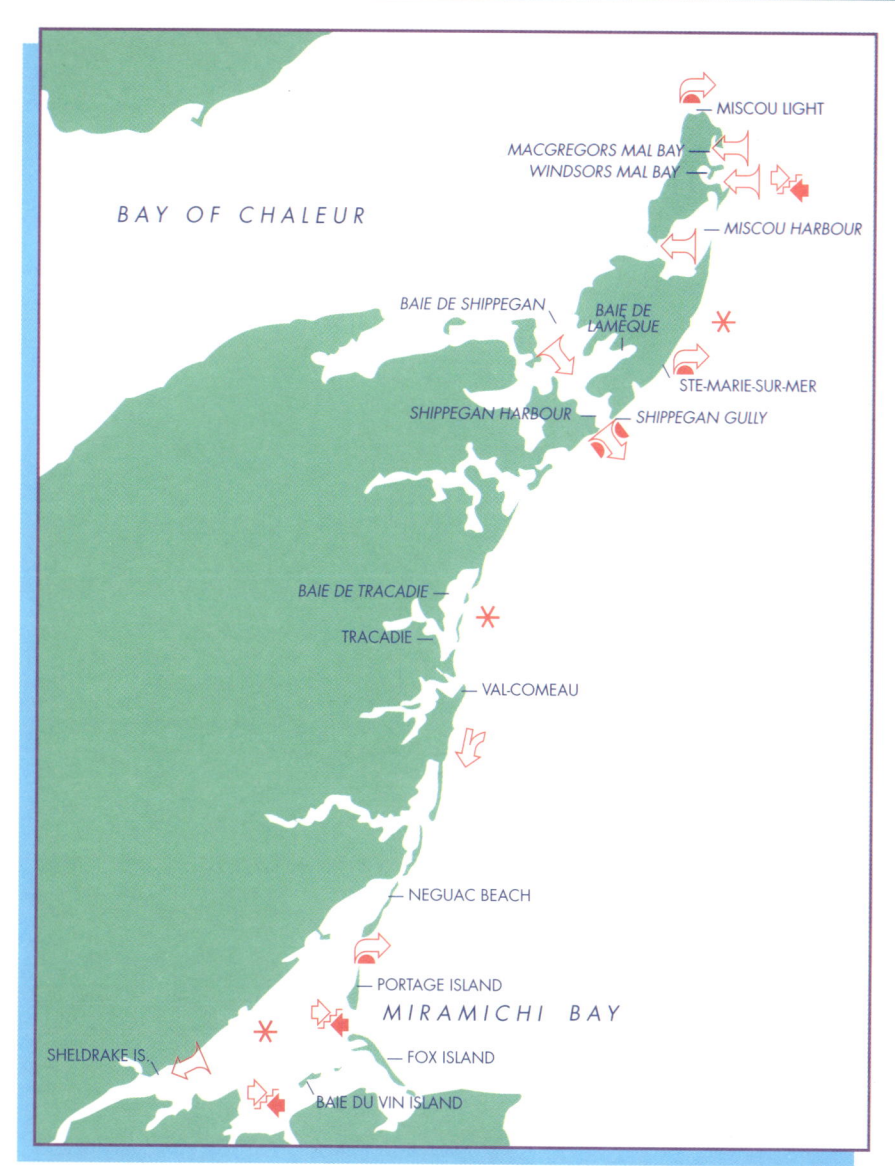

MIRAMICHI BAY TO MISCOU ISLAND

The ebb tidal current coming out of Miramichi Bay can be as strong as 3 1/2 knots between Fox Island and Portage Island. Steep seas develop in this area when an east-to-northeast wind runs against the tide.

The coast from Neguac Beach to Miscou Lighthouse is exposed to winds and seas from northeast-to-southeast. Serious storm-surge conditions under persistent northeast gales. Seas steepen and break in the shallow water off the coast.

- Off Val-Comeau, access to the area can be restricted by onshore winds and seas.

- Off Tracadie, strong southeast winds and seas are dangerous.

- Along eastern Miscou Island, and south from there, dangerous seas develop, causing sand dunes to shift. After each storm the dunes must be relocated and buoys moved to mark the safe passage.

Sea breezes along this coast are generally northeast to east, but this varies in bays and inlets. According to one local fisherman, "Spring has not come until breezes from offshore have occurred."

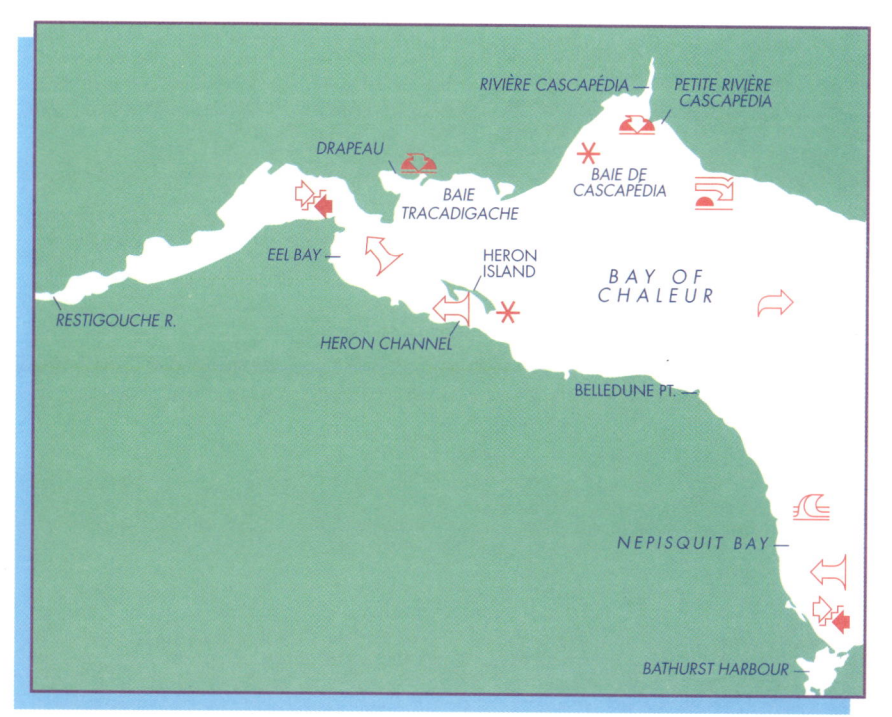

BAY OF CHALEUR (WEST)

Easterly winds become funnelled in the western end of the Bay of Chaleur. This effect produces choppy waves, especially when the wind blows against an ebb tide combined with outflow from the Restigouche River. The high ground of the Gaspé Peninsula makes coastal areas along the north shore of the bay prone to drainage winds and arctic sea smoke in winter.

105

LOCAL WEATHER New Brunswick and P.E.I. North

BAY OF CHALEUR (EAST)
Under certain conditions, lee waves develop off the mountains of Gaspé in northwesterly flows. These winds can vary greatly in speed and direction and cause strong northwesterly gusts. This effect is experienced in the inner bay and along the north coast of the outer bay, to the tip of the Gaspé Peninsula.

Marine Weather Tip
The marine forecast for the Chaleur-Miscou area usually reflects conditions at the mouth of Bay of Chaleur and over open water. Conditions are often considerably better in the inner bay than the forecast indicates.

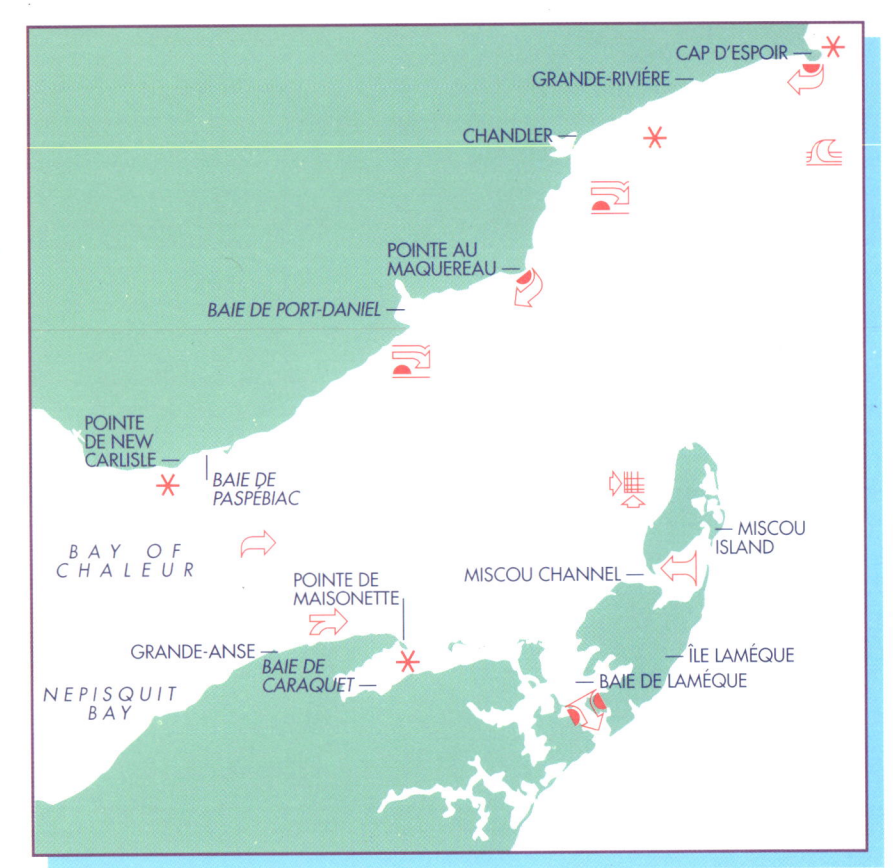

ANGRY SEAS WEST OF MISCOU ISLAND
The area west of Miscou Island can be dangerous. When winds are generally northwest in the Bay of Chaleur, the coastline along the south steers waves towards the northeast. These waves meet the Wind-waves coming from the northwest, creating crossing seas. The condition is worsened by shallow water, especially over Miscou Flat and Shippegan Flat.

LOCAL WEATHER New Brunswick and P.E.I. North

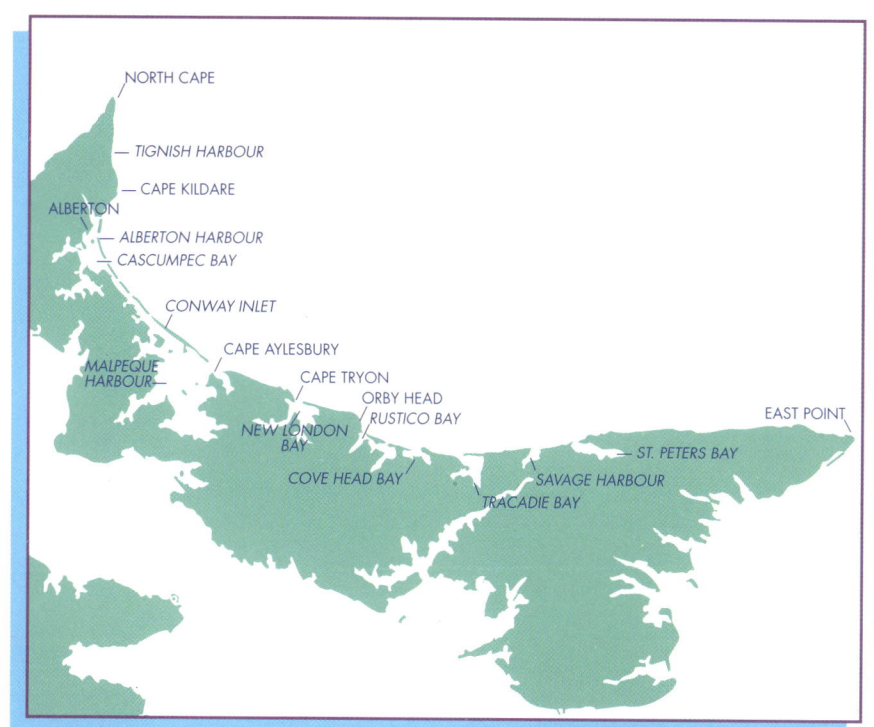

Prince Edward Island North

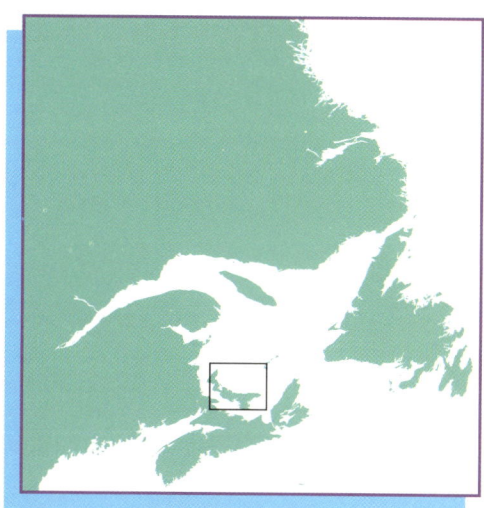

GENERAL CONDITIONS

Prince Edward Island is in the southwestern part of the gulf where the water is shallower. Consequently, water temperature varies considerably throughout the year. The water freezes early in winter and becomes very warm in summer. Fog is less frequent here than elsewhere in the gulf, especially in summer, partly because of warmer water temperatures and partly because southwesterly winds are drier.

Sea breezes are more common in spring just after ice break-up, when the water is still cold. They become weaker and less frequent by mid- or late summer, as the water warms up. The waters around Prince Edward Island are subject to line squalls and waterspouts in late summer and fall.

For easier reading, this coastline has been divided into two sections.

Caution: Complicated Channels

There are many bays along this coast, connected to the sea by narrow channels. A lot of water must pass through the channel with each change in the tide, so tidal currents are strong near harbour entrances, especially during spring tides. There is usually a sand bar just offshore with a shallow channel through it; these channels are liable to shift in storms. At times the buoys, leading lights, and other markers are moved to mark the best channel. In strong winds and heavy seas it is often impossible to find the channel—conditions aggravated by northwest-to-northeast winds and waves moving against the current.

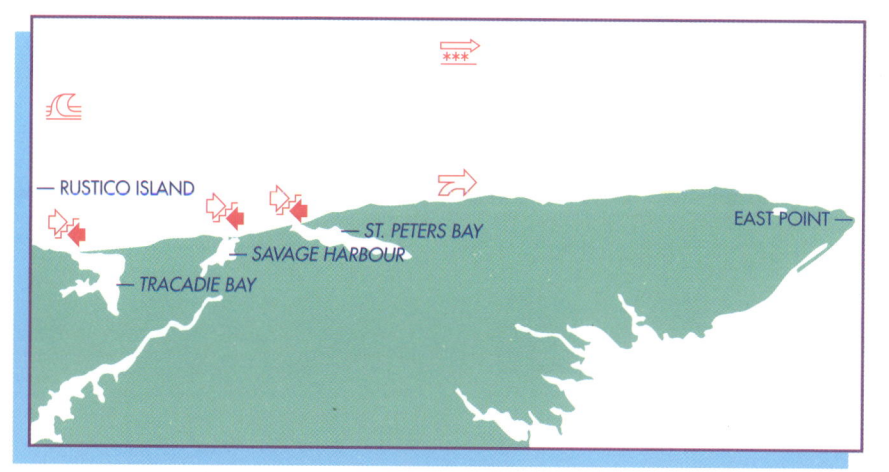

EAST POINT TO TRACADIE BAY

Winds from any direction between northwest and northeast bring the heaviest seas onshore in this area. In addition, winds from between west and northwest align with this coast and strengthen within 2–3 miles of the coast between East Point and Rustico Island, due to coastal convergence.

107

LOCAL WEATHER New Brunswick and P.E.I. North

COVE HEAD BAY TO NORTH CAPE

Northwest winds align with this coast and are stronger within 2–3 miles of the shore between Orby Head and Alberton. Northwesterly winds may be further strengthened near Cape Tryon, due to cornering. Winds from between north and northeast bring maximum seas onshore between Rustico Island and Alberton, making the coast dangerous between Cape Tryon and Cape Aylesbury.

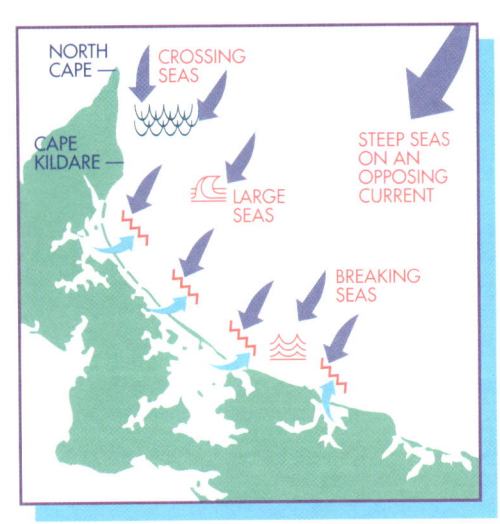

NASTY NORTHEASTERLIES

Winds from between north and northeast will become aligned with the coast and strengthened within 2–3 miles of the shore between Cape Kildare and North Cape. Northeast-to-east winds will bring maximum seas onshore along this coast.

Caution: Deceptive Conditions

In summer, when winds are most often southwesterly, sand dunes along the north shore of P.E.I. provide some shelter. A sea-breeze circulation offsets the southwest winds and the wind becomes nearly calm at the coast. This is deceptive to board and dinghy sailors, who set off from the beach only to encounter southwesterly winds a little way out. These conditions can make it difficult to return to shore, especially for inexperienced board sailors. Anticosti is worth a visit—but it's a long way on a sailboard!

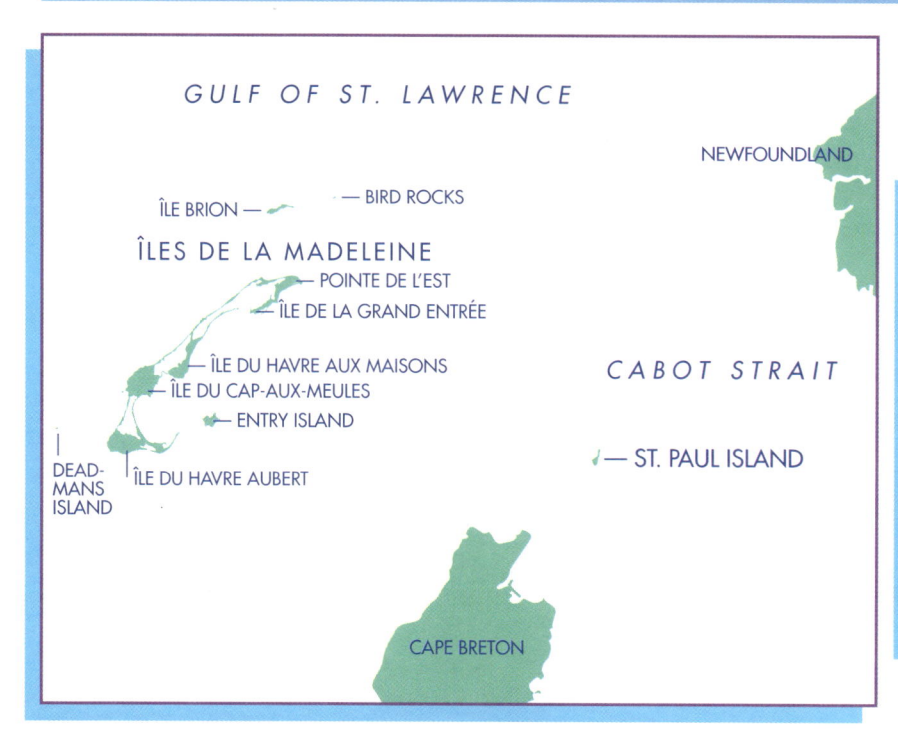

Southeast Gulf

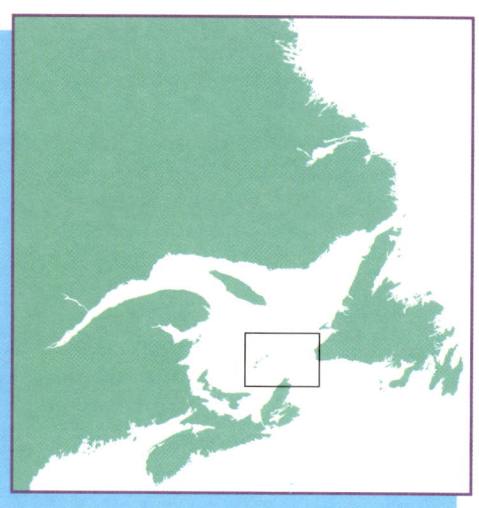

GENERAL CONDITIONS

The Cabot Strait is the main shipping entrance to the Gulf of St. Lawrence and all inland ports. Normally, there is a moderate current coming out of the gulf near the Cape Breton side of the strait and a weak ingoing current on the Cape Ray side. These can cause choppy seas when they run against the wind. Sustained periods of wind modify the currents considerably.

Ice usually moves into the Cabot Strait in late January, and most years there is considerable ice cover until mid-April. The ice continues to thicken as it drifts southeastward across the gulf. Strong winds put the ice under pressure, especially along sections of coast where the winds are blowing onshore.

The Cabot Strait has one of the harshest climates in the region. It often remains ice-free in winter, yet water temperatures can drop below zero, creating freezing spray. The expanse across the strait between Cape Breton and Newfoundland is wide enough to be open water: similar to the Gulf of St. Lawrence on one side (in north-to-west winds) and to the Atlantic on the other (in south-to-east winds)—often the worst of both worlds. Many mariners feel that the wind report from St. Paul Island—a very windy spot—is representative of wind conditions in the strait.

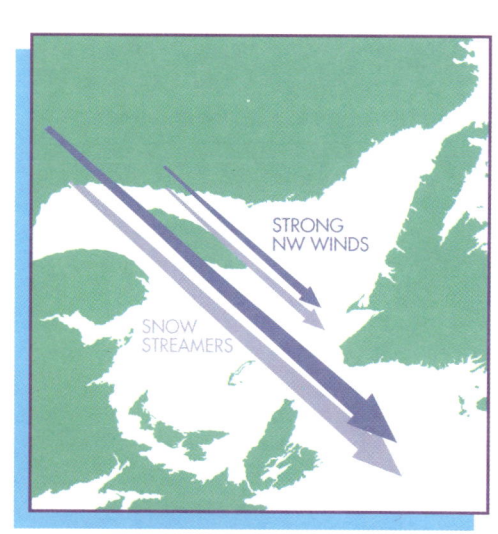

FETCH

Cabot Strait is exposed to very long open-water fetches. From the northwest, it is open all the way to the Gaspé Passage (Détroit d'Honguedo), about 250 miles. To the southeast, there is an unlimited fetch out into the Atlantic. The fetch from the northeast is limited in the strait itself, but as you move into the gulf towards the Magdalen Islands, this fetch stretches to almost 250 miles. These long fetches allow very large seas to form in the area, and waves continue to roll long after the wind dies down. This is one of the roughest areas in Atlantic Canadian waters.

SNOW STREAMERS

In fall and winter, when there is enough ice-free water, snow streamers can develop in cold northwesterly winds. Within the streamers, visibility may be reduced to almost zero in heavy snow, while the sky is clear a few miles away. A frequent source of streamers is the Gaspé Passage. Depending on the wind direction, the streamers can affect the Magdalen Islands and the waters around them, the waters downstream to the Cape Breton coast, Cabot Strait, or the Newfoundland coast. A slight shift in wind direction will move the streamers a couple of miles north or south.

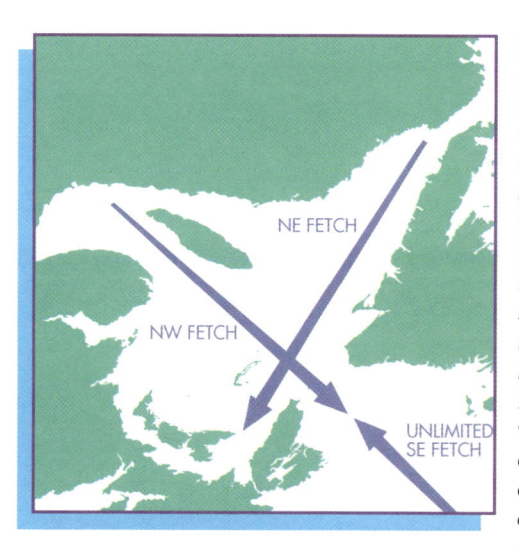

LOCAL WEATHER Southeast Gulf

ST. PAUL ISLAND

The water around St. Paul Island deepens rapidly, and the island rises steeply from the ocean floor. Waves reflect off the island, causing steep confused seas close to the cliffs. Variable currents compound the effect.

Near St. Paul Island, northwest winds are particularly strong off Northeast Point, due to cornering. The same effect strengthens east-to-southeast winds off Southwest Point. Atlantic Cove and South Martin Powers Cove are sheltered from west to northwest but are exposed to east-to-southeast wind and seas. North Martin Powers Cove is sheltered from the east but is exposed to west-to-northwest wind and seas.

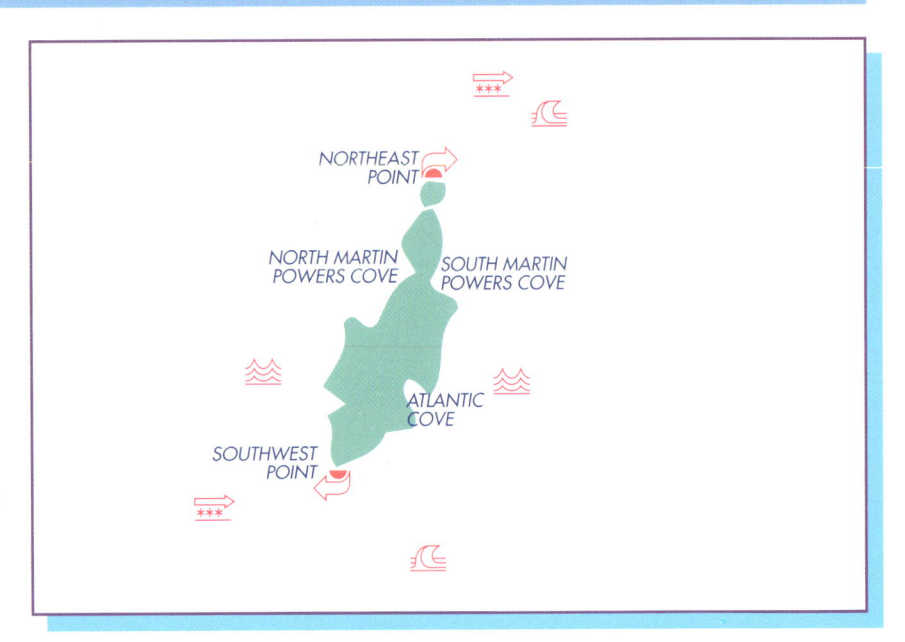

MAGDALEN ISLANDS

The water around the Magdalen Islands is cooler in spring and summer than the shallower waters of the southwestern gulf. Air that has picked up a lot of moisture before reaching the islands becomes chilled by the cooler water, and frequent fogs result.

The main semi-diurnal tides of the Gulf of St. Lawrence rotate around the Magdalen Islands. This means that there is a small tidal range and, on the western side of the main islands, only one high and one low tide per day; however, around the islands, currents are quite variable in direction and speed.

In spring, northeasterly winds tend to dominate. The onset of sustained northeasterlies coincides with the end of the ice season.

There are many shoals around the islands, most of them on the eastern side. Strong easterly winds bring rough seas and breaking waves to these areas. Some noteworthy locations are: (1) A little more than 1 mile southeast of Pointe de l'Est; (2) Within 1 mile east of Old Harry Point; (3) A second shoal, which extends from about 1 mile southwest of Old Harry Point for about 2 miles southeast to Les Colombines; (4) Alright Reef, which extends eastward nearly 4 miles from Cap Alright.

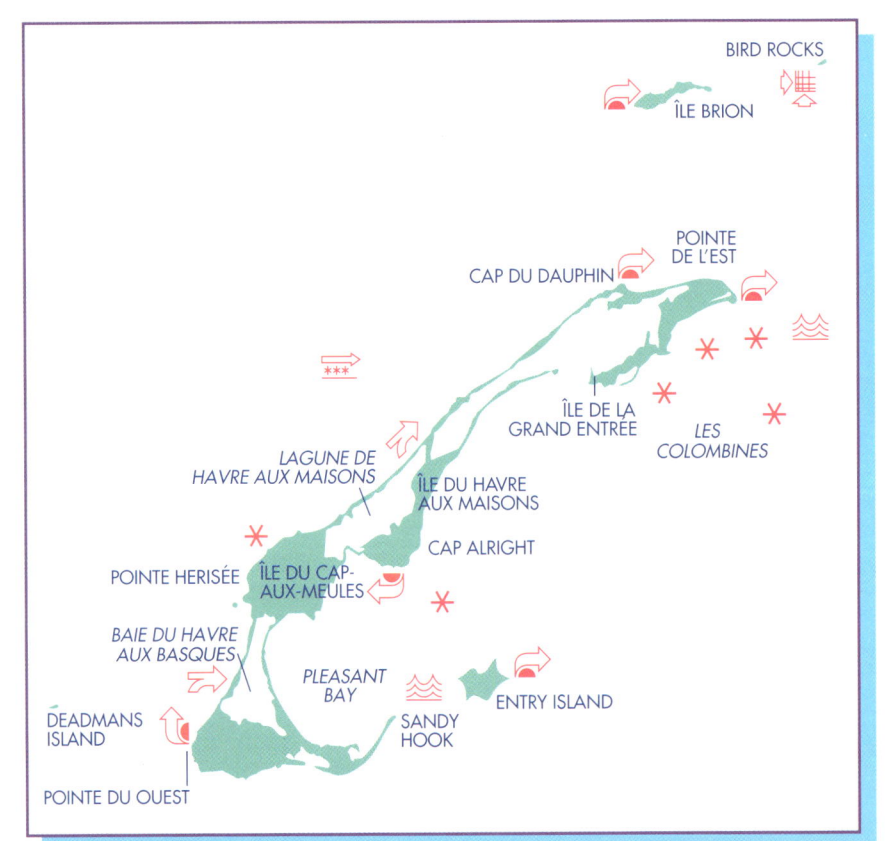

Caution: Choose Shelter Wisely

The Magdalen Islands provide some shelter on the leeward side, but the strongest winds are usually associated with moving storms. For example, strong southeasterly winds normally accompany an approaching storm, and northwesterlies signal its departure. The storm often intensifies as it moves, so the northwesterly winds can be much stronger than the initial southeasterlies. This can make a once-sheltered location the most dangerous place to be; therefore, for shelter from any particular wind direction, be sure to follow the forecast so you can anticipate changes in wind direction. There are harbours where more secure shelter can be found. Check your Sailing Directions!

LOCAL WEATHER *Southeast Gulf*

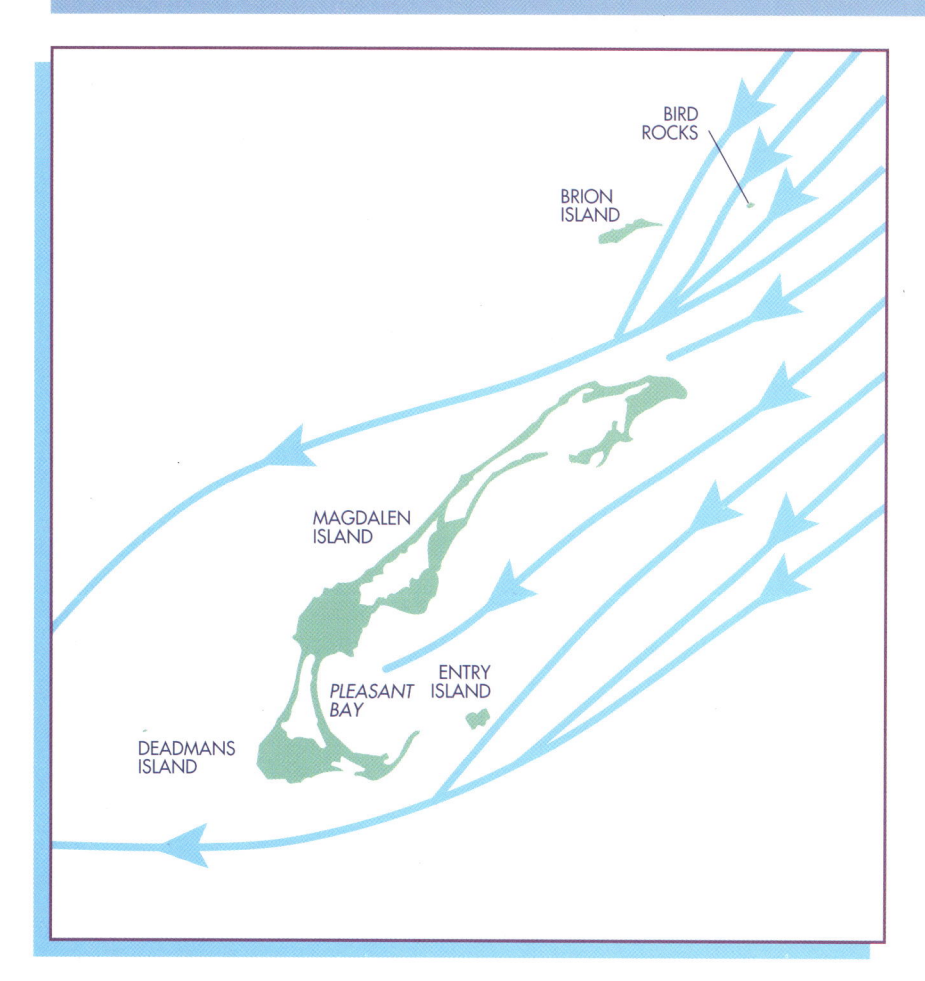

WAVE REFRACTION
Magdalen Islands and the surrounding smaller islands have many significant shoals, which cause waves—generated by strong northeasterly winds—to split as they pass the islands. The waves refract gently around the Magdalens, but separate much more dramatically around Bird Rocks. The refracted waves meet on the lee side of the island, creating a challenging sea of crossing waves.

Haven of Rest: Lagoons' Dunes
The islands' large, enclosed lagoons offer an ideal, relatively safe haven for recreational sailing, especially for board sailors. Sand dunes create an enclosed area: there is little danger of being swept out to sea, except possibly near the entrance at ebb tide. The dunes are low enough to allow winds of the gulf to blow over the lagoons, creating near-perfect sailing conditions in summer.

LOCAL WEATHER Newfoundland West

Belle Isle

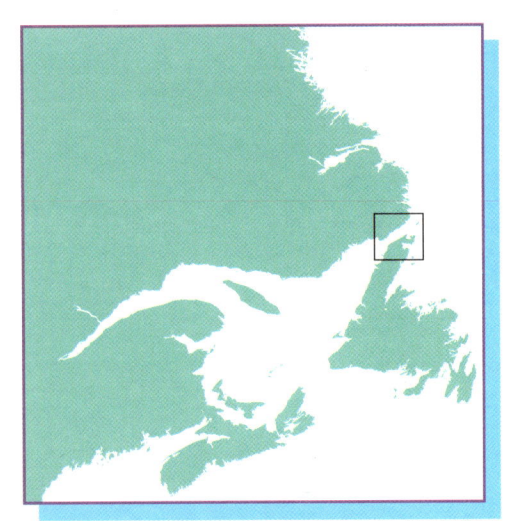

GENERAL CONDITIONS
Winds tend to blow along the axis of the Strait of Belle Isle from the southwest or northeast. Larger waves—associated with these wind directions—are carried into the strait from the Gulf of St. Lawrence and the Atlantic. Currents run back and forth with the tide, creating steep and choppy seas when the current runs against the wind. The choppiest seas usually are encountered in the narrow part of the strait.

Westerly winds produce flat seas on the Labrador side of the strait and choppier seas on the Newfoundland side. The reverse is true for easterly winds. The area is subject to fog in summer when warm southwesterlies blow across cooler water; fog in the gulf is often pushed into the narrow confines of the strait. Average currents show an inflow of cold water occurs on the Labrador side and an outflow of warmer Gulf water on the Newfoundland side. Consequently, average water temperatures in July are 4°C colder on the north side; so fog is more prevalent along this coast.

For easier reading, this coastline has been divided into two sections.

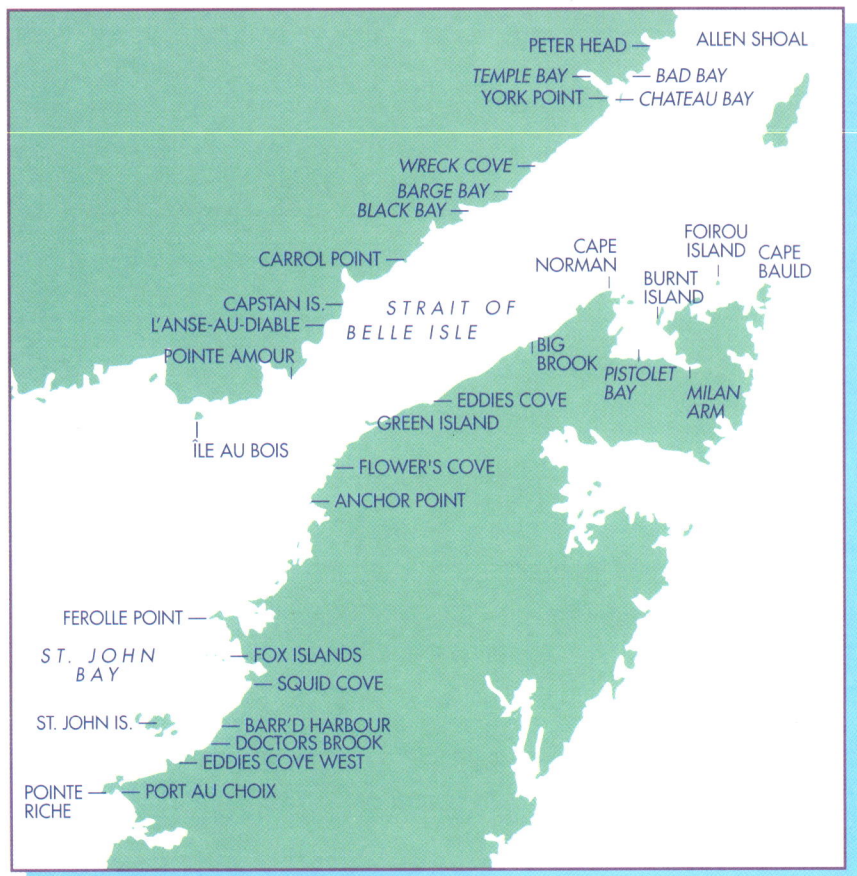

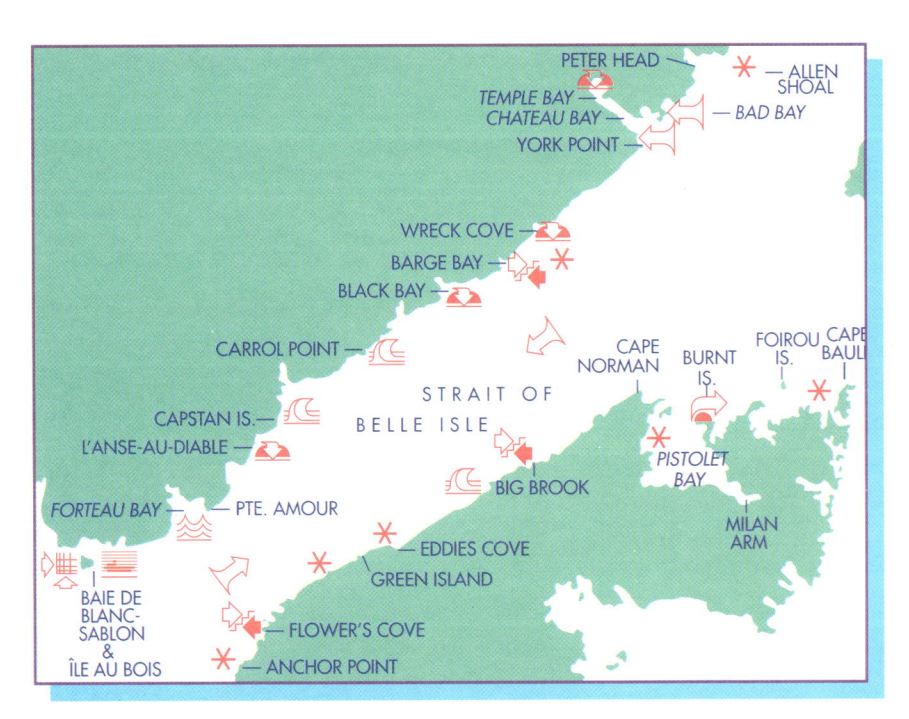

STRAIT OF BELLE ISLE
The Newfoundland side of the Strait of Belle Isle is shallower than the Labrador side. Shoaling occurs at several places along the coast, and choppy seas develop near the coast from Cape Norman to Flower's Cove when the wind opposes the current.

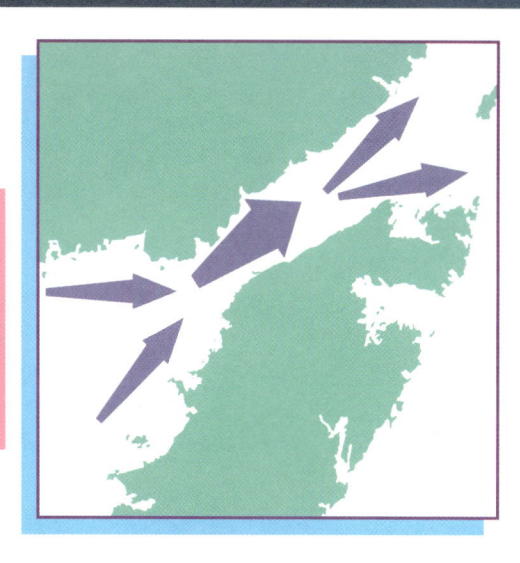

LOCAL WEATHER Newfoundland West

Caution: Katabatic Winds
Steep hills line the Labrador coast along the Strait of Belle Isle, and katabatic winds can be common. Since these usually occur when prevailing winds are light to moderate, the offshore winds may be only 15 knots; however, in this area, the katabatic winds are funnelled by valleys that cut through the hills from the north or northwest. The effect can cause a four- or five-hour blow of 35-to-40-knot northerlies near the shore, while offshore winds remain light to moderate.

STRAIT OF BELLE ISLE: FUNNELLED WINDS
Funnelling increases certain winds through the narrow part of the strait. A west-southwest to south-southwest wind will become southwesterly and increase in speed as it encounters the strait. Similarly, a north-northeast to east wind becomes northeasterly and increases in speed as it moves through the strait.

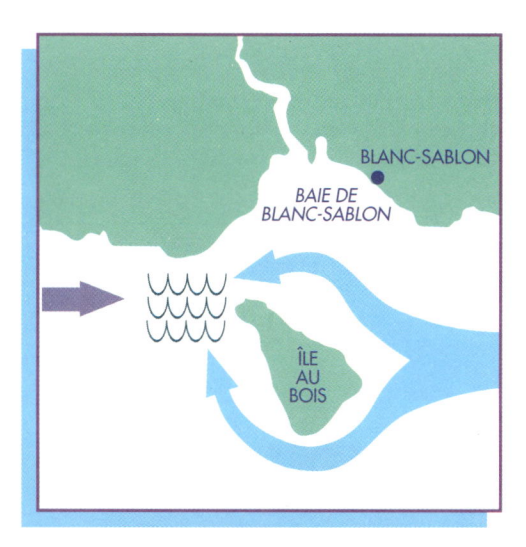

HEAVY SEAS NEAR ÎLE AU BOIS
Heavy seas occur north of Île au Bois when the wind opposes the currents. The west-going current forks around Île au Bois. The two streams then converge off the northwest end of the island, causing rough seas.

DIFFERENCES IN FOG
When it is foggy at Blanc-Sablon, visibility will sometimes improve farther east, as the southwest winds that bring the fog remain offshore.

LOCAL WEATHER Newfoundland West

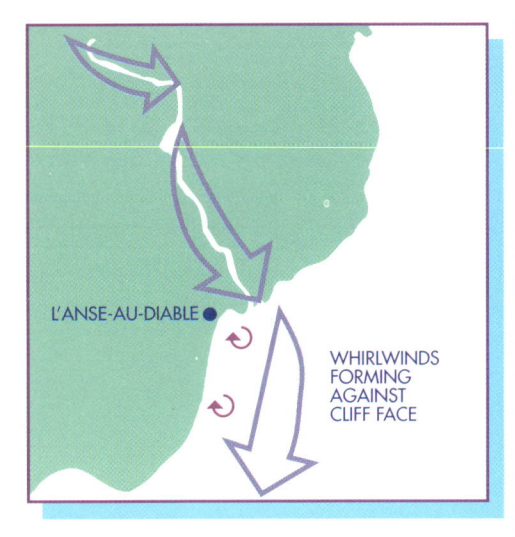

KATABATIC WINDS AT L'ANSE-AU-DIABLE

The katabatic winds that produce strong northerly gusts at L'Anse-au-Diable are felt up to 1 1/2 miles from the coast. A valley to the north channels the air flow southward until it reaches the steep cliffs at the coast. Frictional effects along the cliffs can cause whirlwinds. Winds can be 25 knots at L'Anse-au-Diable and 40 knots near the cliffs.

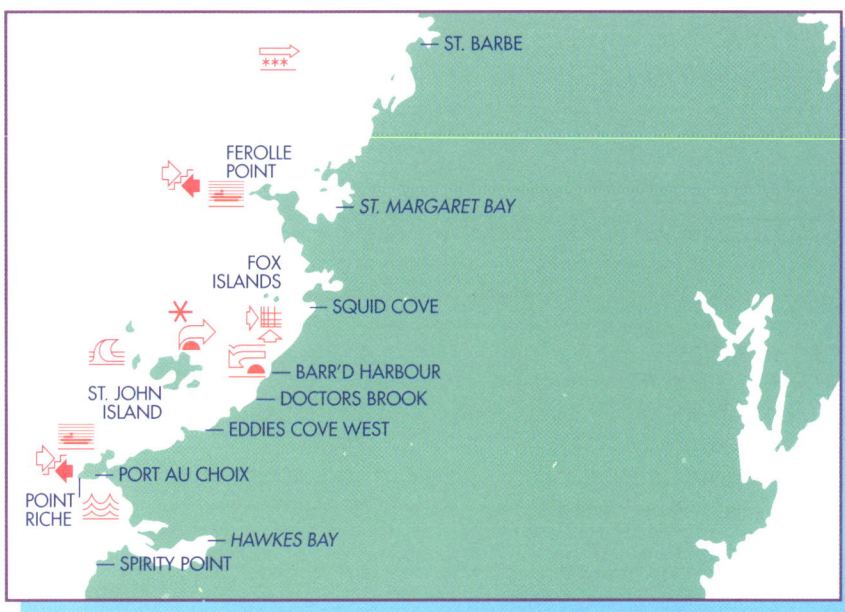

ST. BARBE TO SPIRITY POINT

St. John Bay is a roughly semicircular bay between Ferolle Point and Pointe Riche. The water depth inside the bay is generally less than half that just outside. Southwesterly winds, which have a long fetch over the Gulf of St. Lawrence, carry large seas into the bay. As well, the seas become choppier as the waves cross the shallower water of the bay.

LOCAL WEATHER Newfoundland West

Northeast Gulf

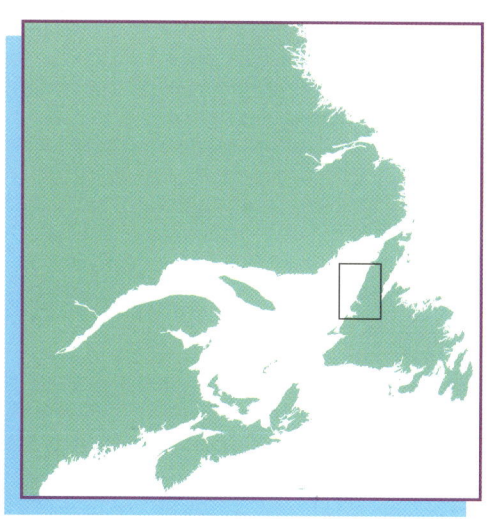

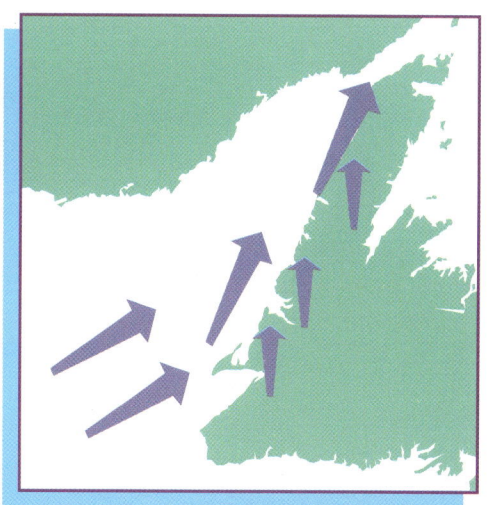

GENERAL CONDITIONS

Strong southeasterly winds occur at several places along the west coast of Newfoundland. They are known locally as squalls but are caused mainly by mountain waves. Drainage and funnelling through mountain valleys also strengthen southeasterlies; which are most common from November through May.

Whirlwinds can accompany these squalls. Known locally as "white wind," they reach speeds of 50–70 knots and can raise swirling columns of water which range from 2–10 m in diameter. White winds appear suddenly, but last only a few seconds at any one place. Fishermen who have been caught in them compare them to a swirling waterfall.

Southwest-to-northwest winds over the gulf generally cause the highest seas. If the wind is northerly, it will blow against the north-going current to create choppy seas.

When there is enough ice-free water in fall and winter, westerly winds bring snow streamers. Most of this coastline receives significant snowfalls.

For easier reading, this coastline has been divided into three sections.

CONVERGING WINDS

The west coast of Newfoundland, below the Strait of Belle Isle, lies in a southwest-to-northeast line. Southwesterly winds undergo coastal convergence, creating a band of stronger winds. Over southern sections of the coast, the Long Range Mountains push these winds some distance offshore. In the north, the mountains are farther inland, so the stronger winds occur at the coast. This effect is observed along the entire west coast of Newfoundland, but is most prominent on this stretch of coastline.

Marine Weather Tip: Weather Signs

Fishermen in this area know the warning signs of strong southeast winds funnelled through local valleys. When cold air begins to drain down a mountainside, it mixes with moist air over the ponds and creates fog at the base of the mountain. This is seen as a sign that squalls will begin in a few hours. Local fishermen can also see the wind generate white water over the ponds a few minutes before the gusts reach the coast.

115

LOCAL WEATHER Newfoundland West

LA FONTAINE POINT TO GULLS MARSH

Several valleys with ponds cut deeply into the western face of the coastal mountains. Mountain waves funnelling through the valleys cause strong southeast winds near the coast. These winds remain strong as they blow across the ponds, unaffected by friction, on their way to the coast.

A strong, north-going current runs over a shallow bank that extends 1/2 mile offshore from La Fontaine Point, occasionally producing rips.

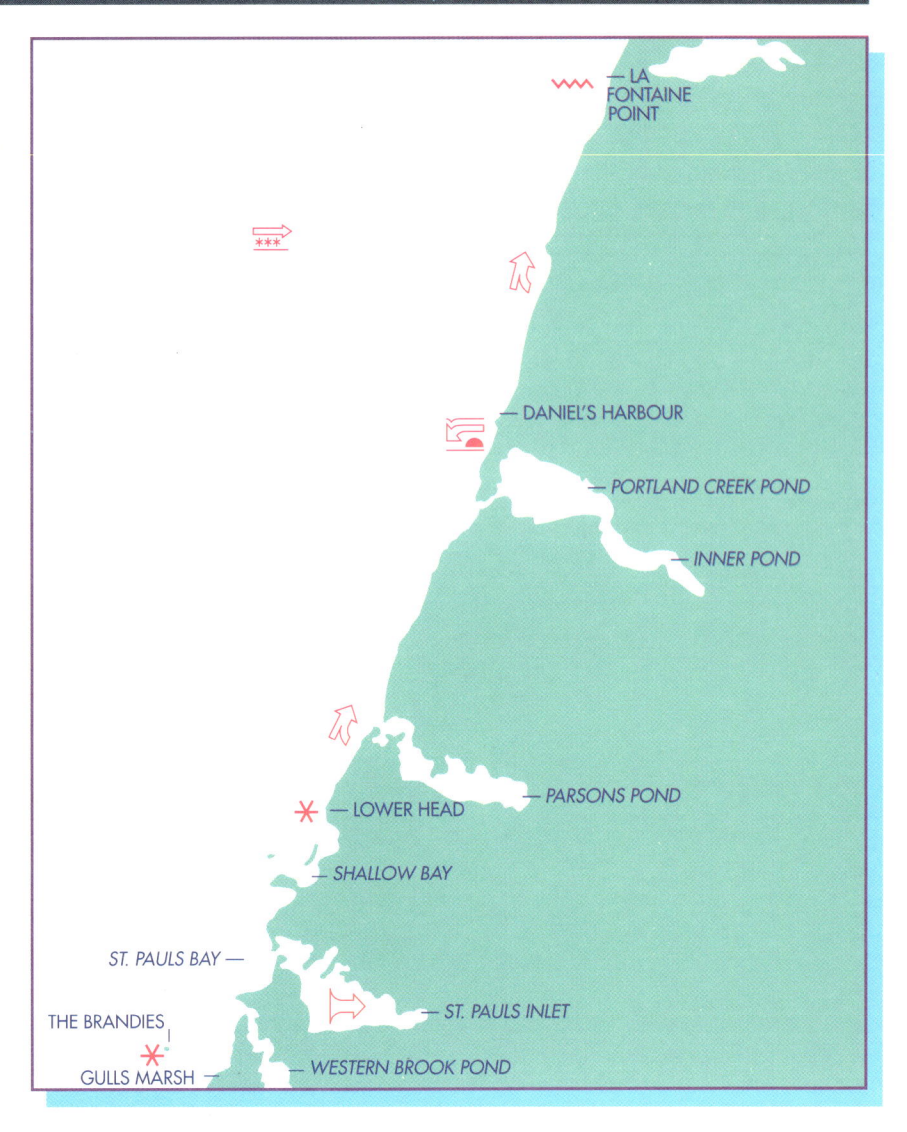

BONNE BAY

Bonne Bay is long and narrow with many steep cliffs. The steepest terrain surrounds East Arm; 2 miles inland it rises to 2,400 ft.. Winds are often funnelled through the bay and its arms, and channelled along their southeast-to-northwest axes.

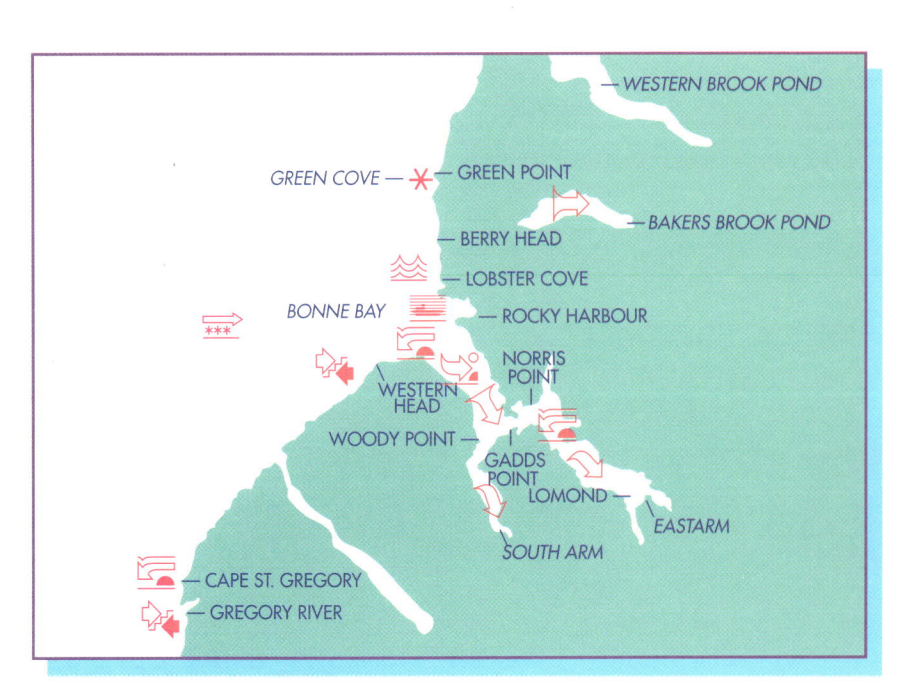

LOCAL WEATHER Newfoundland West

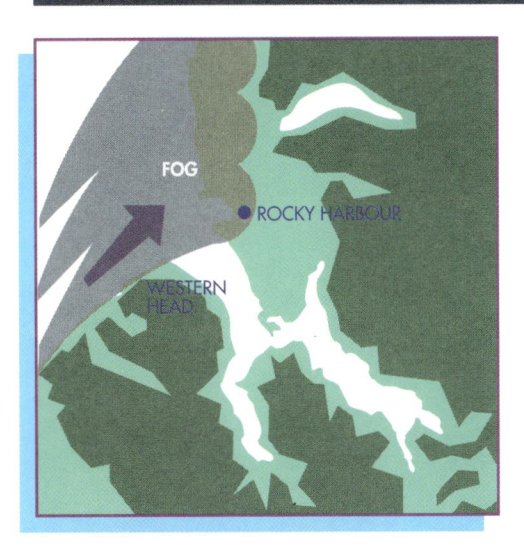

FOG IN BONNE BAY
Under a southwest flow, fog can creep into the mouth of Bonne Bay almost as far as Rocky Harbour. High terrain around Western Head prevents it from pushing farther into the bay.

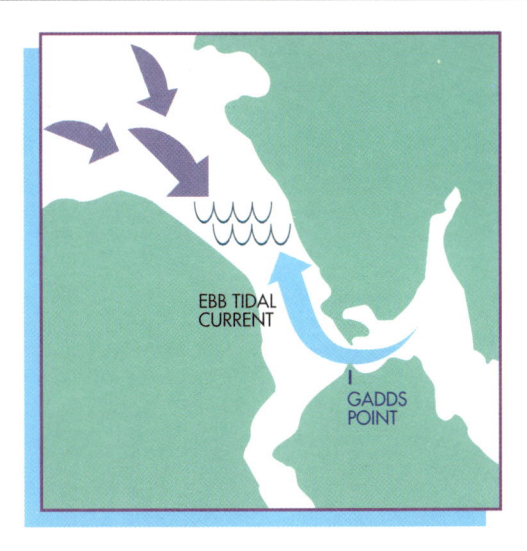

SQUALLY NORTHWEST WINDS
Northwest winds are funnelled into the mouth of this bay and create squally northwesterlies at Gadds Point. Heavy seas occur on the east side of the bay when these winds blow against the ebb tide.

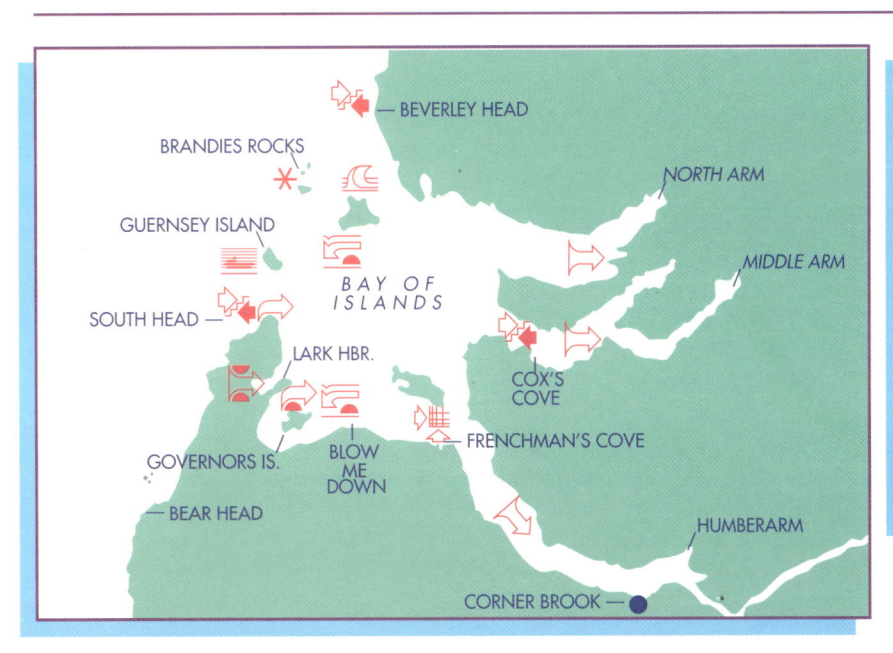

BAY OF ISLANDS
Like Bonne Bay, the Bay of Islands is surrounded by high terrain. Strong winds caused by mountain waves are common in the bay, and funnelling and channelling occur in the arms.

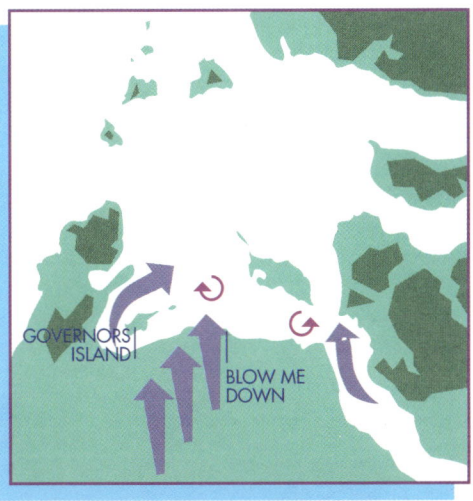

BLOW ME DOWN WHIRLWINDS
In southwest to southeast winds, mountain waves produce strong winds and whirlwinds off Blow Me Down. The winds blow around the southwest side of Governors Island, where they are reinforced by cornering effects. Southwesterly gusts are a much greater problem during the summer months.

Marine Weather Tip: Fishermen's Rule of Thumb
In this area, the strongest winds caused by mountain waves are from the east. A fishermen's rule of thumb is to add 20 knots to a forecast easterly.

117

LOCAL WEATHER Newfoundland West

Gulf-Port au Port

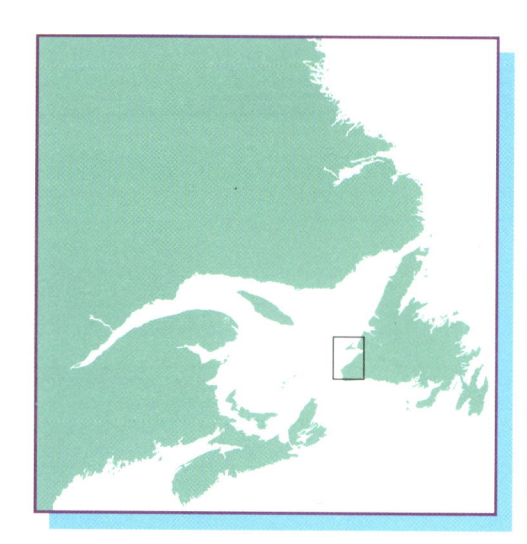

GENERAL CONDITIONS
Southeast winds caused by mountain waves are very strong along the southern part of Newfoundland's west coast. The notorious "Wreckhouse winds" are discussed later in this section.

Most of this stretch of coastline faces open water from the Gulf of St. Lawrence. Prolonged west or northwest winds often bring large seas that can break as much as 1 1/2 miles from the coast. St. George's Bay is protected somewhat against these winds, but open to southwesterly winds, which cause rough seas along the coast, from Cape St. George to Stephenville.

For easier reading, this coastline has been divided into two sections.

FISH HEAD TO ROBINSONS
St. George's Bay is much deeper than Port au Port Bay; nevertheless, rough seas occur along the coast from Cape St. George to Stephenville when winds are southwest. The bay opens to the Gulf of St. Lawrence from the southwest and is protected from sea and swell from any other direction. Fog from the gulf is trapped by the funnel shape of the bay, much of which remains ice-free for most of the winter.

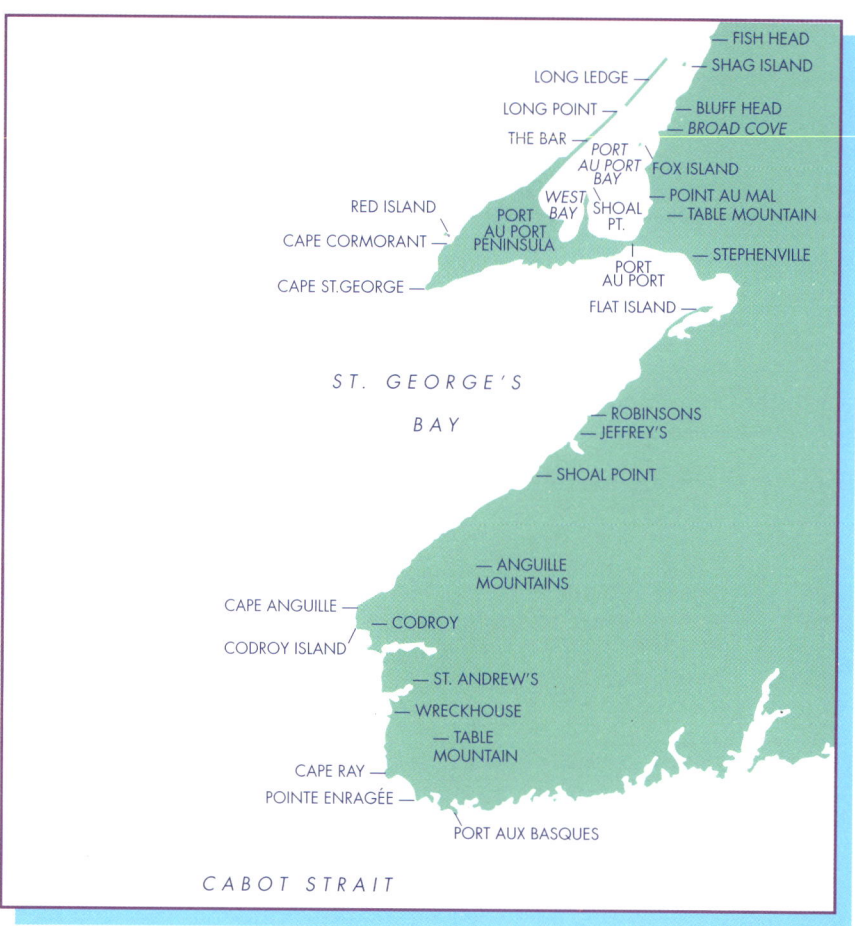

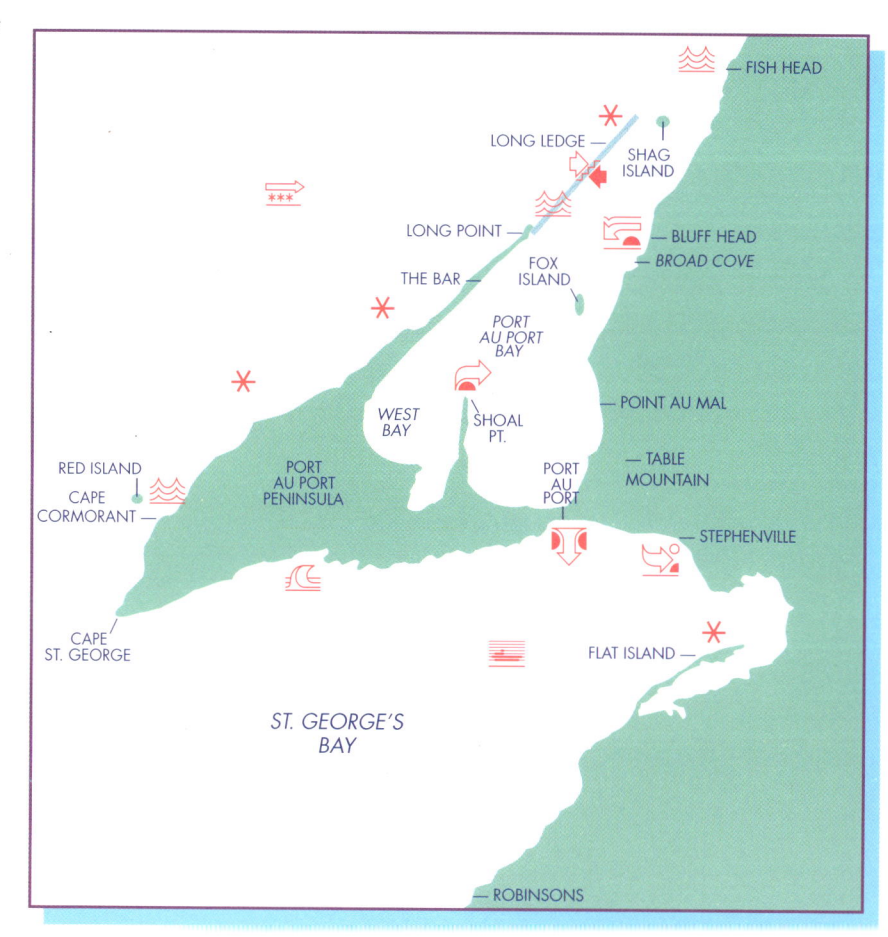

LOCAL WEATHER Newfoundland West

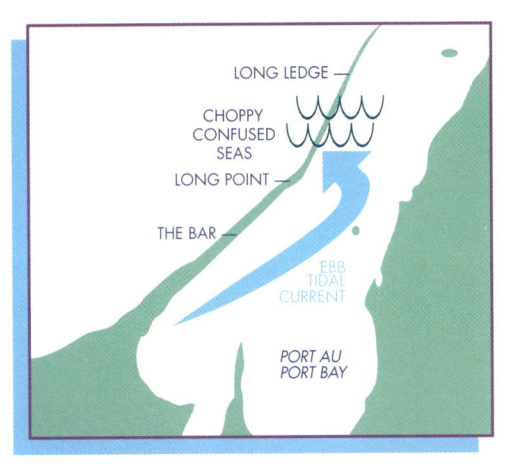

TRICKY TIDES IN PORT AU PORT BAY
The ebb-tide current leaving Port au Port Bay turns west to cross The Bar at Long Point, causing eddies and overfalls. Both flood and ebb tides move quickly across the bar, creating heavy seas when the wind opposes the current.

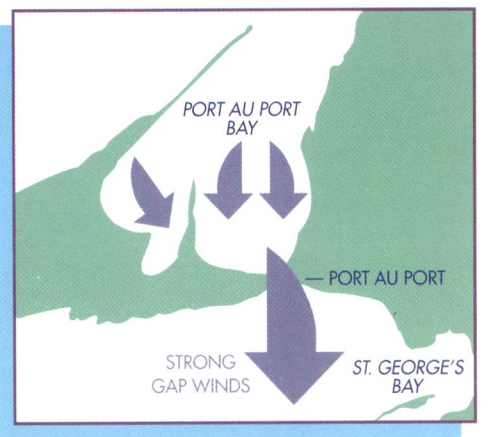

VIOLENT NORTHERLIES IN PORT AU PORT BAY
Violent northerly winds have been reported south of Port au Port to at least 2 miles out. Northerly winds from Port au Port Bay funnel across the narrow isthmus that connects the Port au Port Peninsula to the rest of Newfoundland. These strong gap winds fan out as they enter St. George's Bay.

A local fisherman experienced this effect for some time while carefully making his way to Stephenville. He also described seeing a white wall of water before being hit, suggesting that a lot of spray was picked up by this wind.

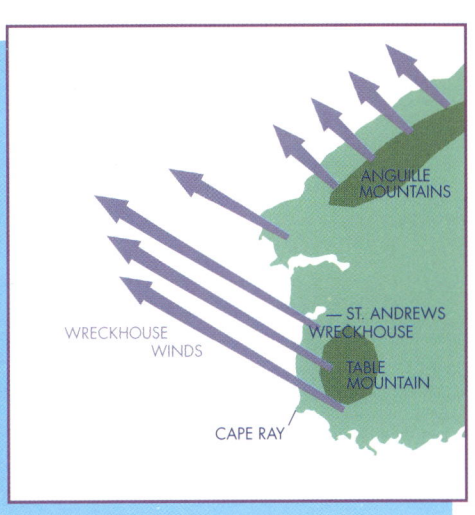

WRECKHOUSE WINDS
The coast from 3 miles south of St. Andrews to Cape Ray is well known for its vicious southeast winds, known as the Wreckhouse winds. These winds are infamous for derailing trains and blowing down power-line towers. Mountain waves off Table Mountain create the effect, which is felt as far as 20 miles out to sea—drainage and funnelling may enhance the effect. Southeast winds of 25–30 knots at Port aux Basques can mean winds of 50–60 knots—or more—at Wreckhouse!

ROBINSONS TO PORT AUX BASQUES
Cape Ray is the southwesternmost point on Newfoundland. The coast to the north is exposed to the northwest and, towards Port aux Basques and beyond, is exposed to the south and southwest. Fog is much more frequent at Port aux Basques than at Cape Ray, but when it's showery at Cape Ray, in west-to-northwest winds, the weather is often much better at Port aux Basques and to the east.

LOCAL WEATHER Newfoundland South

Southwest Newfoundland

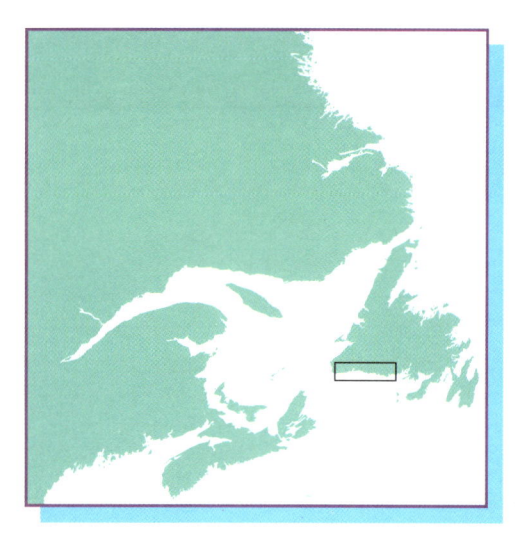

GENERAL CONDITIONS

A series of steep cliffs runs parallel to this stretch of the Newfoundland coastline. They are indented by many narrow, steep-sided bays, which run from north to south. The configuration of the bays produces gap winds when winds blow from the northeast. This effect combines with coastal convergence to create violent winds in and around the mouths of these bays.

The coastline is exposed to an unlimited fetch of open sea to the south, so it takes the full brunt of large waves and swells that have been generated over the deep ocean.

Areas with shoals feel the greatest effect. During the winter, the seas off this coastline cool to slightly below 0°C, but usually do not freeze; therefore, freezing spray is a concern when cold westerlies blow, while thick fog develops when mild southerlies set in.

Southerly and westerly winds are also affected by the coastline's geography. Steep cliffs along the coast block southerly flows, which in turn creates strong easterlies near the shore. This effect will be discussed in detail in this section.

For easier reading, this coastline has been divided into two sections.

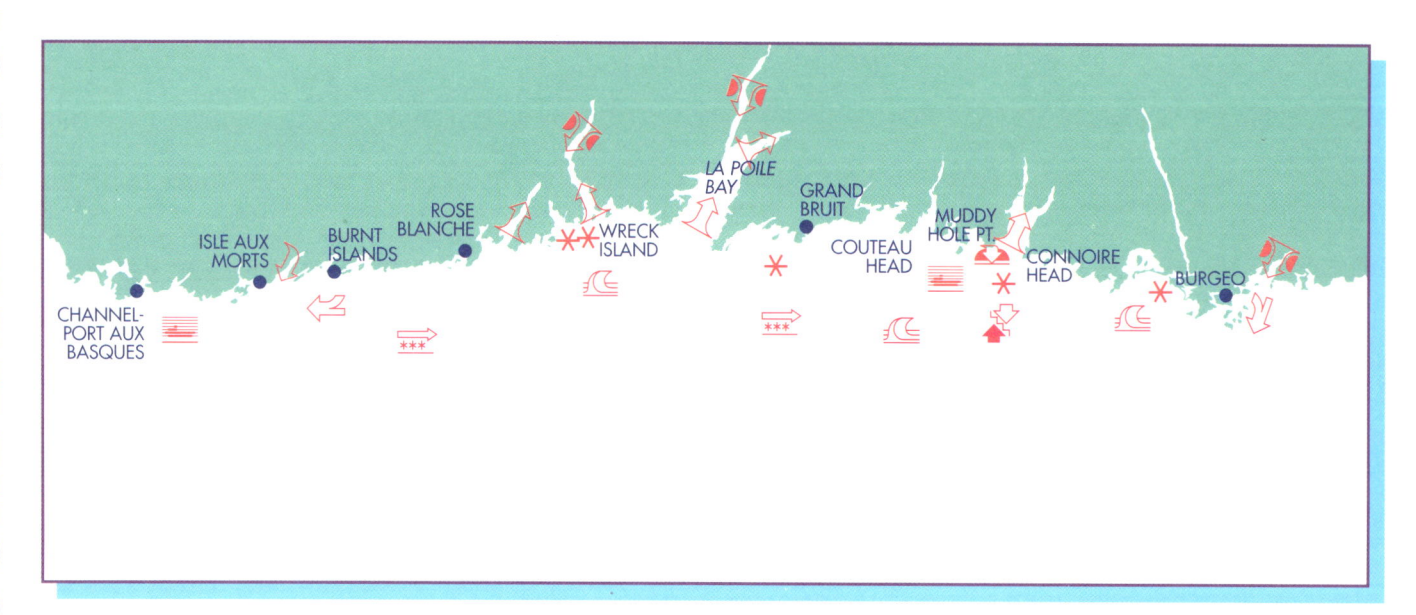

PORT AUX BASQUES TO BURGEO

This stretch of coastline runs from east to west and is marked by steep and rugged cliffs indented with north-to-south running bays and inlets. The topography makes blocking, channelling, and funnelling of winds important effects near the shore.

LOCAL WEATHER Newfoundland South

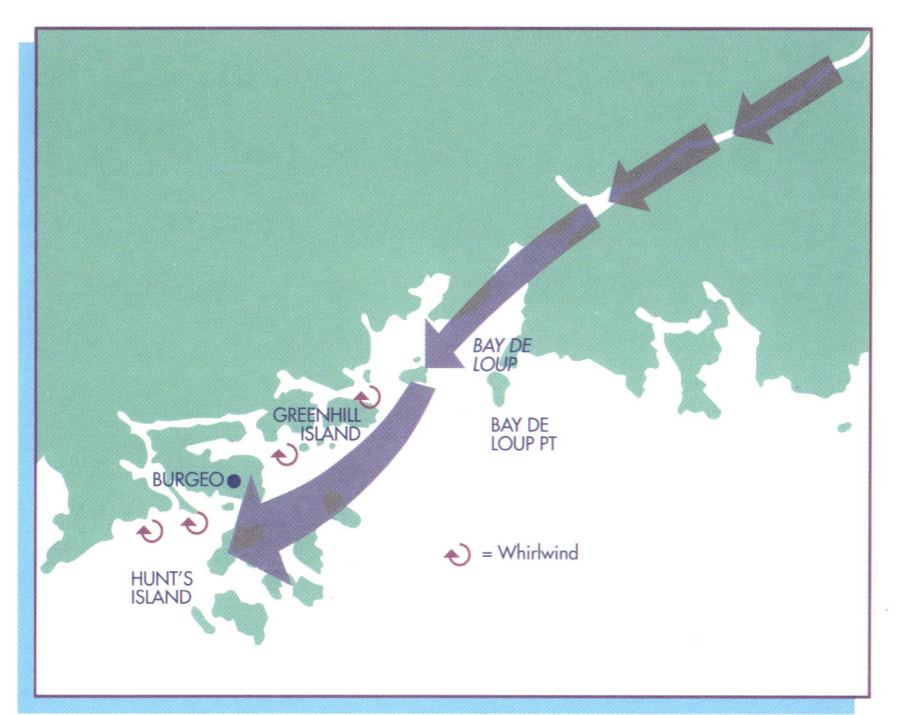

STRONG NORTHEASTERLIES AT BURGEO
At Burgeo, northeasterly winds are funnelled and channelled through Bay de Loup. Coastal convergence further increases their speed. Whirlwinds are often observed near the coast in these conditions, and Burgeo has reported winds of up to 75 knots. This effect is common to northeast channels along this section of the coast.

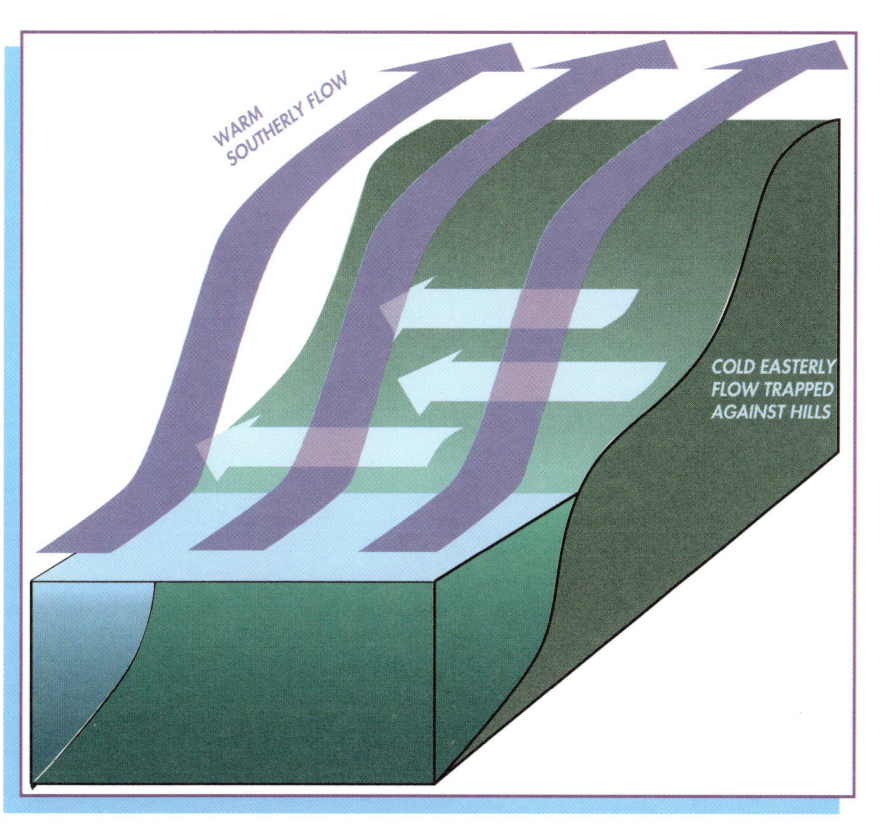

(Map showing Bay de Loup, Bay de Loup Pt, Greenhill Island, Burgeo, Hunt's Island, with whirlwind symbols)

BLOCKING OF SOUTHERLIES
This effect occurs mainly in the spring, when a mild southerly flow pushes cooler air against hills along the coastline. The warm southerlies ride over this trapped cool air; the resulting difference in air pressure between the two air masses leads to the development of an easterly circulation along the coast. This effect is often observed up to 15 miles out to sea.

(Diagram showing WARM SOUTHERLY FLOW over COLD EASTERLY FLOW TRAPPED AGAINST HILLS)

Marine Weather Tip
Many place names provide a clue to potential weather conditions in an area. In Newfoundland, Funnel Head, Wreck Cove, Mistaken Point, Cap au Diable (Cape of the Devil), and several Blow Me Downs all speak for themselves. The shape of the land and the sea bed affects the behaviour of the wind and the sea, providing another clue to weather conditions.
   There are three Blow Me Downs along this stretch of coast, all located in steep-walled valleys. Blow Me Down Point in White Bear Bay is a good example of how these locales earned their names and reputations.

Marine Weather Tip
Local fishermen add 15–20 knots to the forecast wind speed along this coastline when crossing the mouth of a bay in north-to-northeasterly winds. The winds slacken on the far side of the bay.

LOCAL WEATHER Newfoundland South

BURGEO TO HARE BAY

Many factors combine to produce the well-known high seas along this coastline—the most important is its unlimited southern exposure, or fetch, to the Atlantic. Strong southeast-to-southwest winds contribute to the effect. Local conditions, such as wave refraction around Ramea Island and shoaling between Cape La Hune and Recontre West, can produce wave heights three times higher than at open sea.

During the late spring, run-off from the river valleys around the bays generates strong seaward currents. When winds blow onshore against this current, confused seas develop near the bays and around the small islands that dot the shoreline.

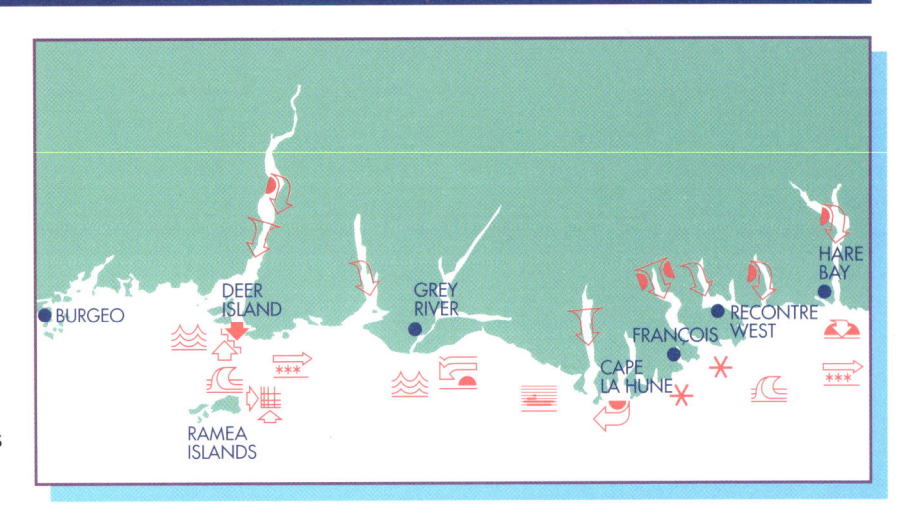

Haven of Rest: Few Gales

During the summer months, westerly gales are rare along this coast, but, they are sometimes observed about 6 miles offshore. This effect is likely due to a combination of coastal divergence and the stabilizing influence of the cooler coastal water.

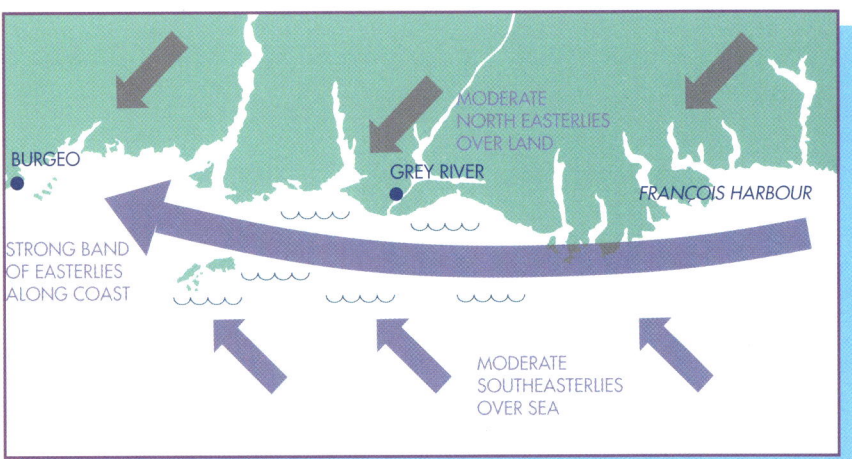

COASTAL CONVERGENCE AND DIVERGENCE

Easterly winds in this area cause coastal convergence—hence stronger winds near the shore. Conversely, strong westerlies here are usually weaker near the shore, due to a divergence effect.

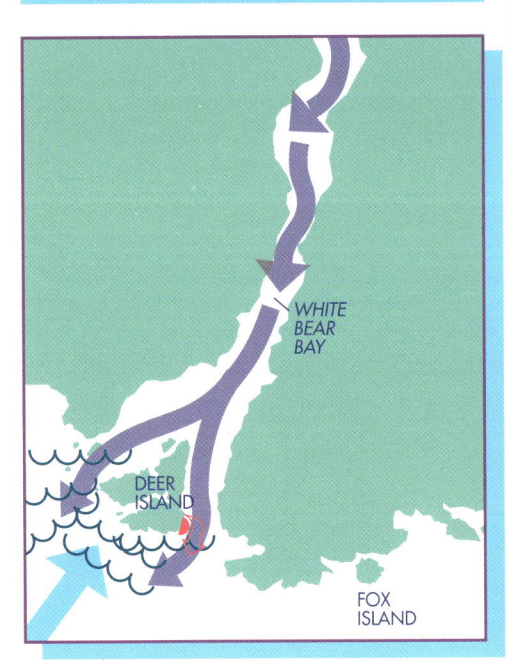

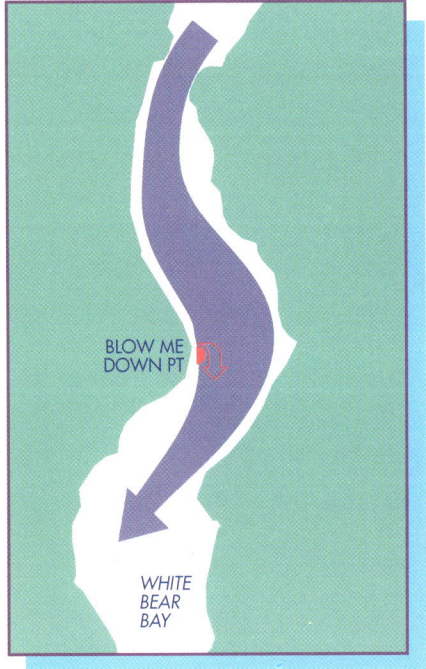

BLOW ME DOWN POINT IN WHITE BEAR BAY

At Blow Me Down Point, several factors combine to create very strong winds. Northerly winds funnel down the bay between steep cliffs. They are subjected to cornering at the point, which further increases their speed.

DEER ISLAND

Deer Island lies at the mouth of White Bear Bay. Northerly winds are channelled and funnelled through the bay, then around the island. This creates confused seas on the leeward side of the island. Seas are roughest on the southeastern side, due to cornering. This is worsened when the northerly wind opposes the north-going flood tide in this area.

LOCAL WEATHER Newfoundland South

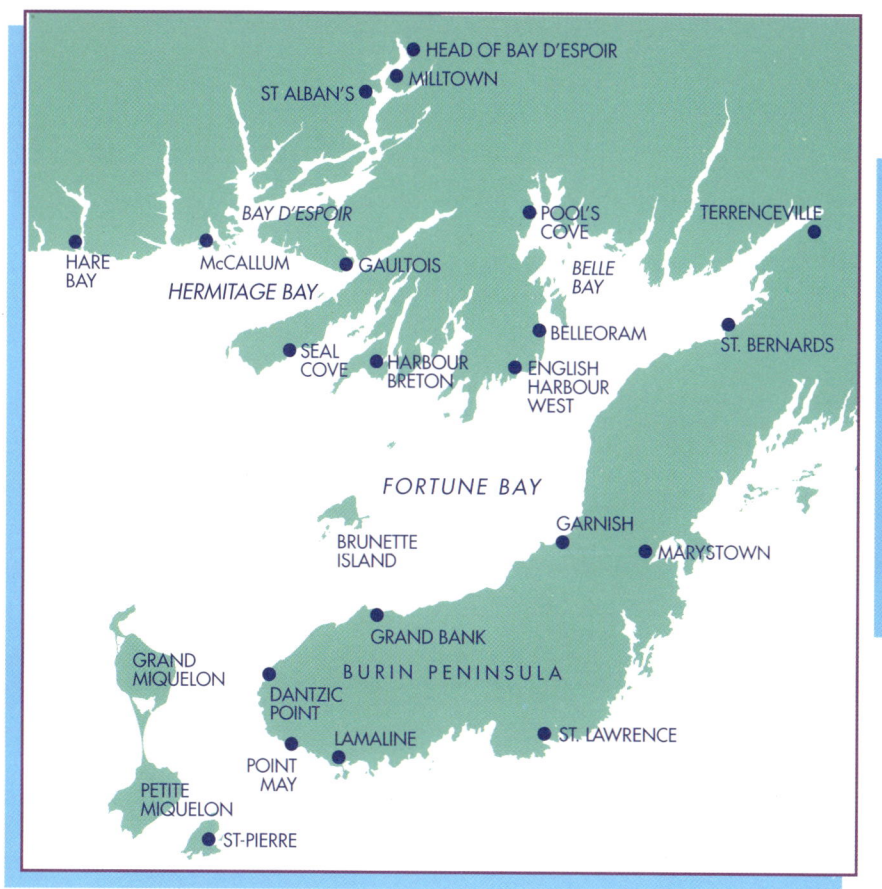

Fortune

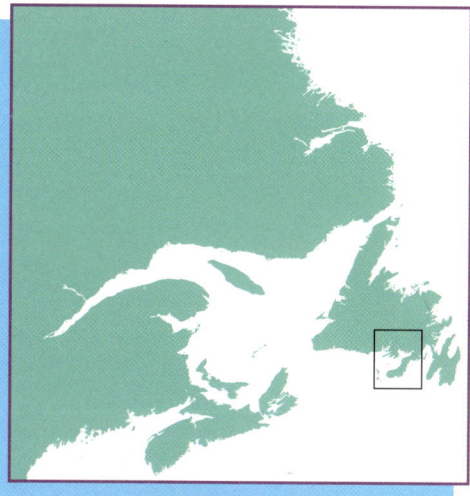

GENERAL CONDITIONS

This coastline has several large bays, running from southwest to northeast. With the exception of Bay d'Espoir, they are fairly open to seas from the southwest, but sheltered from southerly waves by the Burin Peninsula and the Miquelon Islands.

The configuration of the many bays causes southwesterly and northeasterly winds to be channelled and funnelled. Cornering effects are also common through this region, due to the many exposed capes and headlands.

Open water year round makes fog common along this coast, and causes freezing spray and heavy snowsqualls in winter.

For easier reading, this coastline has been divided into three sections.

HARE BAY TO GAULTOIS

Like the coastline from Burgeo to Hare Bay, this stretch of coast has river valleys with late spring run-off, generating strong seaward currents. Onshore winds blowing against these currents create confused and choppy seas near shore.

The dominant feature here is Bay d'Espoir, a large bay running generally from southwest to northeast. It has a small and fairly well-sheltered entrance, which protects the bay from large swells, strong winds from the sea, and fog. During warmer months, in a southwesterly flow, the more exposed coastline is fogged in, while Bay d'Espoir has much better visibility.

123

LOCAL WEATHER Newfoundland South

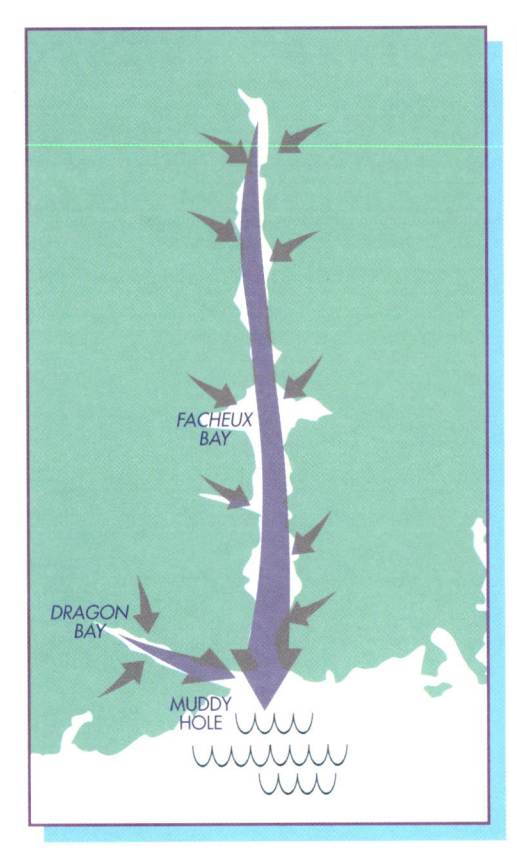

MUDDY HOLE
Cool and gusty drainage winds are a frequent occurrence at the mouths of bays along this coast. These are most common on summer nights, when skies are clear and winds are fairly light.

A good example of this is Muddy Hole, where cool air drains out of Facheux Bay and Dragon Bay. Fishermen familiar with this area report that cold, gusty northerlies are common in the early morning during the summer.

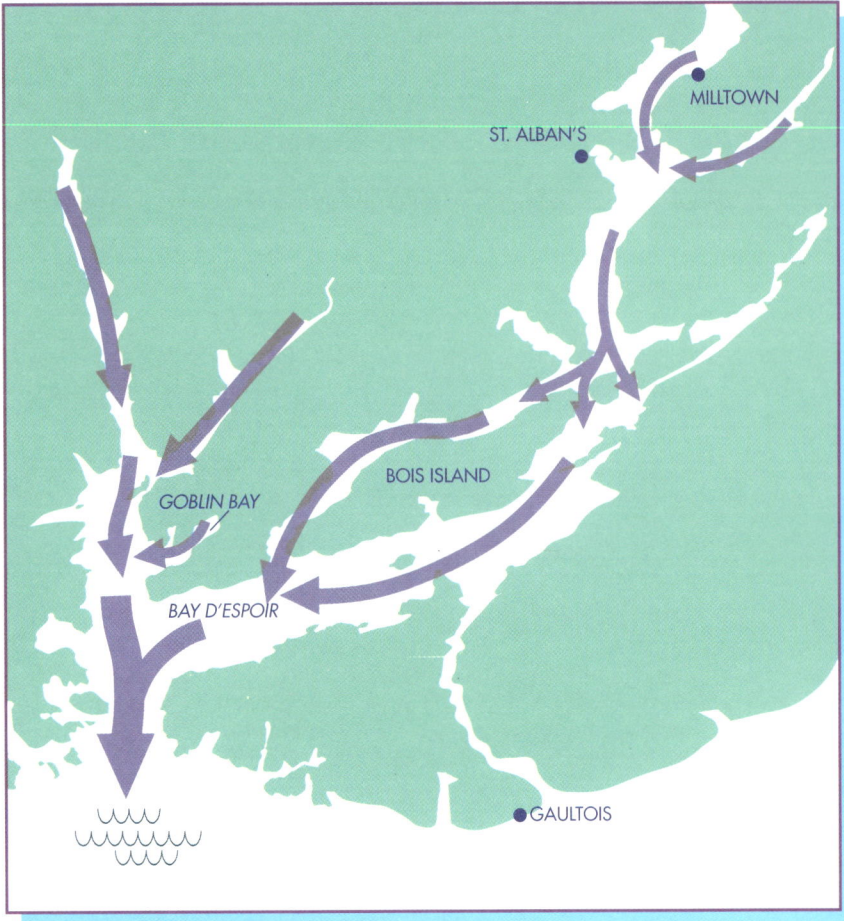

VARIABLE WINDS IN BAY D'ESPOIR
This complex bay is well sheltered from the south and west, but a northerly flow can be drastically altered by the islands and steep-walled valleys in the area.

The many-cliffed bays and coves extending off Bay d'Espoir cause channelling and funnelling of winds into the bay. This is especially noticeable at the mouth of the bay in northerly winds. Northerlies are funnelled down North Bay, then funnelled again as they pass through the north-south cliffs at the bay's entrance.

Channelling causes winds to align themselves with the various bays, whose orientations range from northwest to east. Funnelling through valleys and cornering around islands creates areas of much stronger winds.

Caution: Funnelling
Northerly winds can double in strength across the mouth of Bay d'Espoir as a result of wind funnelling through the bay's narrow entrance.

LOCAL WEATHER Newfoundland South

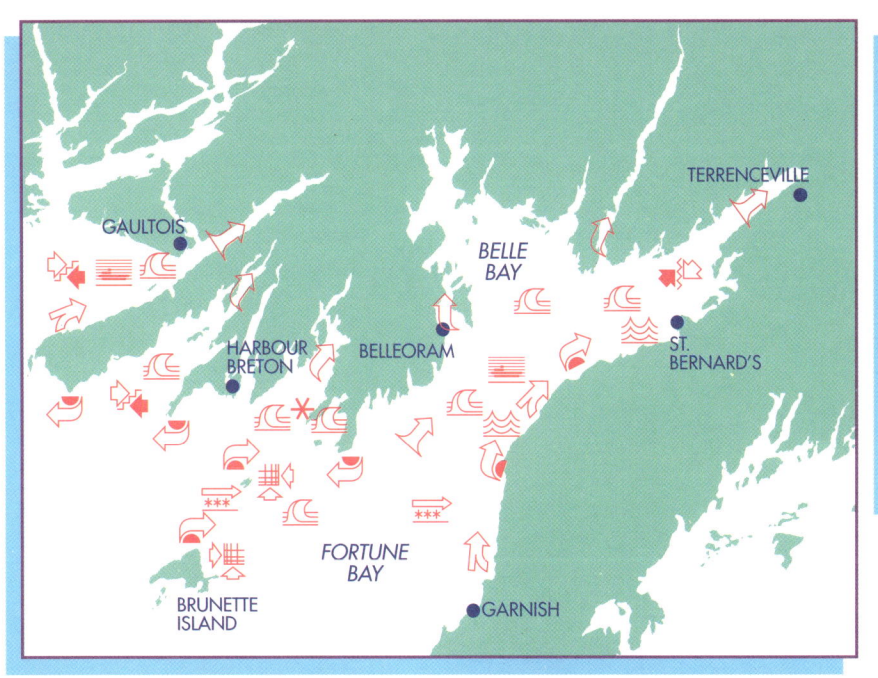

GAULTOIS TO GARNISH

This area includes several large bays extending from southwest to northeast—the largest being Fortune Bay. The orientation of these bays makes funnelling and channelling of northeast and southwest winds critical marine-weather effects in this area. These effects are often magnified by cornering around the many capes between the bays.

Funnelling of southwesterlies at the head of Fortune Bay, near Terrenceville, often makes navigation difficult. Many local ferry operators use Bay L'Argent for shelter.

The bays along the western portion of this coast are fully exposed to the southwest, so large swells are driven onto the shore. When these swells are forced into the many narrow bays along the coast, very high seas can develop. This effect is further enhanced at high tide—especially at spring tide, which creates "an awful sea," as fishermen put it. Farther east, in Fortune Bay and Belle Bay, the upstream land and the Miquelon Islands provide an effective shelter from the southwest.

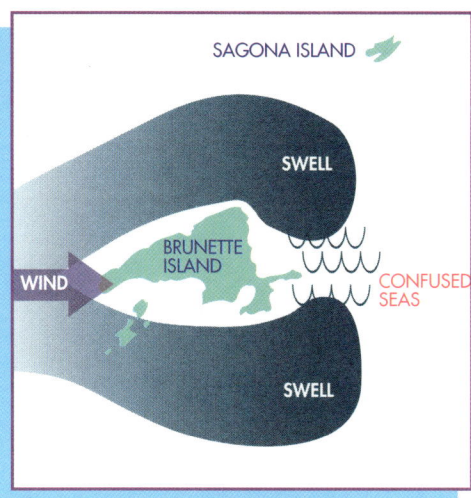

BRUNETTE ISLAND

Strong westerly winds, and the large sea that accompanies them, are blocked by Brunette Island. The wind and waves travel around the island and meet on the leeward side, creating very rough seas. Seas are less rough in easterly winds because the fetch of open water is insufficient to build large waves.

Note that westerly winds are often enhanced around the northern shores of Brunette Island and Sagona Island, due to cornering and convergence. These effects can also enhance snow streamers, causing very low visibility and winds that gust to over 30 knots more than elsewhere.

Marine Weather Tip

Sagona Island is exposed to winds from all quadrants, so the wind report from the automatic station on the island is a good indication of the wind you can expect offshore.

125

LOCAL WEATHER Newfoundland South

Snowsqualls and Freezing Spray
In winter, the waters off this coast do not freeze, making snow-squalls and freezing spray common from late December through February. Freezing spray is especially dangerous during snow-squalls when heavy snow builds up on a boat and adds to the weight of the icing, and during rough seas, when the sea-surface temperature is below 0°C.

Fog
Fortune Bay is known for frequent heavy fogs, mainly in spring, when warm air from the south travels across the cold water. During late spring and summer, the sun is usually strong enough to lift the fog inland and along the coast, but rolls in again at nightfall.

BELLE BAY

This is a medium-size bay extending northwestward from Fortune Bay. Unlike many of the other bays in this area, Belle Bay is well sheltered from the open ocean. It is protected by land from all directions but south and southeast, where there is a fairly small fetch across Fortune Bay. When strong southwesterlies bring fog and large swells to Fortune Bay, Belle Bay usually experiences lighter winds, smoother seas and better visibility.

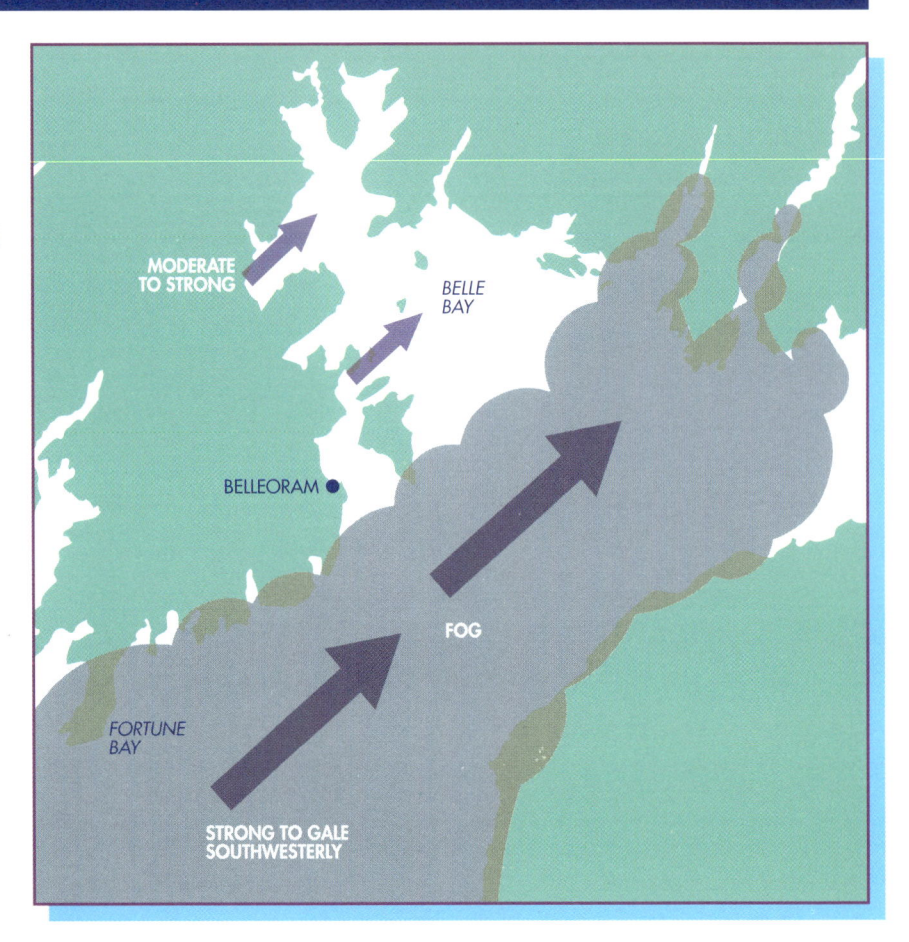

CORNERING AT POINT ENRAGÉE

From Garnish to St. Bernard's, southwest winds undergo coastal convergence, resulting in a band of very strong winds and choppy seas near the shore. This effect is increased at Point Enragée, where cornering makes the winds even stronger.

LOCAL WEATHER Newfoundland South

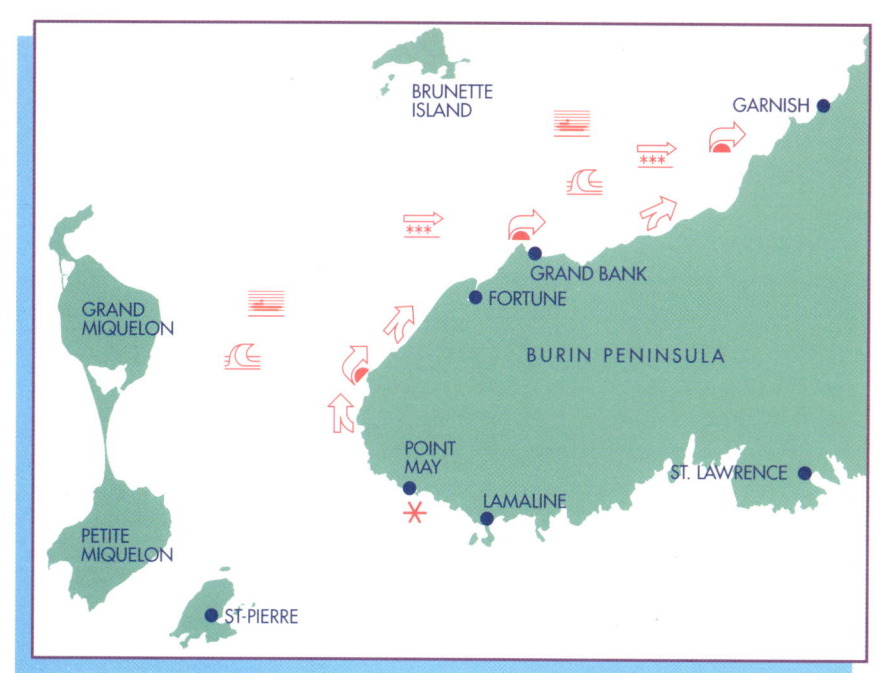

GARNISH TO POINT MAY

This section describes the southwestern portion of the Burin Peninsula. The coastline here is dominated by low rolling hills and several small coves. A few exposed points along this coastline are prone to cornering.

For the most part, this area is fairly well sheltered from the worst effects of the wind. The Burin Peninsula provides protection from the east, while the Miquelon Islands provide some shelter from swells to the southwest. Western exposure, however, is quite extensive, which makes for heavy onshore snowfall.

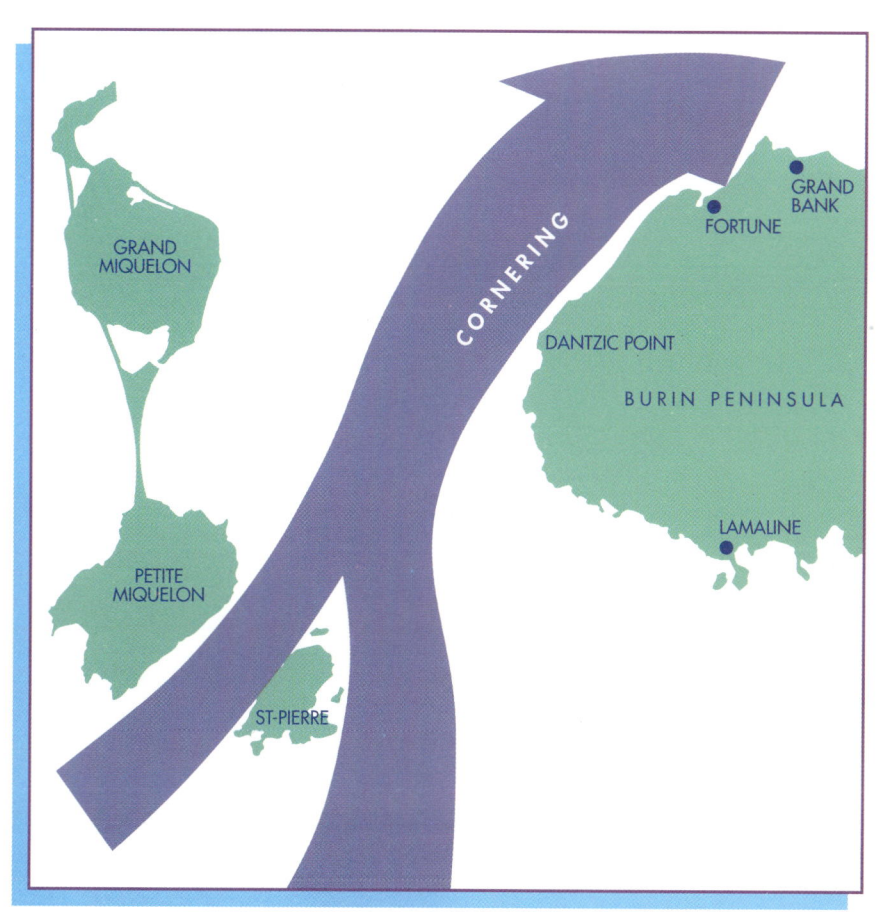

DANTZIC POINT

Strong southerlies are funnelled between the Miquelon Islands and the southwestern tip of the Burin Peninsula. Cornering near Dantzic Point creates even stronger winds.

LOCAL WEATHER Newfoundland South

Placentia Bay

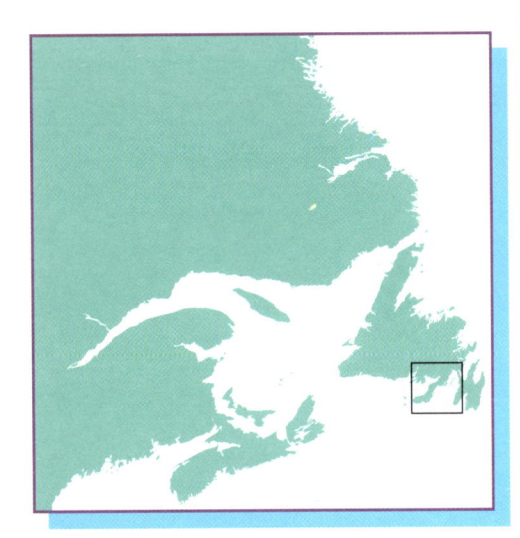

GENERAL CONDITIONS

Placentia Bay is a large, triangular bay bound to the west by the Burin Peninsula and to the east by the Avalon Peninsula. The bay's deep, wide entrance gives way to narrower and shallower waters midway into the bay. Shoals become extensive in the shallow section, causing areas of very rough seas under certain weather conditions.

The bay's wide opening to the south allows large swells to travel into its narrower and shallower reaches, causing frequent rough seas. Storm surges are common over the eastern part of the bay, especially along the eastern coast, north of the town of Placentia.

Coastal convergence increases southwesterlies on the east side of the bay, while northeasterlies are enhanced on the west side. Several large islands near the head of the bay create areas where channelling and funnelling occur.

Southerly winds produce widespread fog throughout this area. Unlike areas west of the Burin Peninsula, the fog here does not lift through the day so long as there is a southerly wind.

For easier reading, this coastline has been divided into three sections.

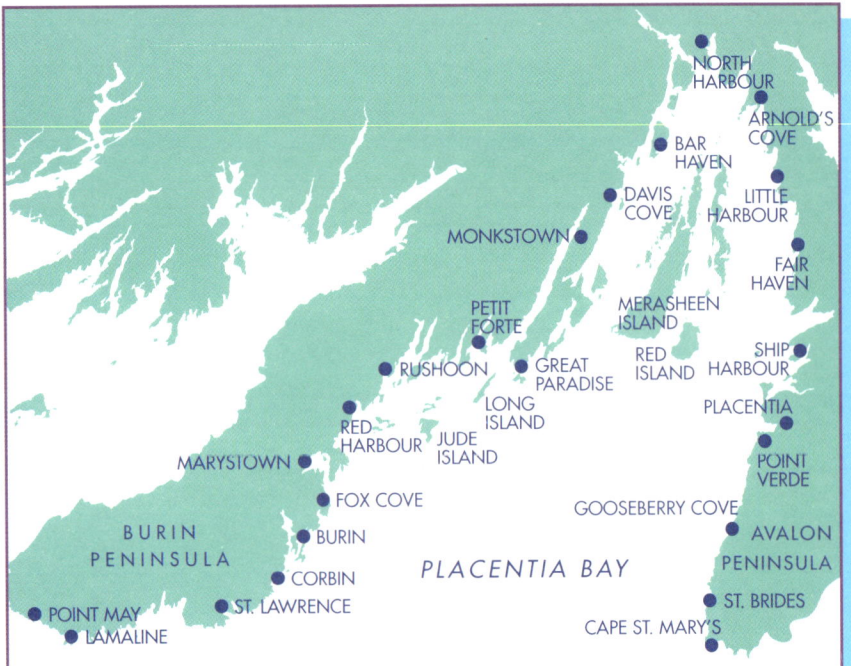

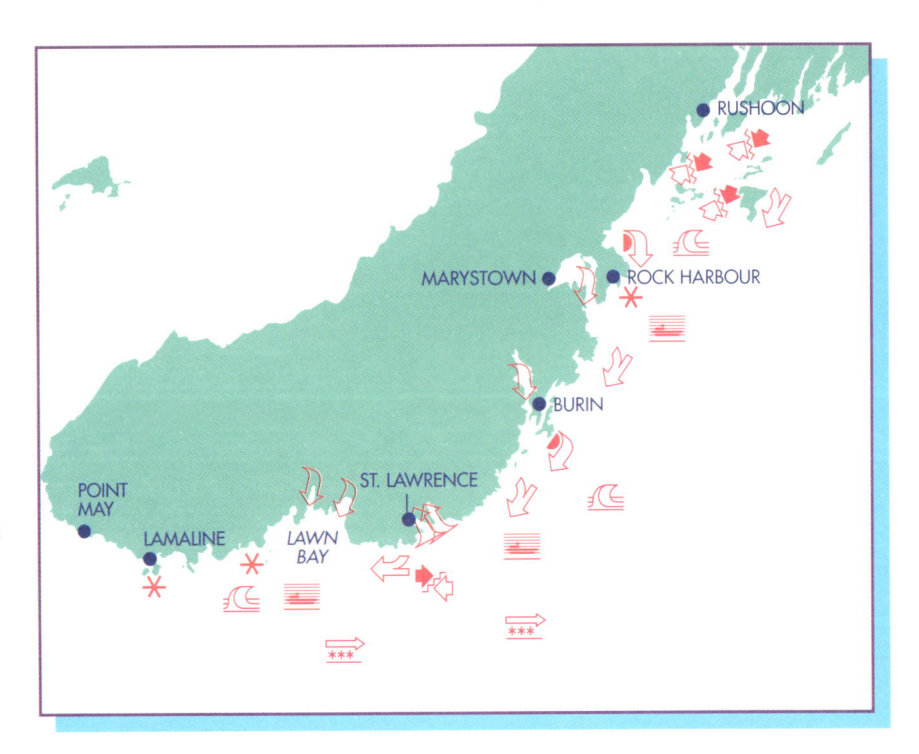

POINT MAY TO RUSHOON

This is a fairly flat stretch of coastline marked by several bays and dotted with small islands. The low terrain does little to block southwesterly winds, while coastal convergence tends to strengthen northeasterlies.

LOCAL WEATHER Newfoundland South

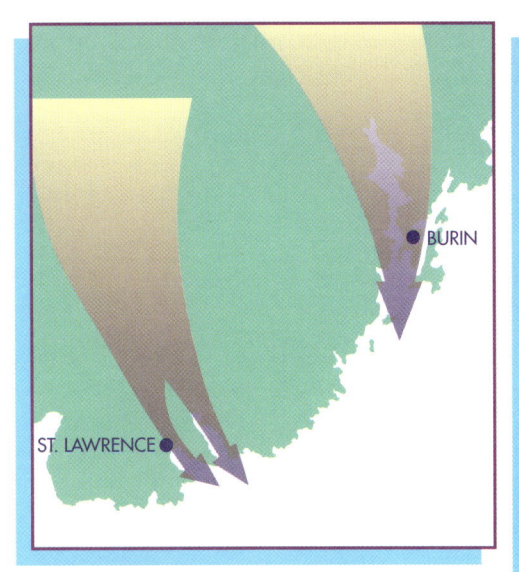

ST. LAWRENCE TO BURIN—FUNNELLING AND CHANNELLING
Northwesterly winds travel virtually unobstructed across the exposed southern part of the peninsula and are then channelled or funnelled through several small river valleys along the coast. This effect causes strong, gusty winds near the mouths of these bays and river valleys.

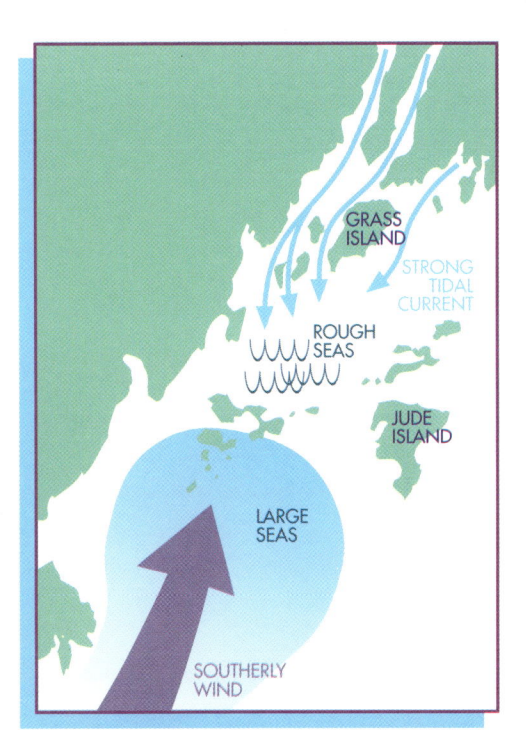

GRASS ISLAND AND JUDE ISLAND
When the tide is falling, there is a strong southward tidal current between the Burin Peninsula and the many small islands offshore. Southerly winds bring large seas into the bay, which oppose the tidal current and cause rough, confused seas.

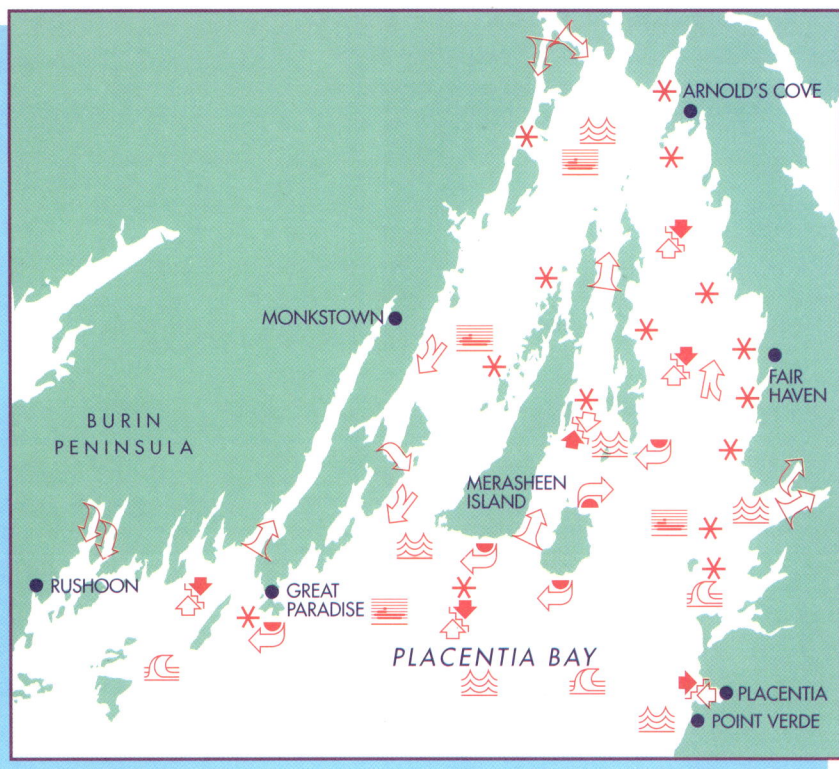

RUSHOON TO POINT VERDE
This wedge-shaped area includes the narrowest and shallowest waters in Placentia Bay and is indented by many narrow bays. Several large islands at the head of Placentia Bay create many long channels where winds can be funnelled. Southwesterly winds drive large waves into this shallow area, causing very rough seas. The geometry of the bay makes for frequent storm surges and seiches.

The shallowness of this section of Placentia Bay makes a knowledge of the many areas of shoaling critical for sailors. Remember to make use of *Sailing Directions*.

Surges and Seiches in Placentia Bay
The bay is noted for its surges and seiches. Deep low-pressure centres with persistent gales create large surges. Seiches set up in the wake of storms once the wind has shifted—the high water sloshes from one side of the bay to the other, continuing for up to a couple of days.

Long Harbour to Placentia: Storm Surges
The most common storm-surge scenario for this part of Placentia Bay occurs when an intense low-pressure centre passes just west of the Burin Peninsula. Gale- to storm-force southerly winds, ahead of the low, push large swells into the bay. The movement of water to the right of the wind forces even more sea onto this coast. Storm surges near the town of Placentia can cause severe flooding due to the bathymetry, especially at spring tide, when the large volume of water is pushed onto the shore at high tide.

Did you hear about Placentia Bay's record storm surge? On the morning of January 5, 1989, an intense low-pressure system crossed the Burin Peninsula. Storm-force southerlies ahead of the low pushed very large seas into Placentia Bay. It happened at high tide, when levels approached spring tide height. When this very high water was forced over the low-lying land near the town of Placentia, extensive flooding resulted. The tide gauge at the mouth of Argentia Harbour registered 3.17 m above the predicted tide—an all-time record.

LOCAL WEATHER Newfoundland South

PARADISE SOUND
A southerly wind opposing a south-moving tidal current in Paradise Sound causes short steep waves in this area. As one local fisherman put it: "You can't fish. Seas become choppy like the devil."

Caution: Unexpected Seas in Placentia Bay
Due to the shape and bathymetry of Placentia Bay, mariners should be aware that it only takes a moderate southerly wind to generate large seas in and around the bay. Because of the sizable fetch to the south, large swells—waves generated well south of Newfoundland—can enter the bay at any time, even if conditions seem benign.

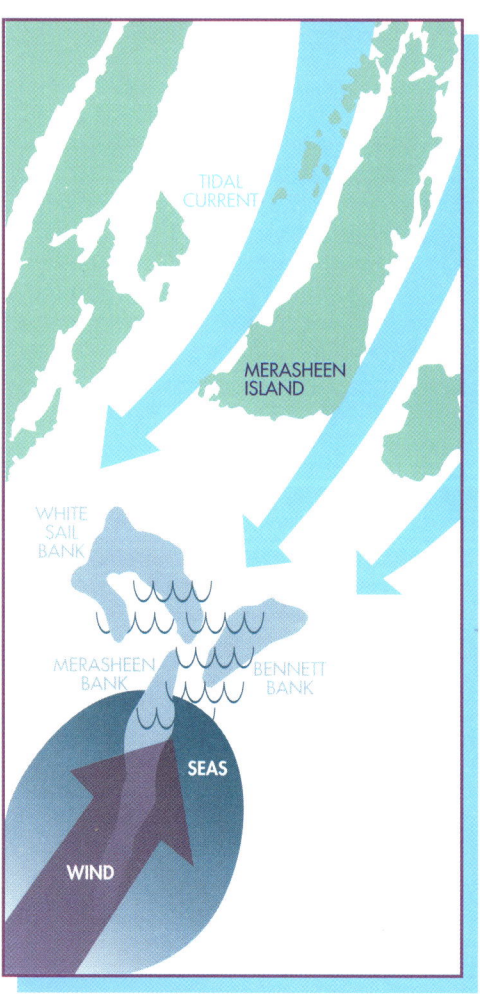

Haven of Rest: Shelter
When caught in the strong westerlies north of Red Island, local fishermen head toward the coast of Merasheen Island, where winds tend to be lighter due to the coastal divergence of southwesterlies.

MERASHEEN ISLAND
Large seas predominate in this area, because of the White Sail Bank, Bennet Bank, and the Merasheen Bank, south of Merasheen Island. Shallow water over these banks becomes especially rough when large seas from the south run against the south-going ebb tide.

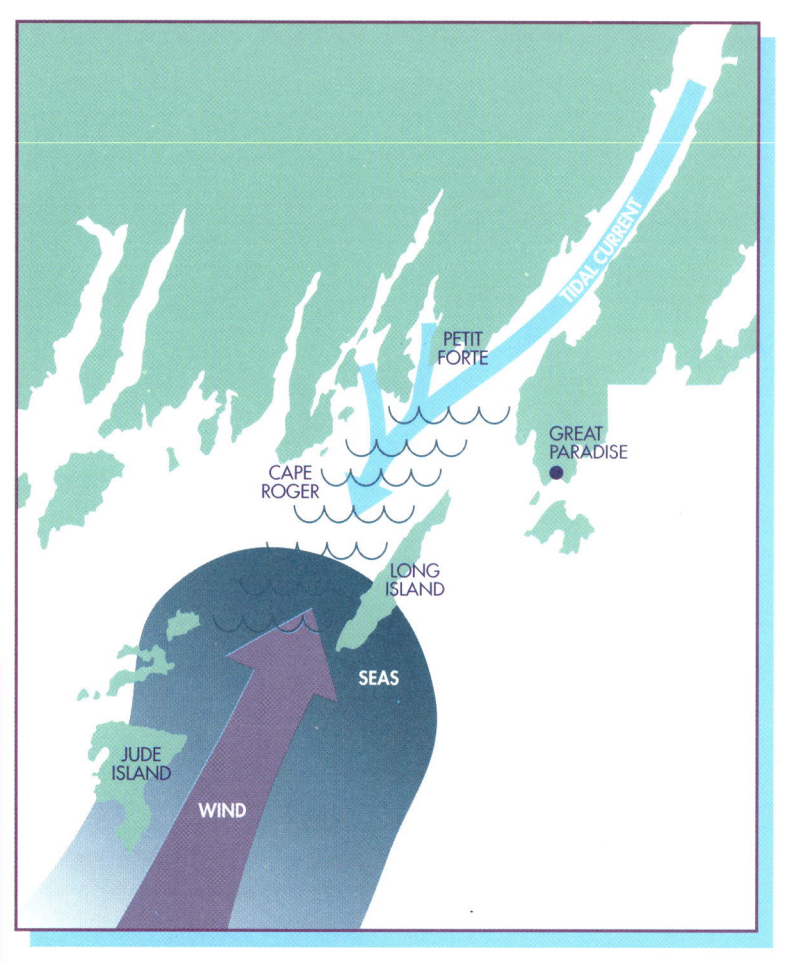

RED ISLAND
Southwesterly winds are funnelled through the Central Channel between Red Island and Merasheen Island, then corner around the northern shore of Red Island, resulting in a strong band of westerly winds.

LOCAL WEATHER Newfoundland South

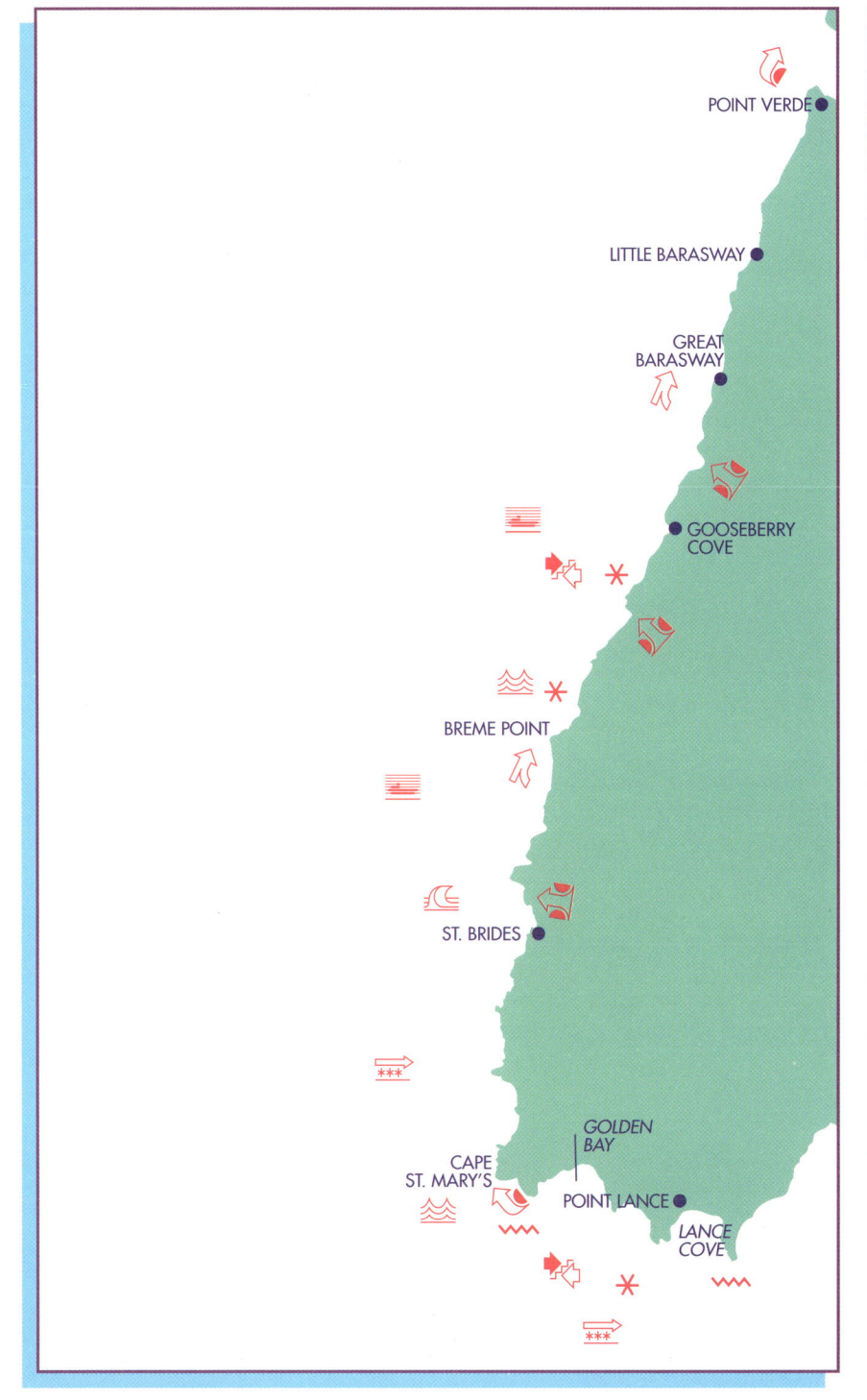

Caution: Tricky Seas
Westerly winds along this coast set up steep, choppy seas, making it dangerous to fish and sail. However, a southerly wind sets up a long swell, which usually doesn't interfere with vessel operations.

Rough Seas from Cape St. Mary's to Point Lance
Local fishermen report that the water within about 3 miles of this stretch of coast is exceptionally rough. The sea here, at its worst when the tides turn, has been described as a "boiling sea where the waves seem to crack against each other."

Seas are also rough when strong westerlies oppose the branch of the Labrador Current that runs along the coast. The strength of this current alone causes seas to "bubble" off Cape St. Mary's, even on a good day.

These rough conditions are created by shallow water and shoals along the coast. Local fishermen use Golden Bay as a shelter.

POINT VERDE TO POINT LANCE
This section of coastline is marked by rolling hills and indented by a few small bays and coves. Several capes, especially Cape St. Mary's, are subject to cornering.

The considerable westward exposure of this coast makes snow streamers possible through the winter months. Large seas generated by strong southerly winds are another major marine weather effect in this area. Shallow water along this coast makes shoaling and tidal rips common hazards, especially between Cape St. Mary's and Point Lance. Seas become rougher to the south of Breme Point, because the water becomes shallower along the coastline to the south.

Caution: Lance Cove a Poor Shelter
Lance Cove is considered a poor location for shelter from high seas, due to its exposure and its shallow waters.

LOCAL WEATHER Newfoundland South

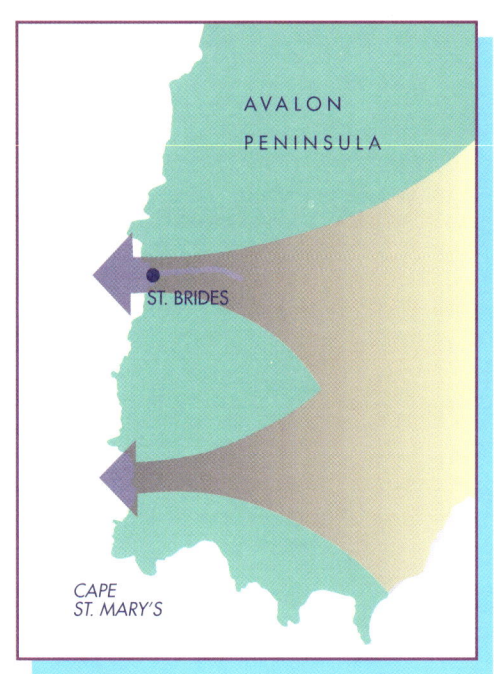

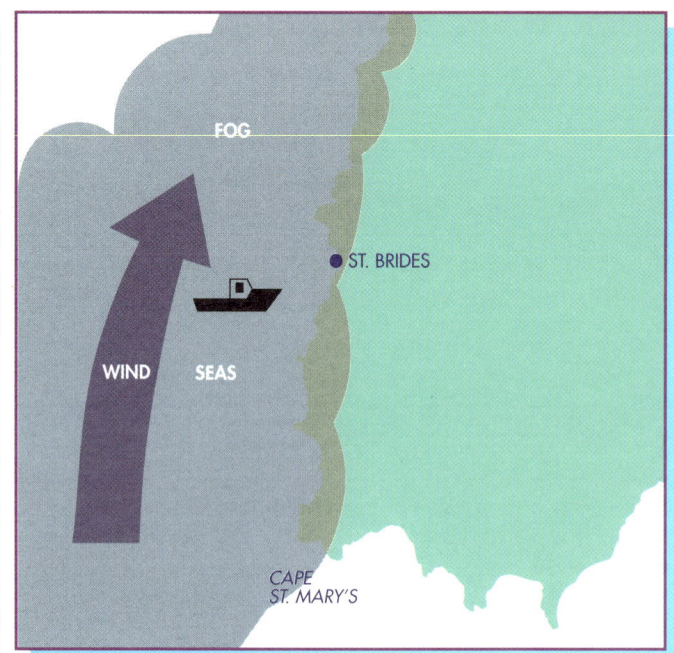

ST. BRIDES
Easterly winds pass over the hills that cover the southwestern Avalon. The valleys between these hills, for the most part, run from east to west. Easterlies increase in strength as they are funnelled through the valleys, resulting in very strong gap winds along the coast.

Smoothing of Seas by Northerly Winds
Despite the limited fetch of easterly winds in this area, mariners report that easterlies make seas high and quite choppy. But the seas "smooth out" when the wind becomes northerly, pushing water out of the bay and away from the coast.

SEAS AND FOG
In this part of Placentia Bay, a southerly wind sets up a north-going sea. When the waves approach the western coast of the Avalon Peninsula, the shallower water refracts the waves towards the shore. Southerlies also bring dense fog into the bay. Fishermen use this knowledge to find their way back to shore when they are lost in heavy fog. Their rule of thumb is: "If you're lost in fog near the shore, go with the swell and you'll make landfall."

When winds shift from southerly to easterly, mariners say that seas become very rough within a few miles of the shore, especially over the shoals, making it very difficult for them to land.

LOCAL WEATHER Newfoundland South

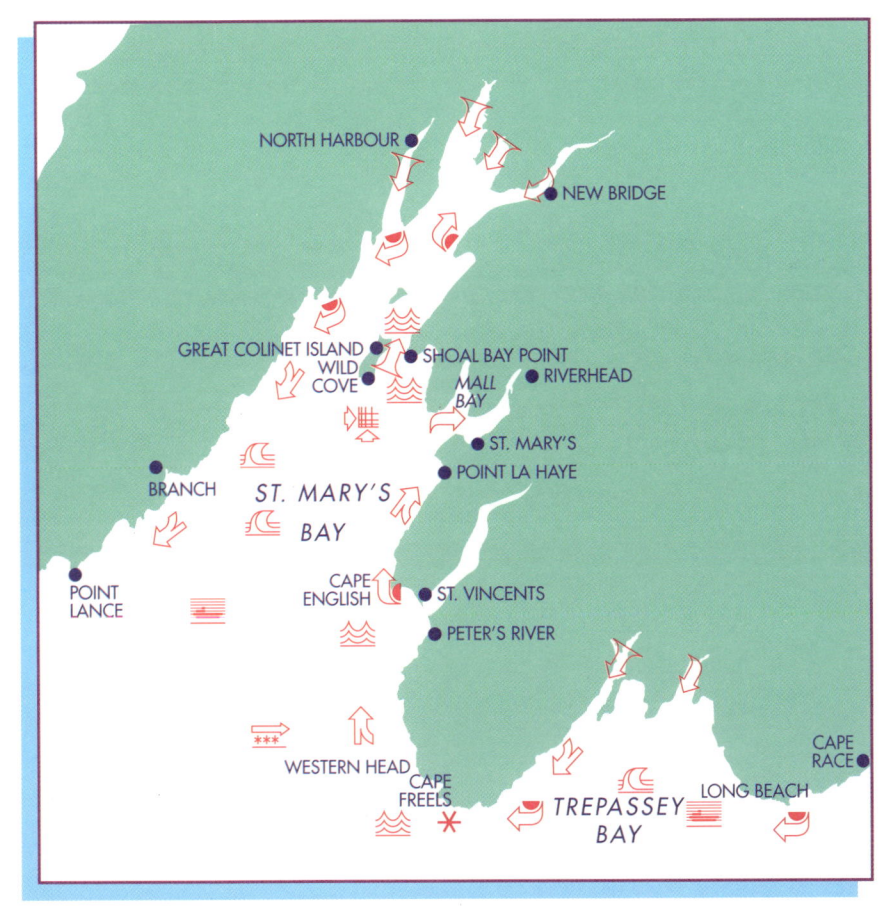

Avalon South

GENERAL CONDITIONS

The southern half of this region is generally flat and barren. St. Mary's Bay, along with many smaller bays and inlets along the southern section, runs from northeast to southwest; channelling and funnelling occur in many areas. The coastline is marked by capes and islands, which significantly affect the wind.

This coastline is fully exposed to the open ocean from the south. Many shoals and banks just offshore can cause very rough seas under certain conditions.

POINT LANCE TO CAPE RACE

This section includes St. Mary's Bay and Trepassey Bay, as well as several smaller bays and harbours. All of these bays run from northeast to southwest. Southerly and northeasterly winds undergo channelling and funnelling through the bays and between their small islands.

The unlimited southern exposure of this coast allows Atlantic swells to move in. Occasional ice cover reduces the magnitude of the swells and southerly winds bring in dense sea fog. In the bays, and just offshore, areas of shoals combine with strong tidal currents to produce rough seas in some spots.

Coastal convergence strengthens southerlies near the eastern coast of St. Mary's Bay. Between Peter's River and Western Head, this also happens with east-to-southeast winds and has been reported as a band of very strong winds within 1–2 miles of the coast. Northerlies are also enhanced along the western

133

LOCAL WEATHER Newfoundland South

coast, due to convergence, and are channelled and funnelled through the many entrances to St. Mary's Bay. These winds may remain quite strong out in the open bay.

Haven of Rest: Effective Shelters
Local fishermen use Wild Cove on the southern shore of Great Colinet Island, for shelter from strong northerlies. Mall Bay provides respite from the rough seas that develop from Shoal Bay Point to Point La Haye during moderate-to-strong southwesterlies.

ST. MARY'S HARBOUR
St. Mary's Harbour has a fairly shallow entrance, open to the west. With only a moderate westerly wind, a sea can develop in St. Mary's Bay and be redirected into the harbour, thus creating larger waves. About three-quarters of the way from the harbour's mouth to Riverhead, the axis of the harbour narrows and turns sharply northward. This causes the waves to pile up as they reflect back upon themselves— resulting in very rough seas. One local fisherman referred to this harbour as "the worst place in the bay" under such conditions. Because of the curve in the harbour, the waters near Riverhead at the head of the harbour are usually calm.

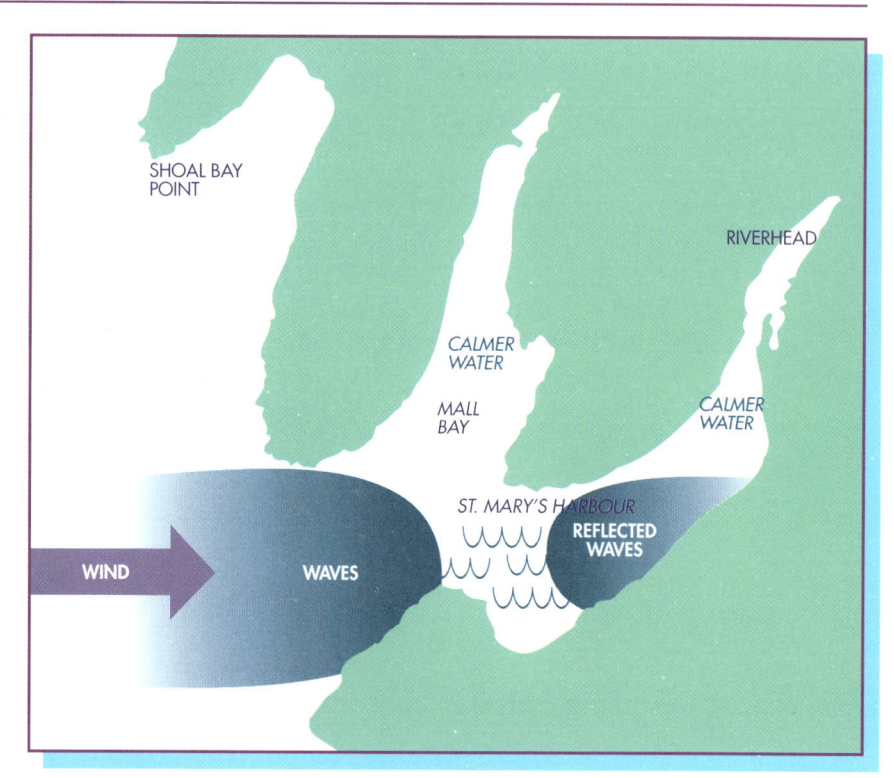

A Caution—and a Haven of Rest
High seas develop under southerly winds throughout St. Mary's Bay. However, seas tend to be somewhat smoother from Cape English to Point La Haye, due to the sheltering effect of the large spit of land that extends down the western side of Holyrood Pond.

LOCAL WEATHER Newfoundland East

Avalon East

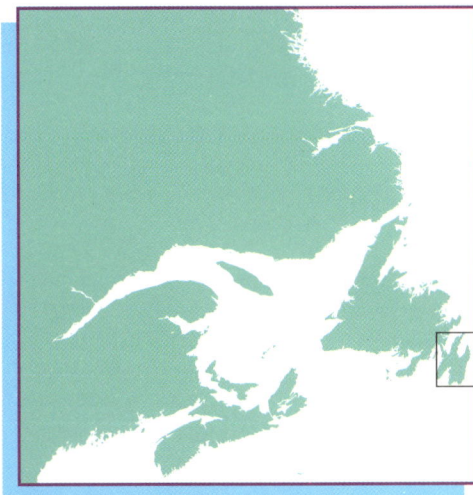

GENERAL CONDITIONS

The eastern portion of the Avalon Peninsula becomes hillier to the north and is marked by several small bays that run from east to west. Conception Bay is the dominant feature of the coastline's northern section. The entire coast is marked by capes and islands, which significantly affect the wind.

This coastline is fully exposed to open ocean from the north, east, and south. Many shoals and banks just offshore can make for very rough seas.

For easier reading, this coastline has been divided into two sections.

LOCAL WEATHER Newfoundland East

CAPE RACE TO CAPE ST. FRANCIS

This section of the Avalon runs generally from north to south. It is indented by several small, but fairly well sheltered east-to-west running harbours. The terrain ranges from flat in the south to hilly in the north.

Coastal convergence strengthens northeasterly winds, which further intensify because of the cornering that affects the many capes and headlands.

Large swells are possible to the east, where there is unlimited exposure to the ocean. Rough seas are common over the Bantam and Ballard Banks, just off the southern half of this coast, and off the northern section, with its steeply sloping ocean floor.

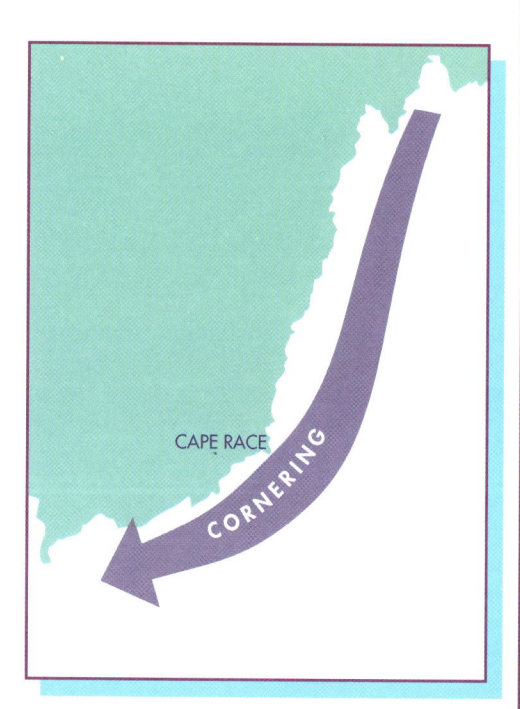

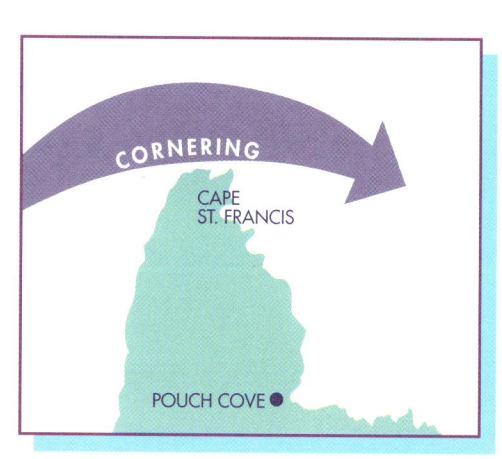

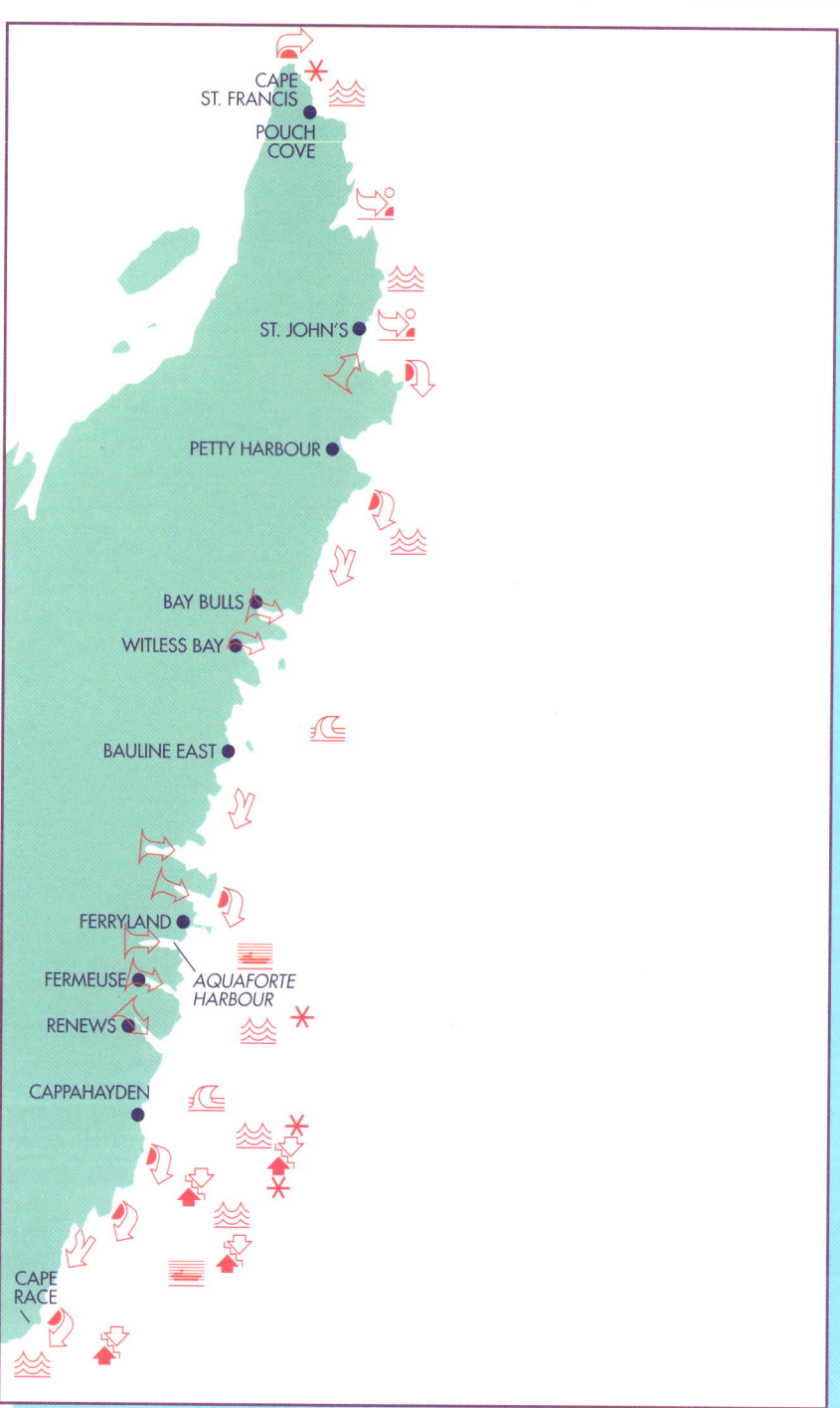

CORNERING: CAPE RACE and CAPE ST. FRANCIS

Cornering occurs at several places along this coast, but the most extreme example is Cape Race. Northeasterly winds undergo coastal convergence as well as cornering, producing local winds up to 25 knots stronger than those elsewhere.

The same effect occurs, but to a lesser extent, with a westerly wind at Cape St. Francis.

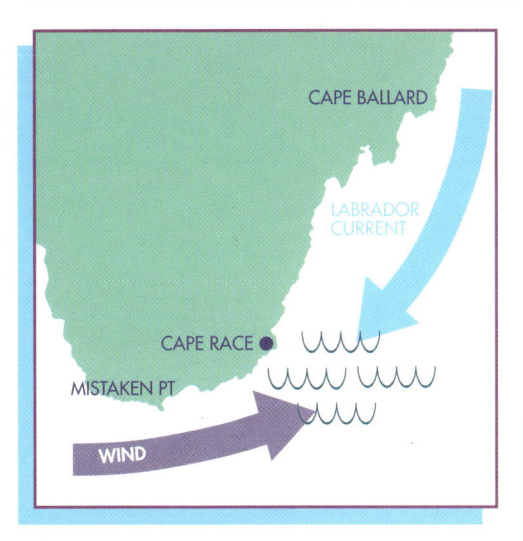

LOCAL WEATHER Newfoundland East

CAPE RACE IN WESTERLY WINDS
Westerly winds oppose the Labrador Current around Cape Race, producing very rough seas in this area and making it very difficult to round Cape Race.

Rough Seas with Northerly Winds
A northerly wind blows parallel to this section of coast.; if persistent, it can result in fully developed seas with large swells refracted onto the fairly shallow shoreline. This can create rough near-shore conditions. The longer the northerlies persist, the longer it will take the sea to settle down.

Caution: Shallow Water
Renews Harbour is very shallow. This makes navigating these waters difficult in rough weather.

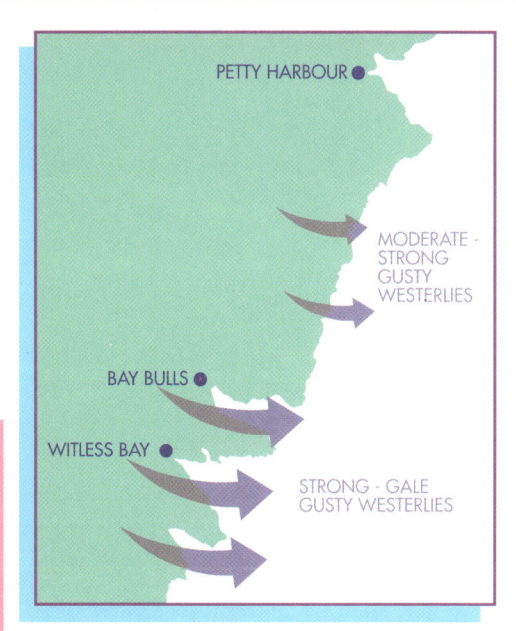

Haven of Rest: Sheltered Harbours
From Cappahayden to Bauline East are several sheltered harbours. One of them, Aquaforte Harbour, is sheltered by Ferryland Head. Fishermen report that although a gale can be blowing at the head, there are only light-to-moderate winds in the harbour.

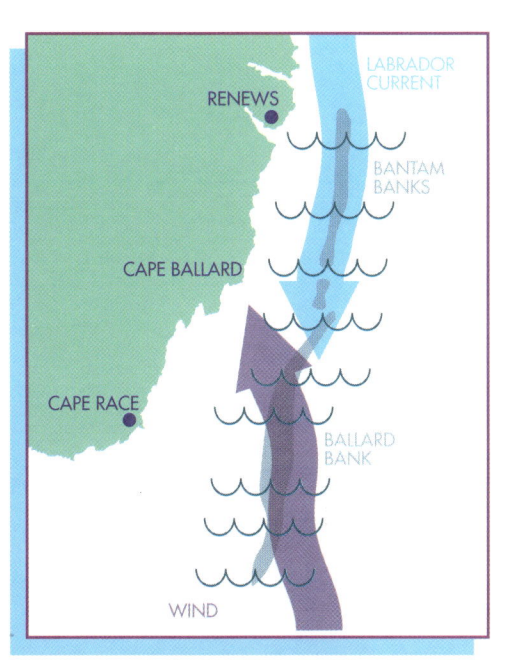

GUSTY WESTERLIES IN SUMMER
During the summer months, light-to-moderate westerlies often become very gusty in the afternoon near the coast, due to the instability of the air over the land. These westerlies are often funnelled through the many east-to-west-running bays and harbours, making the gusty winds even stronger. The effect of these winds can be felt as far as 10 miles offshore.

THE BALLARD BANK AND THE BANTAM BANKS
Just a few miles off Cape Ballard is a long stretch of banks, running southward. The shallowness of these banks, 7 or 8 fathoms in some places, helps create steep-breaking seas, even during moderate easterly winds. When winds become south to southeasterly, conditions worsen, because the wind opposes the strong southward arm of the Labrador Current, which crosses this area.

As mariners say, "Fishermen caught in this area during a storm are at the mercy of God."

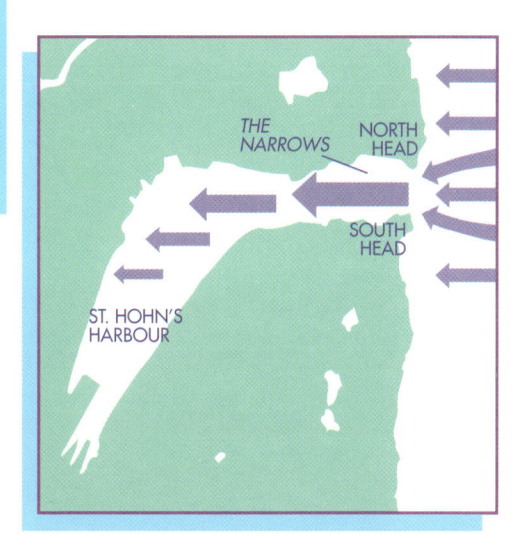

St. John's Harbour
Southwesterly winds funnel through this harbour, because of its shape. These winds can be magnified at the narrow mouth of the harbour since it is very narrow; easterlies are funnelled there but tend to weaken at the harbour's head.

The exposure of the harbour to the east allows large waves to enter, growing as they funnel through the narrow harbour entrance. Large storm surges can occur here, but the steepness of the land on either side of the harbour reduces the risk of flooding.

During the winter, the harbour's entrance is often hampered by ice. Sea ice and small icebergs move in and out of the harbour with the changing wind; easterlies push ice in while southwesterlies force it out. An open water lead (see **ICE** or **APPENDIX C**) may appear along the coast as the ice moves east.

LOCAL WEATHER Newfoundland East

ST. JOHN'S TO CAPE ST. FRANCIS
This section of coast is very rugged and steep, as is the sea bottom, which ranges from the shoreline level to the Cordelia deeps (100 fathoms), only a few miles off the coast. Extremely steep breaking seas develop along this section during prolonged onshore winds, producing conditions that fishermen call "brutal." Except for St. John's Harbour, there is little shelter along this coastline.

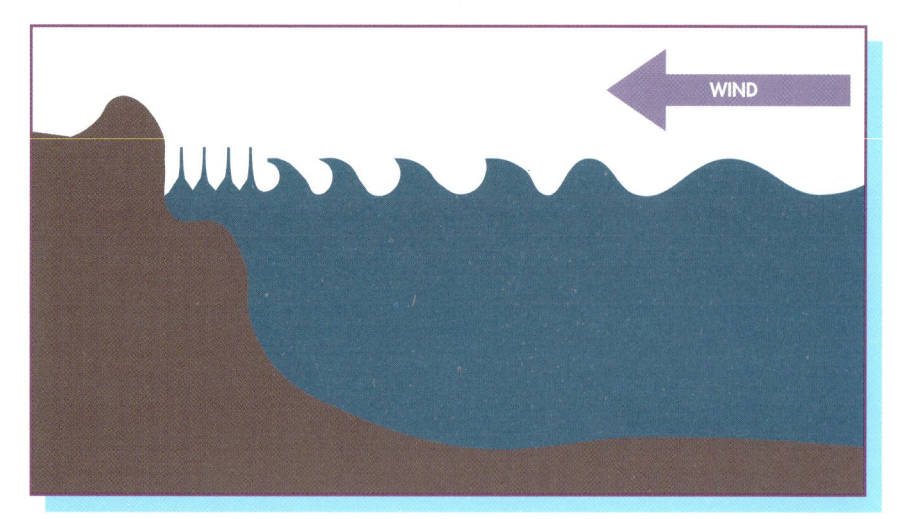

CONCEPTION BAY
Conception Bay is a large and deep V-shaped bay marked by sheer cliffs on the eastern side and rolling terrain to the west. The southwestern portion of the bay is indented with numerous northeast-to-southwest bays that are prone to funnelling. Elsewhere, the coastline is made up of rugged cliffs, with little shelter available. Shoals on the western side of the bay can produce treacherous seas in northeast winds.

This bay has a large exposure to the north towards the open ocean. When large waves interact with either the shallow coastline, Bell Island, or the narrow and shallow Baccalieu Tickle, very rough seas result.

Cape St. Francis and Bell Island
A strong tidal current runs northward along the northeastern side of Conception Bay when the tide is falling. A strong northerly wind opposes this current and forces large waves into the bay. This combination of wind, tide, and waves leads to very steep and confused seas to the west of Cape St. Francis and around Bell Island.

Caution: Waves at High Tide
Strong northerly winds generate large seas that get "corralled" into Holyrood Bay. When this occurs at high tide, seas become high enough to break over breakwaters and wharves.

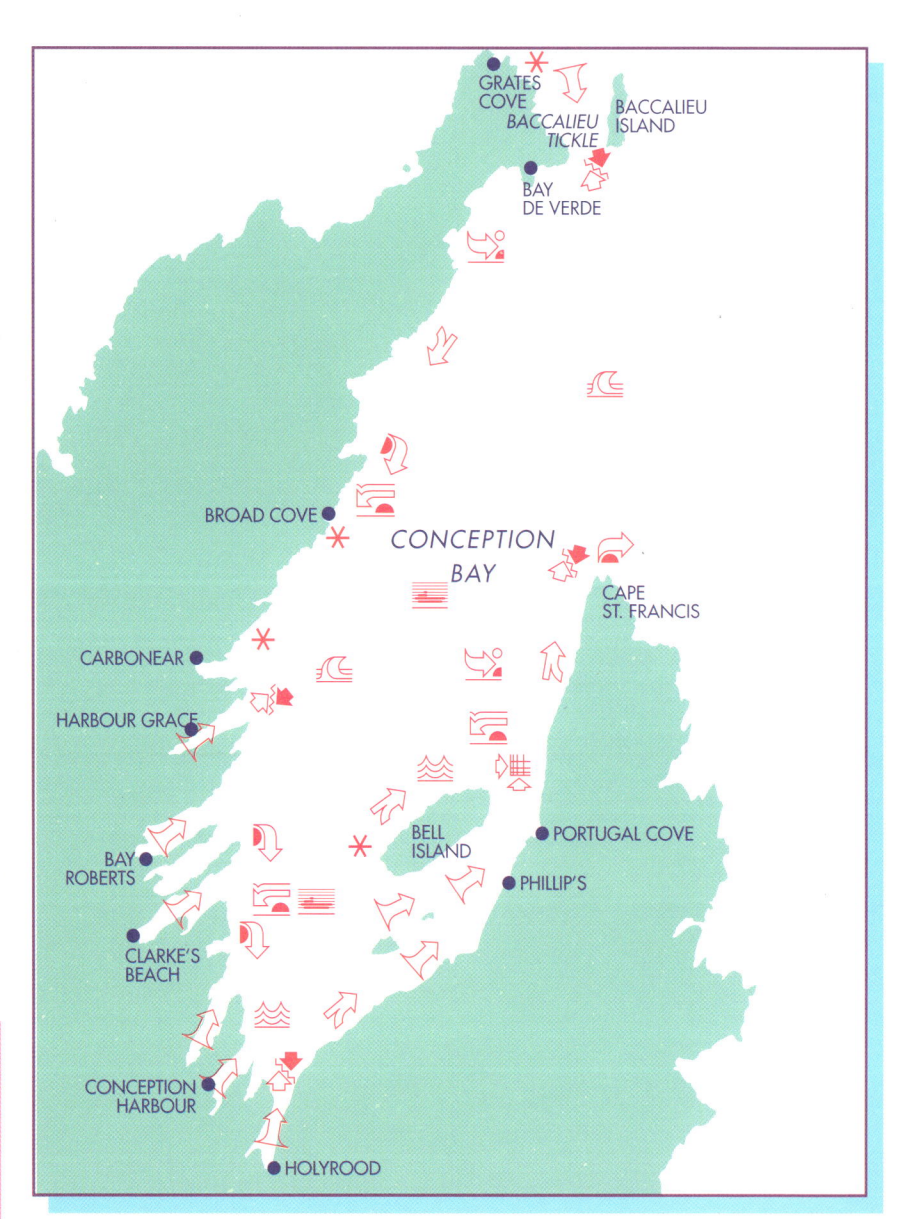

LOCAL WEATHER Newfoundland East

Cape St. Francis to Portugal Cove: Cliff Effects
This stretch of coastline is characterized by very steep cliffs, reaching heights of 900 ft.: usually rising straight out of the water. Strong westerly winds crash against this wall of rock and reflect back upon themselves, leading to gusty, variable winds and confused seas. Southeasterlies "fall" off the cliffs, often causing whirlwinds when they hit the water.

BELL ISLAND
Strong southwesterlies "split" around Bell Island. On the northern side, these winds are intensified by coastal convergence; on the southern side, by funnelling. These stronger winds meet on the northeast side of the island, resulting in rough crossing seas.

Caution: Tickle Winds
Funnelling of southwesterlies in the tickle between Bell Island and the coast results in winds 15–25 knots stronger than in other areas of Conception Bay.

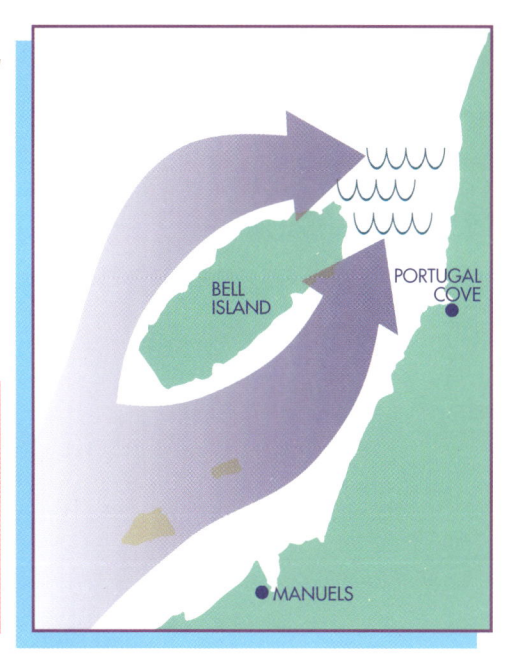

HARBOUR GRACE ISLANDS
Northeasterly winds push large seas into Conception Bay; these waves break when they reach the shallow waters near the northern side of the Harbour Grace Islands. Seas are made even rougher when the waves refract around these small islands. In this area, even a moderate northeasterly will cause confused seas.

This effect occurs within 2–3 miles of shore.

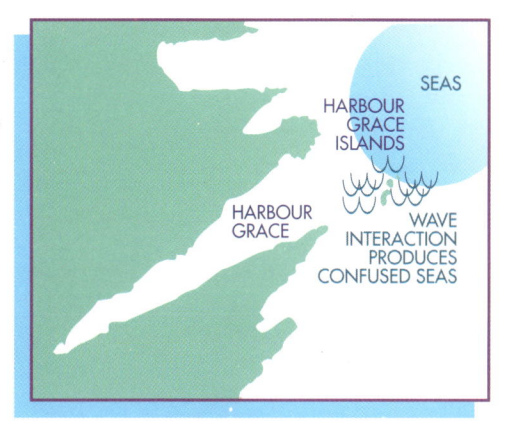

BACCALIEU TICKLE
This small stretch of water is narrow and fairly shallow. Large waves associated with southeasterly winds channel into the narrow passage to create very steep seas. The effect is complicated by a strong tidal current that moves southward through the tickle when the tide leaves Trinity Bay. Very steep and confused seas develop when the winds cross or oppose this current.

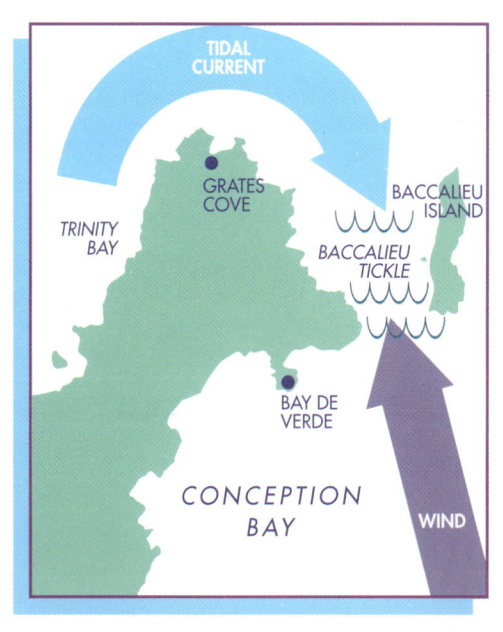

LOCAL WEATHER Newfoundland East

Trinity-Bonavista

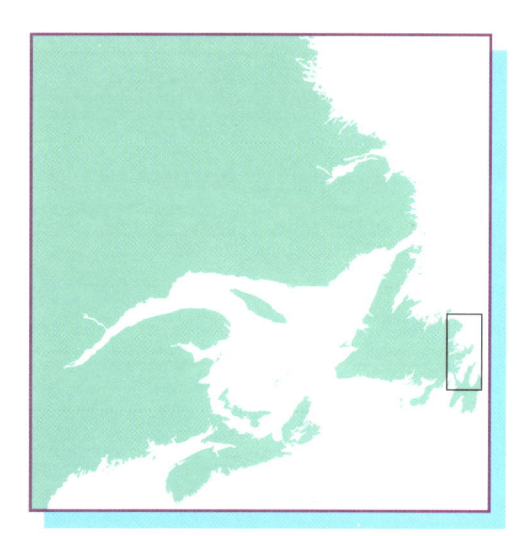

GENERAL CONDITIONS

This area is made up of two large bays, separated by the Bonavista Peninsula: Trinity Bay to the south and Bonavista Bay to the north. Both bays are indented by several sounds and inlets, and dotted by numerous islands. The terrain is rugged and rocky, with many steep cliffs along the coastline.

Shoals are common in both bays, but they become more frequent to the north. The area around Cape Freels alone has over a dozen shoals, and both bays have strong tidal currents. When currents oppose one another, and interact with the wind and shoals, very rough seas develop.

During the winter, sea ice moves into these bays; its motion depends on the winds and ocean currents.

For easier reading, this coastline has been divided into two sections.

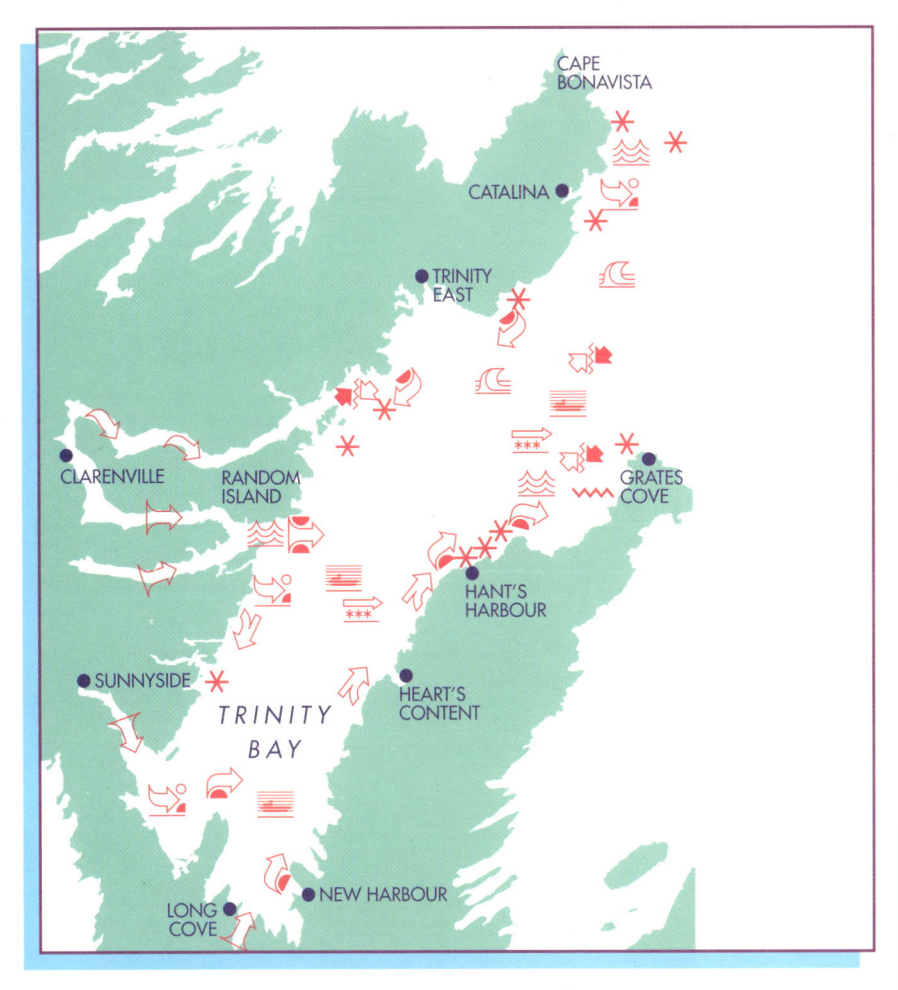

LOCAL WEATHER Newfoundland East

TRINITY BAY

Trinity Bay is deep and rectangular, with a very rugged coastline, a few small inlets on the eastern side, and numerous large inlets and arms to the west. Funnelling and cornering are common, due to the many sounds and headlands. The inlets along this section of coast are prone to strong winds, but fortunately their entrances are fairly well sheltered from waves. Snow streamers are common in the bay from late October to December and during the spring. Gusts, due to the instability of the streamers, can reach values of 25 knots more than the average speed elsewhere.

Although the centre of the bay is very deep, it quickly becomes shallow near the shoreline. Large Atlantic swells from the northeast break upon the many shoals and rocks along the shore. The "Back of the Knife," the "Skerries," and the "Haypooks" are notoriously rough areas, where seas break with a vengeance.

Caution: Northeasterlies
Local fishermen avoid the coastline from Grates Cove to Winterton during strong northeasterly winds. Northeasterlies push in large waves, which break against the many shoals that line this shallow section of coast.

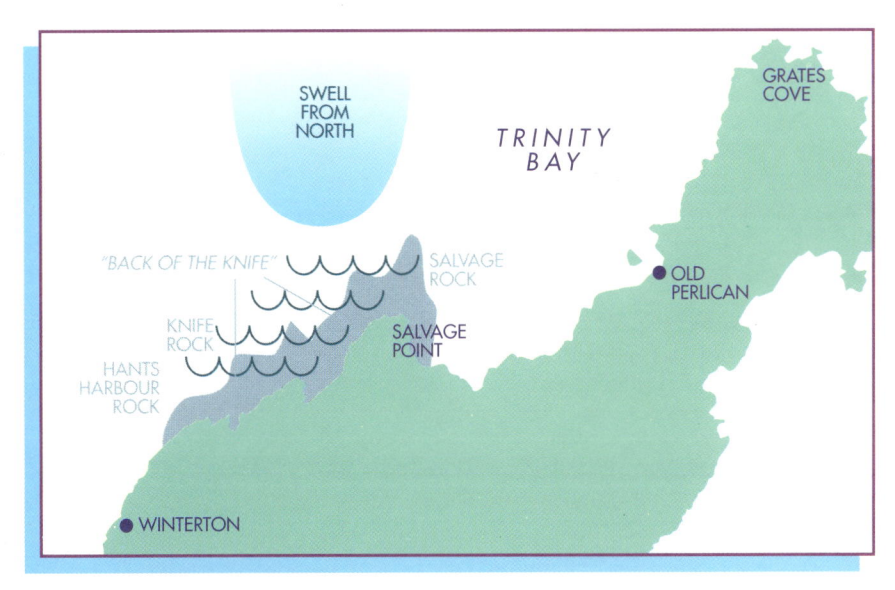

Winterton to New Harbour
Strong northerly winds push large seas into the bay, and the curve of the eastern shore of Trinity Bay leaves areas north of Winterton exposed to these seas from the north. However, south of Winterton, the water is deeper and the coastline is usually sheltered from the wind and swell.

Sea Ice
Sea ice is a common sight along the northeast coast of Newfoundland through the winter and spring, and many Newfoundland fishermen work on, or near, the ice edge during the winter. The strong tidal currents from Salvage Point to Grates Cove makes working near the ice in this location hazardous. These currents can cause an ice pan to split and head in different directions, and converging currents can push masses of ice together.

BACK OF THE KNIFE
This area of shoal—also known as "the Rif Raf"—lies within a few miles of the coast, from Salvage Point to Winterton. The sea bed here becomes shallow quickly and is dotted with shoals and rocks.

LOCAL WEATHER Newfoundland East

TICKLE HARBOUR POINT
Tickle Harbour Point lies at the tip of a small peninsula at the head of Trinity Bay. Southwesterly winds blow unobstructed across the narrow and barren isthmus that joins the Avalon Peninsula with the rest of Newfoundland. These winds therefore blow strongly in Trinity Bay, but particularly at Tickle Harbour Point, where cornering results in very strong and gusty winds.

Fog over Southern Sections of Trinity Bay
Southwesterly winds frequently bring good weather to Trinity Bay. However, from winter until early summer, when fog moves into Placentia Bay with the southwesterlies, a persistent wind carries the fog across the isthmus into the southern half of Trinity Bay.

Caution: Tricky Sea Breezes
The higher terrain along the eastern shore of Trinity Bay tends to prevent sea breezes from developing. However, strong sea breezes do develop along the western shore. During the spring and summer, easterly-to-northeasterly sea breezes can develop, reaching speeds of 20–25 knots.

Smith Sound
Smith Sound is a narrow and well-protected waterway that snakes from east to west along the north shore of Random Island. Winds are channelled through the sound, but they usually are not funnelled, due to the sound's width and many curves. The mouth of Smith Sound is well sheltered from the large swells that roll into Trinity Bay, although an ebb tide with northeast winds can cause problems near Bonaventure Head.

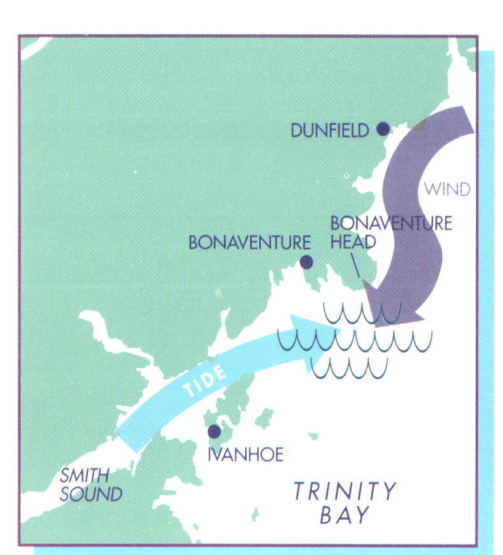

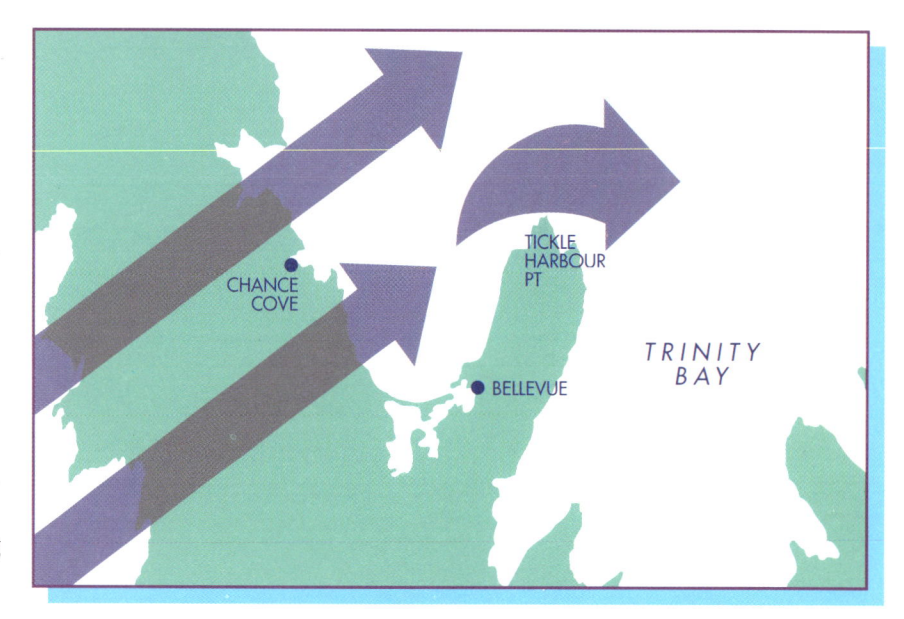

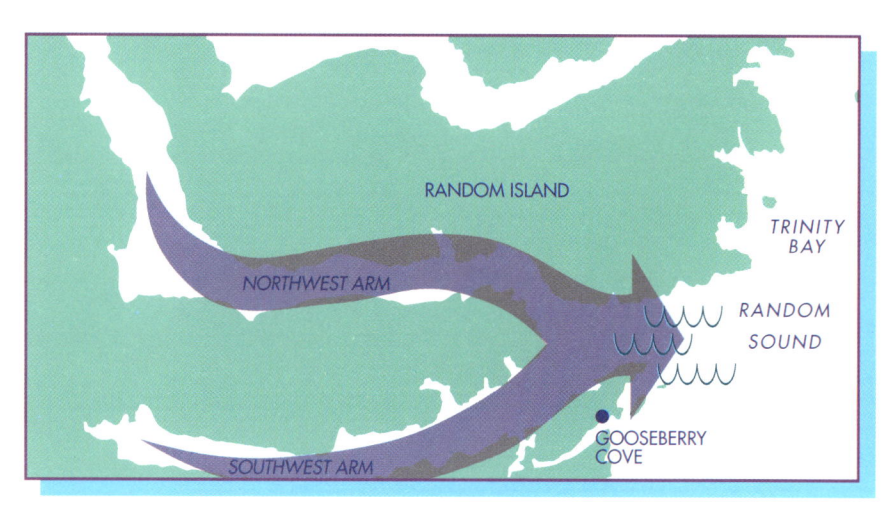

RANDOM SOUND
Strong westerly winds funnel down the Northwest Arm and the Southwest Arm, converging in Random Sound and producing choppy seas. Mariners should also note that southwest winds in the Southwest Arm are often up to 20 knots stronger than the winds in the bay, due to funnelling.

BONAVENTURE HEAD
Northeasterlies bring large seas into the bay, particularly along the western shore. When the tide is going out of Smith Sound, confused seas develop near Bonaventure Head. The effect is compounded when northeasterly winds corner around the head and become even stronger. Under these conditions, local fishermen say, "The sea comes at you in all directions."

LOCAL WEATHER *Newfoundland East*

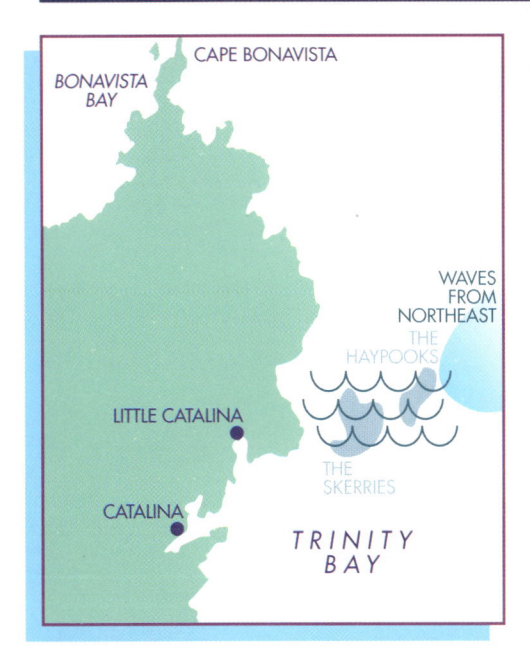

THE SKERRIES AND THE HAYPOOKS

This is an area of submerged rocks, as shallow as 4 fathoms just a few miles northeast of Little Catalina. This area becomes treacherous in northeasterly winds of moderate or greater strength. Large Atlantic waves, driven by northeasterlies, hit these submerged rocks, then "pile up like a haystack." The sea then breaks unexpectedly, with waves sometimes reaching 50 ft. The northeasterly wind also blows across the branch of the Labrador Current in this area, intensifying the rough conditions. One local fisherman refers to the Skerries as "scary as hell."

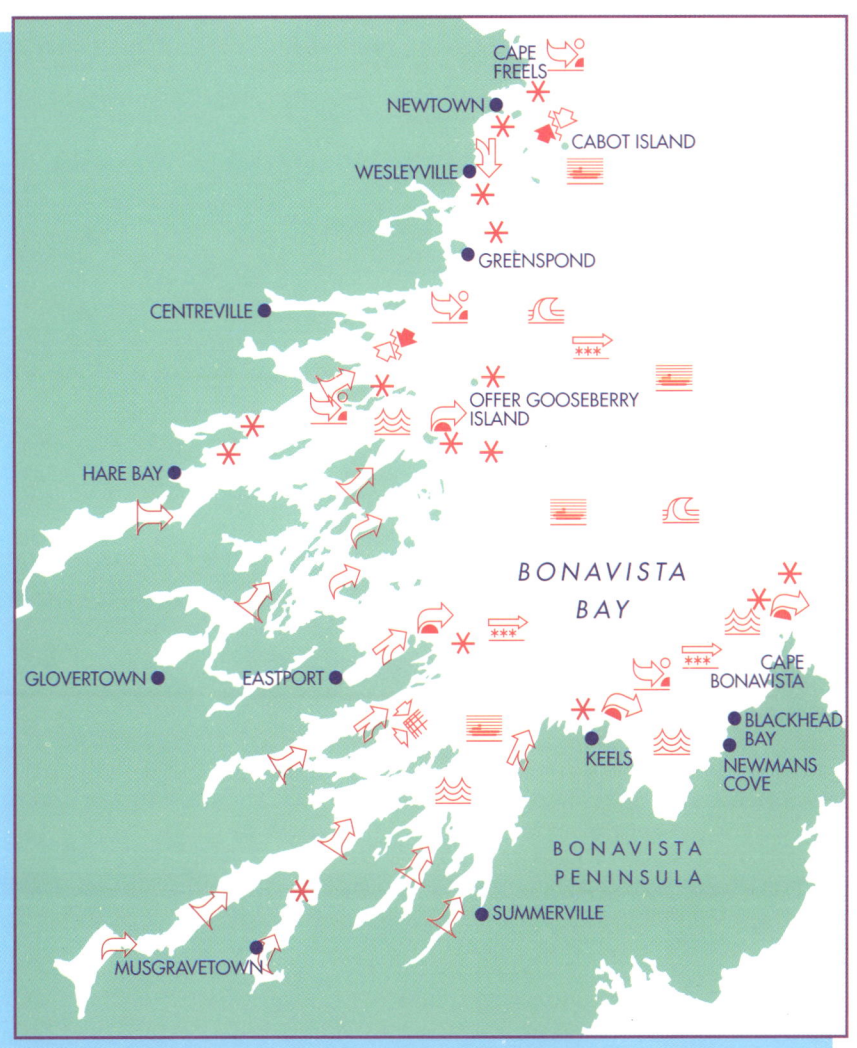

BONAVISTA BAY

Bonavista Bay, a large, irregularly shaped body of water, is completely exposed to the northeast. The bay is indented by many large channels and sounds, and dotted with numerous islands. A rugged coastline borders the bay with many rocks and cliffs. This varied geography makes funnelling and cornering very common.

The main body of the bay is deep, as are many of the channels. However, the waters around much of the coast, and nearly all of the islands, are quite shallow—many are characterized by shoaling and rough seas.

The bay is also subject to strong tidal currents, which create rough seas when they are opposed by the wind, or crossed or opposed by large waves. The currents also influence the motion of the thick sea ice that moves into the bay every winter. As well, ice will move into the bay with a north or northwest wind.

Shelter from Large Ocean Swells

The many small islands in the western bay, and the shallow waters surrounding them, offer excellent shelter from large Atlantic swells. Seas break on the shoals, rocks, and steep shelf that lie between the islands and the deep water of the bay. The large seas have been reported to diminish inside Offer Gooseberry Island.

Fog in Summer

During the summer months, when the waters in the Bonavista Bay reach their maximum temperature, fog usually remains offshore from about 15 miles east of Cabot Island to 30 miles northeast of

LOCAL WEATHER Newfoundland East

Cape Bonavista. As the fog is pushed into the bay by an east or northeast wind, the warm water will cause it to lift into a deck of low cloud instead. It is difficult for fog to form in the bay because warm winds, like those from the southwest, are usually fairly dry, while winds from other directions are too cold.

Cape Bonavista
This barren point of land is exposed to the full force of the wind from virtually every direction. Westerlies here undergo cornering around the cape, making them even stronger. Wave energy is also focused at the headlands because they are shallow. The shallow water and shoals just offshore make this area very rough whenever the wind is strong. Local mariners go 4–5 miles offshore to escape the turbulent seas.

Caution: Freezing Spray
Freezing spray is common along this coast in winter, especially along the eastern coast from Blackhead Bay to Cape Bonavista, where there is usually enough fetch over open water for it to develop. Even the road that runs along the coast from Blackhead Bay to the Cape is prone to freezing spray in west-to-northwest winds. At times, frozen spray has to be ploughed from the road.

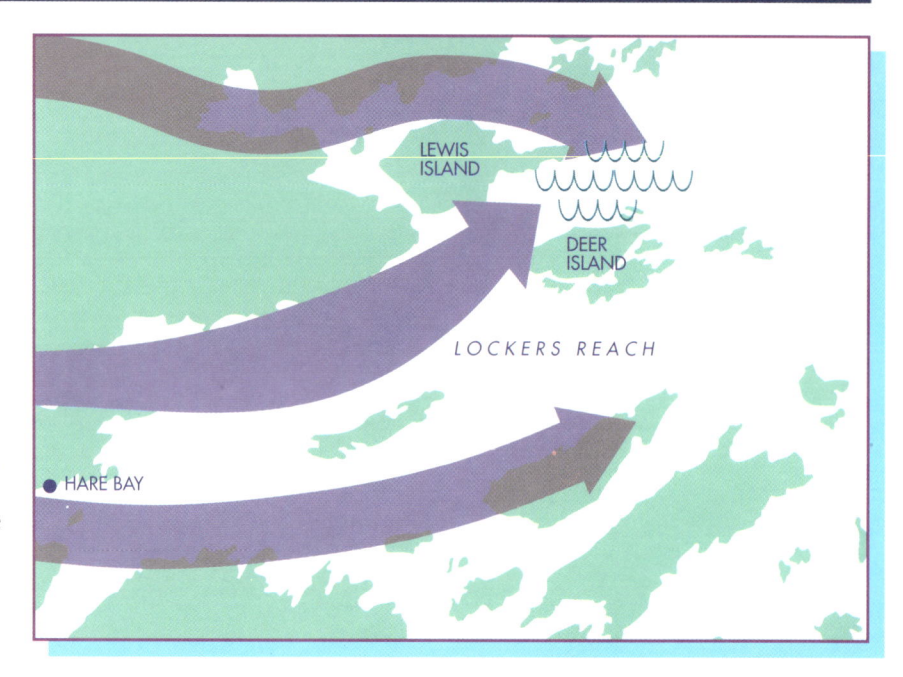

LEWIS ISLAND
Westerly winds undergo funnelling and coastal convergence on the north side of Lewis Island. These winds are channelled to southwesterly through Lockers Reach, then funnelled between Deer Island and Lewis Island. When they intersect on the east side of Lewis Island, they result in strong winds and choppy seas.

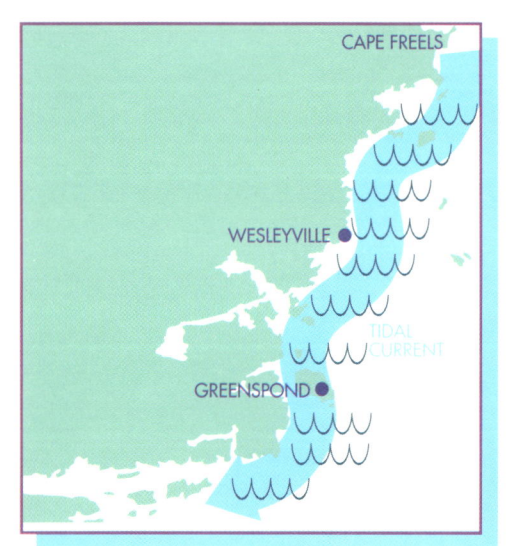

CAPE FREELS TO GREENSPOND
Seas in this area are known to be rough, even on a calm day, because of a strong tidal current that runs along the shallow stretch of coast. Seas become even choppier when a southwesterly wind opposes this current; local mariners venture up to 10 miles offshore to escape them.

LOCAL WEATHER Newfoundland East

Notre Dame

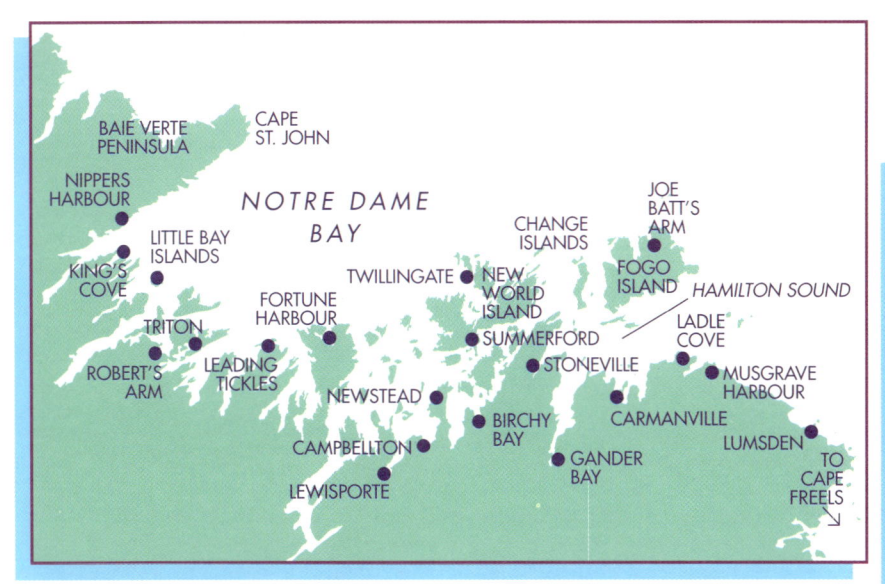

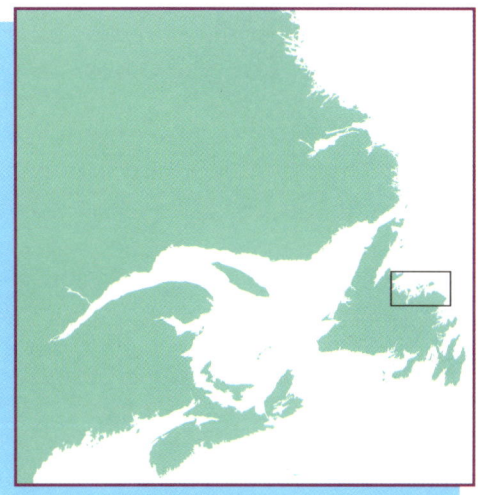

GENERAL CONDITIONS
This area of coastline runs generally from east to west, from Cape Freels to the Baie Verte Peninsula. It is indented by many north-to-south bays and inlets; and several large islands lie off the coast, most notably New World Island and Fogo Island.

There are numerous shoals and shallow areas along the coast, especially around the many islands. These shallow areas, combined with strong tidal currents and strong spring run-off, produce many areas of very rough seas.

Sea ice reaches the area by late January; the mobile pans of ice create many hazards for winter and spring shipping activity. Icebergs move in along the coast in the spring, transported by the Labrador Current.

Gusty southwesterlies are common on sunny summer afternoons. The sun heats the land, creating unstable, gusty conditions. Light-to-moderate southwesterlies can often gust to strong or gale force in the afternoon, ending with sunset. This usually occurs within 5–6 miles of the coast.

For easier reading, this coastline has been divided into two sections.

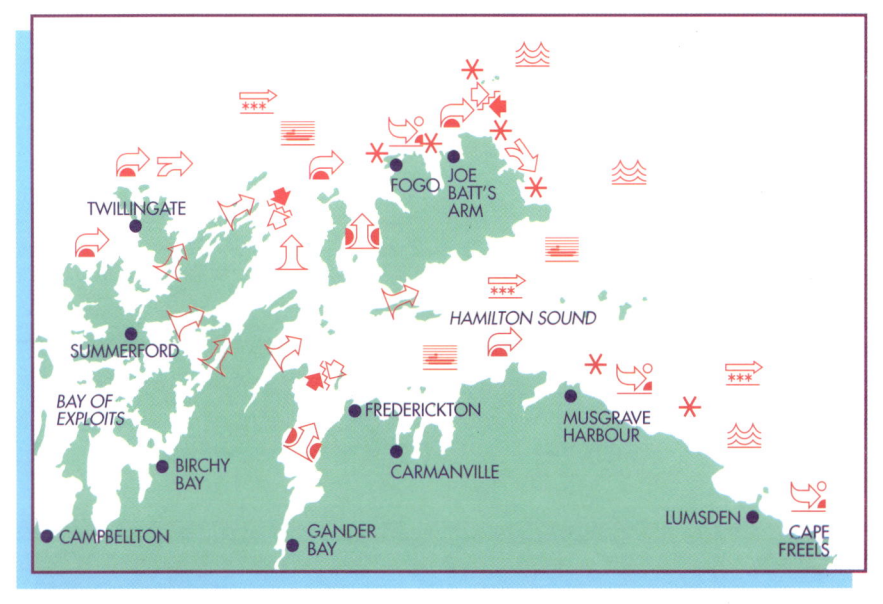

CAPE FREELS TO CAMPBELLTON
This section of coastline contains a chain of large islands running northeastward from the Bay of Exploits. The many channels between these islands cause winds to be channelled and funnelled. The terrain is fairly flat to the east, with higher ground to the west. There are many shoals around the islands, with strong tidal currents between them. This makes rough seas a significant hazard.

The weather along this coast can be extremely harsh. To the north, the islands are completely exposed to the cold Atlantic; snow, fog, and freezing drizzle are common. Icebergs are a common sight in spring, as tidal currents bring them close to shore. These 'bergs present a serious threat to navigation and marine operations.

The coastline from Cape Freels to Frederickton is generally quite flat; thus there is little difference in friction between the sea surface and the land. As a result, westerly winds do not experience significant convergence along this section of the coast.

145

LOCAL WEATHER Newfoundland East

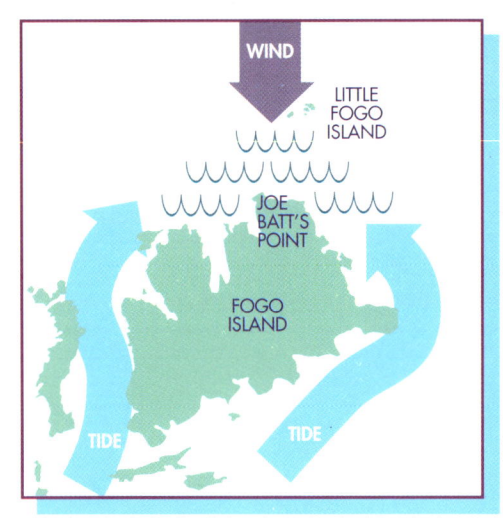

FOGO ISLAND
Fogo Island lies a few miles off the northeast coast of Newfoundland. On the north side of this island there is a gently sloping shelf extending to the Atlantic. The large northern exposure, along with the shallow waters offshore, leads to very rough seas when winds are from the northwest or north. Conditions are often worsened by strong tidal currents that run between Joe Batt's Point and the Little Fogo Islands.

Seas remain much calmer on the south side of the island under these conditions, due to the shelter provided by Fogo Island.

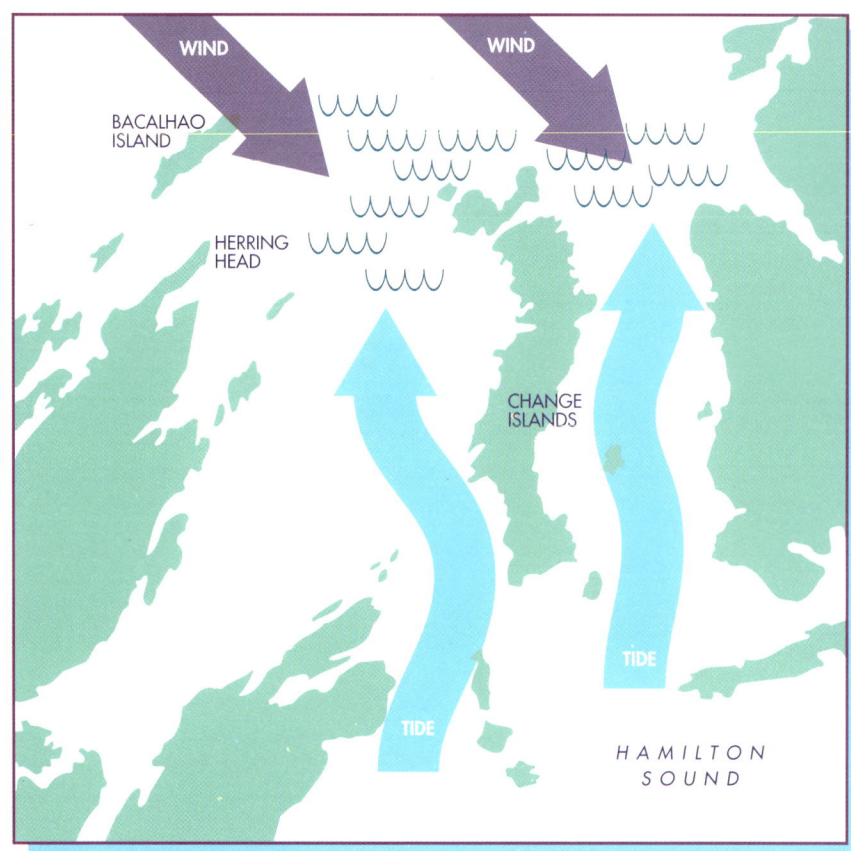

THE CHANGE ISLANDS
Seas become very rough when the tide ebbing out of Hamilton Sound meets a strong northwesterly wind. This effect is reported to extend nearly 10 miles out to sea. Local mariners use extreme care under these conditions.

Caution: Rough Seas
East-to-northeast winds cause very rough seas along this coast, which is exposed to open sea and characterized by shallow coastal waters.

Haven of Rest: Shelter
When seas are rough between Bacalhao Island and the Change Islands, the waters inside Herring Head are usually much calmer.

Sea Breezes
During the summer months, especially August and September, sea breezes are common, especially when a ridge of high pressure lies over Newfoundland. Under these conditions, the large-scale winds are generally from the west at 10–15 knots. However, they are light enough to be "overpowered" by the flow of air created by the land-sea temperature difference, which increases as the land is heated. As a result, a 10–15-knot westerly wind with sunny skies in the morning often switches to a cool easterly wind of 15–20 knots in the afternoon, as the sea breeze sets in. Fog offshore can be driven to the coast with these sea breezes.

Icebergs
Every spring, icebergs can be seen off the northeast coast of Newfoundland. Tidal currents often bring 'bergs close to shore, where they can enter harbours and become grounded in shallower water.

Marine Weather Tip: Fickle Sea Ice
Mariners report that if the sea ice is blocked in Bonavista Bay and the wind is from the northwest, then sea ice tends to move into Hamilton Sound. If, however, Bonavista Bay is free of ice when the wind is from the northwest, then the ice usually stays out of Hamilton Sound.

LOCAL WEATHER Newfoundland East

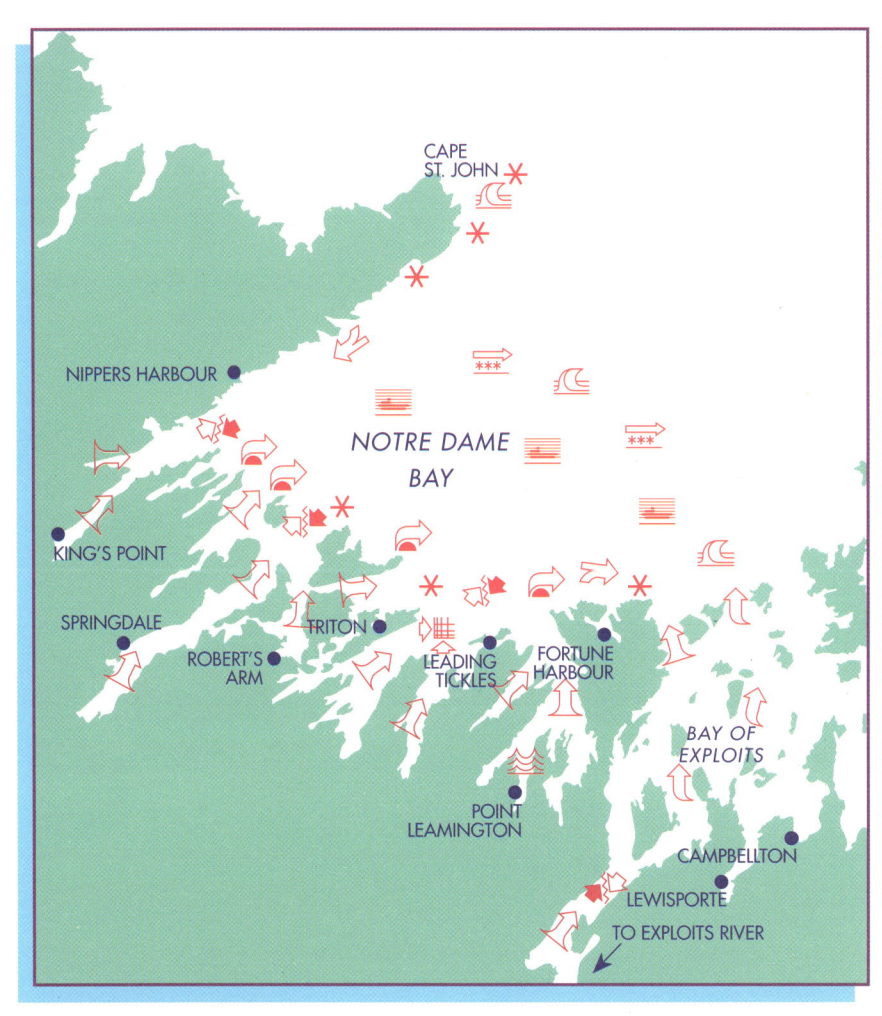

CAMPBELLTON TO CAPE ST. JOHN

This is a very rugged stretch of coastline, marked by fairly steep cliffs that contain several northeast-to-southwest bays. Channelling and funnelling of southwesterlies and northeasterlies through the bays and between a few of the small islands along this coast are common in this area.

Like most of the bays and inlets that indent this coastline, Notre Dame Bay is fairly deep. There are a few shallow areas near the coast where shoaling occurs, especially near the islands. Rough seas also occur when winds blow against the strong tidal currents in the bays.

Spring run-off can contribute to rough seas and strong currents in and near many of the bays, especially in the Bay of Exploits, where the Exploits River releases large volumes of fresh water into the bay every spring.

Freezing Drizzle

Freezing drizzle is a common nemesis during the spring, when sea ice and cold open water are present offshore. Northeasterly winds push cool air over this mixture of ice and water, making the air very moist. When the temperature is between 0°C and -7°C, freezing drizzle and fog result.

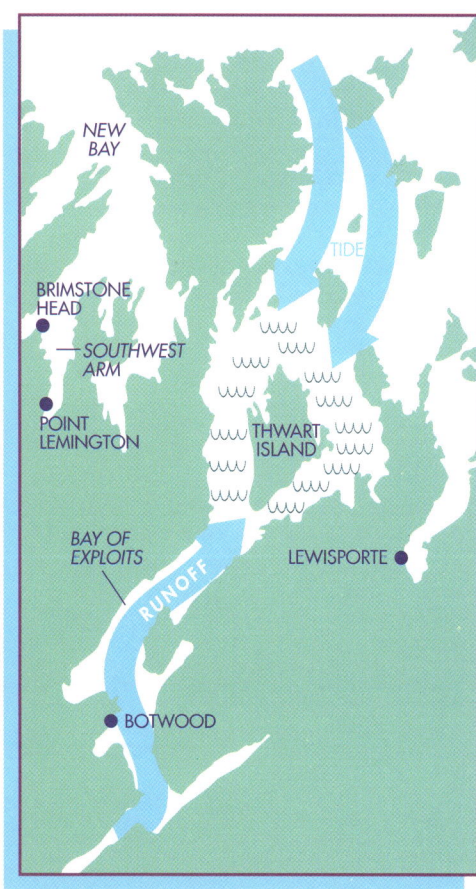

BAY OF EXPLOITS

The Exploits River runs from central Newfoundland to the northeast coast, where it empties into the Bay of Exploits. During the spring, when much snow and ice melts into the river, a strong current of fresh water flows into the bay. When this current meets an incoming tide, or is opposed by the wind in the bay, very choppy seas result. These conditions are compounded by local tidal currents, which are strengthened by the bay's funnel shape.

Caution: Tricky Tides in New Bay

Tidal currents running into New Bay, then into the Southwest Arm, refract around Brimstone Head. This causes steep and choppy seas from Point Leamington to Brimstone Head.

147

LOCAL WEATHER Newfoundland East

NOTRE DAME BAY

Southwesterly winds are funnelled between the cliffs that line the many northeast-to-southwest-running bays emptying into Notre Dame Bay. The winds are intensified by funnelling through the bays and between the islands.

Caution should be taken when crossing the entrances of the bays and when leaving the shelter of the islands in southwest winds. The funnelled southwesterlies converge in the bay, creating even stronger winds. This effect is strongest in the summer, when the land is heated to its maximum.

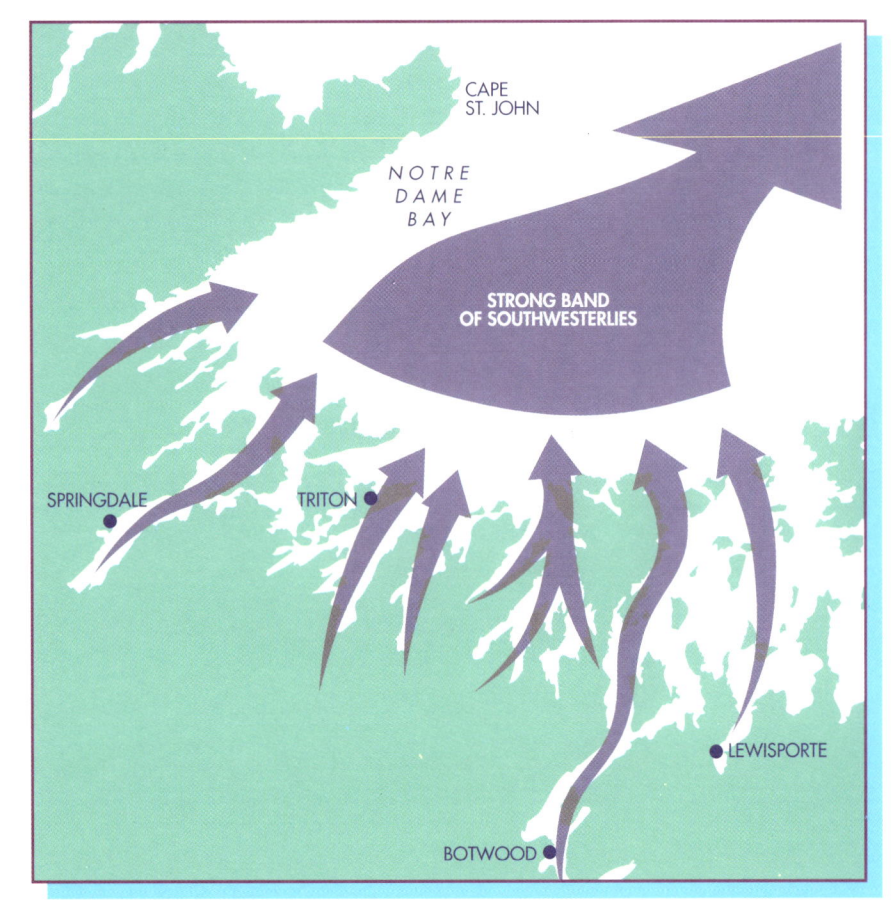

GREEN BAY

The orientation of the many bays within Notre Dame Bay produces funnelling of both southwesterly and northeasterly winds. Northeasterlies undergo funnelling and coastal convergence along the eastern side of the Baie Verte Peninsula. When these strong winds oppose the tide ebbing out of the Southwest Arm and Middle Arm, very rough seas can develop.

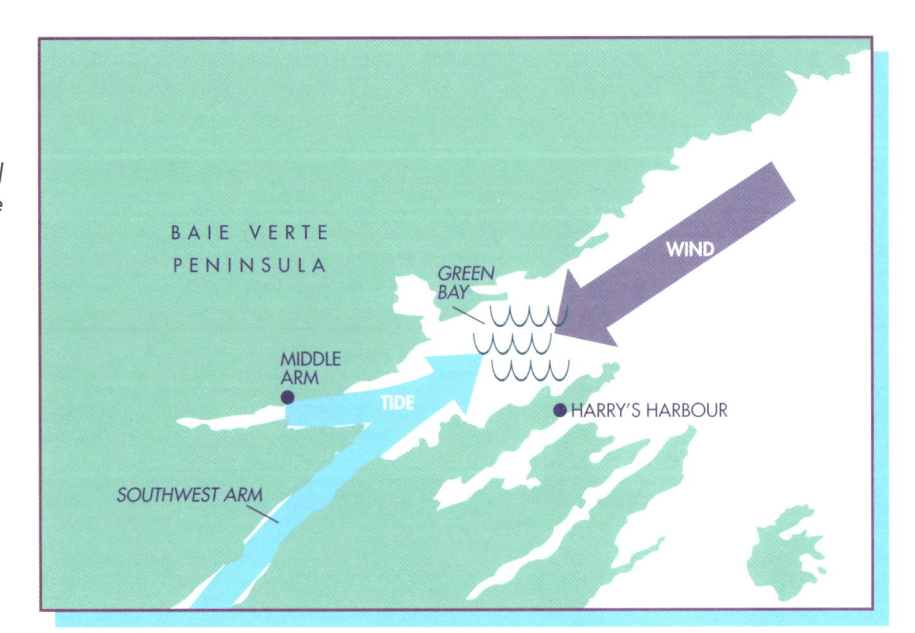

LOCAL WEATHER Newfoundland East

Newfoundland North

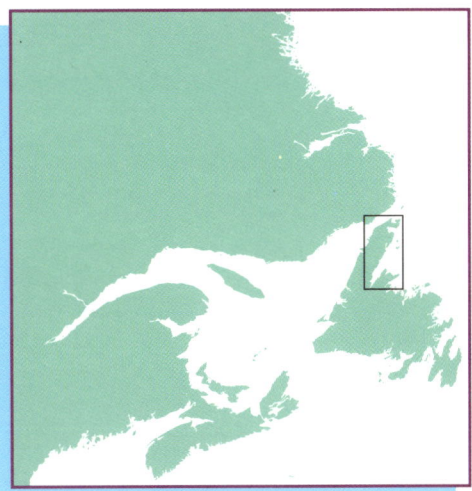

GENERAL CONDITIONS

The Long Range Mountains dominate this section of the Newfoundland coast. The range is indented by several bays that open into the Atlantic. Lee-wave effects are common, because of mountains, while funnelling affects the steep-walled bays.

This coast is exposed to the full force of the north Atlantic Ocean from the northeast. The abundance of cold water and ice leads to frequent, heavy snow in winter, and freezing precipitation and fog are common in spring.

Most of the water along this coast is quite deep, and shoaling is infrequent. However, rough seas do develop when large seas or strong winds interact with the vigorous tidal currents that run throughout the region.

For easier reading, this coastline has been divided into two sections.

149

LOCAL WEATHER Newfoundland East

CAPE ST. JOHN TO HARBOUR DEEP

This section of coast begins on the extreme eastern end of the Baie Verte Peninsula and is bordered by the Northern Peninsula to the west. On the Baie Verte Peninsula, the bays run from southwest to northeast; on the Northern Peninsula, from east to west. The largest bay in this section is White Bay, a large and deep V-shaped bay that extends from northeast to southwest.

Seas in this area are often very rough. Hazardous conditions produced by shoals along the northern shore of the Baie Verte Peninsula, strong tidal currents, the Horse Islands, large ocean swells, and several exposed capes.

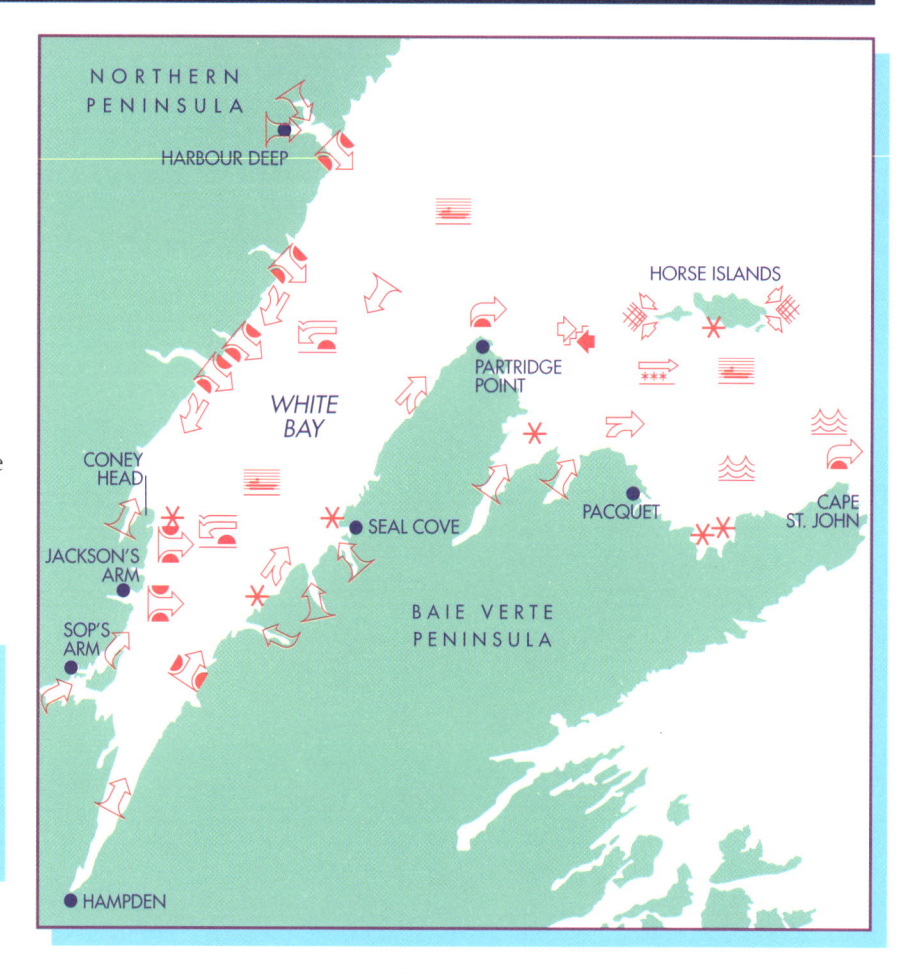

Haven of Rest: No Ice
Mariners report that when sea ice is 20–30 miles off the coast of the Horse Islands, the ice will stay offshore—even if a northeast wind blows for a few days.

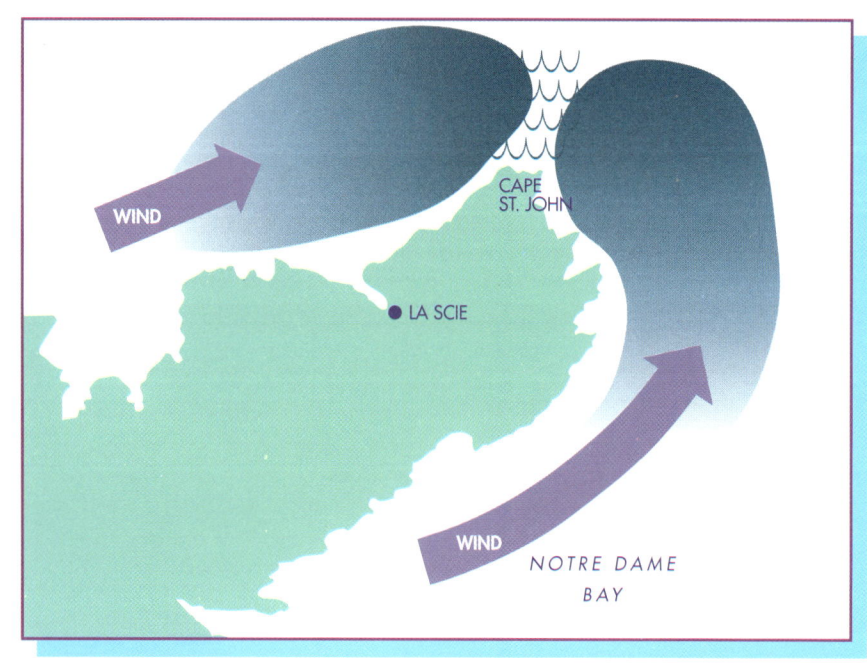

CAPE ST. JOHN
South-to-southwest winds generate northeast-running currents in Notre Dame Bay and along the coast just west of Cape St. John. The currents are redirected around the cape, which causes them to cross just to the north. Under these conditions, seas can become very rough within 3–15 miles north of Cape St. John.

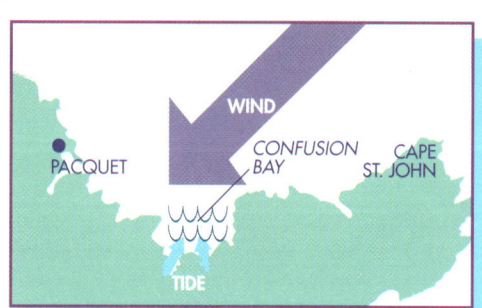

CONFUSION BAY
This aptly named bay on the north shore of the Baie Verte Peninsula is quite shallow, with shoals along its shore. Seas become very confused when an onshore wind forces large ocean waves onto the shoals, and conditions worsen when the tide in the bay opposes the wind. Local mariners use caution when navigating this bay during northeasterlies.

LOCAL WEATHER Newfoundland East

> **Caution: Crossed Seas**
> The refraction of waves around the Horse Islands leads to crossed seas on the leeward side.

West of the Horse Islands
When the tide runs out of White Bay, a strong eastward tidal current sets up between the Horse Islands and the Baie Verte Peninsula. Very strong seas result when a brisk easterly or northeasterly wind opposes this current.

White Bay: Southwesterlies
Southwesterlies are funnelled between the steep cliffs that border White Bay near Hampden, and are channelled through Sops Arm. The result is strong and sustained southwesterlies in White Bay, even when moderate southwesterlies are being reported elsewhere.

Coney Head to Sop's Arm
Northeasterlies undergo funnelling in White Bay; they also are increased by coastal convergence along its western side. These strong winds push large waves into the bay, which break along the relatively shallow shoreline. Thus, seas are extremely rough over this part of the coast.

> **Cautions in White Bay**
> **Coastal Convergence**
> Coastal convergence strengthens southwesterlies along the eastern shore of White Bay more than along the western shore.
>
> **Storm Surges**
> Deep low-pressure centres that pass east of the Baie Verte Peninsula are characterized by strong northeasterly winds and accompanying storm surges in White Bay. The bathymetry of this V-shaped bay makes it prone to flooding from storm surge, especially at the head of the bay at high tide.
>
> **Whirlwinds**
> Whirlwinds near the coast usually accompany strong mountain waves when the wind speed exceeds 30 knots. These can be very hazardous to small boats.

TRICKY WINDS IN WHITE BAY
The western side of White Bay is bounded by steep, high cliffs. Strong cliff effects result when westerly winds blow off these cliffs and "fall" to the water below. Mariners report a band of fairly light winds within 5 miles of the coast (except as noted below) increasing to very strong westerlies farther into the bay. These intensified westerlies are often strong enough to trap boats along the eastern side of the bay.

The wind patterns near the western coast of the bay becomes complicated near the mouths of the smaller bays on the western side, and mariners need to exercise caution. Westerly winds intensify as they pass through these steep-walled bays; across the mouths of these bays, winds can reach 50–60 knots, while winds in White Bay are at 20–30 knots. Therefore, the wind bands along the western coast of White Bay can range from light to storm-force, depending on your location in the bay.

LOCAL WEATHER Newfoundland East

HARBOUR DEEP TO CAPE BAULD

Along this section of coast, the Long Range Mountains dominate the south, while flatter and swampier land lies to the north. Two fairly large bays indent the coast: Canada Bay and Hare Bay. The presence of the mountains makes lee-wave effects common; and the bays are prone to funnelling and channelling. Local wind effects are also pronounced around the Grey Islands, which lie just offshore.

The water off this shoreline is relatively deep. This limits shoaling to only a few areas around Hare Bay, the Grey Islands, and near Cape Bauld. Rough seas in this area are created mainly by the combined wind, tide, and wave-refraction effects around the islands.

As along most of the Newfoundland coastline, the weather in this area can be very harsh. By December, sea ice covers most waters and remains until early summer, leading to long, cold, and snowy winters and springs.

Caution: Fjords
Extreme caution should be used when crossing the fjords along the southern half of this coast under westerly winds. Funnelling and channelling of westerlies through the fjords makes for winds up to 30 knots stronger near the opening.

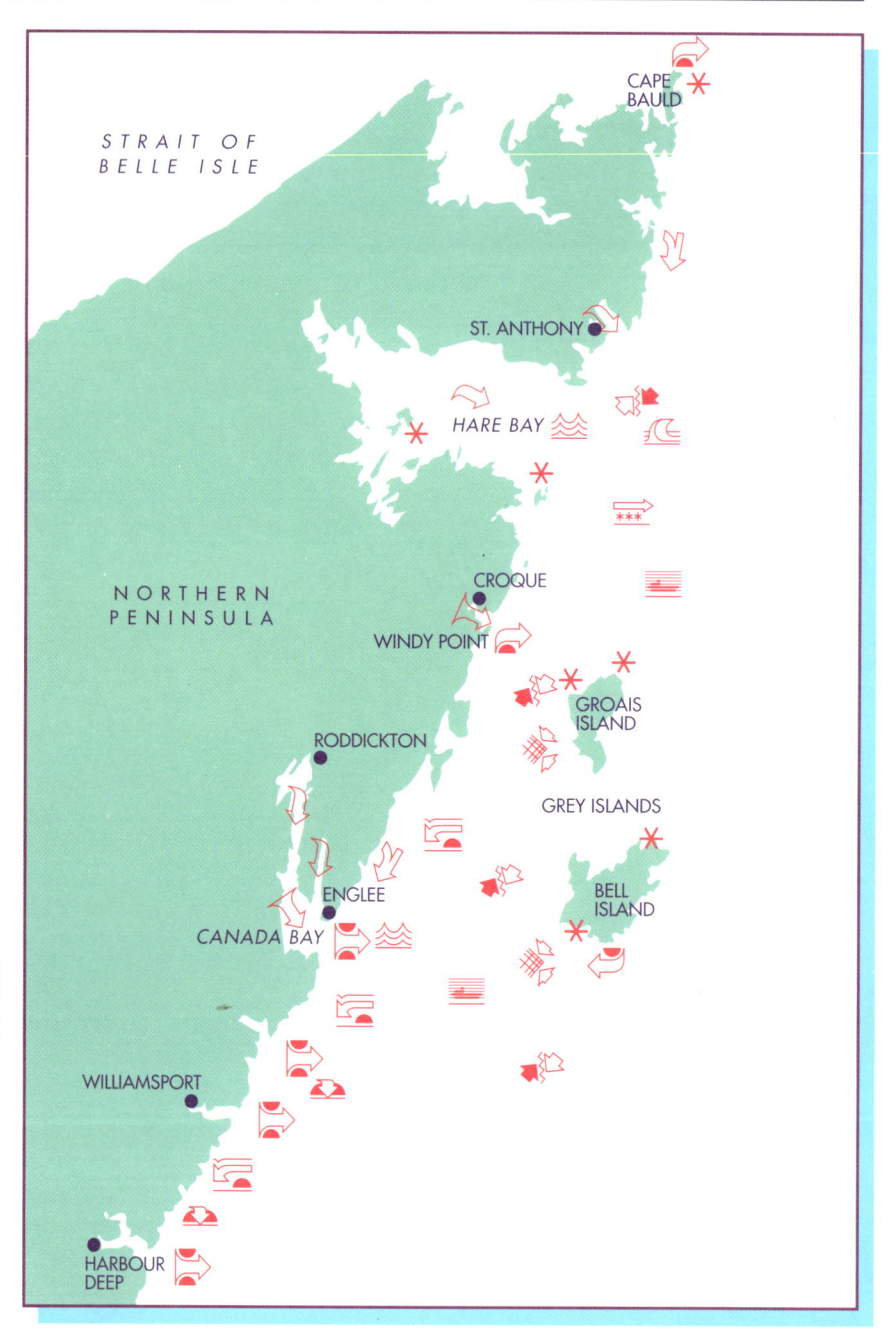

Marine Weather Tip: Forecasting the Wind
Local mariners use the sea state as a rough forecasting tool. Strong northwesterly winds along the Labrador coast generate a large ground swell; fishermen find that strong northwesterlies develop along this coast within a day after the ground swell moves in from the south.

LOCAL WEATHER Newfoundland East

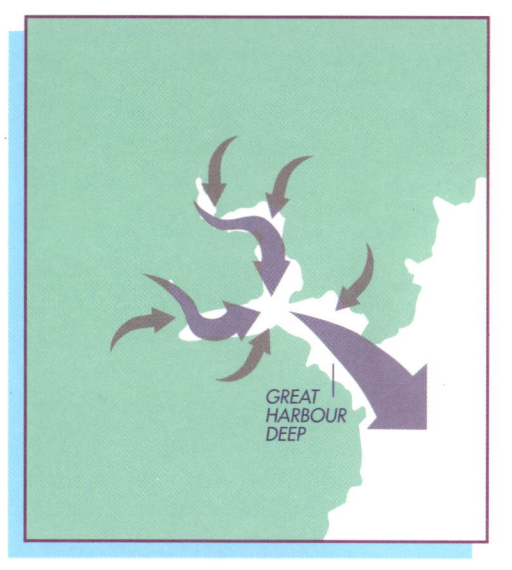

GREAT HARBOUR DEEP
Drainage winds are quite common through the summer months in most bays along this coast. They result in cool westerly winds, usually around 20 knots, in the bays in the morning. Winds diminish soon after sunrise, as the sun begins to reheat the air.

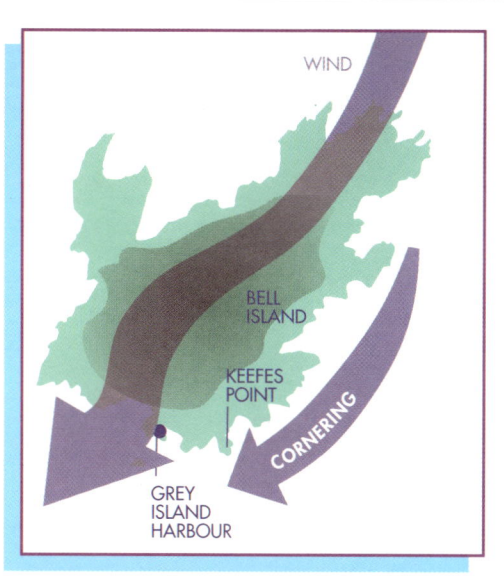

GREY ISLAND HARBOUR
Northeasterly winds undergo cornering at Keefes Point, on the southeast corner of Bell Island (the southernmost of the Grey Islands). Northeasterlies are also strengthened by mountain waves produced by the 500-ft. hills that dominate this island. The resulting northeasterlies gust up to 20 knots more than those 10 miles to the south.

Caution: Spring Melt
Seas can be rough near the coast in the spring, when strong currents are created by the run-off. Local mariners report that the roughest seas are found at the mouth of Hare Bay.

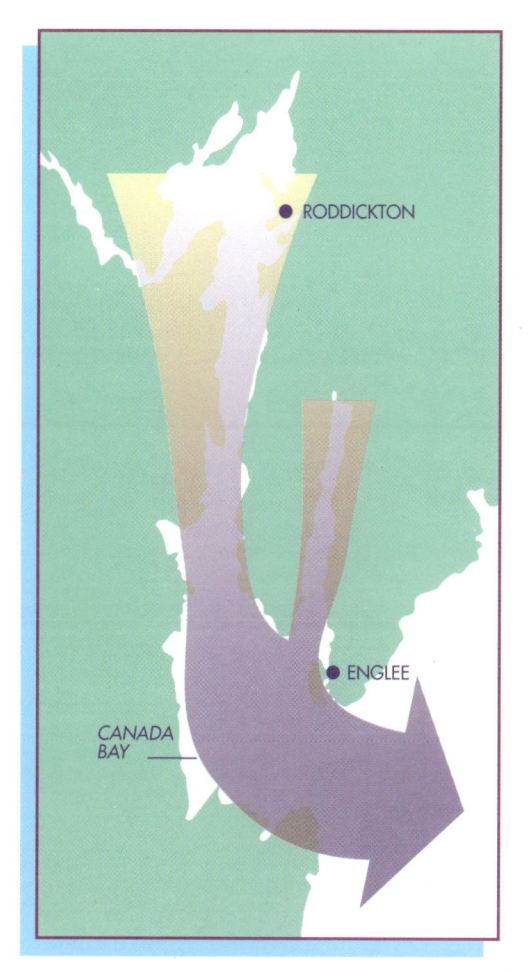

CANADA BAY: STRONG WINDS
Westerly and northwesterly winds are channelled and funnelled through the high cliffs that line Canada Bay. This produces particularly strong westerlies at the mouth of the bay. Winds reported from the automatic observing station at Englee can be usually 2–3 times faster than those recorded farther north. It is suspected that mountain waves are also a factor in these strong winds.

Caution: High Seas
Along this coast, seas tend to be higher between Croque and Cape Bauld, because the water is shallower and there is a greater exposure to the open ocean north of the Grey Islands.

Windy Point
This well-named point lies at the southern end of the mouth of Croque Harbour. Westerly and northwesterly winds intensify as they funnel through the harbour and are further strengthened by cornering at the point. Northeasterlies, too, are increased when they undergo coastal convergence.

LOCAL WEATHER Labrador

Labrador South

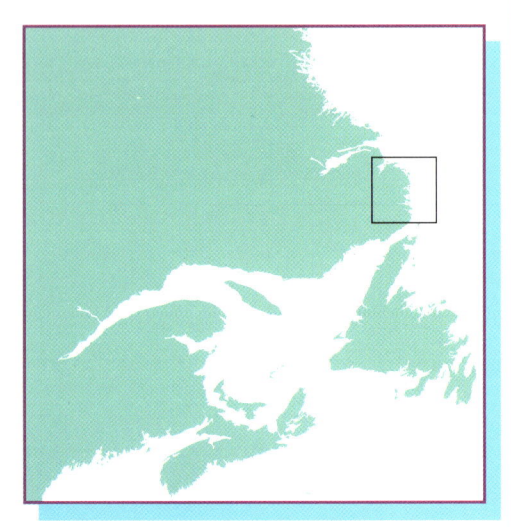

GENERAL CONDITIONS

This steep rugged coast is dotted with numerous islands and east-to-west-oriented bays that cause funnelling and channelling. Exposed to the full fury of easterly gales, the coast is pounded by large waves, making navigation hazardous. The Labrador Current runs southward, parallel to the coast. Southerly gales opposing this current create steep seas off the headlands.

Fog remains offshore under a south-to-southwesterly flow, but is common and often dense over the cold waters of the Labrador Current. Ice begins to form along the north Labrador coast by late November and moves quickly southward to cover the south coast by early- to mid-December. Melting usually begins in May or June.

The coastline between Island of Ponds and West Bay is oriented northwest to southeast and is somewhat flatter and less rugged. The water here is shallower, which leads to a large area of breakers when strong winds blow onshore. There is little shelter from these winds, creating hazards for small vessels.

For easier reading, this coastline has been divided into two sections.

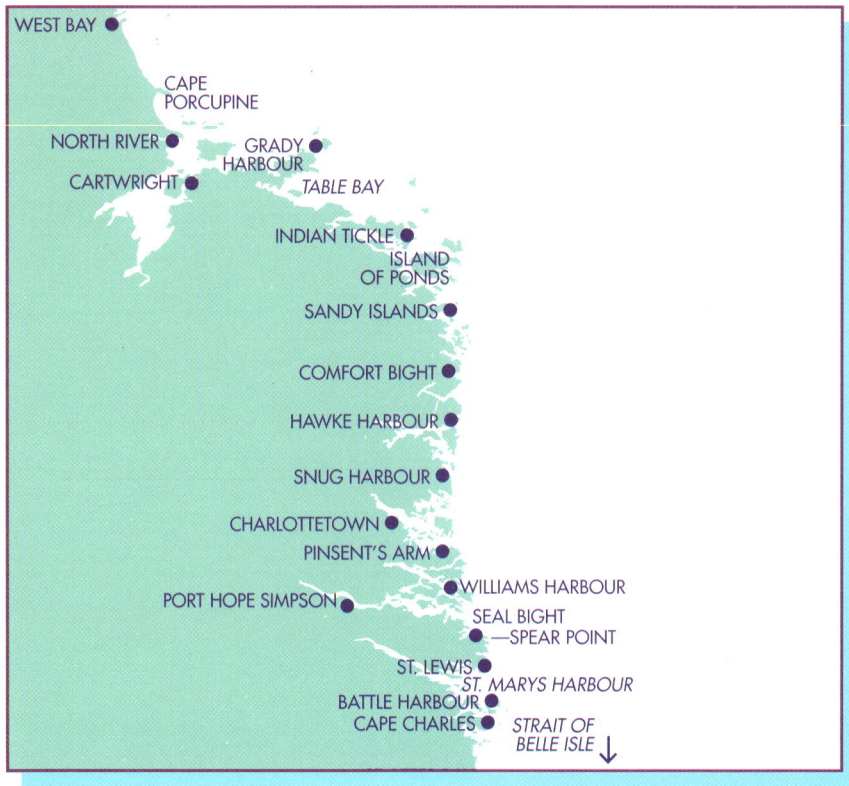

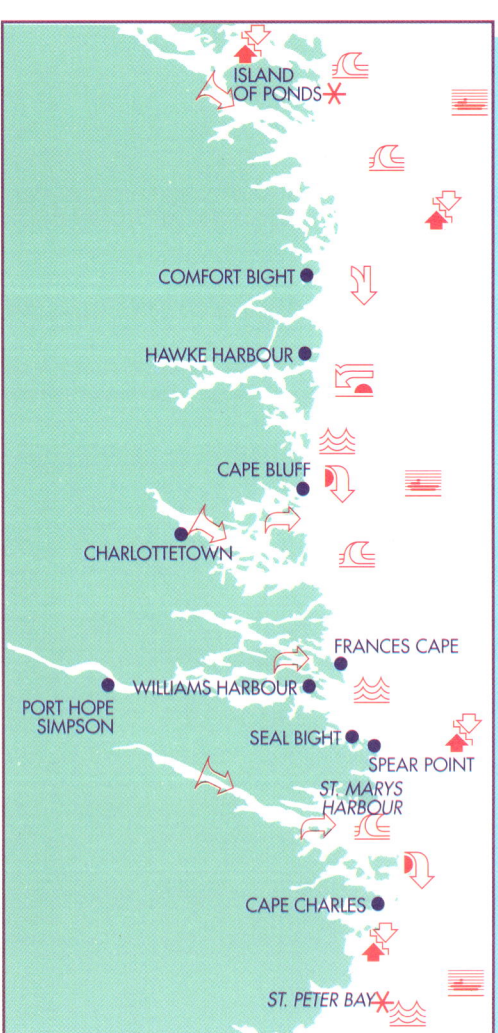

ST. PETER BAY TO ISLAND OF PONDS

The numerous islands and bays that indent the coastline cause the wind to funnel and channel along their axes. Winds blowing offshore during the warmer months can be very gusty near the land, but become calmer over the colder waters of the Labrador Current.

During the summer months, dense fog lingers offshore over the cold waters of the Labrador Current. When winds blow onshore, the dense fog bank moves onto the coast, creating very low visibility. Northerly winds undergo coastal convergence, causing a band of stronger winds near the coast.

Large waves pound headlands during strong onshore winds. This makes navigation hazardous—even for large vessels—but narrow bays and inlets provide shelter from these seas.

Following a period of persistent onshore winds, it can take a day or more for the ground swell to settle, because of the unlimited fetch of open ocean to the east.

LOCAL WEATHER *Labrador*

Wind Opposing the Labrador Current
Steep seas develop off the headlands, then move seaward when strong southerly-to-southeasterly winds oppose the Labrador Current. Spear Point, Frances Cape, and Cape Bluff, are exposed points along the coast, which are particularly prone to choppy seas under these conditions.

Wave Refraction and Onshore Water Transport
Northerly winds run parallel to this stretch of the coast; wave refraction brings the seas from these winds onshore, and rough seas develop in shallow areas of the coastline. As well, strong northerlies can create a storm surge along the coast producing higher water levels.

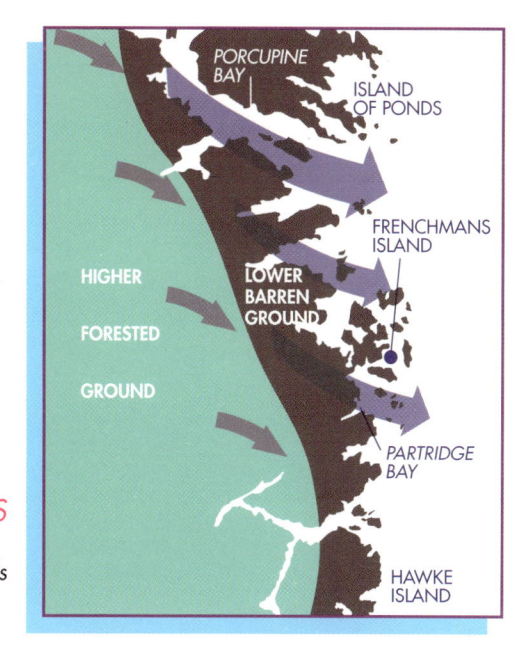

SOUTH OF CAPE CHARLES
Weather conditions can change drastically when a mariner rounds Cape Charles, heading south. Moderate westerly winds and sunny skies north of the cape can change to gusty southwesterlies, fog, and rough seas to the south of it. The gusts are caused by the funnelling of southwesterly winds out of the Strait of Belle Isle. When these meet the south-going Labrador Current, choppy seas result. As well, the warm southwesterlies can cause fog when they become chilled by the cold waters of the Labrador Current. Southwesterlies may also bring fog into the southern part of this area from the Strait of Belle Isle.

NORTH OF HAWKE ISLAND
Westerlies tend to blow more strongly and more steadily in this area, because the land near the coast is low and barren. Without any physical barriers—such as the forests farther inland—to create friction and reduce its speed, the wind is free to increase as it blows across the barrens.

Northwesterly winds are particularly strong in Porcupine Bay and Partridge Bay, due to funnelling

Island of Ponds
An unstable air mass is created around the island when frigid arctic air settles over the area. There is a transfer of heat to the air from leads of open water—even through the ice itself—that can create localized areas of instability. Small areas of strong, gusty winds can develop, producing low visibility in blowing snow.

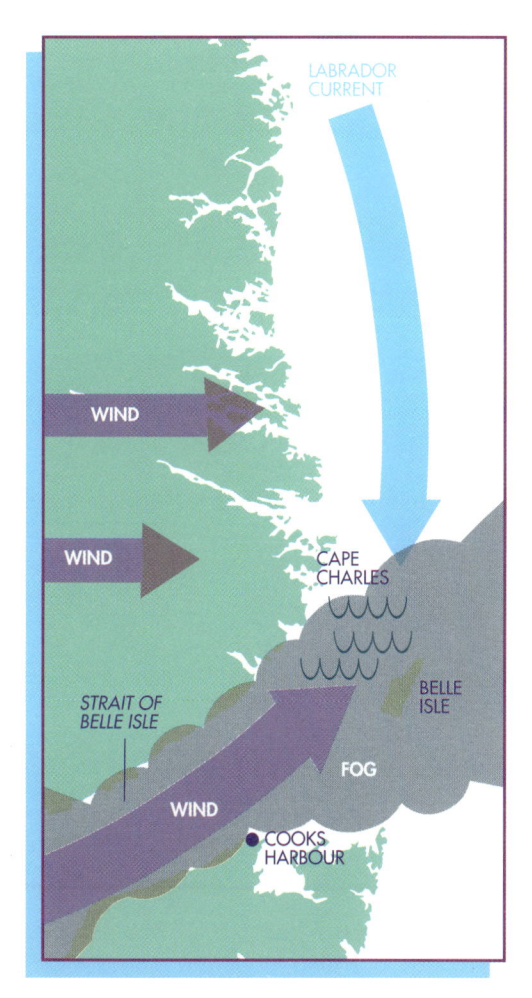

DOMINO RUN
Exposed to the east, Domino Run has a fearsome reputation for rough seas during strong onshore winds. The eastern entrance is particularly bad because large seas break over the shoals, causing steep seas. Farther west, Domino Run is sheltered from the full fury of the waves by its narrow channel; however, rough seas still occur here when strong winds oppose the current.

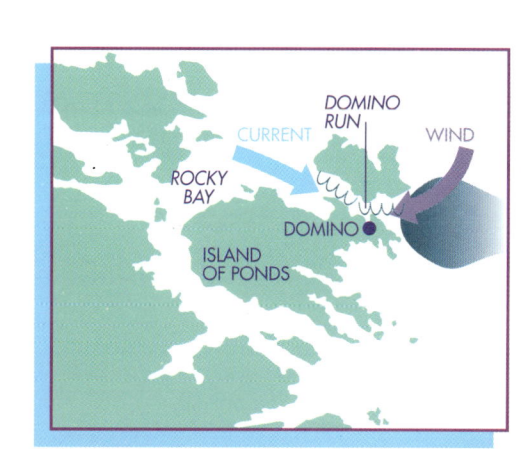

LOCAL WEATHER *Labrador*

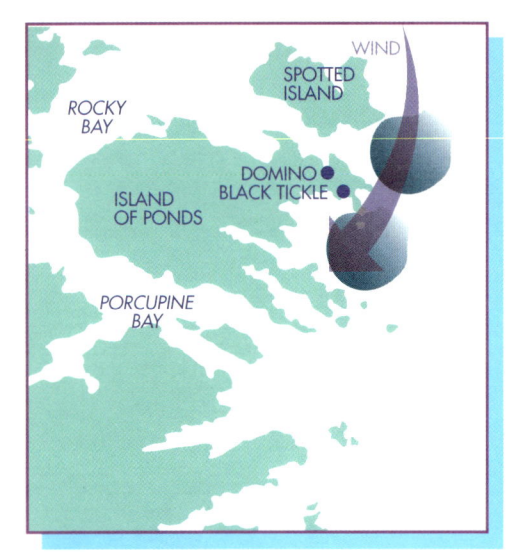

BLACK TICKLE
Northeasterly winds are enhanced by cornering from the eastern end of Spotted Island to Black Tickle. Local fishermen say they can't go to sea when the northeasterly is on. During persistent northeasterly winds, large seas heave up on the land, causing hazardous conditions.

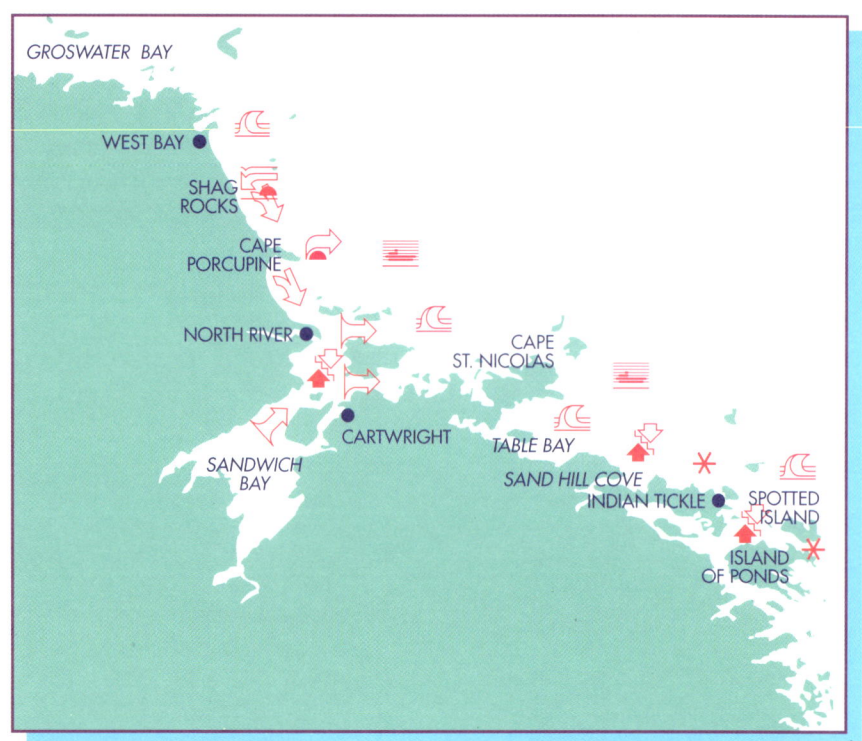

ISLAND OF PONDS TO WEST BAY
North of Island of Ponds, the coastal orientation changes to northwest to southeast. Coastal elevations up to 500 ft. at Sandwich Bay rise to 1,000 ft. farther north. North-to-northeasterly gales cause large waves to break on exposed shores. Table Bay is sheltered from all directions but the east; farther north, Sandwich Bay is protected from Atlantic swells by a narrow channel and numerous islands dotting its entrance.

Strong tidal currents, up to 3 1/2 knots, out of Sandwich Bay and approaches to Groswater Bay cause very choppy seas to develop when the wind opposes them.

Northwesterly winds undergo coastal convergence between North River Point and West Bay, creating a band of stronger winds.

Sand Hill Cove
In the late spring or early summer, melting snow and ice cause a strong current of fresh water to empty into Sand Hill Cove from the Sand Hill River. Very choppy seas result when this current meets an incoming tide in the bay, or is opposed by the wind.

LOCAL WEATHER *Labrador*

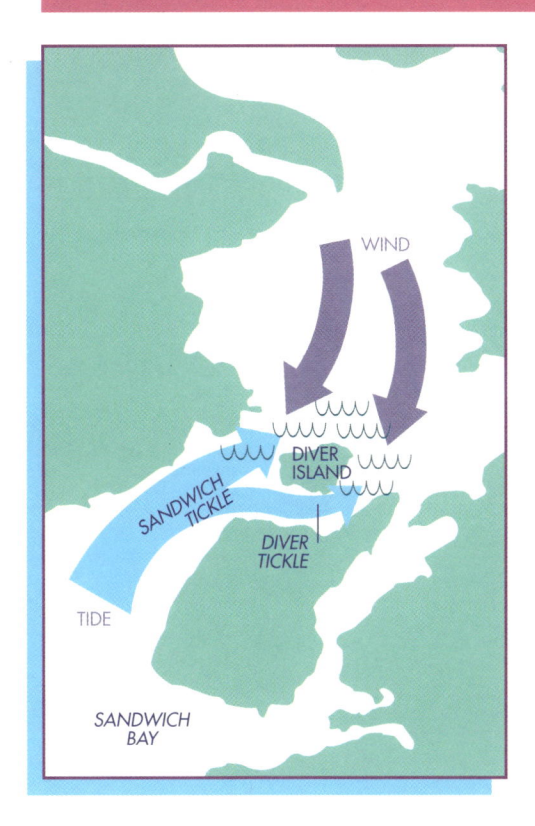

ENTRANCE TO SANDWICH BAY

When strong tidal currents out of Sandwich Bay oppose a strong northerly wind, large steep waves develop in Sandwich Tickle and Diver Tickle. Funnelling enhances these effects.

Caution: Dangerous Waves
The large waves in the entrance of Sandwich Bay are known locally as "rampers," and can be very dangerous to small open boats—and to larger ones. These unpredictable waves rise straight up and can fall in any direction.

Marine Weather Tip: Cartwright's Winds

Cartwright's wind report does not generally represent the wind conditions over open water, since the site is well exposed only to the northwest. Mariners should therefore use caution when consulting this report.

Between North River Point and West Bay

Northwesterly winds experience coastal convergence that causes a band of strong winds to develop along the coast. These winds are intensified south of Shag Rocks by mountain waves created by terrain that rises to approximately 1,200 ft. inland.

Northwesterlies and Rough Seas

A small peninsula extending from Cartwright to Cape St. Nicolas shelters the area from Spotted Island to Table Bay from the full brunt of northwesterly winds. North of the islands off the tip of this peninsula, the northwesterlies are stronger and the seas rougher, because of coastal convergence and the increased fetch of water. Conditions improve near the outer approaches of Groswater Bay, where the fetch is once again limited.

LOCAL WEATHER Labrador

Hamilton Inlet

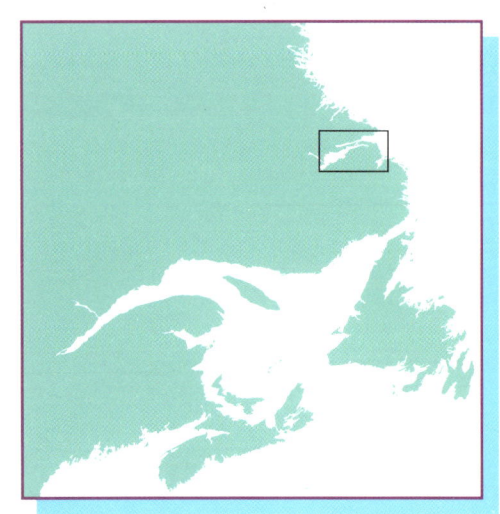

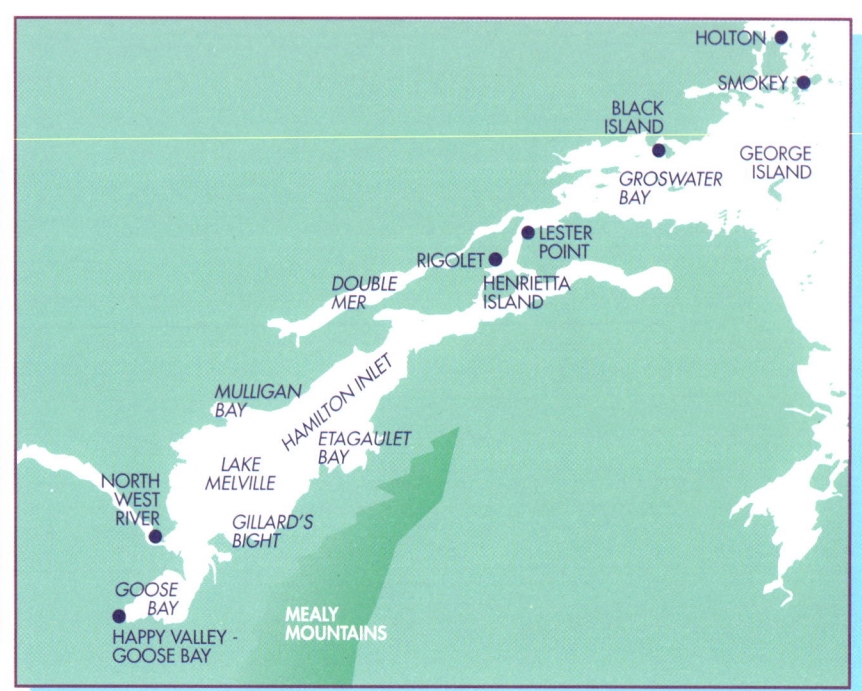

GENERAL CONDITIONS

Hamilton Inlet is a waterway that extends from the coast, approximately 140 miles inland.

At the outer portion of the inlet is Groswater Bay, dotted on its northern entrance by numerous islands and inlets, which cause localized funnelling and channelling. The hilly, barren terrain gives an indication of the harsh coastal climate. In the fall and winter, in particular, storms bring gale-force winds and heavy precipitation. Fog is frequent and is related to the onshore airflow off the cold Labrador Current.

The Narrows, which connects Groswater Bay with Lake Melville, is surrounded by steep, hilly terrain. The effects of the harsh coastal climate diminish farther inland, where more extensive vegetation and forest cover are found. The Narrows rarely freezes over, due to the strong tidal currents there.

The final section of Hamilton Inlet is Lake Melville, a large body of water running from northeast to southwest. Because of the orientation of the lake, winds are funnelled and channelled in these two directions. The Mealy Mountains, just south of the lake, cause mountain waves.

GROSWATER BAY

This V-shaped bay, the largest on the Labrador coast, is bounded by a variety of terrain, ranging from barren, hilly land to the north, and flat, swampy land east of Nats Discovery Point to the south.

A large exposure to the Labrador Sea to the east produces rough seas under strong easterlies, especially near the shoals and islands at the mouth of the bay. In addition, strong tidal currents can interact with high seas and strong winds to create rough conditions.

Cornering, funnelling, and channelling occur around the islands and the narrow channels between them. Coastal convergence leads to intensified westerlies along the southern coast, while easterlies are strengthened in the north.

George Island

Southeast gales bring large breaking seas over shallow water between the island and the mainland. These effects, combined with strong tidal currents, create hazardous conditions. On the west side of the island, crossing seas develop under strong easterlies, the result of large ocean waves refracting around the island.

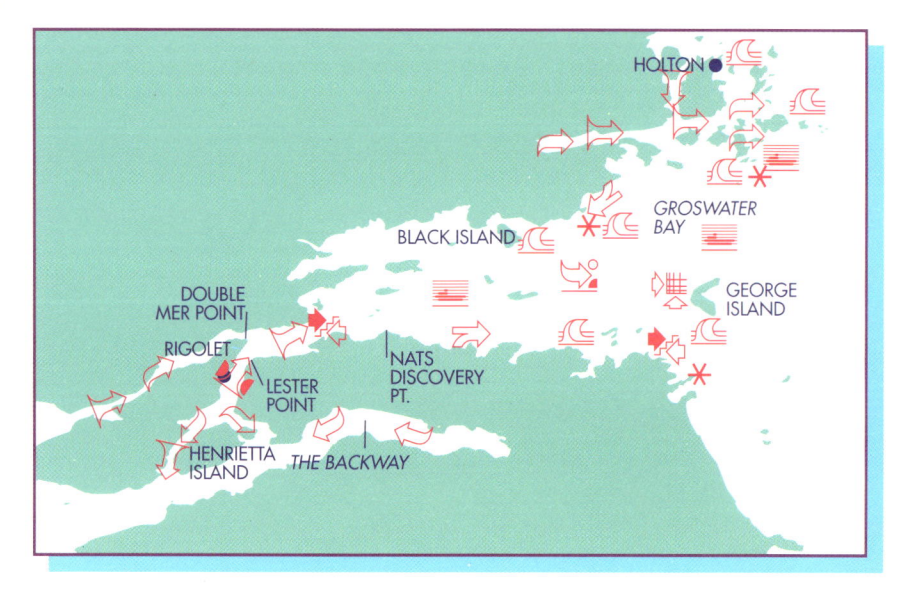

LOCAL WEATHER Labrador

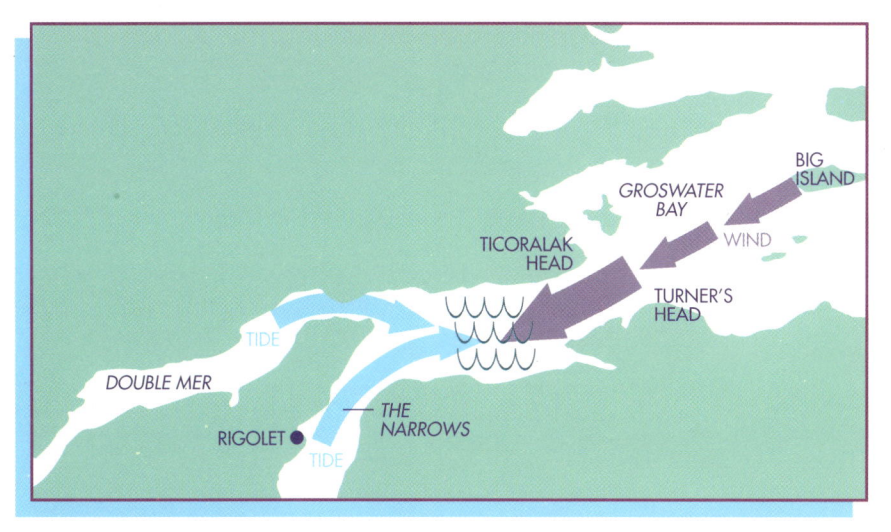

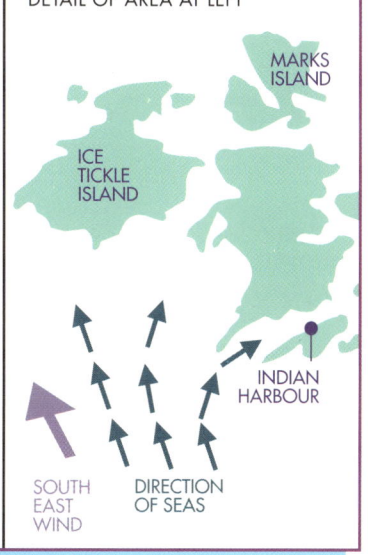

HEAD OF GROSWATER BAY
Northeast and southwesterly winds funnel between Ticoralak Head and Turner's Head, causing strong winds that can increase by 15 knots. Combined with strong tidal currents, these winds can create steep, choppy seas.

Caution: Ice Changing Direction
Sea breezes affect Groswater Bay during the warmer months; westerly winds early in the day can shift to moderate easterlies in the afternoon. Sea ice can drift with the wind; an ice drift that is offshore in the morning can move to the shore in the afternoon, as the sea breeze becomes established.

TWIN ISLANDS TO CUT THROAT ISLAND
Seas can become fully developed along this coast when prolonged, strong southeasterly winds blow across the south Labrador coast and Belle Isle Bank marine areas. When these deep-water waves run over shallow water, seas steepen and break—and hazardous conditions result. Large swells can enter Indian Harbour when these conditions prevail, due to the refraction of the waves at the harbour's entrance.

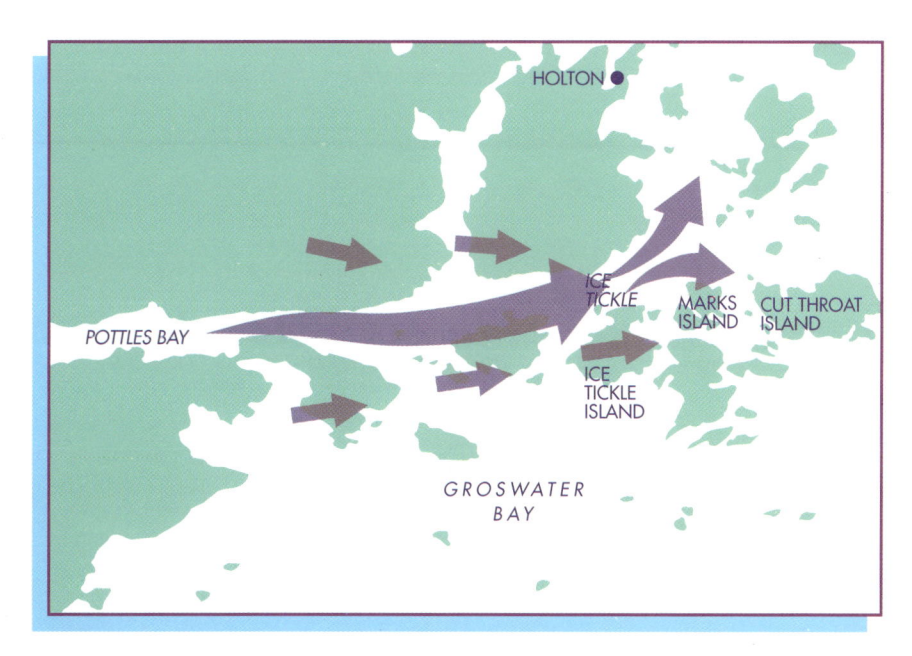

POTTLES BAY TO ICE TICKLE
Strong, gusty winds result when westerly winds are channelled and funnelled from Pottles Bay to Ice Tickle. During summer thunderstorms, these winds can increase to storm force.

LOCAL WEATHER Labrador

The Narrows
The appropriately named channel, bordered by steep, hilly terrain, connects Groswater Bay with Lake Melville. Northeast and southwest winds undergo funnelling and channelling, and strong southwest gap winds can be expected between Double Mer Point and Lester Point. As well, winds funnel and channel in the arms around Henrietta Island and in The Backway, an arm of Lake Melville. Mariners should note that these effects make it difficult to predict the prevailing wind direction when navigating the Narrows and adjacent arms.

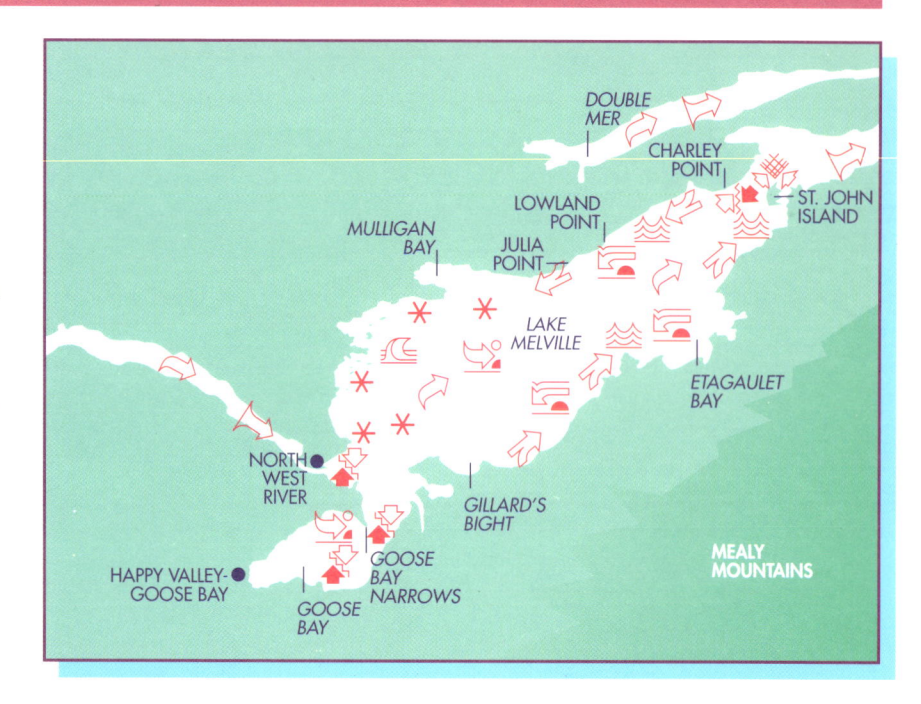

Haven of Rest: Shelter in Northeast Gales
During northeast gales, mariners can find shelter in a small cove on the eastern end of Pike Back Run.

LAKE MELVILLE
Lake Melville, oriented northeast to southwest, is tidal and generally deep. Winds funnel and channel along its axis, resulting in strong northeasterlies and southwesterlies. Most of the shoreline is bounded by high terrain, especially on the southern coast, where the Mealy Mountains rise to nearly 4,000 ft. about 7 miles inland. Heavy squalls can develop off the mountains in southeasterly winds.

The high terrain surrounding the lake, along with its inland setting, result in a continental type of climate rather than the maritime one on the Labrador coast. Fog in this area is less frequent, and greater temperature extremes occur. The mean daily temperature at Goose Bay is 3°C colder than Cartwright in winter and 3°C warmer in summer.

During the summer months, thunderstorms that form over land can cause squalls over the lake. Ice begins to form over shallower western sections of the lake by mid-November and spreads eastward to cover remaining areas by mid-December. Breakup usually begins in April.

St. John Island
Strong southwesterly winds split around St. John Island. Coastal convergence produces a band of stronger winds on the northern side; on the southern side, the winds are strengthened by funnelling and channelling. The sea becomes confused where the two wind streams meet on the northeast side, and turns even rougher during a flood tide.

Marine Weather Tip
When crossing the mouth of Etagaulet Bay in east or southeasterly winds, mariners generally add 20 knots to the forecast wind speed. Take note as well that winds here can reach 50 knots in squalls.

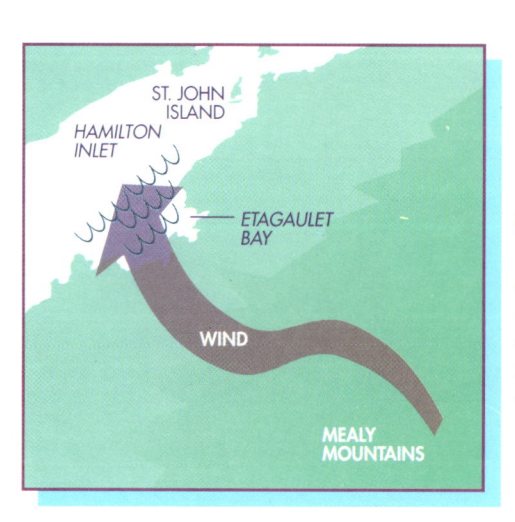

ETAGAULET BAY
This area is known for very strong east-to-southeasterly winds. Waves off the Mealy Mountains can quickly produce storm conditions from the mouth of the bay to well out in the lake.

LOCAL WEATHER *Labrador*

Haven of Rest: Shelter in Southeast Gales
Small vessels can find good shelter from southeasterly gales in the bay between Eskimo Paps and Long Point.

LONG POINT TO THE EPINETTE PENINSULA
Southwesterly winds undergo coastal convergence along this low, swampy stretch of coast from Gillards Bight to 4 miles west of Eskimo Paps. This effect results in a band of strong winds that hug the coast. Elsewhere, the terrain is higher and more rugged, which tends to deflect this band of strong winds 2–3 miles offshore.

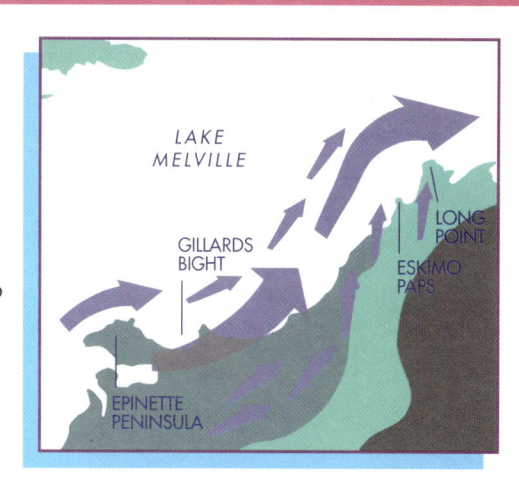

Goose Bay Narrows
When strong northerly winds oppose the ebb tide out of Goose Bay, short, choppy seas are created. Conditions are usually worse during the spring run-off, when large volumes of fresh water run into the bay from the Churchill River, causing even stronger currents.

Goose Bay
The prevailing winds in this area are westerly and are somewhat influenced by the Churchill River basin under light to moderate flows. The sheltered bay is fringed by extensive wooded vegetation, which has a calming influence on the wind. Winds, especially southwesterly, are generally lighter here than elsewhere in Lake Melville, where a longer fetch over the ice or water leads to stronger winds.

Marine Weather Tip
The observation site at the Goose Bay Airport, which is sheltered from most directions, does not represent typical wind conditions on Lake Melville. Mariners usually add 10–20 knots to Goose Bay's wind report in order to determine exposed conditions on the lake.

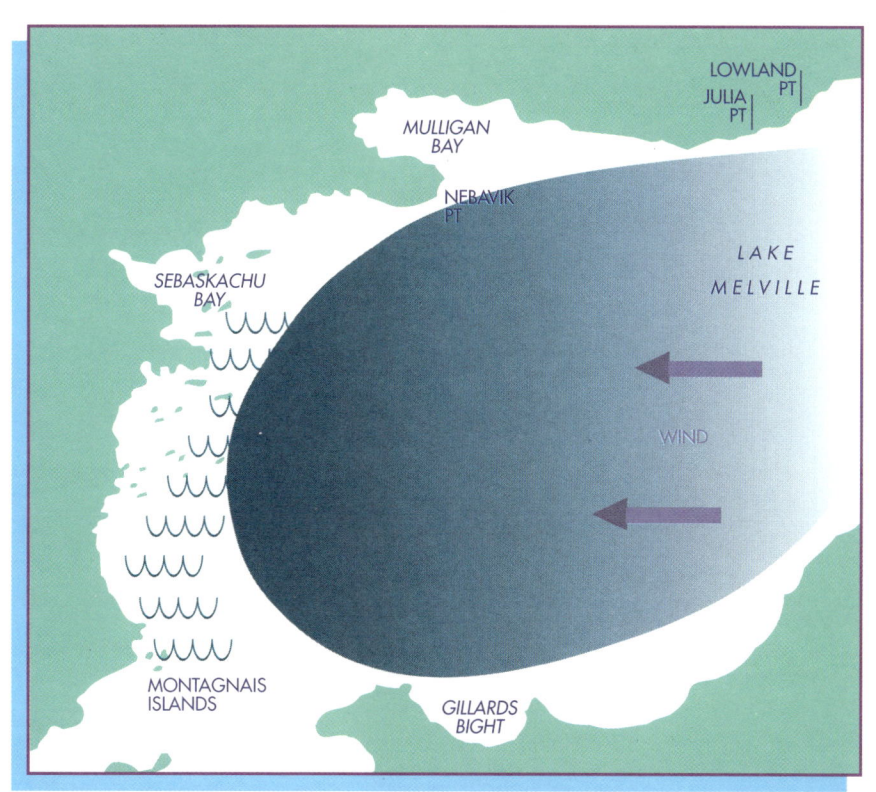

MONTAGNAIS ISLANDS AND SEBASKACHU BAY
This area is perhaps the shallowest in the lake. Waves pile up on the western shore of Lake Melville under strong easterly flows, creating short, choppy seas. Easterly winds blowing along the length of the lake produce higher waves due to the long fetch of water. When the waves move into shallow water, shoaling results, and the waves steepen and break.

161

LOCAL WEATHER *Labrador*

THUNDERSTORMS

During the summer months, air-mass thunderstorms often develop around Lake Melville. These storms form over the warm land and tend to weaken as they move over the colder waters of Lake Melville. Lightning, heavy rain, and strong, gusty winds accompany the storms, which are usually more severe near the shoreline than over the lake, where they are weakened by the stabilizing effect of the cold water. Sea breezes along various parts of the shore can converge, resulting in more thunderstorm activity.

Caution: Line of Thunderstorms

Line, or frontal, thunderstorms rarely weaken over Lake Melville. They often form a continuous line of active weather, offering little opportunity to avoid them by altering course.

Charley Point to Julia Point

East-to-northeasterly winds undergo coastal convergence along this shoreline. The terrain between Charley Point and Lowland Point is high, which deflects the band of stronger winds 3–4 miles offshore. When north-to-northwest winds blow off the steep cliffs, turbulent eddies form in the lee of the cliffs. A band of gusty winds is usually found within 4 miles of shore, where it creates choppy seas. Between Lowland Point and a few miles west of Julia Point, the terrain is lower and swampy; this creates a band of stronger winds within a mile of shore.

LOCAL WEATHER *Labrador*

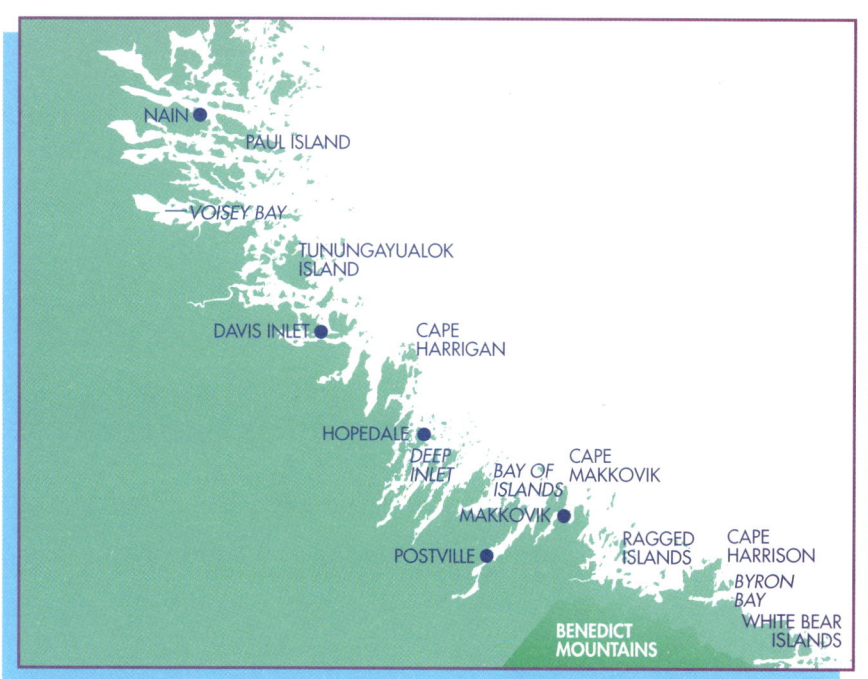

Labrador North

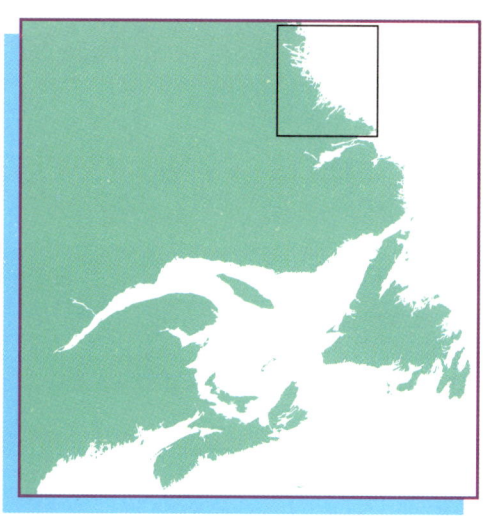

GENERAL CONDITIONS

This coastline is deeply indented by numerous bays and steep-sided inlets fronted with hundreds of islands. The terrain becomes more mountainous with fjordic inlets north of Cape Harrigan. This topography results in drastic local effects, especially funnelling and channelling. Funnelling, in particular, can give rise to storm-force winds, while gap winds can surprise mariners as they pass by the mouths of bays and inlets.

During the fall and winter, intense low-pressure systems moving through the Labrador Sea bring gale- to storm-force winds and heavy precipitation (mostly snow) to the coast. Winds vary from calm to storm force; gales are less frequent in the summer but can still occur in the narrow channels and fjords. During the summer months, thunderstorms form inland, moving towards the coast and causing heavy squalls.

Local variations in climate are evident everywhere from the outer islands to the inner reaches of the lengthy inlets. Gales, fog, and precipitation tend to be more prevalent along the coast than farther inland.

The Labrador Current generally flows southeastward parallel to the coast. When strong winds oppose the current, seas become choppy and steep.

Land and sea breezes are common and enhanced considerably by the topography.

The long fetch of water over the Labrador Sea causes large waves to pound the exposed coastline during strong, persistent onshore winds.

Ice begins to form over northern bays and inlets by late November and moves quickly southward to cover remaining areas by early December. Melting usually begins in May or June.

Note: This manual details the marine weather conditions in northern Labrador only as far as Nain. Beyond Nain, the coastline is similar to those described here, and mariners can apply the generic information in this chapter to the fjords, capes, and islands that compose the remainder of the coastline.

For easier reading, this coastline has been divided into two sections.

LOCAL WEATHER Labrador

WHITE BEAR ISLANDS TO CAPE HARRIGAN

This coastline is dotted by numerous islands and indented by lengthy inlets oriented northeast to southwest; southwesterlies and northeasterlies are the strongest and most common winds along this coast.

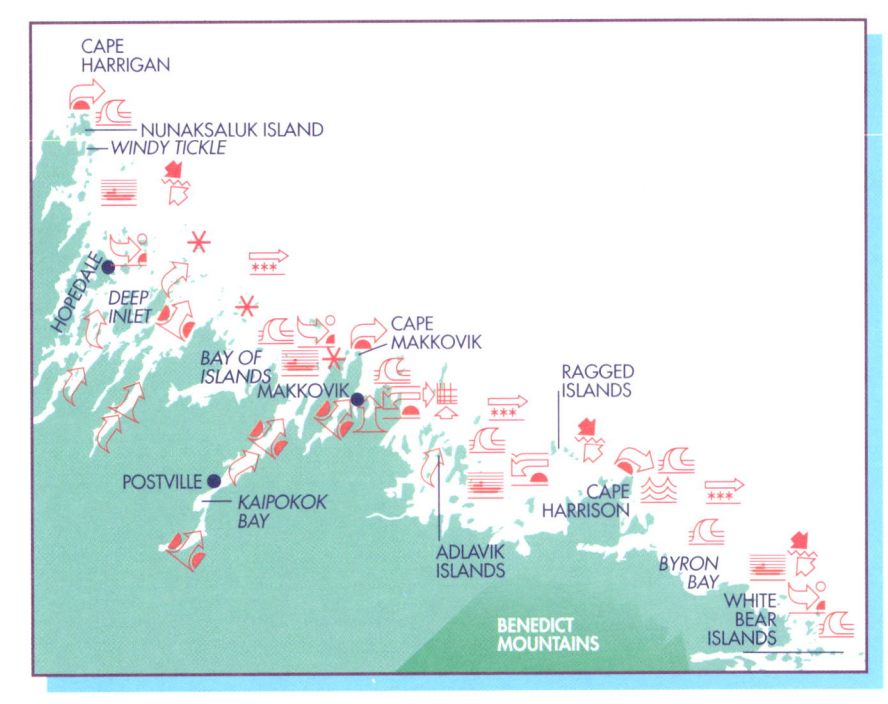

FJORDS

The coast of Labrador contains many deep and steep-walled fjords, which can create tricky local wind conditions for mariners.

Winds inside a fjord usually blow along the fjord's axis, or length. In an east-to-west-oriented fjord, for example, a northwest (or southwest) wind over the open water will shift—or channel—to west within the fjord.

When winds blow along the fjord's axis, they are funnelled by the steep walls and can double in speed, inside the fjord and at its mouth. Strong winds that exit a fjord—gap winds—can be violent, catching inexperienced mariners by surprise. Under these conditions, experienced mariners add 20–30 knots to the open-water wind speed when they are crossing a fjord. Waves moving towards a fjord can be corralled, resulting in tricky seas.

However, a fjord's steep walls can provide shelter to mariners when winds blow across the fjord's axis. For example, strong southerlies over the open water outside an east-to-west fjord will be significantly lighter inside.

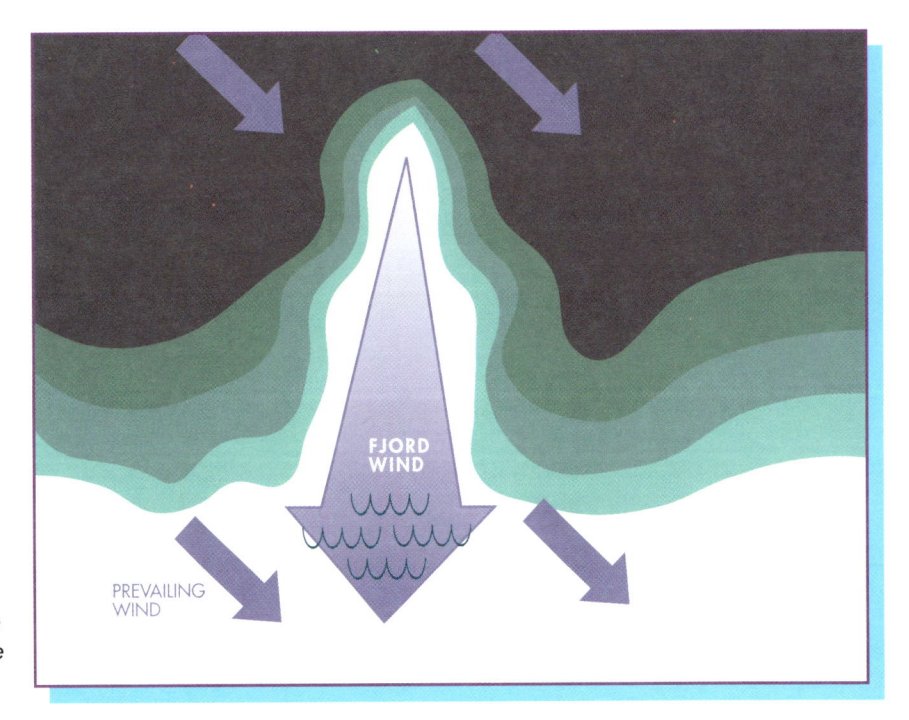

Northwesterly Winds and Rough Seas

Seaward of the areas from Cape Harrison to Cape Makkovik to Cape Harrigan, the ocean exposure can intensify northwesterly winds and seas. During cold outbreaks in the fall, before sea ice forms, conditions can become dangerous, due to freezing spray. Conditions improve inside the capes and inner islands.

Wind Opposing the Labrador Current

When gale-force southeast winds oppose the Labrador Current, seas steepen and become dangerous. Prominent headlands such as Cape Harrison, Cape Makkovik, and Cape Harrigan are particularly prone to steep, choppy seas.

LOCAL WEATHER Labrador

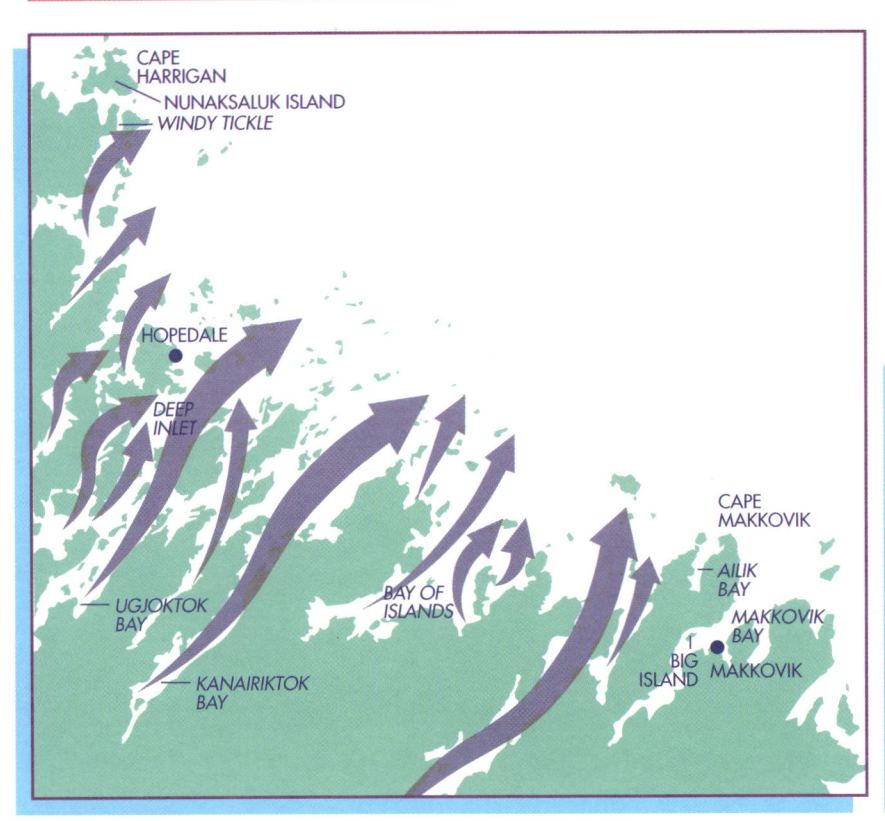

Marine Weather Tip
Local mariners add 15–20 knots to the open-water wind forecasts when crossing the mouths of larger bays in winds blowing off the land.

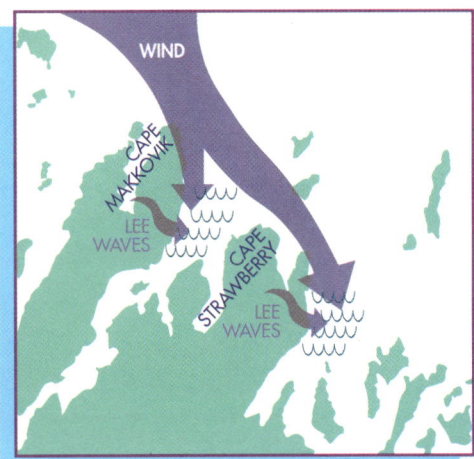

CAPE MAKKOVIK TO CAPE HARRIGAN
Westerly flows across Labrador shift to south to southwesterly, due to channelling along the axis of the inlets. Localized areas of strong gap winds occur at the mouths of inlets.

Makkovik Bay and Aillik Bay
In strong and persistent northeast winds, large seas can push into the mouth of these bays, causing confused seas. As well, significant ground swell can move into Makkovik Harbour. A band of stronger northeasterly winds, enhanced by coastal convergence between Cape Makkovik and Big Island, can cause seas to steepen even more.

Kaipokok Bay, Kanairiktok Bay and Udjuktok Bay
Kaipokok Bay is a narrow bay bordered by steep, hilly terrain. Funnelling, channelling, and coastal convergence make for strong winds here, along the length of the bay. Where the bay narrows, between Postville and Post Hill, gap winds occur, sometimes accompanied by whirlwinds. Similar conditions affect Kanairiktok Bay and Udjuktok Bay.

Sea Breeze
Strong temperature contrasts characterize the summer months, when warm offshore winds meet the cold waters of the Labrador Sea. Moderate offshore winds in the morning can give way to brisk onshore winds (sea breezes) in the afternoon. Funnelling causes these winds to increase from 10–15 knots outside the bays to 25 knots inside, where channelling turns the winds northeasterly in Kaipokok Bay, Kanairiktok Bay, and Udjuktok Bay.

Windy Tickle
This spot, as the name implies, is known for its wind—particularly violent northerly squalls. Cornering on the east side of Nanaksaluk Island produces a narrow band of stronger northerly winds, intensified by funnelling and channelling through the Tickle. Whirlwinds or swirling columns of water can accompany these squalls.

STRONG WINDS AROUND PROMINENT HEADLANDS
Capes Harrison, Strawberry, Makkovik, and Harrigan are exposed high points of land subject to very strong winds from every direction. North and northwesterly winds are particularly fearsome, due to cornering. These winds, added to small-scale lee waves east of these capes, make for gustier winds and choppier seas.

The diagram shows this effect in the Cape Makkovik and Cape Strawberry areas. Similar effects can be expected around other headlands.

Caution: Mountain Waves
Strong, gusty southwest winds, caused by mountain waves off the Benedict Mountains, can be felt as far as the Ragged Islands.

LOCAL WEATHER *Labrador*

CAPE HARRIGAN TO NAIN

The bays and steep-sided inlets here are oriented more east to west than those south of Cape Harrigan: winds tend to be more westerly. The terrain is mountainous right up to the coast, many inlets have fjordic characteristics, and hundreds of islands dot the coast. Funnelling and channelling are the main local effects in this area, often resulting in violent winds.

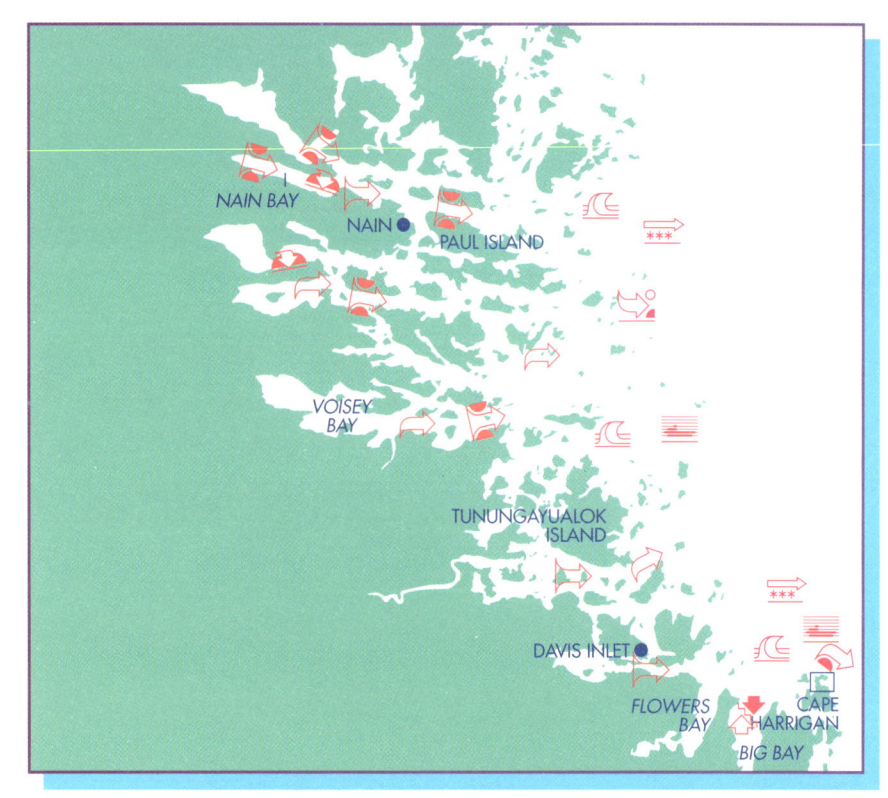

NAIN BAY

Strong westerly winds blowing down the fjordic Fraser River valley undergo both funnelling and channelling. When these winds blow out of Nain Bay, they can be violent. The west-to-east orientation of the passages allows these squalls to reach the outer islands virtually unimpeded. Similar, but less violent winds are felt at Voisey Bay and the Bridges Passage. This effect has been known to occur even under moderate westerly circulations.

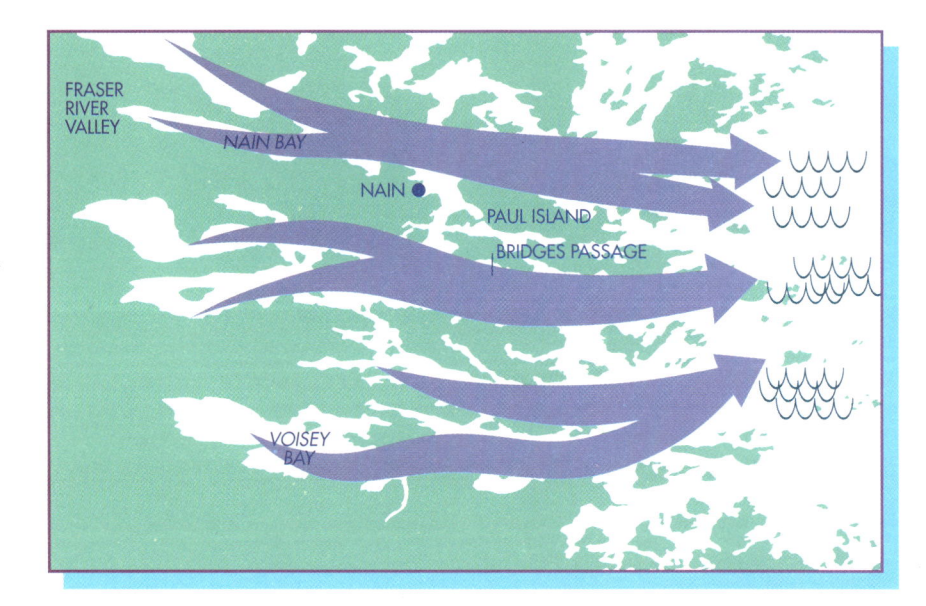

Marine Weather Tip

Since Nain is a sheltered site, wind reports from the community do not generally represent conditions outside the islands. North-to-northeast winds tend to be lighter at Nain than those farther offshore, and the terrain often causes winds to shift to the west at Nain.

Big Bay and Flowers Bay

When strong northerly winds oppose the ebb tide out of Big Bay and Flowers Bay, seas become very rough. Conditions can worsen if the onshore winds are persistent, causing seas to become fully developed.

Caution: Strong Sea Breezes

Sea breezes can be 25 knots or greater in the narrow passages and inlets along this coast, because they are enhanced by funnelling.

APPENDIX A Conversion Tables

WIND SPEEDS

Descriptive	knots	mph	km/h	Beaufort
Light	≤11	≤13	≤20	≤4
Moderate	12–19	14–22	22–35	4–5
Strong	20–33	23–38	37–61	5–7
Gale	34–47	39–54	63–87	8–9
Storm	48–63	55–73	89–117	10–11
Hurricane	≥64	≥74	≥118	≥12

1 knot = 1.15 miles per hour
1 mile per hour = 0.87 knots

1 knot = 1.85 kilometres
1 kilometre = 0.54 knots

1 kilometre = 0.62 miles per hour
1 mile per hour = 1.61 kilometres

ATMOSPHERIC PRESSURE

millibars	inches	kilopascals
950	28.1	95
970	28.6	97
990	29.2	99
1000	29.5	100
1013.25	*29.92*	*101.3*
1020	30.1	102
1040	30.7	104
1060	31.3	106

global average pressure (in italics)

1 inch of mercury = 33.87 millibars

1 inch of mercury = 3.387 kilopascals

1 kilopascal = 10 millibars

1 millibar = 0.1 kilopascals

DISTANCES

metres to feet

1 m	=	3.28 ft.
2 m	=	6.56 ft.
3 m	=	9.84 ft.
4 m	=	13.12 ft.
5 m	=	16.40 ft.
6 m	=	19.69 ft.
7 m	=	22.97 ft.
8 m	=	26.25 ft.
9 m	=	29.53 ft.
10 m	=	32.81 ft.
15 m	=	49.21 ft.
20 m	=	65.62 ft.

kilometres to nautical miles

1 km	=	0.54 n.miles
10 km	=	5.4 n.miles
100 km	=	54.0 n.miles
1,000 km	=	540 n.miles

nautical miles to kilometres

1 n.mile	=	1.85 km
10 n.miles	=	18.5 km
100 n.miles	=	185 km
1,000 n.miles	=	1,852 km

TEMPERATURE

°F	°C
110	43
100	38
90	32
80	27
70	21
60	16
50	10
40	4
30	-1
20	-7
10	-12
0	-18
-10	-23
-20	-29
-30	-34
-40	-40

°F = °C × 9/5 + 32

°C = (°F − 32) × 5/9

APPENDIX B *Wind-chill Factor*

Everyone knows how much colder the weather feels on a windy day—particularly in the winter. The wind's rapid cooling effect makes it feel colder than it really is. This effect can create serious and often dangerous conditions.

Wind-Chill Factor is a measure of the combined chilling effect of wind and temperature. The calculation is based upon how fast water cools with the combination of low temperature and wind, but it has been found to be equally applicable to the cooling effect experienced by the human body and by an inanimate object.

	5°C	0°C	-5°C	-10°C	-15°C	-20°C	-25°C	-30°C	-35°C
5 kts	5	0	-5	-10	-15	-20	-25	-30	-35
10 kts	0	-6	-11	-17	-23	-29	-35	-41	-46
15 kts	-3	-9	-16	-22	-28	-35	-41	-47	-53
20 kts	-5	-11	-18	-25	-31	-38	-45	-52	-58
25 kts	-6	-13	-20	-27	-34	-41	-48	-55	-62
30 kts	-7	-14	-21	-28	-36	-43	-50	-57	-64
35 kts	-8	-15	-22	-29	-37	-44	-51	-58	-66
40 kts	-8	-15	-23	-30	-37	-45	-52	-59	-66
45 kts	-8	-16	-23	-30	-38	-45	-52	-60	-67

WIND-CHILL TEMPERATURES

In the past, it has been common practice to use an equivalent wind-chill temperature to relate wind and temperature. Here is an abbreviated table with some sample temperatures.

For example, if the temperature is -20°C and the wind speed is 25 knots, the equivalent wind chill temperature is -44°C.

While quite popular, the wind-chill temperature does not correspond to the combined effect of wind and temperature on the human body. The graph below is a better guide for the effects of wind chill.

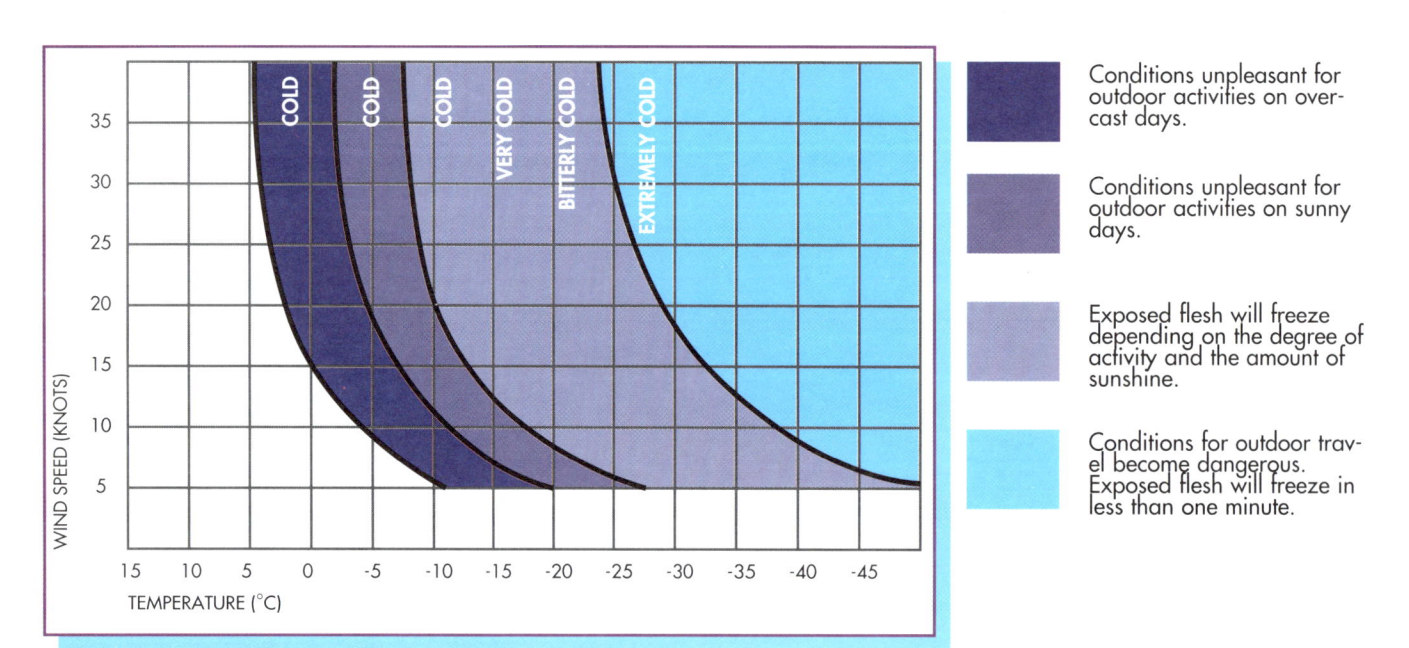

- Conditions unpleasant for outdoor activities on overcast days.
- Conditions unpleasant for outdoor activities on sunny days.
- Exposed flesh will freeze depending on the degree of activity and the amount of sunshine.
- Conditions for outdoor travel become dangerous. Exposed flesh will freeze in less than one minute.

WIND-CHILL EFFECTS

This graph is a good tool to determine the effect of wind chill. Follow the temperature across and the wind speed up until the two lines intersect, then read off the description from the graph. For example, at a temperature of -10°C with a wind speed of 30 knots, the point of intersection lies in the band that describes conditions as, "exposed flesh will freeze depending on the degree of activity and the amount of sunshine."

APPENDIX C Ice Terminology

Ice bulletins for fishermen and facsimile charts of ice conditions use unique terminology that mariners have to understand. Below is an abbreviated list of these terms.

FLOATING ICE

Any form of ice floating in water should concern mariners. These include:

Sea Ice: Any ice at sea formed by the freezing of salt water.

Ice of land origin: Ice formed on land or in an ice shelf, found floating in water.

Lake Ice: Ice formed on a lake, regardless of observed location.

River Ice: Ice formed on a river, regardless of observed location.

The first two categories are highlighted below.

STAGES OF DEVELOPMENT OF SEA ICE

The names given to an area or piece of sea ice usually describe its thickness, age, and size.

New Ice: A general term for recently formed ice—composed of ice crystals only weakly frozen together (if at all), which have a definite form only while they are afloat.

Frazil	Fine plates of ice suspended in water.
Grease	Coagulated ice crystals forming a soupy layer on surface.
Slush	Snow that is saturated and mixed with water on ice surfaces, or as a floating mass in water after a heavy snowfall.
Shuga	Spongy lumps of ice formed from grease ice or slush.

Nilas: A thin elastic crust of ice that bends easily on waves and under pressure; it grows in a pattern of interlocking "fingers"; it can be up to 10 cm thick.

Young Ice: ice that is in the transition stage between nilas and first-year ice; 10–30 cm thick.

Grey Ice	10–15 cm thick; less elastic than nilas; breaks on swell; usually rafts under pressure.
Grey-White Ice	15–30 cm thick; under pressure it is more likely to ridge than to raft.

First-Year Ice: sea ice of not more than one winter's growth; at least 30 cm thick.

Thin First-Year/White Ice	30–70 cm thick.
Medium First-Year Ice	70–120 cm thick.
Thick First-Year Ice	More than 120 cm thick.

Old Ice: Sea ice that has survived at least one summer's melt; surface features generally are smoother than first-year ice.

Second-Year Ice:	Old ice that has survived only one summer's melt; thicker and less dense than first-year ice; stands higher out of the water; surface marked by "puddles" and "thaw holes"; bare patches of ice are a greenish-blue.
Multi-Year Ice:	Old ice that has survived at least two summers' melt; hummocks are smoother than on second-year ice and the ice is almost salt-free; where bare, the ice is usually blue; the melt pattern consists of large interconnecting, irregular puddles and a well-developed drainage system.

ICE OF LAND ORIGIN

Ice of land origin in the waters of Atlantic Canada has broken away from a glacier in the north. Icebergs, either afloat or aground, are massive pieces of glacier ice that vary in size and shape. A mass of ice that breaks away (calves) from an iceberg can create smaller hazards. The threats to waters of Atlantic Canada are:

Very Large Iceberg: Piece of glacier ice extending more than 75 m above the water; length greater than 200 m.

Large Iceberg: Piece of glacier ice extending 46–75 m above the water; length 121–200 m.

Medium Iceberg: Piece of glacier ice extending 16–45 m above the water; length 61–120 m.

Small Iceberg: Piece of glacier ice extending 5–15 m above the water; length 15–60 m.

Bergy Bit: Piece of glacier ice, generally showing 1–5 m above the water; length of 5–15 m—the size of a small house.

Growler: Smaller piece of glacier ice than a bergy bit, often transparent, but appearing green or almost black in colour; extending less than 1 m above the water; length of less than 5 m—the size of a large piano.

FORMS OF SEA ICE

Pancake Ice: Predominantly circular pieces of ice from 30 cm to 3 m in diameter, up to about 10 cm thick, with raised rims due to the pieces striking against one another; it may be formed on a slight swell from grease ice, shuga, or slush, or the breaking of nilas or—under severe conditions of swell or waves—the breaking of grey ice; can also

APPENDIX C *Ice Terminology*

form at some depth at an interface between water bodies of different physical characteristics, from where it floats to the surface; may rapidly form over wide areas of water.

Brash Ice: Accumulation of floating ice made up of fragments not more than 2 m across; the wreckage of other forms of ice.

Ice Cake: Any relatively flat piece of ice less than 20 m across.

Fast Ice: Ice that forms and remains fast along the coast; may be attached to the shore, between shoals or grounded icebergs.

Floe: Any relatively flat piece of ice 20 m or more across:

Small	20–100 m across.
Medium	100–500 m across.
Big	500–2,000 m across
Vast	2–10 km across.
Giant	Greater than 10 km across.

ARRANGEMENT OF THE ICE

Drift Ice or Pack Ice: Term used in a wide sense to include any area of ice, other than fast ice, no matter what form it takes or how it is disposed; when concentrations are high, i.e., 7/10 or more, the term pack ice is normally used; when concentrations are 6/10 or less, the term drift ice is normally used.

Ice Cover: The ratio of an area of ice to the total area of water surface within some large geographic locality.

Concentration: The ratio, expressed in tenths, describing the area of the water surface covered by ice as a fraction of the whole area.

Ice Free	No ice present.
Open water	Large area of freely navigable water in which the ice concentration is less than 1/10.
Very Open Drift	1/10 to 3/10 concentration.
Open Drift	4/10 to 6/10 concentration with many leads and polynyas; floes generally not in contact with one another.
Close Pack/Drift	7/10 to 8/10 concentration, composed of floes mostly in contact with one another.
Very Close Pack	9/10 to less than 10/10 concentration.
Consolidated Ice	10/10 concentration with floes frozen together.
Compact Ice	10/10 concentration with no water visible.
Bergy Water	An area of open water with no sea ice present but in which ice of land origin is present.

Ice Distribution

Ice Field	An area of floating ice more than 10 km across, consisting of any size floes.
Ice Patch	An area of ice less than 10 km across.
Belt	An elongated feature of drift/pack ice; from 1 to more than 100 km wide.
Strip	A narrow area of drift/pack ice less than 1 km wide.
Ice Jam	An accumulation of broken ice caught in a narrow channel.

Openings in The Ice

Fracture	Any break or rupture through very close pack ice, compact ice, consolidated ice, fast ice, or a single floe—caused by deformation processes; their lengths range from a few metres to many kilometres.
Crack	Any fracture of fast ice, consolidated ice or a single floe ranging from a few centimetres to 1 m.
Flaw	A narrow separation between fast ice and floating ice, where the pieces of ice are in a chaotic state; flaws form when ice shears under the effect of a strong wind or current along the fast ice boundary.
Lead	Any fracture or passageway through ice that is navigable by surface vessels.
Shore Lead	A lead between ice and the shore or between the pack and the permanent ice.
Flaw Lead	A passageway between ice and fast ice that is navigable by surface vessels.
Polynya	Any irregular opening enclosed by ice; similar to a lake, this opening may contain brash or be newly frozen but still navigable.

APPENDIX C *Ice Terminology*

ICE SURFACE FEATURES

Rafted Ice: Deformed ice formed by one piece of ice overriding another.

Ridged Ice: Ice piled haphazardly one piece over another in the form of ridges or walls. Usually found in first-year ice.

Hummocked Ice: Ice piled haphazardly one piece over another to form an uneven surface. When weathered, has the appearance of smooth hillocks.

STAGES OF MELTING

Puddle: An accumulation of water on ice, mainly due to melting snow, but in the more advanced stages melting ice enlarges the puddle.

Thaw Holes: Vertical holes in ice formed when surface puddles melt through to the underlying water.

Rotten Ice: Ice that has become honeycombed and is in an advanced state of disintegration.

APPENDIX D Cold Water Survival

Hypothermia (lowered deep-body temperature) can be life-threatening to anyone exposed to Atlantic Canada's cold, coastal waters. Wise weather decisions can be critical to marine safety. The following information on cold water survival is reprinted from *Sailing Directions, Nova Scotia (SE Coast) and Bay of Fundy, Tenth Edition* (Fisheries and Oceans, 1985).

"Without special clothing such as an immersion suit or Personal Flotation Device (PFD) with good thermal protection, even a short period of immersion in cold water causes hypothermia, which can be fatal.

In cold water, the skin and external tissues cool very rapidly but it takes 10 to 15 minutes before the temperature of the heart, brain and other internal organs begins to drop. Intense shivering occurs in an attempt to increase the body's heat production and counteract the large heat loss. Once cooling of the deep body begins, body temperature falls steadily and unconsciousness can occur when the deep-body temperature drops from the normal 37°C to approximately 32°C. When the body core temperature cools to below 30°C, death from cardiac arrest usually results.

In a water temperature of 5°C, persons without normal thermal protection become too weak to help themselves after about 30 minutes. Even if rescued, the chances of survival after an hour of immersion are slim.

The body, in almost all weather conditions, cools much faster in water than in air, thus the less body surface submerged, the better. The parts of the body with the fastest heat loss are the head and neck, the sides of the chest and the groin. To reduce body heat loss, protect these areas. Two ways of reducing heat loss are:

◆ HELP (Heat Escape Lessening Position): arms held tight against the sides, ankles crossed, thighs closed together and raised.
◆ HUDDLE: two or more persons in a huddle with chests held close together.

To use these methods successfully a person must be wearing a lifejacket or PFD.

Survival time is greatly increased by wearing clothing that gives thermal protection, including a hood to prevent heat loss through the head. Do not swim to keep warm as this causes heat to be lost to the cold water due to more blood circulation to the arms, legs and skin. Tests show that a person in a lifejacket cools 35 percent faster when swimming than when holding still.

If you have no lifejacket or other flotation, tread water: remain as still as you can, moving your arms and legs just enough to keep your head out of the water. Although tests show that the heat loss is faster when treading water than when holding still in a lifejacket, this is much better than the "drownproofing" technique with which the heat loss is 82 percent faster, mainly due to the head (a high heat loss area) being periodically submerged.

Rewarming after mild hypothermia—If the casualty is conscious, talking clearly and sensibly and shivering vigorously, then:

◆ get the casualty out of the water to a dry sheltered area;
◆ remove the wet clothing and if possible put on layers of dry clothing; cover the head and neck;
◆ apply hot, wet towels and water bottles to the groin, head, neck and sides of the chest;
◆ use electric blankets, heating pads, hot baths or showers;
◆ use hot drinks but never alcohol as it does not warm a person.

Rewarming after severe hypothermia—If the casualty is getting stiff and is either unconscious or showing signs of clouded consciousness such as slurred speech, or any other apparent signs of deterioration, immediately (if possible) transport the casualty to medical assistance where aggressive rewarming can be initiated.

Once the shivering has stopped, there is no use wrapping casualties in blankets if there is no source of heat as this merely keeps them cold; a way of warming them must be found quickly. Some methods are:

◆ put the casualty in a sleeping bag with one or two warm persons, with upper clothing removed;
◆ use hot, wet towels and water bottles as described previously;
◆ warm the casualties lungs by mouth-to-mouth breathing.

Caution:
Warm the chest, groin, head and neck but not the extremities of the body; warming the extremities can draw heat from the area of the heart, sometimes with fatal results. For this reason do not rub the surface of the body."

APPENDIX E *Naming of Hurricanes*

WHY HURRICANES ARE NAMED

Experience shows that using short, distinctive given names in written and spoken communications is quicker, and less subject to error than traditional latitude-longitude identification. Speed and accuracy are critical when exchanging detailed storm information between hundreds of widely scattered stations, airports, coastal bases, and ships at sea.

Easily remembered names are especially important when two or more tropical storms occur at the same time; for example, one hurricane may be moving slowly westward in the Gulf of Mexico, while another one is moving rapidly northward along the Atlantic coast. In the past, confusion and false rumours have arisen when storm advisories have been mistakingly applied to another storm occurring hundreds of miles away. The potential danger of such confusion is obvious.

BRIEF HISTORY OF HURRICANE NAMES

For several hundred years many hurricanes in the West Indies were named after the particular saint's day on which they occurred. Australian meteorologist, Clement Wragge, began giving women's names to tropical storms before the end of the nineteenth century. This practice came to an end in 1978 when men's and women's names were included in the Eastern North Pacific storms lists. Lists for the Atlantic and Gulf of Mexico followed suit in 1979.

THE SIX-YEAR LIST OF NAMES FOR ATLANTIC STORMS

1995	1996	1997	1998	1999	2000
Allison	Arthur	Ana	Alex	Arlene	Alberto
Barry	Bertha	Bill	Bonnie	Bret	Beryl
Chantal	Cesar	Claudette	Charley	Cindy	Chris
Dean	Dolly	Danny	Danielle	Dennis	Debby
Erin	Edouard	Erika	Earl	Emily	Ernesto
Felix	Fran	Fabian	Frances	Floyd	Florence
Gabrielle	Gustav	Grace	Georges	Gert	Gordon
Humberto	Hortense	Henri	Hermine	Harvey	Helene
Iris	Isidore	Isabel	Ivan	Irene	Isaac
Jerry	Josephine	Juan	Jeanne	Jose	Joyce
Karen	Kyle	Kate	Karl	Katrina	Keith
Luis	Lili	Larry	Lisa	Lenny	Leslie
Marilyn	Marco	Mindy	Mitch	Maria	Michael
Noel	Nana	Nicolas	Nicole	Nate	Nadine
Opal	Omar	Odette	Otto	Ophelia	Oscar
Pablo	Paloma	Peter	Paula	Philippe	Patty
Roxanne	Rene	Rose	Richard	Rita	Rafael
Sebastien	Sally	Sam	Shary	Stan	Sandy
Tanya	Teddy	Teresa	Tomas	Tammy	Tony
Van	Vicky	Victor	Virginie	Vince	Valerie
Wendy	Wilfred	Wanda	Walter	Wilma	William

Notes: After the sets have all been used, they are used again (although the names of extremely destructive storms are often "retired" and replaced with another name beginning with the same letter). The 1995 set, for example, will be used again to name storms in 2001. The letters Q, U, X, Y, and Z are not included because of the scarcity of names beginning with those letters.

GLOSSARY

Words in italics are also defined elsewhere in the glossary.

ADVECTION FOG—See sea fog.

AIR MASS—A large volume of air with uniform properties of temperature and moisture.

ALTOCUMULUS—Mid-level cumulus clouds.

ALTOSTRATUS—Mid-level stratus clouds.

ANABATIC WIND—A *wind* that blows up the slope of a hill or mountain due to the sun heating the land.

ARCTIC SEA SMOKE—A type of fog formed by very cold air moving over relatively warm water. Also called "steam fog" or "ice fog."

BACKING—A counterclockwise change in *wind* direction; opposite of *veering*.

BACKWASH—A term used to describe reflected waves from a *steep-to* shoreline. When waves encounter land that rises steeply from the ocean bottom, they will "reflect" or bounce off the land, rather than break, or "*refract*" as they would in shallow water. Reflected waves interact with oncoming seas to create confused *crossing sea* conditions.

BATHYMETRY—The shape of the sea bed.

BEAUFORT SCALE—A scale of *wind* force, based on behaviour of the sea under varying degrees of wind speed.

BREAKER—A wave that has broken into foam.

BUYS-BALLOTS LAW—States that over the open sea, if the *wind* is from astern, then lower *pressure* will be to *port* (in the northern hemisphere).

CIRROCUMULUS—High-level cumulus clouds.

CIRROSTRATUS—High-level stratus clouds.

CIRRUS—Wispy clouds that form high in the sky, often preceding the lower clouds of an approaching frontal *low*.

COLD FRONT—A boundary separating cold and warm *air masses* at which the cold air is advancing.

CONVECTION—Describes the vertical air motions that occur when the atmosphere is *unstable*. Convection often gives rise to the formation of convective clouds (*cumulus, towering cumulus,* and *thunderstorms*) and showery precipitation.

COLD LOW—A *low-pressure* centre that has been flooded by cold air, at all levels. It is the remains of a frontal low, following an *occlusion process*.

CORIOLIS FORCE—An apparent force exerted on moving objects due to the earth's rotation.

CROSSING SEAS—The result of a train of waves moving at an angle to a second train of waves.

CUMULONIMBUS—The *thunderstorm* cloud. It has grown upwards from a smaller *cumulus* cloud.

CUMULUS—Heaped or lumpy clouds that form in an *unstable* atmosphere. Without the "alto" or "cirro" prefixes, it refers to low-level heap clouds.

DEWPOINT—The temperature at which the air, cooled at constant *pressure*, becomes saturated with *water vapour*.

EBB TIDE—The portion of the tide cycle between high water and the following low water. It is sometimes called the "falling tide."

EDDY—A region of rotating air or water.

EKMAN TRANSPORT—The bulk movement of sea water to the right of the *wind* direction and waves.

FETCH—The distance over which the *wind* blows from a constant direction.

FATHOM—A nautical unit of length equal to six feet.

FLOOD TIDE—The portion of the tide cycle between low water and the following high water. It is sometimes called the "rising tide."

FOG—Cloud that comes in contact with the surface. Visibility is 1/2 mile or less.

FRONT—The boundary between two *air masses*.

GALE-FORCE WIND—A sustained *wind* speed of 34–47 knots.

GAP WINDS—Often very strong, these winds blow out of a gap—generally seaward—and are usually the result of channelling and funnelling.

GEOSTROPHIC WIND—The *wind* that results from a balance between the pressure gradient force and the Coriolis force. This wind blows parallel to the isobars on a weather map and its strength is proportional to the closeness of the isobars: the closer the isobars, the stronger the wind.

GUST—A sudden, brief increase in *wind* speed, generally lasting less than 20 seconds.

HIGH—A region of high *pressure*. Air flows outwards and clockwise around a high. Highs are usually associated with fair weather.

HIGH CLOUD—Clouds based 6 km or more above the surface.

HIGH WATER SLACK—See *slack water*.

GLOSSARY

HURRICANE—A storm of tropical origin in which maximum sustained surface *winds* are greater than 63 *knots*.

HURRICANE-FORCE WIND—*Winds* greater than 63 *knots*.

ICE—See Appendix C for a complete listing of ice-terminology.

ICE FOG—See Arctic Sea Smoke.

ICEBERG—A chunk of fresh water ice "calved" from a glacier. Icebergs are harder than *pack ice*.

INVERSION—Also known as a "temperature inversion." This occurs when warm air resides over colder air. Inversions give rise to *stable* conditions.

ISOBAR—Line on a weather map joining points of *equal pressure*.

KATABATIC WIND—A *wind* that blows down the slope of a hill or mountain due to cooling of the land.

KNOCKDOWNS—Local name for strong, blustery, katabatic winds.

KNOT—A unit of *wind* speed in the nautical system equal to one nautical mile per hour.

LAND BREEZE—A small-scale *wind* circulation set off by differences in water and land temperatures along the coast. The land breeze develops at night and always blows from the land. Its daytime counterpart is the *sea breeze*.

LEE WAVE—Also called *mountain waves*, it results from air flowing over a range of highs or mountains. Extremely strong winds can develop from lee waves.

LEE TROUGH / LOW—A trough or low that forms on the lee side of a range of hills or mountains when westerly *winds* flow across the top.

LEEWARD—Downwind, situated away from the *wind*; opposite of *windward*.

LIGHT WINDS—*Wind* speeds less than 12 *knots*.

LOW—A region of low *pressure*. Air flows inwards and counterclockwise around a low. A low centre is usually accompanied by precipitation and strong *winds*.

LOW CLOUD—Cloud based below 2 km above the surface.

LOW WATER SLACK—See *slack water*.

MAGNETIC WIND DIRECTION—The direction, with respect to magnetic north, from which the wind is blowing. It is distinguished from *true wind direction*.

MESOSCALE—A scale of distance and time used by meteorologists to describe weather disturbances on a scale larger than the *micro-scale*, but smaller than the *synoptic-scale*. Systems of this scale span hundreds to thousands of square kilometres and last for many hours. *Cornering, coastal convergence, thunderstorms,* and small *tropical storms* are examples of mesoscale weather systems. This is the scale of most of the local effects discussed in this guide.

MICRO-CLIMATE—The peculiarities of the climate of a small region, caused by local effects. It does not deal exclusively with weather events occurring on the *micro-scale*.

MICRO-SCALE—A scale of distance and time used by meteorologists to describe small weather disturbances. *Wind* flow around a boat and weather events that last for only a few minutes are examples of micro-scale systems.

MIDDLE CLOUD—Clouds based between 2 to 6 km above the surface.

MILLIBAR—A unit used to measure air *pressure*.

MIST—Cloud in contact with the surface such that visibility is greater than 1/2 mile.

MODERATE WINDS—*Wind* speeds in the range of 12 to 19 *knots*.

MOUNTAIN WAVE—Also called *lee waves*, it results from air flowing over a range of hills or mountains. Extremely strong winds can result from mountain waves.

NAUTICAL MILE—The unit of distance in the nautical system. There are 60 nautical miles in one degree of latitude. 1 nautical mile = 1.15 statute miles = 1.85 kilometres.

NEAP TIDE—The tide with smallest ranges between high and low water. It occurs near first and last quarter moons when the moon, earth, and sun are at right angles.

NIMBOSTRATUS—Cloud that is layered to great heights ahead of a frontal *low* producing steady precipitation.

NIMBUS—A rain cloud (see also *nimbostratus* and *cumulonimbus*).

OCCLUSION—The end result of a *cold front* overtaking a *warm front*. It marks the dying stages of a frontal *low*.

PACK ICE—Also known as "sea ice," it is different from *icebergs*. It is sea water that freezes and forms into large floes.

POLAR LOW—A small *low-pressure* centre that forms in very cold air that has driven out over a relatively warm ocean or large lake. Usually about 100 km in diameter, it can have *storm-force* or *hurricane-force winds*.

PORT—The left-hand side of the ship, when facing the bow.

GLOSSARY

PRESSURE—The force exerted by the weight of the atmosphere. It is also known as atmospheric or barometric pressure.

PRESSURE GRADIENT—The difference in *pressure* between two points divided by the distance between them. On a weather map, the closeness of the *isobars* is a measure of the pressure gradient.

RADIATION FOG—Ground fog formed when night-time cooling allows temperatures to drop to the *dewpoint*.

REFRACTION—The bending of waves that pass over shallow water at an angle to the shoal.

RIDGE—An elongated area of high *pressure*. Like a high, it is usually associated with fair weather.

SALINITY—A measure of the quantity of dissolved salts in sea water.

SEA BREEZE—A small-scale *wind* circulation set off by differences in water and land temperatures along the coast. The sea breeze develops in the daytime and begins by blowing from the sea towards the land, although it usually veers in the afternoon and may end up blowing parallel to the coast. Its night-time counterpart is the *land breeze*.

SEA FOG—Fog formed by warm moist air moving over colder sea water.

SEA STATE—A description of the properties of wind-generated waves and swell on the surface of the sea. "Sea state forecasts" are actually only deep-water *wave-height* forecasts.

SEAS—This term is used to describe wind-waves.

SEICHE—The "sloshing around" of a body of water in its basin.

SHALLOW WATER—Water depths less than or equal to one half of the *wavelength* of a wave. Therefore, water may be "shallow" for some waves, but not for others.

SHOALING—The changes in wave characteristics when *shallow water* is encountered by the wave.

SIGNIFICANT WAVE HEIGHT—Average height of the highest one-third of the waves present.

SLACK WATER—This occurs as the tidal flow changes direction, and the current momentarily ceases flowing. Because of momentum, some *tidal bores* continue moving after the time of high and low water; so the times of low-water slack and high-water slack do not correspond to the times of low, or high tide.

SNOW STREAMERS—A line of *convective* cloud giving significant *snowsqualls*. These usually form when cold air passes over relatively warm waters. Streamers align themselves nearly parallel to the *wind*.

SNOWSQUALLS—Snow with low visibility from a *convective* cloud: often accompanied by gusty *wind*.

SPRING TIDE—The tide when ranges between high and low water are greatest. It occurs near full and new moons when the moon, earth, and sun are in line.

SQUALL—A brief, violent windstorm, usually, but not necessarily associated with rain or snow.

SQUALL LINE—A line of *thunderstorms*, or other heavy weather, often running parallel to, and ahead of, *a cold front*.

STABILITY—The buoyancy of the air. Air that has a tendency to rise, when warmed, is *unstable*, while air that resists this tendency is *stable*.

STABLE—A non-*convective* state in the atmosphere, opposite of *unstable*. This occurs when warm air resides over cold air.

STARBOARD—The right-hand side of the ship when facing the bow.

STEAM FOG—see *Arctic Sea Smoke*.

STEEP-TO—An expression used when water depth increases rapidly away from shore or away from shallow underwater features such as reefs.

STORM-FORCE WINDS—Sustained *wind* speeds in the range of 48 through 63 *knots*.

STORM SURGE—A change in water level caused by atmospheric forces such as *pressure* and *wind*. A storm surge can cause coastal flooding, especially when it occurs at the same time as high tide.

STRATUS—A uniform, featureless layer of cloud that forms in a *stable* atmosphere. Without the "alto" or "cirro" prefixes it refers to the low-level layered clouds that are sometimes accompanied by drizzle.

STRONG WINDS—Sustained *wind* speeds in the range of 20 to 33 *knots*.

SWELL—Ocean waves formed by *winds* blowing over a distant area.

SYNOPTIC SCALE—A scale of distance and time used by meteorologists to describe large weather disturbances. Synoptic-scale weather systems span thousands to millions of square kilometres and exist for several days. Highs, fronts, frontal lows and large hurricanes are examples of synoptic-scale weather systems.

GLOSSARY

THERMAL TROUGH / LOW—A *trough* or *low* formed when cold air moves over a relatively warmer surface.

THUNDERSTORM—A local "storm," produced by a cumulonimbus cloud, accompanied by thunder, lightning, strong *winds,* and occasionally, hail and *waterspouts*.

TIDAL BORE—The body of water that rushes up some rivers (that empty into the sea) at times of exceptional tides.

TIDAL RANGE—The difference between the heights of high and low water.

TIDAL RIPS—The result of strong currents running over irregular shallow sea bottoms.

TOPOGRAPHY—The shape of the land.

TORNADO—A violent swirling vortex, or funnel cloud, that extends beneath a thunderstorm and touches the ground. It is the most locally destructive force in the atmosphere. Tornadoes that move over water are called *waterspouts,* although, all waterspouts do not necessarily begin as tornadoes.

TOWERING CUMULUS—A *cumulus* cloud that "towers" to significant heights.

TROPICAL DEPRESSION—A circulating *low-pressure* area of tropical origin with maximum sustained *wind* speeds less than 34 *knots*.

TROPICAL DISTURBANCE—A moving area of thunderstorms in the tropics that has maintained its identity for 24 hours or more.

TROPICAL STORM—A *low-pressure* area of tropical origin with maximum sustained *wind* speeds in the range 34 to 63 *knots*. When *tropical depressions* reach this stage, they are given a name.

TROUGH—An elongated area of *low-pressure*. When troughs pass, winds veer and showery weather can be expected.

TROWAL—A **T**rough **O**f **W**arm air **Al**oft. It is one of the possible stages of an *occlusion* process in a dying frontal *low*.

TRUE WIND DIRECTION—The direction, with respect to true north, from which the wind is blowing. It is distinguished from *magnetic wind direction*. In weather observations and forecasts, it is the true wind direction that is reported, usually in terms of tens of degrees in the 360° compass.

TSUNAMI—Massive coastal-waves that result from submarine earthquakes, bottom-slides, or volcanic eruptions.

UNSTABLE—A turbulent state in the atmosphere, often caused by cold air moving over warm air. Unstable conditions are also induced by cold air moving over warm water and by strong heating of the ground by the sun. *Convection* develops when the atmosphere is unstable.

VEERING—A clockwise change in *wind* direction; opposite of *backing*.

WARM FRONT—A boundary separating cold and warm *air masses* at which the warm air is advancing.

WATER VAPOUR—Invisible molecules of water in the air. It is the gaseous form of water.

WATERSPOUT—A small whirling storm over water which can either be spawned from the base of a *thunderstorm,* or formed in a cold outbreak of Arctic air. They are similar to, but generally not so severe as *tornadoes*.

WAVE LENGTH—The horizontal distance between two successive wave crests (or troughs).

WAVE PERIOD—The time interval between the passage of successive crests (or troughs) at a fixed position.

WAVE STEEPNESS—The ratio of *wave height* to *wave length*.

WAVE HEIGHT—The vertical distance between an adjacent wave crest and trough.

WHIRLWIND—General term for a small-scale rotating column of air. They can be caused by uneven frictional effects.

WIND—The horizontal movement of air relative to the earth's surface.

WIND SHADOW—A shelter from the wind, usually to the lee of an island or range of hills.

WIND-WAVES—Waves produced by the *wind* blowing in the area where the waves form.

WINDWARD—Upwind, or the direction from which the *wind* is blowing; the opposite of *leeward*.

BIBLIOGRAPHY

BARKS, E.A. (1985): *The Climatology of Tropical Cyclones in Atlantic Canada;* Unpublished Manuscript.

BISHOP, DR. JOSEPH M. (1988): *A Mariner's Guide to Radiofacsimile Weather Charts;* Alden Electronics.

BOWYER, PETER J. (1988): *Marine Wind Forecasting;* Atmospheric Environment Service, Atlantic Region Technical Notes 88-003(N); Unpublished Manuscript.

CANADA. SCIENTIFIC INFORMATION AND PUBLICATIONS BRANCH, FISHERIES AND OCEANS (1979, 4th Edition): *Sailing Directions—Labrador and Hudson Bay;* Minister of Supply and Services Canada.

CANADA. SCIENTIFIC INFORMATION AND PUBLICATIONS BRANCH, FISHERIES AND OCEANS (1985, 6th Edition): *Sailing Directions—Gulf and River St. Lawrence;* Minister of Supply and Services Canada.

CANADA. SCIENTIFIC INFORMATION AND PUBLICATIONS BRANCH, FISHERIES AND OCEANS (1985, 10th Edition): *Sailing Directions—Nova Scotia (SE Coast) and Bay of Fundy;* Minister of Supply and Services Canada.

B.EID, C.MORTON, C.CALNAN, and V.CARDONE (1991): *Wind and Wave Climate Atlas—Volume 1, The East Coast of Canada;* Transport Canada Publication No. TP10820E.

DAVIS, JR., RICHARD A. (1977, 2nd Edition): *Principles of Oceanography;* Addison-Wesley Publishing Company.

ENVIRONMENT CANADA ATLANTIC REGION (1990, Revised): *East Coast Marine Weather Manual;* Minister of Supply and Services Canada.

ENVIRONMENT CANADA ONTARIO REGION (1990, 2nd edition): *Marine Weather Hazards Manual;* Minister of Supply and Services Canada.

ENVIRONMENT CANADA ATLANTIC REGION (1991): *Gulf of St. Lawrence Marine Weather Guide;* Minister of Supply and Services Canada.

ENVIRONMENT CANADA ATLANTIC REGION (1992): *Scotia/Fundy Marine Weather Guide;* Minister of Supply and Services Canada.

ENVIRONMENT CANADA ATLANTIC REGION (1993): *Newfoundland and Labrador Marine Weather Guide;* Minister of Supply and Services Canada.

ENVIRONMENT CANADA ONTARIO REGION (1992): *Great Lakes Marine Weather Guide;* Minister of Supply and Services Canada.

ENVIRONMENT CANADA ARCTIC REGION (1991): *Marine Guide to Local Conditions and Forecasts: Great Slave Lake; Lake Athabasca; Lake Winnipeg; Lake of the Woods; Lake Nippigon;* Minister of Supply and Services Canada.

HAGGERTY, D. (1985): *Rhymes to Predict the Weather;* Springmeadow Publishers, Seattle.

HORNSTEIN, RUEBEN A. (1980): *The Forecast Your Own Weather Book;* McClelland and Stewart Limited and Minister of Supply and Services.

HOUGHTON, DAVID (1986): *A Yachtmaster's Guide—Weather at Sea;* Fenhurst Books, West Sussex.

ICE CLIMATOLOGY AND APPLICATIONS DIVISION, ATMOSPHERIC ENVIRONMENT SERVICE (1985 REVISED): *Ice Observer Training Course—Ice Climatology Notes;* Environment Canada, Unpublished Manuscript.

KNAUS, JOHN A. (1978): *Introduction to Physical Oceanography;* Prentice-Hall, Inc.

PAUL J. KOCIN, LOUIS W. UCCELLINI (1990): *Snowstorms Along the Northeastern Coast of the United States: 1955 to 1985;* American Meteorological Society.

L.D.MORTSCH, T.AGNEW, A.SAULESLEJA, and V.R.SWAIL (1985): *Marine Climatological Atlas—Canadian East Coast;* Canadian Climate Centre Report No. 85-11, Unpublished Manuscript.

Marine Weather Guide REPLY CARD

To help us determine the success and usefulness of this guide, please fill in the brief form below, and return this card to our weather centre in Bedford.

1. **Which of the following best describes you?**

    ❏ Full-time fisherman ❏ Part-time fisherman ❏ Educator

    ❏ Commercial seaman ❏ Pleasure sailor / Boater

    ❏ Other (explain): _____

    _____

2. **Where did you get this guide?** _____

    _____

3. **How did you first hear about this guide?** _____

    _____

4. **Did this guide help you to better understand marine weather and local effects?**

    ❏ Yes ❏ No

5. **How easy was the information to understand?**

    ❏ Very easy ❏ Somewhat easy

    ❏ Somewhat difficult ❏ Very difficult

6. **Is there anything missing from the guide that you think should have been included?**

    ❏ Yes ❏ No

    Explain: _____

    _____

    _____

7. **Are there any corrections that you think should be made?**

    ❏ Yes ❏ No

    Explain: _____

    _____

    _____

REPLY CARD *Marine Weather Guide*

8. If there are MARINE WEATHER HAZARDS or LOCAL EFFECTS that you would like to bring to our attention, please mark the location(s) on the map and explain:

_____
_____
_____
_____
_____
_____
_____
_____
_____

To mail this card please fold it along the dotted line and **tape** it closed—do **not** staple!

Name _____

Address _____

_____

Phone _____

Director,
Atmospheric Environment Branch
Environment Canada
1496 Bedford Highway
Bedford, Nova Scotia B4A 1E5